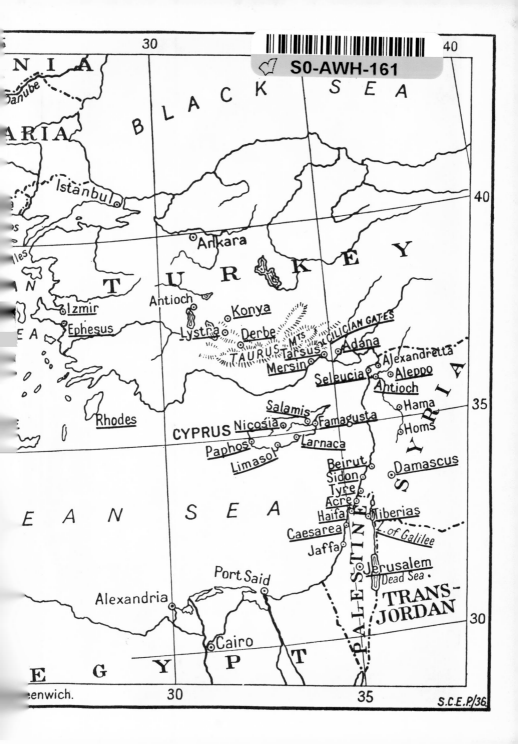

IN THE STEPS OF ST. PAUL

IN THE STEPS
OF ST. PAUL

By

H. V. MORTON

WITH ENDPAPER MAPS

DODD, MEAD & COMPANY
NEW YORK

CONTENTS

CONTENTS

INTRODUCTION

THE modern traveller who takes the *Acts of the Apostles* as his guide-book, as I have done, journeys into a part of the world which once enjoyed the unity of the Roman Empire and is now divided among many nations. Where he is held up at national frontiers, to pass onward under a different flag and among men who speak a different tongue, St. Paul moved forward over a Roman road, speaking Greek all the time.

It follows, therefore, that travel was easier for St. Paul than for those who follow him, for the great commercial highways along which he moved, and the famous ports from whose harbours he set sail, are no longer the main highways of the world. What was to St. Paul a progress along the best-known roads of the Roman Empire, becomes, to the modern traveller, a series of explorations from the beaten track. The harbour of Antioch is desolate, and Ephesus is a nesting-place for the stork.

In the course of four journeys to the Near East, I was fortunate enough to traverse the varied territory of the three Pauline missions. For the guidance of those who may feel a desire to make this journey, or a part of it, I should say that there is nothing that cannot be done, given time and patience, and only in very remote places will the visitor feel compelled to make the Aristophanic inquiry: "Which inn is the least interesting—entomologically?"

Palestine and Syria are now, of course, well known to travellers, but Antioch and Aleppo are, naturally, more familiar to the French than to the English. Apart from the cities of Istanbul and Ankara, Turkey offers neither the freedom of movement nor the comfort which the general traveller demands, but, to the Pauline student, no country promises a richer reward. I believe that if the condition of the world justified the construction by the Turkish Government of a good motoring road from Istanbul, through Troy, Pergamum, Smyrna, Ephesus, to Miletus, the venture would be a great success, and an area of enormous archæological and historical interest would be opened to the ordinary traveller.

Greece is a land which, of course, needs no praise. It is one of the few countries in the world which does not disappoint the most ardent admirer. The hotels in all the important places are either excellent or adequate, and the road system is being improved. Greece has the additional attraction of being one of the cheapest countries in Europe for those who travel with the pound sterling.

The British Colony of Cyprus deserves a much greater popularity than it can claim at present with the British travelling public. Its distance from England is, of course, a difficulty, but, if communications were improved, this exquisite island, covered by excellent roads, notable for its small, but admirable, hotels, for its superb winter climate and the perfection of its bathing, should attract people who are in the habit of going fairly far afield for their holidays.

In writing this book I have described the actions of St. Paul the Traveller. My route is set down in the *Acts of the Apostles*. I have introduced the Epistles only so far as they seemed to me to illuminate local conditions, or to explain the conduct of the Apostle. Every word written by St. Paul has become a battleground on which the scholars, not only of this country, but also of Europe and America, have for generations matched learning against learning and have launched theory against theory, until, to the respectful eye of a non-combatant, it seems at times that the battlefield itself has become obscured in the conflict.

I have no qualifications for this contest, and therefore the theological aspect of St. Paul is outside the scope of this book.

If, however, I have innocently strayed on the field of action and seem, to a regular combatant, to be armed, I would take this opportunity of declaring my neutrality.

My debt to those who have written before on this subject is immense. The bibliography at the end of this book will indicate in what directions my acknowledgments are due. I should like especially to mention the Pauline works of Sir William Ramsay, and also those wonderful standard books: *The Life and Epistles of St. Paul,* by Conybeare and Howson, and the volume with the same little title by Thomas Lewin. My thanks are due to Messrs Hodder and Stoughton for permission to quote the Epistles of St. Paul in the modern translation of Dr. James Moffatt.

I wish to thank my friend, Demetri John Travlos, of Athens, for so much generous and enthusiastic help.

H. V. M.

London.

CHAPTER I

In which I set out in the steps of St. Paul, see the Holy Land again, visit Jerusalem, mount the wall above the Gate of St. Stephen, receive permission from the Grand Mufti to climb the minaret overlooking the site of Solomon's Temple, and journey to Damascus.

1

I WENT on deck before sunrise. The storm had backed to the north-west, the sky was clear, and the ship rolled in a long, sullen swell. I hoped to see the pin-prick of the lighthouse on Mount Carmel, but we were still too far from land.

St. Paul must have known this moment: the grey light, the last star, the cold wind, the fusty cargo, the smell of beasts and tar, the movement of the mast against the sky, the smooth pressing forward and the rhythmic hiss of water running back along the sides of the ship. It was good to stand on deck, thinking that this ship might be the *Castor and Pollux*.

After all, the Mediterranean coaster has not changed much since Roman times. These ships still carry corn from Egypt, and leave Cyprus in summer, heavy with pomegranates, the fruit of Aphrodite. As they pass slowly south from Alexandretta, which is now the port of Antioch, they stir old memories; and the ghosts of Tyre and Sidon beckon vainly as they pass.

I looked down to the fo'c'sle-head, where, grey in a grey light, mules tied to the rails were unaware that the worst was over. These creatures, so improbably at sea, so firmly linked in association with hill-paths and olive trees, now stood heads down before grey hills of water that launched themselves monstrously in a dim light.

It was a sight as old as travel in the Mediterranean.

Through a square hole in the deck emerged Nubian and Egyptian faces, and deck-hands moved softly in the half-light, the wind shaking their thin garments. Timidly, with propitiatory noises, they approached the mules, and the ship bowed to the sea.

Land was still far off, but I could see in the east, where I knew the mountains of Lebanon to be, the first troubled movement of dawn. As I waited for the sunrise, I thought of the strange roads I was about to travel, of the ruined cities I hoped to visit, and of the harbours into which I should sail by light of sun or moon. And when I whispered the names of these places—Tarsus, Ephesus, Philippi, Corinth, Antioch, Iconium, Salamis, Paphos—they sang gloriously in my mind; and I thought how fortunate I was to be standing on this ship in the grey light before morning, with nothing before me but the adventure of following the path of St. Paul across the ancient world.

Light grew in the east as the sun fought his February battle with the night clouds of the Lebanon. A cold blue light grew over the sea, and colour slowly returned to the world. The mules were no longer grey, but brown and dark brown. Suddenly, with only the shortest preamble of bright cloud, the sun came into the sky with the air of a miracle performed, and the sea was gold.

In that moment I saw, far off, a ridge harder than a shadow and more solid than a cloud. And I knew that I was looking at the Holy Land.

2

On the freshness of the morning we swung in past the head of Mount Carmel, where the Carmelites would be saying Mass above a cave hung with lamps. I could see the blue bay curving northward and palm trees on the sand, and the little town of Acre lying out to sea, its honey-coloured ramparts edged with spray. Beyond Acre the coast-line curved in fainter blue, and I saw the distant outline of the Ladders of Tyre, like a cobweb pinned against the sky.

As we moved into dock at Haifa, all the smells and sounds of a growing port were about us. I looked down on lines of concrete sheds, crowds of Arab porters in their cone-shaped Phœnician caps and loose robes of hair-cloth, Arab guides standing beside saloon cars, Palestine police in their blue uniforms, and sunburnt Jews in khaki shorts.

I was glad to step ashore among the violent, shouting crowds. I sought out the Armenian who had once driven me through Palestine. Stephan, standing beside his car, was childishly delighted to see me. He crushed his shabby velour hat in his hands and wrinkled up his brown face into a radiant smile, trying painfully to excavate English words from his scanty vocabulary.

"Stephan," I said, "when I wrote to you, I told you that we should go to Damascus and then to Antioch. But I have changed my mind. We are going instead to Jerusalem."

"As you say," replied Stephan with a smile.

I motored to Jerusalem through a land already awake to spring time. With intense pleasure I saw again the familiar sights of Palestine: camels padding softly in the dust; the ploughman goading a recalcitrant ox at the turning of the furrow; the patient, burdened donkeys; the swarthy girls at the village well—petrol-tin, alas! on shoulder; the brown hills strewn with a million grey boulders; and on the hillcrests those small white Moslem shrines which, whether the Arabs know it or not, occupy the high places of Baal.

I felt my excitement rise mile by mile as we approached the mountain road that swings up towards Jerusalem, with Nebi Samwîl towering to the west and scattered brown villages lying terraced on the slope of hills.

But of all the approaches to Jerusalem, this is the least attractive. When you come west from Jericho, or north from Bethlehem, there is one moment when the whole city of Jerusalem lies before you. From the west you see the sweep of the great Wall as it overhangs the Kedron Valley; from the south you see the splendid vista of the city piled on the brown hill, with the southern angle of the wall standing like a challenge in the sun. From this northern road, however, the traveller who has never before made the journey expects a climax that never comes. The road mounts so steeply, and so fierce and barren are the hills, that they promise more than they give; almost before you know it, you are running tamely into Jerusalem past the clock tower by Barclay's Bank.

In the afternoon, after I had settled down and read my letters, I walked along the Jaffa Road, as every visitor to Jerusalem does, to enter the Old City. The little Arab shoe-blacks were still sitting in the dust under the Jaffa Gate. The same hideous gramophone was grinding out Arab music from the café at the corner. The lemonade-seller was still clashing his brass cups and crying the snow-coolness of his drink. Bedouin, walking with the fierce disdain of minor prophets, strode with dust on their eyelashes and beards, tapping their staves on the ancient stones. Veiled women waddled past like black ghosts, and vivid, big-boned peasant girls, unveiled and bold, marched with their infants astride their shoulders or on their backs. Town Arabs in striped suits still stood in conference on the pavement, their red tarbushes almost touching. The same Armenian, standing in the door of a curio shop, murmured, "Come inside, please, sir, no need to buy." And, with the sunlight flooding down over them, the gold-brown stones of Herod's tower stood defiant even in decay, their turrets against the sky and their feet in history.

When I descended that dim stone stairway which is called David Street, I was enchanted by its apparent immutability.

The same fat old men, a little fatter, it seemed, and maybe slightly darker in the face, sat behind their ramparts of purple aubergines, oranges, colossal cabbages, red and green peppers, lifting cigarettes to their lips. The same incoherent press of dust-smelling men and beasts filled the narrow place. Camels loomed above the heads of the people, brushing past with their immense loads, and burdened donkeys pressed neatly through the crowds.

As I walked along Christian Street, I saw the shops hung with fringes of coloured and gilded candles, four feet long. Even the thin linen shroud was still exposed to view near the Holy Sepulchre, a sample of those shrouds, cheaply printed with sacred scenes, which Russian pilgrims once bought in thousands and took home with them against the day of their release from earth.

Just before you descend the flight of steps leading into the courtyard of the Holy Sepulchre, there is a wrought-iron gateway. Beyond the black arabesques of the grille you can see a sunny little court with a well in the middle of it, where sometimes men may be seen lowering a bucket and drawing water. As I looked, someone came out of a low door and, standing over the well, flung down the bucket and began to wind it up again.

It is always pleasing to return to a place and to discover life going on just the same. The little street was still musky with incense. The merchants have been burning it there for centuries, in thin black sticks and small black pyramids.

I went down the steps into the glare of the courtyard and passed into the Church of the Holy Sepulchre. It was cool and dark. Small wicks, burning in glasses of olive oil, pricked the darkness. Brazen lamps, hanging on chains, also held these little tongues of flame. In the Rotunda there was silence. On the marble floor before the Tomb of Christ, a peasant woman was kneeling in prayer. There was no one else.

3

Leaving the silent church, I walked through the lanes of Jerusalem until I came to the Gate of St. Stephen. It is the only gate that opens towards the Mount of Olives. The road passing under it descends into the Valley of the Kedron.

It was that hour in the afternoon when the sun lies above Jerusalem, blazing over the Mount of Olives, but leaving in shadow the eastern Wall of the city. When the sun sinks, the shadow of the Wall grows longer, travelling down into the Kedron Valley and ascending the opposite slopes until it steals among the ancient trees in the Garden of Gethsemane. But that time was still far off.

I walked a road of powdered limestone white as chalk dust. Not far from the Garden of Gethsemane I found an olive tree, and in its shade I rested. Taking the New Testament from my pocket, I began to read the opening chapter of the *Acts of the Apostles*, but my eyes kept wandering from the page to the Wall of Jerusalem. And I sat in the warm sunlight near the Garden of Gethsemane, thinking of St. Paul and of the world in which he lived.

We see in St. Paul the first full-length portrait of a Christian missionary. His loving "care of all the churches" was something new in the world: never before had a man felt himself responsible for the moral and spiritual welfare of his fellowmen, and never before had any man struggled as he did to save his flock from falling into sin.

This greatest of all missionaries had not read the Gospels, for they had not been written in his time. Unlike all missionaries from the end of the first century onward, he advanced across the world preaching the good news, but without the written Gospel in his hand. This invests all the writings of Paul with a singular interest, because his knowledge of the words and deeds of Jesus Christ came not from documents, but from the lips of St. Peter and those who accompanied our Lord during His Ministry.

Our authorities for the life of St. Paul are the *Acts of the Apostles* and the letters, called by the forbidding name of Epistles, which the Apostle wrote for the instruction of the various churches he had founded. Some of these letters were written to settle questions of conduct and behaviour which naturally puzzled people who were in a transitional stage from paganism to Christianity; others were written to explain his conception of the Christian life. He had no idea that he was writing for any but the first generation of Christians, which lends to his writing something of the charm of a diary; and he would have been astonished had he known that his letters would be cherished for centuries and eventually incorporated in the New Testament. Letters written by Paul nearly nineteen centuries ago still inspire Christians, because he dealt with fundamental matters which are as real to-day as they were in the time of Nero.

St. Paul's letters are, therefore, the earliest Christian writings on record. The fact that they were written before any of the four Gospels is not, perhaps, generally appreciated, because the scholars who produced the Authorized Version of our Bible in the reign of James I. did not arrange the New Testament in the order in which it was written. St. Paul's Epistles are, for instance, arranged according to their length. Readers interested in the complicated subject of Pauline Chronology should turn to the note at the end of this book.

While the Epistles illuminate the mind of St. Paul for us—and we feel that we know him more intimately than any man of antiquity except, perhaps, Cicero—the *Acts of the Apostles* describes his missionary journeys. This book tells us where he went and what he did. The only Apostles who play any prominent part in the narrative are St. Peter, the central figure of the first part, and St. Paul, the central figure from chapter nine to the end. The theme of the book is the spread of Christianity from Jerusalem to Rome in the teeth of violent Jewish opposition. That Roman officials are shown to be fair to Christianity accords well with the theory that St. Luke wrote the book while St. Paul was in Rome, awaiting his appeal before Cæsar, and hoped to enlist on his behalf the influential support of the capital.

I have mentioned St. Luke as the author of *Acts*. This ancient tradition is now accepted by most scholars. He was, of course, the author of the Gospel that bears his name, and is assumed to have been a man of Gentile birth, possibly a Macedonian. St. Paul's reference to him as the " beloved physician," and St. Luke's frequent use of Greek medical terms, prove that he was a doctor by profession.

St. Paul and St. Luke were fellow travellers. Even if we did not know this, we should assume as much because of the vivid, first-hand observation which distinguishes the narrative. As if to emphasize his presence as an eye-witness, the author on many occasions breaks from the third person into the first person plural, portions of the book which are known as the "We-passages." These are: chapter sixteen, verses ten to seventeen; chapter twenty, verses five to fifteen; chapter twenty-one, verses one to eighteen; chapter twenty-seven, verse one, to chapter twenty-eight, verse sixteen.

Although it would be rash to imagine that Luke was absent except during the events described in the "We-passages," we can, at least, be certain that he was present on those occasions: Paul's first visit to Europe; his return voyage to Palestine, after his third mission; his journey to Jerusalem; his voyage from Cæsarea; his shipwreck on Malta; and his two years detention in Rome.

Apart from its importance in Christian history, the *Acts* is the most interesting travel narrative of antiquity. The attempts made in the last century to discredit it as a later and untrustworthy document have failed largely through the researches of such men as Sir William **Ramsay**. Its reputation **as** a piece of meticulously accurate topography has never stood higher than it does to-day. *The Acts of the Apostles* outlines the background and structure of the pagan world in the time of Claudius and Nero. The central figure, pressing on from land to land, crossing mountains and seas, suffering imprisonment, poverty, persecution and shipwreck, is shown to us as a man of iron will and lion-like courage. If we supplement this picture with the unconscious self-portrait given in the epistles, we see the same determination and courage, but we see also a more complex personality: a man in whose nature tears of tenderness and tears of rage are often close together.

From these sources, therefore, we can build up an accurate picture of St. Paul. It is only the first few years of his life, and the last year or two, that are hidden in obscurity. For the rest he walks in the full daylight of history.

He was born at Tarsus, in the opening years of the Christian Era. It was a Greek-speaking city of Cilicia, in Asia Minor, famous as a University town, as a port, as a caravan city, and as a big lumber and spinning centre. Like all the great commercial cities of the Roman world, Tarsus contained a colony of Jews; and to a family of this colony Paul belonged. His family possessed the privilege of the Roman citizenship. This meant that Paul could never be crucified or scourged, and had the right of appeal to Rome against the sentence of any provincial law-court. How Paul's family obtained this privilege is unknown. Their position as Roman citizens, however, suggests that the traditional idea of Paul as a humble tent-maker, and the son of a poor weaver, is not correct. Some of the greatest authorities to-day believe that Paul sprang from one of the leading families in Tarsus, a family of wealth and influence. That he was by trade a tent-maker is no argument against this, because it was the rule throughout

Orthodox Jewry to train sons, no matter what their financial prospects, to a trade.

In his home at Tarsus Paul would be called by his Hebrew name, Saul, and he retained this name during his youth and for the first thirty years or so of his life. In Roman, or Greek, surroundings, however, he would use his alternative name, Paul. The language which he spoke, and in which his epistles are written, is Greek, which was the common tongue of the world in his day. We know that he spoke Aramaic, the Semitic dialect that was spoken by our Lord and was the language of the Jews in the first century. It is also possible that Paul understood Latin, the language of proclamations and of official intercourse with the Roman authorities.

All we know about Paul's childhood and early life is that he was sent at some period to study theology under the rabbi Gamaliel in Jerusalem. Thus Jesus and Paul trod the soil of Palestine at the same time. We do not know whether Paul ever saw Jesus in the flesh. Some scholars believe that Paul may have seen Jesus, but just as many believe that he did not. If Paul were in Jerusalem during the Crucifixion, it would seem impossible that so ardent a young Pharisee would not have followed the crowds to Golgotha. On the other hand, is it feasible that a man of Paul's emotional nature would not have mentioned this in one of his letters or speeches?

Paul emerges in history as Saul, a fiery young anti-Christian bent on the death of Stephen, the first Christian martyr. This event was swiftly followed by Saul's vision on the road to Damascus and his conversion to the Faith that he had persecuted. Was he a young boy, or a man in the prime of life, when he was converted? Alas, we do not know. Some say one thing, some the other. It is impossible to determine Paul's age at any period of his life, because we do not know the year of his birth. There is an ancient tradition that he served God for thirty-five years and died in Rome, aged sixty-eight, in the year 67 A.D. If we accept this tradition, we must imagine his birth to have occurred in the year 1 B.C., and that he was a mature man in the thirties when he was converted at some time between the years 32–37 A.D. Sir William Ramsay argues that the Greek word used to describe Paul—*neos*, "a young man"—was used to describe a person of from twenty-two to forty years of age. The only other indication of his years is given by the Apostle towards the end of his life, when, probably about 60 A.D., he writes of himself as "Paul, the aged."

Paul's life of sixty-eight years covers a spectacular period of Roman history. He lived during the reigns of five Cæsars. He was born in the reign of Augustus, and grew to manhood in the reigns of Tiberius and Caligula; he spent his middle-age in the reign of Claudius, and his old age in the reign of Nero. When St. Paul was a middle-aged man, Britain was invaded by the legions of Claudius and London was founded as a Roman city. Vespasian was a young cavalry officer, serving with the army in Britain—Vespasian, whose son, Titus, was to command the armies that, three years after Paul's death, destroyed the Temple of Herod and burnt Jerusalem to the ground. When Paul was an old man in Rome, he may have heard talk of the terrible revolt in Britain under a queen called Boadicea. It is probable that he heard of the burning of London, of the annihilation of the Ninth Legion, and of the flight of the Procurator of Britain to Gaul.

Among famous men of antiquity who were contemporaries of St. Paul, in the sense that they were alive during some portion of his life, were Seneca and Pliny the Elder. An older generation, including Livy, Ovid, and Strabo, died while Paul was a young man. His countryman, Philo of Alexandria, was about twenty years older than Paul. In the year of Paul's death Josephus, the Jewish historian, was about thirty; Martial was a struggling young writer in Rome; Tacitus was a boy of twelve; and Epictetus was a child of seven. The world that is so well known to us in the writings of the historians of Imperial Rome was also the world in which St. Paul lived. . . .

I watched the sunlight falling over the brown walls of Jerusalem. Above me, in the north-east angle of the wall, was that enclosed space where the Mosque of the Dome of the Rock stands on the site of Solomon's Temple. If a Christian goes there to-day, he must conform to certain rules, just as the Gentile was obliged to conform to the rules of the Jewish Temple. Something of the atmosphere of the one has descended as a birthright to the other. I suppose this is natural, because the main formative influences in Islam are Judaism and a fainter tinge of Christianity. This explains, no doubt, why so many people who visit this mosque to-day feel the shadow of the Temple upon it.

Within that brown wall, I thought, Jesus had taught His disciples. St. Peter and the Apostles walked there after the Resurrection. Saul had called down death on Stephen there, and in after years, as Paul the Apostle, had faced for Christ's sake the same fury against the Faith that he himself had once instigated.

If a Roman visitor, who had been in Jerusalem at the time of the Crucifixion, had returned to it a few years afterwards, about the time of Stephen's death, he would have seen no outward change. Pontius Pilate was still the Procurator of Judæa, and Herod Antipas was the puppet Tetrarch of Galilee. The Temple worship was still the very heart and soul of Jerusalem. The altar before the Holy of Holies smoked all day long. The trumpets of the priests awakened Jerusalem at the first streak of dawn. The smell of incense and of roast flesh would drift with a west wind over the Mount of Olives.

And if this Roman visited again the Outer Court of the Temple, which was one of the things that every Greek and Roman tourist did, he would see the same kind of crowd that he had seen years before: the eager hucksters sitting under the cedars of Annas, selling sacrificial doves, the acute money-changers at their little desks, changing Greek and Palestinian money into the Temple currency, the scribes, and the Pharisees. Many of the merchants would remember how, some few years before, a Prophet from Galilee had made a whip and had driven them from the Temple courts.

He would see with curiosity and with astonishment, especially if it were the Passover month, that Jews had come to Jerusalem from every part of the civilized world. As a Roman, he would recoil from contact with them, because the Roman despised the Jew as heartily as the Jew despised the Roman. He would probably whisper to himself, as he saw the rich variety of Jews from every corner of the Empire, those words which Strabo had applied to the race:

"It is not easy to find a spot in the world that has not sheltered this people, and is not in their power."

He would notice that there was a marked difference between the native Palestinian Jew and the Jew from overseas. The strict Palestinian Jew was a man so firmly bound up in the Law that he could hardly move without suffering ceremonial defilement. He read the scriptures in Hebrew and he spoke Aramaic, a Hebrew dialect. The overseas Jew was, in comparison, a man of the world. He spoke Greek and he read the scriptures in the Greek version, the Septuagint which had been made at Alexandria.

It is interesting to imagine this Roman, so secure in his sense of superiority, watching, with a faint curl of the lip, a crowd of Jews thronging the Temple a few years after the Crucifixion. He would not know that among the stern Palestinian Jews, and among the more human Jews from foreign parts, were some who were conscious of the Divinity of Jesus Christ, and that from these Jews of both parties was to spring the new Faith of the world. This stranger would perhaps have followed with his eyes the tall figure of a Galilean fisherman. Suppose he had been told:

"That is Peter. He will die for the Faith and will lie in the heart of Rome, and his fame will go out over all the world. That other man—that eager, burning man—is Paul. When everything you see around is dust and ashes, his words will be alive. He, too, will lie in Rome, and men will come from all parts of the world to kneel at his grave."

4

The overseas, or Hellenistic, Jews, play a large part in *Acts*, and in the story of Paul's mission. These Greek-speaking Jews were resident in various cities in the Roman Empire. They came to Jerusalem on pilgrimage, just as devout Moslems visit Mecca.

Some people imagine—it is difficult to know why—that the Jewish race did not scatter over the earth until the Temple of Herod was destroyed in 70 A.D. This scattering, or Diaspora, as it is called, began centuries before Christ. It was Alexander the Great who gave impetus to it, three hundred years before Christ was born. That mighty conqueror wished to found not only a great empire, but to spread Hellenistic culture all over the world. If Napoleon's soldiers carried a marshal's baton in their knapsacks, Alexander's carried Homer and Aristotle.

One result of Alexander's brief career was to cover the stupendous area of his conquests with countless new and vigorous Hellenistic cities. Safe new roads were drawn across the world, and new opportunities for commerce were opened up. The new world offered enormous attractions to the Jews. Their synagogues were soon to be found everywhere. By the time of Christ, the majority of the Jewish nation was living outside Palestine, and it has been estimated that these Jews numbered seven and a half million, or seven per cent. of the total population of the Roman Empire.

Jews of the Diaspora, who were making money and living in the defiling presence of the Gentile, were looked down on by the conservative and exclusive Palestinian as Jews of a weaker and less reputable religious caste. Although the Greek-speaking Jew had to adapt himself to Gentile surroundings and was brought into the main current of Gentile thought, he often retained his Jewish identity with passionate intensity. He looked towards Jerusalem as the Holy City, just as the Moslem looks towards Mecca. He made an annual contribution to the Temple, that was taken once a year to Jerusalem with solemn ceremony. Among the more pious overseas Jews were some who dreamt of retiring to the sanctity of Jerusalem in order to be buried there, and certain of the communities even maintained special Hellenistic synagogues in the city.

Therefore the Jews of the Diaspora belonged to the Roman Empire only in a geographic sense. Just as the Romans planted colonies of retired soldiers about the world, which were really little bits of Rome set down on foreign soil, so the Jewish colonies in the various big cities might be compared to little bits of Jerusalem in a foreign country. And the ordinary inhabitants of such cities resented and disliked this.

The unpopularity of the Jew was world-wide ages before the Crucifixion. The Greeks and the Romans loathed the Jew with equal intensity. Such closed communities, living apparently eccentric lives, adopting curious diet laws, abstaining from pork and shell-fish, and disappearing into their mysterious synagogues on the Sabbath, were not regarded as pleasant neighbours. As religion and politics were closely related in the mind of classical antiquity, the refusal of the Jews to make even a formal genuflection towards the municipal or Imperial deities led to constant charges of disloyalty to the city and to Cæsar.

Another source of hatred were the privileges which Jews enjoyed under the Romans. These included freedom from military service. Why, asked the Gentile fellow-townsman, should this Oriental people, who made money out of the city and sent a portion of it abroad to Jerusalem, who behaved with such arrogant contempt towards the Gentile and his institutions, why should they be so favoured by the Government? Pogroms were frequent, and Jewish insistence on privileges led to demonstrations which often ended in riots, so that throughout the Empire the Jew had a bad name as an agitator. In Rome the political influence of the Jews was such that, on one occasion, when Cicero was defending Flaccus, he warned the judges that he would drop his voice so that they only could hear him, because he was speaking in a turbulent Jewish district.

The official attitude towards the Jews was, on the whole, favourable, but it varied from reign to reign with the anti- or pro-Jew influences surrounding the Imperial throne. In addition to the millions of poor and middle-class Jews throughout the Empire, there were numbers of enormously rich Jews whose political influence was sometimes very great. At the head of these wealthy Jews were the princes of the Herodian House, who were educated in Rome just as the sons of Indian rajahs are to-day educated at Eton and Oxford. These young princes became sophisticated Romans and numbered among their friends all the "best people" in Roman society, including, of course, the members of the Imperial family. Their influence on politics was, from time to time, immense.

Julius Cæsar was a great friend of the Jews. He never forgot how much he owed to Antipater, the father of Herod the Great, who, realizing that Cæsar was coming out on top, swiftly changed sides and extricated him from a perilous military position in Egypt. When Cæsar lay murdered, the Jews of

Rome wailed round his funeral pyre for many nights. Tiberius, the Cæsar of the Crucifixion, was not partial to the Jews, and his chief minister, Sejanus, was a violent anti-Semite. This is, perhaps, one of the reasons why Pontius Pilate was able to rule the Jews with a firm hand for ten years. His firmness was supported in Rome, and it was not until Sejanus fell from power that Pilate's enemies among the Jews were able to bring about his downfall. During the reign of Tiberius, the Jews were expelled from Rome.

In the following reign, Caligula, the mad Emperor, had as his boon companion the clever young Jewish prince who became Agrippa I., and during this reign the Jews returned to Rome. Apart from a crazy desire to have his statue erected in the Temple at Jerusalem, which was averted by the skill of Agrippa, Caligula did nothing to affect the Jews during his short period of power. It was also Agrippa who was partly responsible for placing the next emperor, Claudius, on the throne. After the murder of Caligula, Claudius, who was a timid man, was hiding behind a curtain in the Imperial palace, unconscious that his feet were visible. Some prætorians, wandering through the palace, pulled him out and laughingly cried: "Why, here is Germanicus; let's make him Emperor!" Agrippa was in Rome, and decided to take the joke seriously. He went to the Senate, who were thinking of reviving the Roman Republic, and managed to sway their opinion; and the result was that Claudius, to his astonishment, became Cæsar.

Although Claudius was of pro-Jewish sympathies, he was unable to prevent another expulsion of the Jews from Rome during his reign: the expulsion that drove St. Paul's friends, Aquila and Priscilla, to Corinth. During Nero's reign, there were close pro-Jewish influences near the throne. It was said that Poppæa was a convert to Judaism. It was the Fire of Rome, and the necessity of giving the crowd some enemy on which to vent its rage, that caused Nero to persecute the Christians. If there had been no Christians, no doubt the Jews would have suffered instead.

It is necessary to understand the attitude of the Roman world towards the Diaspora before one can understand the time of St. Paul. It was among the Jews of the Diaspora that his missionary life was spent. This widespread settlement of commercially adroit and religiously aloof Orientals puzzled and irritated the Latin mind.

"Amongst themselves," wrote Tacitus, "there prevails a persistent combination and ready liberality, but towards all others an intense hatred. They never eat, they never sleep with strangers. Those who go over to them they instruct in contempt of the gods, in the disowning of one's fatherland, the despising of one's parents, children, brothers and sisters."

This "going over to the Jews" is a reference to the large number of Gentiles who sought consolation in the uplifting monotheism of the synagogue because they were sickened by the oriental sex-cults that masqueraded as religion in Asia Minor, or by the empty fables which were all that Greece or Rome had to offer. It is sometimes forgotten that in the time of Christ, Judaism was an active missionary faith. Our Lord referred to Pharisees who would compass sea and land to make one proselyte.

Each synagogue throughout the Diaspora had attached to it a ring of proselytes, some who were merely friends of the Jewish faith, who observed the fasts and the Sabbath, and believed in God; others who actually became Jews, changed their names, and were in the course of three generations indistinguishable from the people who had adopted them.

Such synagogues were a powerful factor in the growth of Pauline Christianity. They gave the Apostle a starting-place for his preaching. St. Paul knew that the whole Roman world was studded with such synagogues, that wherever there was a

Jewish colony there would he find a prayer-house willing to give him a hearing. He was invariably driven away as a blasphemer; but that did not matter. Sometimes the seed fell on good ground. Often, even though the Jews drove him away, the proselytes became Christians.

Therefore, among the main factors in the westward spread of Christianity, were the synagogues of the Diaspora; the universal character of the Greek language, which St. Paul spoke and in which his epistles were written; the unity of the Roman Empire, which made his journeys safe; and the splendid Roman roads which made such journeys possible.

These were some of the reasons why a missionary, in the short space of probably less than twenty years, could found a chain of churches across Asia Minor, in Macedonia, in Greece; and testify to the Divinity of Christ in the Imperial Capital itself.

5

The sun had not set when I retraced my steps across the valley. Swifts, which at this time of year come up from Africa, were flying like darts over the Wall of Jerusalem. They flashed and dived with shrill cries up and down the gash of the Kedron Valley, turning my thoughts to villages at home and to grey churches standing among elm trees. Whenever I see the swifts flying now, or watch them flattened against the eaves of an English barn, I wonder if they have cut the air above the Garden of Gethsemane.

On the city side of St. Stephen's Gate, a flight of steps goes up to the Wall. Mounting them, I found myself on the sentry-walk, with a breast-high, crenellated rampart before me; through the openings I gazed down at the Moslem cemeteries clustering fifty feet below, at the foot of the Wall. I could see the white ribbon of road disappearing beneath St. Stephen's Gate, and in the stillness of the evening I could hear every word spoken by Arabs on the Jericho Road as they turned and urged their donkeys up the little path to the gate.

In Old Testament times this Gate was known as the Sheep Gate, because sheep required for sacrifices in the Temple of Solomon were gathered here and passed into Jerusalem this way. Jesus must have used the Gate many a time as He passed from the Temple to the Mount of Olives. I like to think that when He said, "I am the door of the sheep," He was standing on the opposite hill, watching the white flocks pressing past into the city.

It is an interesting commentary on the tenacity of Eastern tradition that, although the last sheep was sacrificed on the Altar of Burnt Offerings in the year 70 A.D., this Gate remained the sheep market of Jerusalem until the British occupation. The market was then moved to the Damascus Gate, and then to Herod's Gate, from which it drifted into the valley at the north-east corner of the city, where it now remains.

The present Sheep Gate dates only from the sixteenth century, for the Gate has, of course, been rebuilt time and again during the stormy history of Jerusalem. The name of St. Stephen was associated with it in Christian times, for the path to the valley leads to the traditional spot of St. Stephen's death.

St. Stephen, St. Peter, and St. Paul, were the three men who released Christianity from the cage of Judaism and sent it speeding in freedom over the early world.

St. Stephen is the forerunner of St. Paul. One thinks of him as the only man who might have been, had he lived, another Apostle of the Gentiles. It is almost as though his fiery spirit returned to earth and, driving out the spirit of Saul the Pharisee, created Paul the Apostle.

At the time of Stephen's death, a few years after the Crucifixion, the infant Church was still in the arms of the syna-

gogue. Jews who believed in Christ did not differ in any of
the outward signs from Jews who did not believe. The Christian Jews still offered sacrifices in the Temple, and still observed the Mosaic taboos and lawful feast days and fasts. There
were about five thousand of them in Jerusalem, under the
leadership of St. Peter and the other Apostles. The whole of
Jerusalem rang with stories of the power that had descended
on the Apostles at Pentecost. St. Peter had healed a man who,
as everyone who frequented the Temple knew, had been lame
since his birth. There was much talk of wonders and of the
strange gift that had descended on the men who had known
Jesus Christ.

"The primitive Apostles were indubitably endowed with
miraculous powers," wrote Dr. David Smith. "The evidence
is irrefragable. It is no mere legend of a later date, but their
own personal and direct testimony. They repeatedly refer to
the phenomenon in their letters, and always as a recognized
fact, familiar to their readers. It was only temporary, but it did
not immediately vanish from the Church on the departure of
the Apostles. It gradually diminished until in the fourth century, as St. Chrysostom certifies, it had quite disappeared;
but on the testimony of St. Justin Martyr and St. Irenæus, it
still persisted in the second century and, on the testimony of
Tertullian, lingered on into the third. Nor, indeed, is either
the gift or its withdrawal inexplicable. It was a providential
dispensation. At its first planting Christianity required special aids, but once it had taken root, these were no longer
needed, and it was left to its normal development."

St. Stephen was a Hellenistic Jew "full of grace and power,"
who, in the course of his contentions in the synagogues, was
charged with undermining the Law of Moses and belittling
the sanctity of the Temple. Like the Founder of Christianity
before him, and like St. Paul after him, this saint was taken
before the Sanhedrin to explain what was regarded as his

blasphemy.

The Sanhedrin met in three places: at the gate of the Temple Hill; in a hall at the south-east corner of the Temple building; and in the *Lishcath hag-gazith*, the Hall of Hewn Stones, the most important assembly-place of the three. There is a passage in the Talmud which tells us that forty years before the destruction of the Temple in 70 A.D., the Sanhedrin had ceased to meet in the Hall of Hewn Stones: therefore the trial of St. Stephen, which occurred just after this hall had been closed, must have taken place either in the open air near the gate, or in the subsidiary hall in the Temple area.

The rabbinical writings contain minute descriptions of such occasions, so that it is easy to reconstruct the scene. The judges sat in a semi-circle, with the president in the centre. At each end of the semi-circle stood a secretary, one taking down evidence for the defence, the other for the prosecution. On three benches in front of the judges sat the law students, or the disciples of the scribes. The prisoner was supposed to stand before the judges in an attitude of sorrow and humiliation.

Stephen did not adopt this attitude. Those who looked at him "saw his face as it had been the face of an angel." When they asked him if he had said that Jesus of Nazareth would change the customs handed down by Moses, Stephen made a long and remarkable speech in which he voiced for the first time, and with fiery conviction, his belief that the Law of Christ replaced the Law of Moses.

He was speaking to men who believed with an immutable rigidity that the Law given to Moses was for ever complete, for ever perfect, and that only in the Temple at Jerusalem was God on terms of intimacy with man.

But Stephen's heresy was not yet blasphemy. They listened while he detailed the well-known backslidings of Israel; they listened even while he told them that "the most High dwelleth not in temples made with hands"; but all the time we can hear, in imagination, a rising murmur of horror, indignation, and fury, which, gathering volume, provoked Stephen to his final tremendous denunciation:

"Ye stiffnecked and uncircumcised in heart and ears, ye do always resist the Holy Ghost: as your fathers did, so do ye. Which of the prophets have not your fathers persecuted? and they have slain them which showed before of the coming of the Just One; of whom ye have been now the betrayers and murderers . . ."

The tumult gathered and broke. They were "cut to the heart." They "gnashed their teeth on him." But, suddenly, over this amazing piece of writing there seems to fall a miraculous hush, in which one hears the voice of Stephen saying:

"Behold, I see the heavens opened, and the Son of Man standing on the right hand of God."

He saw the Son of Man *standing*, not sitting, on the right hand of the Father: he saw Jesus standing as if ready to welcome into heaven the first of the army of Christian martyrs.

As Stephen said this, they stopped their ears at the blasphemy and, with a shriek of rage, "ran upon him with one accord, and cast him out of the city, and stoned him: and the witnesses laid down their clothes at a young man's feet, whose name was Saul."

And Saul "was consenting unto his death." He stood there, watching Stephen die. He saw the executioners cast him from a high place, as detailed by the Talmud, in the hope that he would break his back and die. He saw them hurl the first stones at his head. But perhaps the formal horror of a Jewish execution was forgotten in that mad riot; for we learn that Stephen knelt down and prayed. As the stones fell about him, Saul heard him cry:

"Lord Jesus, receive my spirit."

As the stones came faster, he sank down and repeated with

a loud voice the cry of his Master on the Cross:

"Lord, lay not this sin to their charge."

"And when he had said this, he fell asleep."

After the martyrdom of Stephen, Saul, like a madman, "made havock of the church, entering into every house, and haling men and women, committed them to prison."

But he had heard Stephen. He had seen him die. The seed had been sown. Stephen had voiced the New Testament; Saul, although he did not yet know it, had already been chosen to take the New Testament out of the hands of Jewry and to proclaim it in the far places of the world.

6

As the sun was setting over Jerusalem, I walked along the sentry-walk to the northern angle of the wall, where, turning to the west, it runs above Herod's Gate to the Damascus Gate. There is nowhere in the world a walk more wonderful than this.

Except for a few yards at the Jaffa Gate, the old City of Jerusalem lies encircled by its wall as it has been since the earliest times. The modern houses that are being built round Jerusalem are all outside the walls, so that the magnificent appearance of the old city has not been destroyed. Excavations made during the last century proved that in certain places the Wall goes down from fifty to eighty feet below the present earth level. These invisible courses are of huge, undressed blocks, laid without mortar, and many of them belong to the wall that encircled Jerusalem in Old Testament times.

The sentry-walk is about a yard wide. There is a high rampart on one side, and, on the other, an easy drop to back gardens and the roofs of bazaars. Descending at the Damascus Gate, I walked down the road to the Monastery of the Dominicans, on whose property is a lovely little basilica of St. Stephen, consecrated in the year 1900.

Father Simeon Vailhé, of the Augustinian Fathers of the Assumption, has proved beyond question that a church of St. Stephen, enshrining his relics, was consecrated in the valley not later than the year 438 A.D. When Eudoxia, wife of the Byzantine Emperor, Theodosius II., paid a second visit to Jerusalem in 444 A.D., as an exile from the Court of Constantinople, she devoted herself to solemn studies and decreed the erection of a great basilica to St. Stephen, her special patron. The site chosen for the basilica was not to the east of the city, on the traditional site of his death, but to the north. As she felt death approaching, she hurried on the consecration of the church, which took place on June 14th, 460 A.D., before the building was completed. In this church the Empress was buried.

When the Crusaders occupied Jerusalem, the basilica built by Eudoxia had fallen into ruins. A camp was established near it, and after they had captured Jerusalem, the Crusaders proceeded to rebuild the basilica as a Romanesque church, believing it to be the actual site of the martyrdom.

The Crusading church did not, however, remain for very long. The Crusaders pulled it down when Saladin approached the Holy City, for they feared that the church of St. Stephen, so near the walls, would give the enemy a platform for siege engines.

Curiously enough, when Christian pilgrims began to visit Jerusalem in the Middle Ages, they reverted, no one knows why, to the traditional site in the Kedron Valley. This is another notable instance of the tenacity of traditional beliefs in the Holy Land; and it was at this period that the gate to the Kedron Valley began to be called St. Stephen's Gate.

In 1881 those great archæologists, the Dominican Fathers, digging near their monastery to the north of the city, discovered the confusing mass of ruins that marked the Byzantine basilica of Eudoxia and the Crusading church. On this spot they have erected a beautiful little basilica in honour of the great proto-martyr, whose death near by in the Kedron Valley was the first signal that the Church of Christ was unfolding its wings in readiness for its flight from the synagogue.

7

One evening at dinner in a house not far from the Mount of Olives, I met the Grand Mufti of Jerusalem, Haj Amin el Husseini. He is an Arab aristocrat, a smiling, quiet man of middle age, whom I had seen a year or two ago riding out of Jerusalem on a white horse during the Feast of Nebi Musa, while cannon boomed from the cemeteries under the old wall. At that time I thought that this leader of the Palestinian Moslems looked as I imagine the more spiritual commanders of the Moslem conquest must have looked, a Saladin who, hearing that his adversary was suffering from malaria, would have sent him a basket of iced fruit. Mr. Philip de László, the artist, who has also met the Grand Mufti, told me that he reminded him of the portrait of the Sultan Mohammed II by Gentile Bellini, in the National Gallery.

Sitting near me at this dinner-party was Mr. John Whiting of the American Colony, who was born in Palestine and speaks Arabic like a native. He knows more about the country than anyone of my acquaintance. He asked me if I should like to ascend the minaret to the north-west corner of the Haram-es-Sherif, or Dome of the Rock. This minaret is built on the site of the Castle of Antonia.

"Of course I should," I told him. "But it is forbidden."

"I'll ask the Grand Mufti," said John Whiting, and, choosing the right moment after dinner, he did so. To my surprise, the Mufti gave his permission.

On the following morning Whiting and I set out full of excitement, for such an invitation is seldom given to a foreigner. Calling at the offices of the Arab Council, we found that our permission had come through and that a young Arab had been appointed as our guide.

We entered the Haram area, where I kept my eyes to the ground because I did not wish to see anything until the site of Solomon's Temple would lie below me from the platform of the minaret. Climbing an outer staircase, the Arab opened a door at the base of the minaret and we ascended a spiral staircase inside it. It was a long, stiff climb. We stepped out on a platform, and were temporarily blinded by the fierce glare from the enormous expanse of open ground below.

When we were able to open our eyes, we saw a sight I shall never forget. We were looking down on the ancient area of Solomon's Temple. I have walked about that place many a time, but never have I seen it to such advantage. It is impossible to get an adequate idea of the enormous area covered by the Haram-es-Sherif unless you have a bird's-eye view of it; and its character as a walled, sacred city within a city—which was its character in the Old and the New Testaments and is still its character to-day under Islam—is not obvious, save from a height.

I saw how, in broad outline, the mosque of to-day reflects the general character of Solomon's Temple. Of course the architectural style of the Temple was entirely different. Solomon's Temple was built by Phœnicians, who, having no architecture of their own, borrowed from the architecture of Egypt and Assyria. The later Temple which Herod the Great built, and in which Jesus taught, was no doubt borrowed from Greece and the architecture of the Hellenistic age, for the Jews never created a national architecture. And how curious it is that the building which now stands on the same site is also a piece of borrowed architecture. It was built in 688 A.D. to the orders of the Caliph Abd el Melek; but it was not designed by Arab architects, because Arab architecture had not yet developed. Just as in Solomon's time the Children of Israel were only a few generations removed from the desert and had no skill in architecture—as Solomon frankly admitted to his contractor, Hiram, King of Tyre—so the Arabs who conquered Jerusalem were men of the desert who knew nothing about building and had to employ Byzantine architects to erect their sanctuary.

One may well wonder how it was that such a large portion of Jerusalem remained an open space for centuries, so that all the Arabs had to do was to clear away the rubbish and erect the successor to Solomon's Temple. The reason is that throughout early Christian history the Christians of Jerusalem wished this site to remain a vacant ruin in order that the words of Christ might be literally fulfilled: "Behold your house is left unto you desolate."

When Julian the Apostate attempted to turn the world back to paganism, he created consternation among Christians by giving the Jews permission to rebuild Solomon's Temple, in order that he might confound Christ's prophesy. The story of this project is curious and the failure to carry it out remains one of the mysteries of history. The whole of Jewry flung itself with joy into the rebuilding. Wealth and workers poured into the Holy Land from every part of the world. Nothing seemed lacking; yet the Temple was never re-built. What happened has not been satisfactorily explained. That something unusual did happen is, however, obvious. Early chroniclers speak of miraculous fires and other manifestations which scared the Jews so badly that they gave up the attempt. Modern writers have offered the suggestion that fires and sudden mysterious explosions did actually occur, caused by the opening of underground tunnels which had been closed for centuries, and the consequent escape of vapours and inflammable gases. Whatever the reason may have been, the work of rebuilding the Temple was suspended, and any hopes the Jews may have cherished of seeing their dream come true ended with the death of Julian, who was killed in battle at the untimely age of thirty-one.

From that time, until the year 635 A.D., the site of the Temple was preserved as a desolate place by the Christians. All the city rubbish of Byzantine Jerusalem was carted to the site of the Temple, so that when the Mohammedans captured the city, the Caliph Omar had to crawl on his hands and knees over accumulated refuse into the place where the Temple had been. So great was the neglect that difficulty was experienced even in finding the *Sakhrah*, the site of the sacred rock.

This was discovered buried deep in debris, and above it in time rose the mosque erected by Omar, described by the pilgrim, Arculf, as "an enormous square edifice of vile construction," built on the ruins of some old buildings, and composed of beams and planks of wood supported on ancient columns. This building occupied the site until Byzantine architects erected the lovely octagonal mosque which stands there to-day.

Only in the East, and on a holy site in the East, can one expect a place to remain unchanged for so long a time. The Dome of the Rock is the same to-day as it was when the Byzantines built it for the Arabs in 688 A.D. It is the building the Crusaders saw when they tied up their chargers in the underground Stables of Solomon. And behind it lies the shadow of that still more ancient Temple of Jehovah in which Jesus and His disciples walked; in which St. Paul studied under Gamaliel; in which St. Stephen defied the Sanhedrin; and in which St. Paul spoke of Jesus Christ and the way of salvation, while a furious mob demanded his death.

8

The night before I left Jerusalem, John Whiting arranged one of his famous picnics. I have never met anyone in whom the picnic sense is more seriously developed.

Having lived so frequently with Bedouin in the desert, he loves to cook and eat out of doors, and watching him at such moments, I can understand why the Arabs treat him as one of themselves. He has the gift, which I suppose men like Burckhardt, Doughty, and Lawrence all possessed, of being able to shed his nationality.

One of the first rules of a Whiting picnic is that no one must know where it is to be. The guests assemble at a given time and place, unaware whether they are to be transported to the Dead Sea or to the Plain of Sharon, until Whiting, in the first car, leads an obstacle race over the hills of Judæa, usually stopping by some overhanging crag where Arab servants, sent on ahead, are seen crouching above a fire and picking up stones before they put down the rugs.

On this occasion we assembled just before sunset and were taken by our leader for some miles along the Bethlehem Road; then, turning to the right along a rough cart-track, we came to a hill from whose slopes the city of Jerusalem was visible, lying some miles below like a scale model on a tray.

Not a word was spoken as we stood watching the afterglow flame for a moment above the Dead Sea and die down into that fifteen minutes of unearthly hushed beauty which is neither dusk nor twilight. The darkness rushed down on the hills and, below us, Jerusalem was lying picked out with thousands of pin-prick lights. We could see the bright lights of the new town and the square of dark that told us where old Jerusalem was lying within the embrace of its wall. All round was a fierce, violet darkness.

The thorn wood crackled and the red glow touched the

earnest faces of the Arab servants. Whiting speared meat on long skewers and grilled the best *kebab* I had ever eaten. He gave us chicken liver as the Bedouin cook it, and legs of chicken with the taste and smell of the thorn fire in them. There were Arabian dates and native sweets and wine.

About fifteen of us sat in a circle on the ground.

Whiting and the Arab servants came over with a special brew of Bedouin coffee, strong and bitter, with a herb called *hail* added to it.

"Sit down and tell us an Arab story," someone asked.

"All right," said Whiting. "This is a story with a moral—like most Arab stories."

He looked like a Bedouin as he sat in the firelight, translating the story out of Bedouin Arabic into English.

"Once upon a time there was a king who wished to capture a certain town. He summoned his Grand Vizier and ordered him to go in disguise as a pilgrim to spy out the land. The Vizier went through the bazaars of this town to the shops which sold food. 'I wish to buy bread,' he said. The shop-keeper said: 'Friend, my bread is stale, but my neighbour has good, fresh bread.' He asked for olives. 'My olives are naught,' cried the merchant, 'but my neighbour has olives that are fat and oily.' So the Grand Vizier returned to the King and he said 'O King, we cannot conquer that town.'

"In ten years time the King ordered his Grand Vizier to go again to this town. He went to buy bread in the bazaars. 'My lord, I have the best bread, and no man in this town can equal the quality of my olives and my cheeses,' said the merchant, rubbing his hands together and bowing to the ground. 'Look around, my lord, what rubbish do you see in the other shops?' So the Grand Vizier returned to the King, and he said: 'O King, the time has now come for us to conquer that town, because the people are no longer of one heart.' "

"Tell us another story!" came from the circle.

"All right," replied Whiting, "I shall tell you the story of the invention of wine. Long ago, when Adam and Eve were in the Garden of Eden, Mother Eve was sorry to notice that Adam lacked enterprise and was quite content to potter about the garden and waste his time. She said to him one day: 'Why do you remain in Paradise all the time? Why don't you go out and see what lies in the world? If I were a big, strong man like you, I should be ashamed to sit about all day long. Have you no sense of adventure?'

"So Adam, in order to escape from Eve's reproaches, left the Garden and wandered in the world outside, where he discovered a tree that was not in Eden. It was a vine. Small clusters of green grapes grew on it, and these Adam gathered and took home to show Eve. She ate them and said they were very good. This pleased Adam, so he determined to nourish the vine. One day he went out to the vine and saw that its leaves drooped in the heat of a *khamseen*. While he was wondering where he could find water, a monkey passed by. Adam seized it and killed it, refreshing the vine with its blood. He went out again, and again the vine was wilting. This time a peacock passed by. Adam slew it and gave its blood to the vine. A third time he went, and still the vine was parched. A lion came along and, after some difficulty, Adam slew it and poured its blood upon the vine. On the fourth visit the vine, although considerably improved, was still suffering from the heat. As Adam was wondering what to do about it, a wild pig came along, and this Adam killed and with its blood nourished the vine. And the heat passed and the vine thrived.

"One day he went again and saw that the vine was covered with huge bunches of big, red grapes. He gathered some and ran to Eve with them. She cried, 'O Adam, are you hurt? There is blood on you!' But he said, 'No, it is the juice of the vine, which I have watered with blood.' Adam and Eve liked the grapes so much that Eve kept them in a pot and they drank the juice. So wine was discovered."

The speaker paused:

"I have told you," he said, "that most Arab stories have a moral. Here is the moral. One drink of wine, and you act like a monkey; two drinks, and you strut like a peacock; three drinks, and you roar like a lion; and four drinks—you behave like a pig."

Under a starlit sky, and in the silence that enfolds Jerusalem when darkness has fallen, we went back to the city. And in the morning Stephan came round with his car and we set off on the road to Damascus.

CHAPTER II

Describes a journey to Damascus, the Street called Straight, and the scene of St. Paul's escape from his enemies. I leave Syria for Turkey, see Tarsus, discover tent-makers at work, explore the Cilician Gates, and, after a little difference with the police, consider it prudent to retire to Antioch.

1

AFTER the death of Stephen, Paul persecuted the believers in Jerusalem. When he had arrested all those who had not fled from his wrath and had them bastinadoed—a punishment which the Sanhedrin and all the local synagogues seem to have dispensed with an alacrity unexampled except, perhaps, by the old Ottoman Empire—Paul looked round for fresh victims. Such prey existed in Damascus, where faith in Christ had spread among the synagogues with great rapidity: therefore Paul obtained official letters from the Sanhedrin authorizing him to arrest the Believers in Damascus, and to bring them bound to Jerusalem for trial.

It has often been suggested that Paul was himself a member of the Sanhedrin. If so, it has been argued, he must have been married, a qualification necessary for every member of the Sanhedrin on the baseless assumption that married men would be more merciful. From what we know of the Sanhedrin, they seem to have been a singularly violent and merciless gathering. It had been thought that the many tender references made by Paul to his converts, such as the lovely sentence to the Galatians, "My little children, of whom I travail in birth again until Christ be formed in you," suggest that he was a parent. If he were a father, it seems strange

34

that no reference is made to this in his personal letters.

Paul seems to have been in a hurry to reach Damascus and begin his campaign against the Believers there. He probably used a trotting camel, a mule, or a donkey, for his journey. It has been said by many commentators that he went on foot, because after his vision those who were with him "led him by the hand and brought him into Damascus." We must remember that Paul was nervously shattered as well as blind. While they led him by the hand, they would also have led his mule or camel. It seems unlikely that an official delegation from the Sanhedrin at Jerusalem would have travelled on foot. No one in the East walks if he can possibly go any other way.

When Paul set out from Jerusalem with an escort, probably provided by the Temple Guard, he had the choice of two routes. He could go down to Jericho and travel north on the road along the Jordan Valley, crossing the river at Beth-shan. This route would take him round the southern shores of the Sea of Galilee and up to the mountain roads linking the cities of the Decapolis with Damascus. But it is a hot and uncomfortable road in summer time, lying far below sea level until the mountains to the east of the Sea of Galilee are reached. A rather longer, but probably better and more frequented way was that which to-day is still the best road to Damascus: this goes through Samaria and Galilee, and up into the foothills of Mount Hermon. I think that Paul must have used this road.

A traveller can now go from Jerusalem to Damascus in one day, a journey made possible by the excellent roads which Britain and France have built in their mandated territories. This day's journey of one hundred and ninety miles would have seemed fantastic twenty years ago. Residents of Jerusalem, who remember conditions before the War, tell me that camel caravans used to take about twelve days to reach Damascus.

I followed the road from Jerusalem down into Samaria, and across that khaki-coloured land of hills into the broad plain of Esdraelon, where the heights of Nazareth rise up to the north. I went up into these hills and down again to the Plain of Ahma. Beyond the Horns of Hattin, where Saladin brought the Crusading Kingdom crashing over the ears of Europe, I saw, a thousand feet below, a spoonful of bright blue water cupped in a curve of hill. And I descended to the heat of the lakeside of Galilee.

As I stood beside the Sea of Galilee, wishing that I might linger there and wanting very much to take a boat and row down to Capernaum, it occurred to me for the first time how significant must have been this stage of Paul's journey. He would come down into Tiberias and ride through the lakeside villages on the west bank, including Capernaum. He would see villages exactly as they had been only a few years before, when Jesus was preaching there. The fact that Paul's heart was full of rage against the disciples of Christ must have made him think of Jesus as he passed through the scene of His Ministry. All round him, wherever he looked, was some link with the earthly visitation of Christ. As Paul rode through Capernaum, the very stones were those standing when Jesus passed through the streets, the synagogue fronting the lake was the one in which He had preached, the people who would come out to see Paul and his escort pass were the men and women who had seen Jesus.

Paul must have thought much about Christ in Galilee. He was living through the last two or three days of his disbelief. The place where his whole life was to be changed was only a few miles away, on the hills to the north of the Lake. Conversion is often said to be a long, unconscious process of the mind. The subconscious mind goes with hands open to meet conversion, but the conscious mind remains fixed and firm until something happens—some little thing—and a man finds his whole life changed. That seems to have been happening to Paul.

"Saul, Saul, why persecutest thou me . . . It is hard for thee to kick against the pricks."

Those words had not yet been spoken; but they were very near. The moments before an event like Paul's conversion, the moments just before St. Francis entered to pray in the ruined Church of St. Damiano, and before St. Catherine of Genoa knew that her whole life had been lifted to another plane, are moments which, no matter how pointless it may be to speculate on them, cannot fail to provoke wonder. At one moment St. Paul, St. Francis, and St. Catherine were like you or me, and at the next they were translated into another sphere of perception and were for ever different and apart.

And, as I stood beside the Sea of Galilee, I thought that when Paul came that way with his heart full of hate against Christ, and with his conversion only a little way off, he made one of the most interesting pictures in the story of Christianity: Saul the unconverted, riding round that little lake of Galilee, but so soon to carry the Message preached beside that lake to cities washed by the Mediterranean Sea.

2

At the northern end of the Sea of Galilee, the road to Damascus climbs steadily into the southern slopes of the Lebanon mountains. I lost sight of the lake for many a mile as I moved upward through a land of varied hills, some brown and stone-strewn, others aflame with all the flowers of the Palestine spring. After travelling for about fifteen miles, I reached the historic ford of the Jordan, Jisr Banat Ya'coub, the "Ford of the Daughters of Jacob."

When the snows of Hermon are melting in spring, the Jordan, flowing under a stone bridge, pretends for a brief time to be a Highland river in spate. It is about eighty feet in width and the ice-green waters slide with force downhill towards Galilee, between banks lined with oleanders, papyrus, and the box-like *Balanites Ægyptiaca,* which is the name botanists have given to the pseudo-balsam tree, or the "balm of Gilead," from whose walnut-like fruit the Arabs prepare a kind of oil.

This ford of the Jordan has been known from remote ages to travellers from Damascus, Palmyra, and the Euphrates, as they journeyed south to Palestine and Egypt. The modern traveller has plenty of time to admire the scenery and to reflect on the fact that, although he has been climbing hard all the way from Tiberias, he is still forty feet below the Mediterranean Sea, for at this ford he must halt. Here is French territory, with the consequent fuss about passports, motor-car licences, and all the difficulties of a frontier.

Hungry Bedouin dogs slink about, nosing round the halted omnibus loads of Arabs, while drivers and passengers line up before the Customs shed to wait until business-like Syrians in French uniforms stamp their documents. Under a shady tree a couple of gendarmes sit at a table, drinking coffee and playing tric-trac with a visiting sheik.

Stephan had something vaguely irregular about his driving licence. It had either expired or was about to expire. Therefore he put his head on one side, clutched his grey velour hat to his breast, and answered a lot of questions with touching Armenian softness, his whole face lined and irradiated by a disarming smile; and after a time the Arab in khaki, who had been waving his hands, shrugging his shoulders, and making pouting and petulant faces, suddenly lifted the stamp and gave our passports a terrific bang, handing them to us with a conclusive smile that almost put Stephan's in the shade.

So we went on up a tremendous hill road, where a young sheik, cantering in front of us, was breaking in a lovely white

Arab stallion. He rode the bit of quicksilver on a rope bridle, and with his knees. He made the little horse stand while we passed them. The creature's eyes were wild like those of a frightened wood creature, and his pink-lined nostrils expanded and contracted as he tossed his head and danced on the hard road.

At the top of this long hill we paused to look back over Galilee, lying far below us, one of the most exquisite views in the world. I have been told that on a clear day it is possible to see south of the lake, where the river runs into the fiery trench of the Jordan Valley. But to-day a heat mist dimmed the distant view, although the whole lakeside was clearly visible, with Capernaum and Tiberias on the west bank and the wild mountains of Moab lying folded together on the east.

From this point the road runs across a sand-coloured upland almost straight to Damascus, with Mount Hermon towering to the left, magnificent and snow-touched on its summits. In strange contrast to the stuffy heat of Galilee, the wind was cold.

At a point on this road, about twelve miles from Damascus, we saw the low-lying white city shining far off, set on the sand, with domes and minarets lifted above a feathery greenness. Somewhere close by, Paul was converted to Christianity.

3

"And as he journeyed, he came near Damascus: and suddenly there shined round about him a light from heaven; and he fell to the earth, and heard a voice saying unto him, Saul, Saul, why persecutest thou me? And he said, Who art thou, Lord? And the Lord said, I am Jesus whom thou persecutest: it is hard for thee to kick against the pricks.

"And he trembling and astonished said, Lord, what wilt thou have me to do? And the Lord said unto him, Arise, and go into the city, and it shall be told thee what thou must do.

"And the men which journeyed with him stood speechless, hearing a voice, but seeing no man. And Saul arose from the earth; and when his eyes were opened, he saw no man: but they led him by the hand, and brought him into Damascus. And he was three days without sight, and neither did eat nor drink."

From that hour Paul was a changed man. Everything he thought, everything he did, was by virtue of that moment. He was charged with God.

This conversion is described twice again in *Acts*, once in Paul's speech to the mob at Jerusalem, and again in his speech before Agrippa II. There is a remarkable resemblance between Paul's conversion and the recorded ecstasies of Christian mystics: the suddenness of the vision, the burning light unbearable to the eyes, the sound of a voice, the instantaneous change of a man's nature and the dedication of his life to God; and, above all, the knowledge that the purely sensory limitations of the physical body had been outdistanced for a moment, just long enough to permit the visionary to know reality.

Those who have voyaged outside the small world of the senses are, strangely enough, often intensely practical in achievement. St. Paul is an outstanding instance, and so are St. Bernard, St. Joan of Arc, St. Catherine of Siena, St. Ignatius Loyola, and St. Teresa of Avila. It seems to me that one of the first things we have to realize about St. Paul is that from the moment of his conversion he became one of those saints who, in the words of Evelyn Underhill in her book *Mysticism,* possessed a "triumphing force" over which circumstances had no power.

"The incessant production of good works seems indeed to

be the object of that Spirit," writes the author of *Mysticism*.
"We see St. Paul abruptly enslaved by the First and Only
Fair, not hiding himself to enjoy the vision of Reality, but
going out single-handed to organize the Catholic Church. We
ask how it was possible for an obscure Roman citizen, without
money, influence, or good health, to lay these colossal foundations: and he answers 'Not I, but Christ in me.'

"We see St. Joan of Arc, a child of the peasant class, leaving the sheep-fold to lead the armies of France. We ask how
this incredible thing can be: and are told 'Her Voices bade
her.' A message, an overpowering impulse came from the
supra-sensible: vitality flowed in on her, she knew not how
or why. She was united with the Infinite Life, and became
Its agent, the medium of Its strength, 'what his own hand
is to a man.'

"We see St. Francis, 'God's Troubadour,' marked with His
wounds, inflamed with His joy—obverse and reverse of the
earnest-money of Eternity—or St. Ignatius Loyola our Lady's
Knight, a figure at once both militant and romantic, go out
to change the spiritual history of Europe. Where did they
find—born and bred to the most ordinary of careers, in the
least spiritual of atmospheres—that superabundant energy,
that genius for success which triumphed best in the most
hopeless situations. . . . We see St. Teresa, another born
romantic, pass to the Unitive State after long and bitter
struggles between her lower and higher personality. A chronic
invalid over fifty years of age, weakened by long ill-health and
the mortification of the Purgative Way, she deliberately
breaks with her old career in obedience to the inward Voice,
leaves her convent and starts a new life: coursing through
Spain, and reforming a great religious order in the teeth of
the ecclesiastical world. Yet more amazing, St. Catherine of
Siena, an illiterate daughter of the people, after a three years'
retreat consummates the mystic marriage, and emerges from

the cell of self-knowledge to dominate the politics of Italy. How came it that these apparently unsuitable men and women, checked on every side by inimical environment, ill-health, custom, or poverty, achieved these stupendous destinies? The explanation can only lie in the fact that all these persons were great mystics, living upon high levels the theopathetic life. In each a character of the heroic type, of great vitality, deep enthusiasms, unconquerable will, was raised to the spiritual plane, remade on higher levels of consciousness."

So it was with Paul. Remade and inspired, his physical body shattered by contact with conditions for which man's physical body was not designed, those who were with him led him by the hand into Damascus.

4

In the late afternoon I approached Damascus through miles of apricot trees. It was the hour when the Damascene goes at the end of a hot day to drink coffee in pile-dwellings built out over the river Barada. His dream of happiness is a hookah drawing nicely, a plate of *lukoum*, a cup of sweet coffee, and the river flowing silently by.

I wish that I could like Damascus. It seems to me that this city is living on a reputation gained a hundred years ago, before there were electric trams, gramophones, or motor-cars; when our great-grandparents rode painfully to it on horseback, probably wondering whether Lady Hester Stanhope would grant them an interview.

The city has suffered a violent collision with the West in the form of French tramcars, telegraph and telephone wires, gramophones, Renault cars, and a number of new buildings. In the heart of it all, side by side with the main streets where Bedouin from the desert sit dreamily in the dusty tramcars,

are a series of dark bazaars in which Greeks and Armenians
picket their doorsteps and lure the visitor into shops stacked
with brass-ware and inlaid furniture that looks wonderful
until it reaches Cheltenham.

There are whole streets hung with red, yellow, and blue
slippers, while cobblers, sitting under these festoons, are
swiftly adding to the collection. There are streets with shops
full of the crystallized fruits for which Damascus has always
been famous; and there is a gold and silver bazaar, where a
number of swarthy and obliging persons preside over safes
and glass cases full of gold earrings, bracelets, watches, and
old silver. But jewellery made in Damascus is not very good.
There is an Arabic proverb which says that the art was born
in Egypt, grew in Aleppo, and came to Damascus to die.

The finest things in Damascus are the mediæval *khans*, but
now that the camel caravan has been superseded by the motor
lorry, they are merely store houses. And it is only when you
look through an open gate that you realize how many walls
hide visions of lovely courtyards where fountains splash under orange trees.

It was, however, St. Paul's Damascus that I wished to see,
and in the morning I set out to visit those places which the
piety of local Christians has associated with the Apostle.

When Paul was led into Damascus, he was taken to the
house of a disciple named Judas who lived in, or near, the
Vicus Rectus or Street called Straight. It was to this house
that another disciple, Ananias, was directed in a vision.

"And Ananias went his way, and entered into the house;
and putting his hands on him said, Brother Saul, the Lord,
even Jesus, that appeared unto thee in the way as thou cam-
est, hath sent me, that thou mightest receive thy sight, and be
filled with the Holy Ghost. And immediately there fell from
his eyes as it had been scales; and he received sight forth-
with, and arose, and was baptized. And when he had received

meat, he was strengthened. Then was Saul certain days with the disciples which were at Damascus. And straightway he preached Christ in the synagogues, that he is the son of God."

Now the Street called Straight was so named because, like the main streets of nearly all the great Hellenistic cities, it ran straight as an arrow from one end of the city to the other. This street in Damascus was a mile in length—longer than Princes Street, Edinburgh. It was one hundred feet wide, and was divided into three sections; a central track for chariots and horse-men, and a path on each side for foot passengers. Ruins of similar streets are to be seen in Palmyra, Jerash, and Ephesus.

The Street called Straight is one of the main bazaars of Damascus. It is roofed with corrugated iron to keep out the blinding sun, and is lined on each side with hundreds of little shops fitted with pull-down shutters. The modern Arabic name is a memory of its Roman name: they call it the *Souk el Tawil,* which means the Long Bazaar.

Wandering through this dark tunnel, avoiding the horse-drawn carriages which bump over its cobbles, the Arabs on bicycles, the flocks of sheep, the strings of camels, and the Greek and Armenian merchants, I stood lost in delight as I saw again that sight which, for me at least, never loses its absurdity.

Two Armenian carpet-sellers were perambulating the Street called Straight, the leading man with a large carpet draped over his shoulders, the ends upheld by his companion. Solemnly they walked up and down, pausing before any interested person. I have never seen anyone buy a carpet, yet this vaguely ecclesiastical ceremony goes on all the year round. If you were in Damascus now, the two men would probably be mournfully parading, like a caricature of some bishop and his acolyte.

One of the most interesting Roman relics is the Gate of the East, or *Bab esh Sharqi,* which gave admittance to the Street called Straight. The northern bay is still one of the entrances to Damascus, although the central gate and its southern bay are now walled up and partly hidden by warehouses. In many a stone in the wall of Damascus and in the ancient Gate of the East, we have definite associations with the Apostolic Age. Local Christians proudly point to the traditional place on the wall from which Paul was lowered in a basket.

There is a small mosque in the Street called Straight which both Christians and Moslems believe to have been built on the site of the house of Judas. A courteous old sheik took me inside and let me climb a rickety ladder to the balcony that serves as a minaret. He could tell me nothing about the history or tradition of the building, but one of the Franciscan fathers, whom I met later, told me that in the year 1616 Quaresimus was told by Christians in Damascus that the mosque was built on the site of an ancient Greek church dedicated to St. Judas.

5

This Franciscan took me to an underground chapel in the Christian quarter, which used to be the Jewish quarter in Paul's time.

"I am going to show you a chapel which a tenacious tradition associates with St. Ananias, who healed and baptized St. Paul," he said. "I think it will interest you."

We entered quiet lanes which exposed blank walls to the view unless a door happened to be open, when, glancing inside, I would see a whitewashed court in dazzling sunlight, a well, a lemon tree, and perhaps two or three brown children playing with a cat.

At the bottom of twenty stone steps we entered a subterranean vault furnished as a little chapel, with an altar at one end of it. The walls and the vaulted roof were of rough stones, some of them enormous squared blocks of the Byzantine period, or perhaps even earlier. The only light was from a round hole in the roof, through which the sunlight poured in a cobweb-coloured shaft.

"This is the Roman level of Damascus," said the Franciscan, "and you will notice that the same depth of earth has accumulated against the *Bab esh Sharqi*. This building is obviously ancient, and it contains material that is undoubtedly of Roman date."

He opened the door of an adjoining vault, where I saw a number of Roman tiles built into the walls.

"Now the history of this chapel," he continued, "is based on the Syrian tradition of St. Ananias. They say that he was one of the Seventy, and may even have been a follower of our Lord during His life-time. They believe that when the Christians were persecuted after St. Stephen's death, he fled back to his native city of Damascus. Ananias had not long returned, when he received the command to heal St. Paul. That would explain why he knew all about St. Paul, why he seemed to fear his presence and to say—as you remember—'I have heard by many of this man, how much evil he hath done to thy saints in Jerusalem.' However, he was in Damascus when Paul came, and he had the gift of healing. It is further believed that in later years Ananias went with St. Paul to Cæsarea in the capacity of lawyer, and spoke for him before the tribunal of Felix. It is believed that he was slain by the sword of Pol, the general of Aretas, but another tradition says that he was martyred under Lucianus, Prefect of Damascus.

"A church soon rose on the site of his house, of which this chapel is a part. Count Lorey, who came here in 1922 with a French archæological mission, made a survey and came to the conclusion that this was once a large Byzantine church, with foundations extending beneath the street. It has for centuries been venerated by Christians and Moslems as the dwelling of St. Ananias, and the Franciscan Fathers took it over in 1820 and restored it. The chapel was destroyed during the massacre of Christians in 1860, but we rebuilt it again in 1867 and made it as you see it to-day."

After the Franciscan had left me, I entered a church named, I think, Casa Nuova, where I saw one of the most gruesome sights imaginable. One of the attendants switched on a light which illuminated an enormous glass coffin under an altar. A covering of red muslin in front of it gave an added horror to the contents, which were bundles of human bones neatly tied with red watered silk and finished off with little bows. There were several horribly gashed skulls.

"The martyrs of the great massacre," said the attendant.

These were relics of eight Franciscans, seven Spaniards, and a Tyrolese, who died heroically on the altar steps during the Moslem massacre of 1860. This terrible rising against the Christian population was inspired by the Indian Mutiny. More than six thousand Christians were murdered and many young women and girls thrown into Arab harems. The revolt spread to the Lebanon, where Druses massacred the Maronites. France sent out an expedition of ten thousand men to quell the rising, and thus one of the blackest chapters in the history of Damascus was brought to an end.

6

Sometimes the *khamseen* blows for days over Damascus, and the sky is red with flying sand. Trees bow the way of the wind, and Arabs draw the ends of their *keffiehs* over their mouths and walk forward bowed against the storm, only their dark eyes showing above the strip of white cloth.

The sand finds its way everywhere—into food, bed, clothes, wardrobes, suit-cases, and, worst of all, between the pages of books. There is a dusty, maddening smell in the air, and people lose their tempers quickly.

After one of these storms had died down, I went out to find the place in the southern fragment of the city wall which a pious tradition claims as the spot from which St. Paul was let down in a basket.

I left the city by the Gate of the East and followed the wall southwards for some little distance, coming to a blocked-up gate which had been restored in recent times. The wall is here about forty feet in height, but only the lower portions are of ancient construction.

An escape from a city wall seems to me the most dramatic of all forms of deliverance. Even escape from a dungeon has not quite the same romantic quality. For a man to save his life by descending the city wall argues that the city is stirred up against him and that the gates are being watched. It also argues the covering of darkness and a tense atmosphere of danger. Even the moon scudding from behind a cloud may become an enemy, the slightest sound may mean failure and death. One imagines the fugitive dropping down the face of the wall and creeping from shadow to shadow away into the night. I am sure that those who remember their childhood will agree with me that one of the most exciting incidents in the Old Testament is the letting down of Joshua's spies from the walls of Jericho.

Paul's escape from Damascus was equally dramatic. He was forced to fly by the anti-Christian movement he had set out to support. The rage of the Orthodox Jews, when they discovered that their champion had gone over to the other side was, naturally, without limit. They would have done anything to seize him and to send him back to Jerusalem bound with the very bonds he had brought for others.

"But their lying in await was known of Saul. And they watched the gates day and night to kill him. Then the disciple took him by night and let him down by the wall in a basket."

That is the account in *Acts*. Strangely enough, this escape seems in some way to have humiliated the proud spirit of Paul. To his mind there was evidently something undignified, perhaps even ridiculous, about this descent in a basket, and one has the impression that, had he not been ill and weak and still shattered by his emotional storm, he might have resisted the excellent plans of his well-wishers. How otherwise can we explain the fact that when writing to Corinth many years afterwards, Paul remembered this incident as if it still rankled in his memory, and placed it among the most unpleasant events of his life?

"In Damascus," he wrote, "the Governor under Aretas the King kept the city of the Damascenes with a garrison, desirous to apprehend me: and through the window in a basket was I let down by the wall, and escaped his hands."

This mention of Aretas, by the way, is the only indication in ancient literature that Damascus was under Nabatæan government at the time of Paul's escape, a fact which has since been proved by a study of ancient Syrian coins.

Not far away from the traditional place on the wall from which Paul descended to safety are several Arab houses whose upper storeys rise above the rampart and look out to open country beyond. People are still living in these houses and, except for the fact that the windows seem rather small, these dwellings would offer to-day the same facilities for escape as the early Christian house in Damascus which stood on the same spot many centuries ago.

A few paces from the wall is the cemetery of the Orthodox Greeks, where, beneath an erection like a wooden summer house, is the tomb of St. George of Abyssinia, venerated by all sects of Christians in Damascus. An ancient legend says that when Paul escaped from Damascus, one of the officers set to guard the towers was an Abyssinian. This man, having become a Christian, either helped Paul to escape or looked the other way, for which he was put to death.

The Greeks always keep a lamp burning before the ikon of St. George of Abyssinia, and I am told that Moslems also revere the tomb as a place of great sanctity.

7

I was driven out of Damascus by force of circumstances. Stephan had to hurry to Haifa to meet a cruising ship, and looking ahead for once, I had some weeks before engaged a sleeping-berth in the train that leaves Tripoli three times a week for Turkey. Therefore we set off at five o'clock and crossed the Lebanons as the sun was rising.

I was looking forward with intense pleasure to seeing Tarsus. I had an idea that I might go right through Turkey and follow the line of St. Paul's first mission, but I did not know what conditions of travel were like, except that, owing to bad roads, it is not easy to travel by car.

At Beyrout I said good-bye to Stephan and set about finding another car to take me a hundred miles north to Tripoli. On any ordinary day I could have had fifty, but this happened to be a feast day of some consequence, so that "all the good cars are gone," as I was informed with charming frankness. I chose what I hoped to be the best of the bad ones.

This was a desperate, raffish-looking Ford saloon, with an ominous crack across the windscreen. It was the sort of car you see in Syria with twelve Arabs piled inside it, a sheep or two looking out of the window, three men clinging to the running board, sacks and bedding slung across the mudguards, and the whole circus doing about sixty miles an hour round corners.

I viewed it with grave misgiving, which deepened into fear when I saw the driver. He was an enormous person who had suffered badly from smallpox, a man who wore his tarbush at a jaunty angle, who slouched about, chewed gum, and gave contemptuous kicks to his tires, a personality who seemed a compromise between a Chicago gangster and an old-fashioned Lebanon assassin.

We set off and in ten minutes I knew that I had struck the worst driver in Beyrout. I also knew that if I expostulated or attempted to curb his violence, we should probably shoot neatly off the mountain into the Mediterranean. The only thing to do was to sit tight and shut my eyes round corners.

After the first hour, I began to take a morbid interest in the man's technique. He had a habit of crouching down and setting the car at corners, accelerating when he should have slowed down. He had another queer habit, when the speedometer touched sixty, of easing himself in the seat and wriggling as if about to rise and desert the car.

He would rush madly through towns, hooting like a lunatic, scattering donkeys and camels and, crouching over the wheel with a grin, would take a delight in shaving the robes of passing compatriots. When I looked through the back window on such occasions, I saw rapidly diminishing figures standing in clouds of dust, shaking their fists and waving sticks; and I could imagine the kind of curses that were following us to Tripoli.

However, we arrived in the dark, with two hours to spare. I was so pleased to be alive that I took the man out to dinner. In an Arab restaurant where a gramophone played Turkish music, we ate an enormous meal of *kubbeh*, which is crushed wheat and minced meat, and *kafta*, a gay and pungent dish of tomatoes stuffed with meat, pine kernels and

onion, the whole thing reeking of hot olive oil. We finished
with the big, thick-skinned oranges of Syria. After this I was
ready for the night train to Turkey.

Under a sky hung with stars and in a silence broken only
by the croaking of frogs, I went to the dark, forlorn looking
station at Tripoli.

Bedouin were wandering erratically across the rails, their
heads bound in white cloths. There was a little train of five
coaches waiting, engineless, on a track that ended in a set of
buffers. I found the sleeping car in which I had reserved a
berth. A wealthy-looking Syrian stepped into the compartment next to mine. In a first-class coach a few distressed-
looking Levantines were removing their collars and shoes, and
in the other coaches Arabs were lying about in their robes.

A locomotive backed along the rails and attached itself to
the train. A crowd of dark, impassive faces gazed up in the
light from the windows. From the next coach a bare brown
arm shot downwards towards a seller of sugar cane. Frogs
filled the night with their croaking and the huge stars
snapped and winked in answer.

Then the stationmaster, hitherto invisible, came out and
tolled a bell. The engine gave a mournful hoot and, with no
demonstrations of farewell, no waving hands, no parting tears
to speed us on our way, we moved with a grinding shudder
into the blue night.

8

The train rocked and shook all night over flat country.
I could not sleep. Looking out of the window in the small
hours, I saw a wide, featureless plain lying in the starlight, and
I wondered where we were.

I assumed from the flat look of the land that we must still
be plodding steadily north through Syria, because, had we

been nearer Turkey, the country would have been wild and mountainous.

I fell asleep for an hour or two, to awaken in the greyness before dawn. I discovered that the train was standing in the station at Aleppo. Lying like Damascus on the edge of a desert, this big, mud-coloured city with its domes, its minarets, its thousands of flat-roofed houses, was fast asleep. The snores of the rich Syrian in the next compartment shook the frail partition. I wondered why he was going to Turkey.

Then into the silence of Aleppo clanked a weary, dusty train with the stain and grime of long travel on it; and I saw with a thrill that this other wanderer in the dawn was our companion, the Taurus Express from Constantinople, or Istanbul as we must now call it.

So these trains met at Aleppo, one on the last lap of its journey to the south, the other on the first lap of its journey to the north. And as we rested together for a few moments in Aleppo, with the sun rising over the domes and minarets and the mud-coloured houses, those remarkable men in chocolate-coloured uniforms, the sleeping-car attendants, stepped down from their coaches and exchanged a few words in French.

As I looked out on this scene, I thought that the experience of entering Turkey through the Syrian Gates was robbed of nearly all its romance because I was going there in a coach with *Compagnie International des Wagon-Lits* written on it. Similar coaches were running into Berlin, into Paris, into Rome, Vienna, Budapest, and Athens. Men in chocolate-coloured uniforms made the beds at night, roused the traveller in the morning. Then the thought came to me that perhaps these international sleeping-cars are the only features of modern travel which link us with the Asia Minor of St. Paul.

In Roman times something like internationalism had been achieved from Britain on the west to the Caspian Sea on the east. In St. Paul's day you could travel on a Roman Road from Jerusalem to Boulogne, and Greek or Latin would see you through all the way. If you got into trouble anywhere on this long journey, you had only to proclaim Roman citizenship, as Paul did, to receive the same police assistance in Ephesus that you would get in Antioch, in Alexandria, or in Rome itself. But think how many different and unsympathetic authorities you encounter to-day on the same journey: French, Swiss, Italian, Yugo-Slav, Serbian, Bulgarian, Greek, Turkish, Syrian and Palestinian. What was once an open road is now a series of frontiers, with customs men and passport officials lying in wait behind barriers ready to treat the traveller as if he were a spy or a smuggler.

Only the international sleeping-cars, whose beds, sheets and blankets are similar in Paris and Istanbul, who serve food on the same thick blue plates in Belgrade as in Barcelona, reproduce in their uniformity something like the magnificent standardization of the Roman road.

As dawn came up behind Aleppo, we moved north into flat, hot country. A few more coaches and a restaurant car had been added to the train.

I had breakfast: eggs *au beurre noire*, coffee and toast. As I ate, I looked out of the window and admired the wild, unchanging East; the strings of camels crossing the ridges, the horsemen riding to some remote domed village of baked mud with rifles slung on their backs, and it pleased me to think that, in spite of all appearances to the contrary, the restaurant car was really the successor of the Via Egnatia.

The Syrian, shaved and scented, sat in the opposite seat and toyed with a cup of coffee. He wore his tarbush at an arrogant angle. He was going to Istanbul, he told me. It was, he said, a dying city. Kemal, the Dictator of Turkey, or Ataturk, "Father of the Turk," to give him his official title, had decided to let the old city die while Angora grew up to be the capital of republican Turkey.

"But how can you kill Istanbul?" asked the Syrian with a wave of his manicured hand. "Nature has made it the bridge between East and West. It has always been a fortress and a bazaar. How can you kill it?"

I longed to ask him what mission took him to Istanbul, but refrained from doing so. With the tall red tarbush on his head, his scented hair, his flashy suit, and his soft, manicured hands, he looked, against the imaginary background of Istanbul, too like the wrapper of a mystery novel to bear investigation.

In a few hours the train climbed out of Syria into the mountains of the Amanus Range.

The flat country, the palm trees, the mud villages and camel caravans were left behind. We mounted into a bleak land of towering peaks, fir and pine woods, and of dark valleys full of rushing water. The mountains dividing the country of St. Paul from the country of Christ reminded me now of Switzerland and now of Scotland. There were moments during that long climb into Turkey when I could have believed that we were approaching St. Moritz, and there were moments when I could have imagined that the train would soon run into Fort William.

We pulled up at the frontier station of Fevzipasa. A red flag with a white crescent and a star on it proclaimed that we were in Turkey. The Ghazi's decree that all Turks must wear European clothes was pathetically visible. A crowd of men hung about the station, wearing cloth caps and incredibly old Western garments. An Arab in rags can achieve a certain dignity, but there is only squalor in a blue European suit patched with the remains of a brown one.

Police with red bands round their peaked caps, red cuffs to their grey, German-looking overcoats, brown belts from whose holsters shone black revolver butts, entered the train and demanded passports. Customs men came along, prodding earnestly into luggage and even shaking the curtains of the carriages in search of contraband.

Meanwhile the silent, impassive crowd of men in cloth caps walked mournfully up and down the train, gazing into the compartments. Soldiers with rifles on their shoulders patrolled the line. At last the train set off, and I looked out on a landscape that I shall never forget.

On his many journeys from Antioch to Asia Minor, St. Paul must have seen this country as I saw it in the morning sunshine. It is a land of immense, flat plains stretching to foothills and snow-topped mountains, no dwelling for miles, only flocks of sheep in charge of shepherds who wear square-shouldered cloaks. These felt cloaks, called *kepenikler*, are impervious to wind or water. They are so stiff that the owner can step out of them and leave them standing upright. They are made of the tough Cilician goat's hair from which to-day, as in the day of St. Paul, tents, sails and ropes are made.

As I looked at the shepherds standing like scarecrows in their stiff Cilician armour, I thought that in the course of his long journeys Paul must have wrapped himself in a *kepenik*. When he was in a Roman prison, did he not write, in his *Second Epistle to Timothy*, begging his "dearly beloved son" to bring "the cloke that I left at Troas with Carpus"? Surely Paul's cloak was a Cilician *kepenik* which, as no man knew better, would keep out the damp of any Roman cell.

The train sped downwards to a fair plain. At Adana I had to change for Tarsus, which lies about twenty miles to the west on a branch line. As I descended, I saw the Syrian from Tripoli leaning out of a window, but no longer wearing his native tarbush. His head was covered with a black beret. What a queer compromise, yet what a skilful one! The beret was European and would therefore find favour in Turkey, but as it had no brim, the Prophet himself could not have objected to it.

I stood for some moments on the platform, wondering what

was the Turkish word for porter. The station was new and made of pressed concrete. Boys were wheeling trolleys full of chocolate, oranges, *semit*—rings of bread covered with sesame seeds—and also fox and marten furs. More mobile salesmen rushed about holding up sticks of sugar-cane to the mournful-looking faces peering from the high windows.

My indecision was solved by a tap on the shoulder, and I turned to find myself under the puzzled scrutiny of two policemen. I had been told that a stranger cannot move two yards in Turkey without attention from the police, but I did not believe it. I showed them my passport, but this only seemed to make them more suspicious. I was taken to an office in the station, where a superior officer sat behind a desk, with the usual revolver at his waist. I began to feel like a character in a spy film. From the suspicion with which this officer glanced at my passport, and from his air of grave disapproval, his whispered remarks to his companions and his side-glances at me, I realized that I was up against the iron wall of a bureaucracy based on fear and on a complete ignorance of the outside world. To a German, a Frenchman, or an Italian, a thousand little things about me and my luggage would have told their harmless story, but to these men I was a profound mystery. The police officer could speak no English and I did not know what was going to happen, when a policeman appeared accompanied by a young American. I felt a happy sense of delivery. The young man explained that he was attached to the American Mission at Adana.

"They want to know what you are doing here," he said.

"I have come to see Tarsus."

"They want to know why."

"Because I am writing a book on St. Paul."

I could see that this shattered the morale of the police force. The officer got up and, lighting a cigarette, he turned and asked, earnestly:

"Are there politics in your book?"

"No."

After grave deliberation, they decided that I must leave my passport in their charge. They told me politely, but in a manner which left no doubt that I was under police supervision, that I might travel to Tarsus on the daily train at seven o'clock on the following morning.

That first ten minutes in Turkey taught me that in addition to my passport, I should have possessed letters from some Turkish authority proving that I was not a spy.

I am still not sure what would have happened to me had the American Mission not given me a faint status by accepting me as a guest. Owing to the regulations of the republican Government, the work of the Mission has dwindled to that of a clinic in charge of one earnest American doctor, who gave me a bed in what was once the maternity ward of his now disused hospital.

The contrast between this room and the view on the other side of the mosquito-netted window was remarkable. Below my window a tribe of Kurdish refugees were encamped in mud and pools of water. They had built pile dwellings with old wood and had made walls of rusty kerosene tins. Hens strolled in and out of their dwellings. The encampment echoed with every kind of cough, from the asthmatic to the genuine whoop. I was startled to hear a cough of a super-human calibre. I wondered what human frame could stand the shattering effect of it, and was relieved to see that it came from a group of camels crouched in the mud.

The American Mission did wonderful work in old Turkey. It was established in 1819 with the object of giving free medical treatment and education. Colleges, high schools for boys and girls, hospitals and churches, sprang up all over the country; for over a century this Mission kept alight the lamp of

Christian endeavour which St. Paul lit there so long ago. But now that republican Turkey has taken for its motto "Turkey for the Turks," the American Mission has found its powers curtailed.

9

Adana is the third largest town in Turkey. Lying on the rich Cilician plain, it is a centre of the cotton trade. One or two large mills produce cotton-thread for export.

It is a typical old Turkish town, a huddle of ramshackle wooden shops and of narrow streets with a surface of hard earth that becomes a quagmire of sticky mud in the wet season.

Strings of camels come softly through the lanes, laden with bales of cotton. Fat men sitting on donkeys thread their way through the crowds. Loud-speakers bellow Turkish music from cafés. Wild countrymen from the plains, and shaggy mountaineers from the Tarsus, stand looking at humble little shops as if they were in a grand metropolis.

There is one wide new street which leads from the station to the town. It expresses the European urge of the Republic. Pretty villas, which might have been picked up from a suburb of Hamburg, dot its length, and in a park stands one of those statues of the Ghazi which are rising in every town.

Statues are a revolutionary break with old Turkey. Graven images are not permitted by the Moslem religion, and the first statue ever erected in Turkey is only a few years old. It must have caused a tremendous sensation. It stands in Istanbul and symbolizes the birth of the Republic. As if to challenge Moslem opinion, or to make up for lost time, the sculptor has created a crowd of bronze men, so that rarely have so many figures stood on one plinth. The group is almost a "Who's Who" of the Republic. Since that creative moment statues of Ataturk have gone up all over the land, so that they no longer horrify even the most conservative.

I was surprised to see a plaster cast of the Venus de Milo standing at the door of the little museum at Adana, in strange contrast to the Hittite monuments that surround her. I was told that she is a regulation "issue" to all museums, and must be placed on view to educate the people. How strange that a race which has ground down the work of Praxiteles for mortar, and has built statues by Pheidias into the walls of its stables, should now be asked to admire the art it has done so much to destroy.

Yet how significant this is of modern Turkey's break with Islam. The present rulers realize that the Mohammedan ban on graven images has warped the mind and closed the windows of the soul. Century after century the beauty of the human face and form has been a forbidden thing in this country, so that the artist and the architect have been obliged to confine themselves to the tracing of mathematical spirals. What a world of irony there is in the gentle body of the Venus de Milo standing at the door of a Turkish museum to teach the beauty of Greece to people whose ancestors built a mosque inside the Parthenon.

One of the most interesting things in Adana is a fine bridge about three hundred yards in length, spanning the river Sihun, the Sarus of antiquity. There is one arch among the many arches of this structure which is said to have been part of a bridge built by the Empress Helena, when she was on her way from Constantinople to Jerusalem to discover the Holy Cross.

While I was walking in the streets of Adana I heard the call to prayer, and looking up towards the minaret of a mosque I saw the muezzin, not in his flowing robes and turban, but dressed in a blue reach-me-down suit and a cap. The old high-pitched, resonant call was there just the same, but the general effect was rather ridiculous. The man might have been selling fish.

The Ghazi's reforms in Turkey are astonishing. He is the greatest iconoclast in modern history. Just as the Soviet has obliterated the Tsarist regime, so Kemal Ataturk is obliterating all memory of the Sultanate and the Caliphate and building a barrier between modern republican Turkey and the static Turkey of the past.

He has carried his reforms into the strongholds of Islam and no man has dared to object. The great mosque of St. Sophia in Istanbul is a museum. The dervish and other religious orders have been disbanded and their mosques turned into show places. The Moslem holy day, Friday, has been abolished in favour of the Christian Sunday. Religious schools have been closed and no religious instruction is permitted in elementary schools.

Europeans have smiled when they read that all Turks must wear hats instead of the fez, thinking it to be merely a childish imitation of dress in Europe. It is much more than this. It strikes at the root of social and religious custom and is a more sweeping change even than the unveiling of women.

Head-gear has always had a profound significance in the East. One glance at a man's head and you know his religion and also his social position. The fez is not really Turkish, but is Greek in origin. Two centuries ago, when the Turks still wore turbans, the social and religious significance of turbans was carried to fantastic extremes. There was a different kind of turban for every official and dignitary in the Sultan's palace. When these turbans were abolished and the fez was adopted as the national headgear, old-fashioned Turks thought the end of the world had come. Similar feelings were expressed when Kemal abolished the fez. But the hat with its brim— for centuries the sign of the Christian dog—was an astonishing substitute, and in no way has the Ghazi proclaimed his power more surely than by compelling his countrymen to conquer their prejudice against it.

No Moslem hat may have a brim, for a devout Moslem cannot bend forward and touch the earth with his forehead if there is a brim to his hat. Therefore it would be easy to make prayers in a mosque both ridiculous and impossible by decreeing the wearing of bowler hats. Turkey's Dictator has not done that. The faithful are still allowed to pray—in cloth caps.

When you go into a mosque in modern Turkey, you realize at once why this most hideous of Western head-coverings is popular with the devout. By reversing the cap so that the brim is at the back of the head, a smooth, brimless surface lies above the forehead and the ground can be touched with ease. Museum curators, Customs officials, and even policemen who obey the call to prayer, can perform the same act by reversing their peaked service caps.

That evening members of the small Christian community in Adana, a few Syrians, Armenians, and one Greek girl, came to the Mission and, sitting round the stove, we talked, as all people talk to-day, of peace and the need for peace in the world.

I walked out on the flat roof before I went to bed. The stars were enormous in a velvet-blue sky. To the north I could see the dark ridge of the Taurus Mountains, and all round was a gigantic emptiness under the stars. There were no sounds but the pitiful coughing of Khurdish refugees and, far off, the barking of dogs.

10

In the morning I rose before daylight and drove down to the station in good time to get my passport. An American schoolmistress from the Mission had been kind enough to accompany me and afford me the necessary protection of the Turkish language. Of course the police office was locked and barred. I was therefore obliged to make the twenty miles journey without any credentials, an unpleasant prospect in Turkey, even though my companion could speak the language and vouch for the purity of my motives.

As the little train pulled out across the Cilician Plain, I moved from side to side of the carriage in my anxiety to miss nothing of the landscape in which Paul was born and bred. I saw an enormous green plain only slightly above sea level, a semi-tropical expanse sown for miles with cotton, wheat, and tobacco. Much of the plain is the colour of Devon soil, and oxen moved slowly over the cocoa-coloured furrows, breaking the earth with a primitive harrow.

The Cilician Plain has always been famous for timber and goat's hair, and I saw with pleasure that these exports have been unaffected by dynasties and empires. Enormous herds of black goats still wander across the plain. Stacks of timber, house high, stood near all the little country stations into which we drew with an asthmatic panting from the locomotive.

At one of these stations a policeman, observing me in the carriage, entered and asked for my passport. Had it not been for my companion's knowledge of Turkish, and the fact that she was known locally, I should probably have been requested to leave the train. As it was, voluminous notes were made and I was allowed to journey on to Tarsus.

I noticed that country carts and occasional wild-looking horsemen crossed the plain on embanked roads, and I remembered reading somewhere that these highways were originally the work of Romans and crossed the plain in every direction. In Roman times, as to-day, winter floods and heavy rains turn the Cilician Plain to mud on which movement is impossible, and in which helpless gazelles have been caught by hand.

The view to the north was stupendous. About sixty miles away from the railway line the Taurus Mountains rose above the plain, a gigantic blue wall crested with snow.

The trees became more frequent until, in a thicket of vegetation so dense that it hid the town completely, we drew into a little station with "Tarsus" written above the entrance.

11

We took a carriage and drove for some way down a long, straight road and into a shabby little town where rows of wooden shacks faced each other across roadways of hard mud. And this was Tarsus, this dusty malarial little town crouched in a swamp.

I looked for something that might have lingered from the time of its pride, but there was nothing. Invasion, war, and centuries of inertia have obliterated every vestige of the past. I was told that remains of the ancient city lie fifteen and twenty feet below the surface of modern Tarsus. People digging in their cellars and back-yards have felt their spades strike hard against the crowns of arches and the capitals of columns buried in the earth.

I was shown an arch called St. Paul's Arch, but it has nothing to do with the Apostle. It is probably a Byzantine arch to which the Greek Orthodox clergy, who were driven out in 1922, had given a picturesque and obvious name.

The modern town occupies only a small portion of the land once covered with the marble temples, colonnades, baths, and public squares of Roman Tarsus. Miles away in open country, bits of the city wall stand in the cotton fields like old teeth. No longer does the ice-clear Cydnus, the pride of ancient Tarsus, flow through the centre of the town. The Emperor Justinian had made a flood channel to the east of the city to carry off surplus water in the spring. In the days of decadence the people of Tarsus neglected to clean the river-bed, with the result that many centuries ago the Cydnus flowed into the canal of Justinian and no longer traversed the city.

The same terrible ignorance and sloth have caused the once magnificent inland lake and harbour of Rhegma to silt up. It is now a marsh thirty miles wide, a nesting-place for wild duck and a breeding-place for the malarial mosquito.

The ancient Tarsians loved to sit chattering like water-fowl beneath the marble colonnades on the Cydnus bank, and could they see the downfall of the city whose splendour and beauty once rejoiced their hearts, there is probably no word in Greek or Hebrew that could adequately express their sorrow or their incredulity.

I had expected streets of squalid wooden shanties, unmade roads, and patches of waste land where groups of unshaven men stood among shaggy horses, but the contrast between the fair Hellenistic city mentioned by Cicero, Strabo, Apollonius, and St. Paul, was so great that I felt a sense of shock. Had it not been Tarsus, I should perhaps have felt only the traveller's interest in strange sights and sounds. But the thought that Tarsus could have sunk to this seemed to me so tragic that I should have been glad to have escaped from the place.

Yet after all, I asked myself, is such a sight more painful than those houses in the Canongate in Edinburgh, now tenements, above whose ample fire-places stand the defaced arms of Scotland's nobility; or is it any less deplorable than those houses in the slums of Dublin which, until the dealers became aware of it, contained Adams mantelpieces and ceilings blackened by a century's soot? Much the same thing has happened to Tarsus and to all the cities of the Græco-Roman world. They have become slums. That pride which made Asia Minor, in the words of Mommsen, "the promised land of municipal vanity," vanished with the Moslem conquest.

Politicians of Western nations ought not to be eligible for election until they have travelled the ancient world. They should be made to see how easy it is for the constant sea of savagery, which flows for ever round the small island of civilization, to break in and destroy. Asia Minor was once as highly organized as Europe is to-day: a land of large cities whose libraries and public monuments were so splendid that when we retrieve fragments of this lost world, we think it worth while to build a museum to house them, as the Germans have housed in Berlin a fragment of Pergamum and Miletus. Yet a few centuries of occupation by a static race have seen the highest pillars fall to earth, have witnessed the destruction of aqueducts that carried life-giving water from afar, and have seen the silting up of harbours that once sheltered the proudest navies of the ancient world. I cannot understand how any traveller can stand unmoved at the graveside of the civilization from which our own world springs, or can see a Corinthian capital lying in the mud without feeling that such things hold a lesson and a warning and, perhaps, a prophesy.

There is, however, one remarkable relic in Tarsus which may have been there in the time of Paul. It is a piece of ground about two hundred and eight feet long and one hundred and thirty feet wide, which is enclosed within a wall of Roman concrete about twenty-four feet high and twenty feet thick. In the centre of the enclosure are two huge concrete platforms of the same height as the wall. The enclosure and the wall are overgrown with grass and asphodels.

The Turks call this structure the *Dunuk Tash*, or the "overturned stone." They say that the building was once the palace of an ancient prince of Tarsus with whom Mohammed was offended. Therefore the Prophet overturned his palace and buried the offender beneath it. A less elaborate but equally erroneous theory is that it is the tomb of Sardanapalus.

There is an easy way to the top of the wall, and I think

that anyone who examines this structure will agree that it is the *podium*, or platform, of a Roman Temple. It is evident that the concrete now exposed to view was once hidden by stonework which was probably covered with marble.

The wall and the concrete platforms within it have been penetrated in many directions by tunnels made by treasure-seekers, but their spades soon became blunted against the steel-hard Roman cement. William Burckhardt Barker, who was resident in Tarsus in the middle of the last century, gave an account of some of the determined assaults on this Roman wall in a book called *Lares and Penates*, published in 1853. The one or two educated Europeans in the town at that time were convinced that the platform was some kind of tomb, and that if they once found a way into it they would discover rich treasures. One of the most energetic excavators was the French consul, who, after many a bitter disappointment, was rewarded by the discovery of "the first and second fingers of a man in marble, of gigantic size, joined together, but not as if they had belonged to the hand of a statue, but a finished work in itself."

The modern traveller appreciates this ruin because the top of the wall is one of the few places in Tarsus which affords a good view over the low-lying country. But even from its height the Mediterranean Sea is not visible. One can, however, follow the course of the river Cydnus as it winds its way southward through the level plain towards the great marsh of Rhegma, five miles away. When one looks to the north, the ground is seen gradually rising towards foothills which become higher until, thirty miles off, they lie against the tremendous wall of the Taurus.

When Paul was born, Tarsus was already one of the ancient cities of the Hellenistic world. The city owed its importance to its geographical position and to the enterprise and the energy of its people. Like the citizens of Glasgow, who for centuries have dredged and deepened the Clyde, making it one of the great shipbuilding rivers of the world, the citizens of Tarsus dredged and deepened the inland lake of Rhegma into which their river emptied itself before meandering over a sand-pit to the sea.

They cut a channel for ships and deepened the lagoon. Great docks, arsenals, and warehouses, were built, and their foundations still lie in the marsh. As long as the engineers drained and deepened the channel and maintained the harbour works, this splendid sheltered stretch of water remained one of the great ports and anchorages of the ancient world.

The engineers of Tarsus cut a road through the Cilician Gates and thus created one of the historic mountain passes on the main road from the Euphrates to Ephesus and Rome. So, by sea and by land, Tarsus became not only a famous port and a rich caravan city, but it became also the buckle which bound East to West. There is a certain inevitability in the fact that the man who was chosen to interpret Christianity to the West should have come from the city which, above all others in the Hellenistic world, was a perfect amalgamation of Orient and Occident.

Tarsus is also interesting in the history of municipal experiments because it realized, for a time at any rate, the Platonic ideal of government by philosophers. The famous University of Tarsus was known all over the world. In its zeal for learning, Strabo placed it above the universities of Athens and Alexandria. Thus the same persistent energy which drove the sons of Tarsus to reform Nature in the service of commerce, inspired them when they approached the intellectual life. Among the many qualities which everyone must appreciate in St. Paul are his tremendous energy, his single-mindedness, and what to-day we should call "drive." He was a true son of the city that hewed the Cilician Gates out of the rock, and it is important to realize that Paul was not born in the lassitude of an oriental city, but in the proud and virile atmosphere of mental and physical achievement.

The students of Tarsus University were all drawn from Cilicia. Unlike Alexandria and Athens, Tarsus did not attract visitors. But the Tarsians loved to study in order to be able to visit other universities to complete their education, and few such, Strabo says, ever returned home: their zeal and enthusiasm found professional posts for them wherever they settled. If the physical achievements of Tarsus remind us of Glasgow, the mental attitude may possibly suggest a resemblance to Aberdeen.

In the era just before Paul, one of the most remarkable citizens of Tarsus was the Stoic philosopher Athenodorus. Paul must have heard many a story about him, for his name and his works lived on after his death. Like a true son of Tarsus, this learned man lectured in many cities and became the teacher of young Augustus. One of the wise rules of conduct which he recommended to the youthful master of the world was to repeat the letters of the alphabet before he allowed himself to speak in the heat of anger. Teacher criticized pupil with the greatest freedom, and many of the attractive qualities of Augustus may have been due to the influence of Athenodorus. Master and pupil were together when the murder of Julius Cæsar recalled Augustus to Rome to assume the purple, and when the Civil Wars were over and the will of Augustus was unquestioned throughout the world, only the Tarsian Stoic dared to rebuke him.

There was an occasion when a noble Roman lady had received a command to meet Augustus at his palace. Athenodorus happened to arrive at her house as a discreetly veiled litter drew up to the door. Inside the house he found the whole family in the depth of sorrow, for no one had the courage to resist the Emperor. Athenodorus borrowed a sword and took his place in the litter. When this was set down in the presence of Augustus, the curtains parted and out stepped the old philosopher with the sword. "Are you not afraid that someone may enter like this and assassinate you?" he said to Augustus. This was evidently an occasion when the Emperor remembered the teaching of Athenodorus, for he must have repeated the letters of the alphabet to himself before he replied that Athenodorus was quite right and had administered a well-deserved lesson.

The philosopher was the friend of Strabo and Seneca; and Cicero, who thought highly of him, asked his aid in the composition of *De Officiis*. It is from Seneca that we learn what little is known of the philosophy of Athenodorus, a philosophy of a release from the passions. Sir William Ramsay believes that the well-known resemblance between the thoughts of St. Paul and Seneca is explained by the influence which the ideas of Athenodorus exerted on both of them.

"Know," said the philosopher, "that you are free from all passions when you have reached a point that you ask nought of God that you cannot ask openly."

And there is an echo of this in Seneca's rule of life:

"So live with men as if God saw; so speak with God as if men were listening."

With the consent of Augustus, the good and learned Athenodorus returned in his old age to his native Tarsus to fight a municipal scandal, for Tarsus had fallen into the hands of a group of racketeers led by a politician called Boethus. The Emperor had given his old master supreme power to reform the town's constitution, but before Athenodorus revealed his authority, he attempted to improve the municipal morality in less drastic ways. He found eventually that the only thing to do was to make a clean sweep, and he sent the evil-doers into exile. His municipal reforms included a measure which suggests that we are wrong in thinking that Paul

sprang from a humble tent-making family in Tarsus. Athenodorus revised the burgess rolls of the city. Only people of
wealth and standing in the community were allowed to retain their Tarsian citizenship. The others were struck off
the records and had sunk, when Dion Chrysostom visited
Tarsus a century later, to a plebeian position and were nick-
named "Linen-workers." The fact that St. Paul could proudly
assert that he was "a citizen of Tarsus," when asked to give
an account of himself, proves that his family must have been
prosperous. In becoming a Christian, Paul willingly and gladly
cut himself off not only from the good will of his family, but
also from the commercial and civic inheritance which awaited
him. Surely that is what he means when he says in his letter
to the Philippians, chapter three, verses seven and eight: "But
what things were gain to me, those I counted loss for Christ.
Yea, doubtless, and I count all things but loss for the excel-
lency of the knowledge of Christ Jesus my Lord: for whom
I have suffered the loss of all things, and do count them but
dung, that I may win Christ."

The Jewish colony to which Paul belonged had probably
been settled in Tarsus for many centuries. It is interesting
to think that Paul's father may have witnessed the celebrated
meeting between Cleopatra and Mark Anthony, which took
place only forty years before Paul's birth.

Cleopatra sailed from Egypt to Tarsus, where Antony was
resting after the triumphal tour that followed his victory at
Philippi. He had sent for the Queen of Egypt to punish her
for the aid she gave to Cassius. Cleopatra, knowing well how
sternly he punished and fined his enemies, decided to make
the sensational appearance which Plutarch and Shakespeare
have immortalized. When the Egyptian fleet came in from the
sea and entered the lake of Rhegma, Antony, sitting on his
throne in the marble streets of Tarsus, noticed that the crowds
had melted away, leaving him alone. They had gone to watch

the approaching pageant. They saw a vessel with a gilded stern, sails of purple outspread and silver oars moving in time to the sound of flutes, pipes and harps. Dressed like Aphrodite, the Goddess of Love, Cleopatra lay beneath an awning be-spangled with gold, while boys like painted Cupids stood on each side, fanning her. At the helm and at the rigging stood her most beautiful slave women in the guise of Nereids and Graces. The crowds on the river bank could smell the per-fumes burning on the ship.

How often must Paul have heard this story told by old men who had seen Cleopatra.

As I looked over the Cilician Plain, I saw far off a file of camels moving to the north. In the sky above them a flicker of sunlight on white feathers betrayed the passage of migrat-ing storks. They were flying from Syria into Asia Minor, to build their nests upon the broken arches of aqueducts and upon the ruined columns of Ephesus.

It was a sight that Paul must have seen every time spring came to the Cilician Plain. Watching the dusty caravans move north over the hills, he would see them vanish suddenly in the darkness of the pass. He would see the storks flying above them. As he saw them go, he must have wondered, as any boy would wonder, where those men and where those fine white birds would rest that night; and where would the rising sun find them in the morning, over what far hills were they mov-ing and towards what distant cities? I realized that travel was in the very air of ancient Tarsus. The caravans, the migrat-ing storks, and the ships that flung down their anchors in the lake of Rhegma, were all messages from the world behind the mountains and beyond the seas; and I knew why the wandering scholars of Tarsus were famous in antiquity.

Paul must have turned from the north, where the caravans entered the Gates, to the quay-sides of Tarsus. The one clear picture of Paul in Tarsus is of a boy born among the sounds and the sights of departure and return. The harbour must have known him well. He must have stood there many a time, watching the ships lift their sails and pass out "leaning upon the bosom of the urgent west." Perhaps he turned away, saying to himself: "Someday I, too, shall travel like the white ships that go over the sea, and like the white birds that go over the mountains."

12

I walked down a side street in Tarsus where a number of humble little workshops are open to the gaze of any passer-by. In the darkness of these sheds men spin thread from goat's hair and weave it into coarse cloth.

This street of weavers is the only link with the Tarsus in which St. Paul was born, for I saw with a start of surprise and delight that these men were making tent cloth for the nomads of the Taurus.

My interest was so obvious that the weavers invited me to go inside, where, with gentleness and kindliness and a sense of humour which made me feel that I was home in England again, they showed me the whole process of their work.

I learnt that the goat's hair comes from the herds which live on the Taurus Mountains, where snow lies until May. In this cold atmosphere the animals grow magnificent coats, and for centuries the hair has been famous for its strength and durability.

In the East a tent-maker is a weaver of tough fabric. In antiquity the Apostle's birthplace was famed for tent cloth, or *cilicium*, as it was called, after the province of Cilicia; an interesting memory of this survives in the modern French word for hair-cloth—*cilice*.

The method of weaving and spinning is primitive. The spinner, with a bag of goat's hair over his shoulder, advances and retreats from the wheel as he feeds the yarn with pinches of hair. In an adjoining shed the weavers sit at ground level, with their legs in a pit. Their looms are upright, warp-weighted looms of a type that has been used since the dawn of history. The warp threads hang down from the roller and as the cloth is made, it is wound round this roller. Such clumsy, but efficient and picturesque, structures were the only type of loom used in ancient Greece and Rome, and I recalled a painting on a Greek vase in the British Museum which shows Penelope sitting beside a loom of the same design.

As I watched the weavers at work, I knew that I was watching something that St. Paul had seen. If he returned to Tarsus to-day, he would look in vain for the temples, the baths, the statues, the market-place, even the river; but in these little workshops he would recognize the trade that had supported him in Thessalonica, Corinth and Ephesus.

How remarkable it is that such a humble trade can survive empires. The explanation is that it fulfils a common human need, and that no matter what race of barbarians pulled down marble statues or destroyed aqueducts, and no matter how savage the war, the siege or the massacre, the time would always come when life became peaceful again and someone would come to Tarsus anxious to buy a length of tent cloth.

13

I set off one forenoon for the Cilician Gates. The ancient Ford car that I managed to hire would have attracted attention anywhere except in Turkey.

The Turkish driver can coax movement out of a car that would remain dead to any other driver. He can also drive a car containing singularly few of the generally accepted essentials, such as windscreen, mudguards, brakes. As long as the engine can turn over, a Turkish driver will somehow manage to take his car across open country and to the tops of mountains.

We bumped out of Tarsus along a narrow track between fields. A hillman came towards us, sitting on top of two enormous bags which hung down each side of his pony. The animal exhibited every sign of terror, as well he might, but the rider managed to hold his head towards us and to keep him under control. The car, however, swerved to avoid a pot-hole in the road and the pony, turning suddenly, shot bags and driver into a field.

I stopped the car and ran after the pony, while my driver picked his compatriot out of the mud. I expected a first class row, but to my astonishment the driver and the hillman pulled away at the sacks and roared with laughter.

It was my first experience of a characteristic which I was to note time and again during my travels: the remarkable good nature of the Turk in moments of difficulty. Situations that would infuriate most people usually rouse his sense of humour; and his sense of humour might be termed English. It is an ironic wit.

As we jolted on, we left the Cilician Plain and mounted the foothills. We met a string of camels descending from the uplands, and a band or two of Yuruks, or nomads, with their burdened donkeys and dark-eyed children. Then came miles of solitude.

Nothing wilder than the approach to the Cilician Gates can be imagined. The mountain sides fall away into gorges loud with the rush of melted snow water. Now and then I would look up from the depths of some ravine and see pines growing in sunlight above me and the high snow-fields flushed pink in the afternoon light. Sometimes the car skidded on the edge of a narrow road that fell into emptiness; more than once we had to get out and move from our path stones which had been brought down by a landslide.

The worse the road became, the higher grew the spirits of my driver. He knew only one English word—"dance." Whenever the car flung us towards the roof and the springs looked like giving out, or whenever he hit his head on the roof, he would turn to me and, waggling one hand up and down to denote the unsteadiness of the car, cry with amusement:

"Dance, dance!"

A few miles from the Cilician Gates we came to a dizzy little village perched in the cold mountains. A few huts stood round a police post.

A smiling young policeman with a rifle over his shoulder inquired where we were going, although for centuries the Cilician Gates have been the one possible destination on this road! He nodded in a friendly way to me as he glanced inside the car, and all would have been well had not an excited young man with a wild mop of hair rushed out of the police station to see what was happening. He spoke a few disconnected words of French, and I gathered that he was the schoolmaster's son.

He asked me a lot of questions and as the police at Adana had retained my passport, I was in a difficult situation, especially as the policeman, egged on by the young man, now joined in.

"You say you are English?" said the young man. "Your passport, was it issued in Berlin?"

"No," I said, "Berlin is in Germany. My passport was issued in London."

"Why are you in Turkey? Why do you go to the Cilician Gates?"

It was useless to object or to ask what right this young man had to question and cross-examine me. I left the car and sat on a stone, smoking cigarette after cigarette while the young fanatic argued with my driver. I realized that because this young chauvinist was interested in me, I stood a good chance of spending the night in the local cell or of being turned back from the Cilician Gates.

He came up and pointed excitedly to my camera.

"What is that?" he cried. "It is a camera! You cannot take photographs."

He pointed to the policeman.

"This man must go with you," he said.

So the policeman climbed in next to the driver and off we bumped over the mountain track. Every now and then the car would give a lurch that threatened to send the rifle of my escort through the roof. I hoped the safety catch was down.

After a mile or so the memory of the young spy maniac faded slightly, and the driver and the policeman began to sing together and to indulge in cheerful bursts of laughter. Then, with the air growing colder and in a silence broken only by the rush of mountain torrents, we approached one of the most awe-inspiring gorges I have ever seen.

The ancient road through the Taurus Mountains is about eighty miles in length, but the actual pass, the Cilician Gates, is only a hundred yards long. The dark-coloured cliffs narrow to a mere slit. There is just a cleft in the rock, at the bottom of which a torrent roars and tumbles.

I walked for some distance through the Gates and examined several weather-worn inscriptions hewn on the face of the rock. They were cut long ago by the armies that had marched through the Gates. One is, I think, an inscription of the time of Marcus Aurelius.

This is a haunted pass. Since the dawn of war and commerce, soldiers and merchants have poured through this narrow slit in the Taurus. Xenophon tells us how Cyrus and his immortal Ten Thousand came through on their way to Babylon in the summer of 401 B.C. It was the road taken by Alexander the Great with his armies in 333 B.C., after the battle of the Granicus. He stood looking up at the mountains and at the knife-slit through them, fearing an ambush, as every soldier has feared it who ventured to march that way. He ordered his light-armed Thracians to advance and reconnoitre, and learnt with astonishment that the Persians had failed to man the pass, for the Persian garrison, after setting fire to Tarsus to prevent its treasures falling into Alexander's hands, had fled before the conqueror's armies. So Alexander entered Tarsus. He nearly lost his life there by bathing in the cold snow-waters of the Cydnus.

When the Crusaders approached the Cilician Gates after their long march across Asia Minor from Constantinople, they, too, looked with fear at the pass. They gazed with awe at its gloomy defiles and gave it the terrible name of "the Gates of Judas."

But as I stood in the pass that afternoon, it was not of conqueror or of caravan that I thought, but of a man with a staff in his hand, who climbed up through the Cilician Gates to the great plains of Asia Minor with a message of peace.

As a child Paul must have known these mountains well, because in Roman times it was the custom to leave the hot plain during the summer months and live for a time on the heights. Early in his life he must have thought of the Gates as the entrance to another world; the pass where roads from Bagdad and Antioch moved up through the mountains and joined a road that lay straight as an arrow to Ephesus, and over the sea to the heart of the world—to Rome.

I sat so long in the gloomy pass, trying to picture this indomitable wayfarer, that my escort cast suspicious glances at me, possibly wondering what mischief the foreigner was hatching on a highway that is now, as it was in the day of Xenophon, a military road.

The driver came to me and, pointing to the sky, indicated that unless we started back at once we should be held up on the hills. Regretfully I began the homeward journey, and we crept cautiously into Tarsus in the dark.

No footfall broke the silence. Now and then the town dogs barked and jackals would answer far off on the plain. Like a ghost in the moonlight I saw the vanished Tarsus of temple and colonnade, and, like a ghost in the moonlight, I seemed to see the figure of one man pressing westward through the mountains I had left behind, bearing the message of Christ.

14

In the little hotel at Adana, which smells strongly of roast mutton, pilaff and baklava, I fell into conversation with a Turk of about forty, who spoke excellent English.

"During the war I was captured on the Suez Canal," he said, "and learnt English in one of your prisons. I also learnt all your songs. Can you sing: 'This is the end of a perfect day'? And can you sing: 'If you were the only girl in the world'? You know those songs? So do I."

He was travelling for a firm of cotton merchants. In dress, manner, and deportment he was European. An old Turk in a corner of the dining-room called for a *chibouk,* or hookah —a relic of the old regime—and as the waiter filled the pan with charcoal, my friend shrugged his shoulders contemptuously.

"That generation," he said, "does not matter. It will soon die. But a generation worthy of our new Turkey is coming along: young boys and girls who can read and write, who have been educated. We shall then be a great nation."

So might a Russian have spoken in the first years of the Soviet.

"Tell me why you are so suspicious of strangers," I asked. "Why do the police think I am a spy if I take out a notebook or a camera?"

"We have no reason to trust the world," he said. "We have

had a bad time, and we can take no chances. The important thing in Turkey is obedience. We must obey the Ghazi. Any-thing—*anything*—that may endanger Turkey must be stamped out."

"But surely a note-book is harmless enough?" I asked.

"No; a note-book can be very dangerous," he replied.

"I believe you must be in the secret service," I ventured with a smile.

"Why do you say that?" he asked quickly.

"For no reason at all," I replied.

"Well, let me give you a bit of advice. You want to see Turkey. You want to see the great work our President is doing to build up a nation. You want to see the ruins of old cities. Go away and come back with something more than a passport. Get a Turk to accompany you. And then you will see something. But as you are, you will see nothing."

I took this advice, and on the following day said good-bye to my kindly hosts of the American Mission and left Turkey for Syria.

During the slow railway journey back to Aleppo, I read the Epistles of St. Paul, underlining many of the well-known quotations and at the same time wondering how many people would attribute them to the Apostle.

> *The wages of sin is death* (*Romans* 6. 23).
> *Vengeance is mine; I will repay, saith the Lord* (*Romans* 12. 19).
> *Thou shalt heap coals of fire on his head* (*Romans* 12. 20).
> *The wisdom of this world is foolishness with God* (*1st Corinthians* 3. 19).
> *Absent in body, but present in spirit* (*1st Corinthians* 5. 3).
> *It is better to marry than to burn* (*1st Corinthians* 7. 9).
> *The fashion of this world passeth away* (*1st Corinthians* 7. 31).

I am made all things to all men (1st Corinthians 9. 22).

Though I speak with the tongues of men and of angels and have not charity, I am become as sounding brass, or a tinkling cymbal (1st Corinthians 13. 1).

When I became a man, I put away childish things (1st Corinthians 13. 11).

For now we see through a glass, darkly (1st Corinthians 13. 12).

And now abideth faith, hope, charity, these three; but the greatest of these is charity. (Revised Version says "Love" instead of "Charity") (1st Corinthians 13. 13).

Let all things be done decently and in order (1st Corinthians 14. 40).

Let us eat and drink; for to-morrow we die (1st Corinthians 15. 32).

O death, where is thy sting; O grave, where is thy victory? (1st Corinthians 15. 55).

God loveth a cheerful giver (2nd Corinthians 9. 7).

Bear ye one another's burdens (Galatians 6. 2).

Whatsoever a man soweth, that shall he also reap (Galatians 6. 7).

Let not the sun go down upon your wrath (Ephesians 4. 26).

Let no man deceive you with vain words (Ephesians 5. 6).

The peace of God, which passeth all understanding (Philippians 4. 7).

Not greedy of filthy lucre (1st Timothy 3. 3).

Drink no longer water, but use a little wine for thy stomach's sake (1st Timothy 5. 23).

We brought nothing into this world, and it is certain we can carry nothing out (1st Timothy 6. 7).

The love of money is the root of all evil (1st Timothy 6. 10).

I have fought a good fight, I have finished my course, I have kept the faith (2nd Timothy 4. 7).

Unto the pure all things are pure (Titus 1. 15).

My reading was interrupted by the sudden stopping of the train. As so often happens when the snow is melting in early spring, several tons of the mountain had fallen almost on the engine.

We stayed for more than three hours, while Turks from the nearest village cleared the line with spades. As I walked about, gazing down over the precipice into which we should certainly have been flung had the train run into the avalanche in the dark. I noticed with interest that every metal sleeper bore the name of "Krupp." This line was part of the ex-Kaiser's famous Berlin-to-Bagdad railway.

We clanked slowly into Aleppo after midnight, many hours late.

CHAPTER III

I enjoy a brief glimpse of Aleppo and journey to Antioch. I visit the scenes of the first Gentile church and explore the city in which men were first called "Christians." Lost among mulberry gardens, I find the port of Seleucia from which St. Paul, St. Barnabas, and St. Mark set sail for Cyprus.

1

DATE-PALMS stirred in the night wind, Mosques that might have been built of snow stood next to ebony gate-ways cut, it seemed, with a knife against the stars. Aleppo was pervaded by a quality of intense drama. It might have been a city after a massacre, or a city lying hidden, awaiting an enemy. From the dark mass of its roofs minarets rose up clear and white in the starlight, as if they still remained in the light of day. . . .

I opened the slatted shutters in the morning, and the sunshine leapt in like a tiger. It lay in warm, striped bars across the stone floor. I looked with delight on a city set on the edge of a desert, and it seemed to me, as I gazed at the white minarets, the domes and the flat roof-tops, that Aleppo deserves the title so recklessly given to many a haunt of squalor: a city of the Arabian Nights.

I went out prepared for the disillusion that frequently follows closer contact with an Eastern city; but it did not come. Aleppo has accepted the West without losing itself in the process. There are really two cities: the modern French city, and the Arab city whose walls enclose the most picturesque covered bazaars in the Near East.

In general appearance Aleppo is like thousands of little

square boxes arranged haphazardly on an enormous expanse of brown country that fades off into desert. From the uniform flatness of the houses rise mushroom domes and slender white minarets like candles with their snuffers on. In the centre of this picturesque jumble is a cone-shaped hill of great height and girth, crowned by a Saracen castle of such splendour and dignity that I felt as a crusader might have felt who had got behind the enemy lines and was looking with awe on Saladin's reply to the Krak des Chevaliers. The hill was artificially erected, and it seems that a memory of this lingers in the local Arab legend that it is upheld on eight thousand pillars. I am told that on a clear day the distant windings of the Euphrates can be seen from the turrets of this superb Citadel.

Although plagues, massacres, wars and earthquakes have destroyed Aleppo with consistent regularity, the town has always risen again to fulfil its destiny, that of a great caravan city of Eastern commerce. For centuries camel caravans from Bagdad brought the produce of India and the East to Aleppo. It is the route by which the light fabrics of Mosul (called mosuline, or muslin) found their way to Europe. There was a trade connection between England and Aleppo in Elizabeth's day, and I believe that in the reign of James I. one of our earliest consulates was established there. This may explain why the name of the city was known to the English playgoer of Shakespeare's time. The poet mentions Aleppo twice, once in *Macbeth* and once in *Othello*. But the reference in *Macbeth* suggests that Shakespeare's geography was not too good, for the Master of the ship *Tiger* takes his brig into Aleppo, which, of course, would have meant a long voyage across the desert!

Aleppo's trade is slowly decreasing. Once on the great trade route of the world, the town is now side-tracked. The first blow was the discovery of the Cape route to India; the second was the overland route through Egypt to the Red Sea; and the third was the cutting of the Suez Canal.

No Eastern city has impressed me with a greater sense of its mystery. To drift with the crowds in the bazaars, those vaulted avenues cool and dim as cathedral naves, is to enter another world: a fatalistic world where violent emotions are covered with a fine veneer of manners. Such cities are like curved Arab daggers hidden in velvet scabbards. You may handle them and think them soft and attractive, but in a second the steel can flash out naked and murderous.

Looking at the quiet, easy-going crowds, the merchants sitting at their stalls, the old men removing their slippers at the mosque porch, the narrow stone streets, the little court-yards flooded in sun, I wondered what was really behind it all.

It sometimes seems to me that in places like Aleppo every-day life is either a game or an elaborate screen of pretence, and that the beggar at the gate, the merchant among his spices, the camel-driver with his muddy beasts, the patriarch in the sunshine, might rise up at a signal and show themselves to be utterly different characters.

I may be wrong, of course; but that is the atmosphere of Aleppo.

I walked through the bazaars, which are lined on each side with little booths and workshops. Here and there a mag-nificent Saracenic gate leads into a courtyard where a lemon tree grows by a fountain, or into a *khan* where a dozen camels rest under the ancient balcony of the inn.

There is a street of metal-workers, a street of leather-workers, of dyers, of cloth and silk merchants, and a street of spices, where the most remarkable selection I have ever seen lies piled in sacks, stored in trays, drums and jars. I saw sacks of cinnamon, clove, coriander, sumach, aniseed, aloes, nutmeg, saffron, tamarind, henna, camomile, and many spices whose names I did not know.

Two veiled women were buying some kind of root. I asked a young Armenian what it was. He spoke to one of the women, who replied in Arabic with the verve and freedom of women in a London market.

"She says it is orris root, and when pounded and mixed with honey it is good for rheumatism. She rubs it on after a hot bath."

I wandered for an hour or so in the dark labyrinth of these vaulted bazaars, watching the protracted process of purchase: the hands held up in horror and dismay, the shrugging shoulders, the forceful gestures, and the violent bargaining which usually ends with smiles and compliments and little cups of sweet coffee.

Near the Street of the leather-workers I took off my shoes and entered the great Mosque, the *Jami Zakariya,* where the tomb of Zacharias, father of John the Baptist, is to be seen behind gilded railings and covered with a heavily embroidered cloth. In the brilliant sunlight of the courtyard kneeling men faced the direction of Mecca, lost in prayer, swaying their bodies slightly and every now and then bending forward and touching the coloured tiles with their foreheads.

2

I had heard several people in Aleppo talk about "the sheik." "He's a curious character," I was told, "and everybody who comes to Aleppo should visit him. By profession he is a dealer in antiquities."

I set off one morning with a native of Aleppo to call on the Sheik. We plunged into ancient streets where gates swung protestingly on hinges forged in the days of the Sultan Selim, and arrived at length in a quiet lane. Two veiled women melted into a gateway like black ghosts. At the end of the lane was an arched door studded with rusty nailheads about the size of a shilling. My companion picked a stone from the road and hammered on the door, which was opened by an

Arab boy.

We walked into a courtyard and, climbing a flight of rickety stairs, entered a remarkable room. In a corner, with his back to a small window, sat a dignified and bearded patriarch. He wore the green turban of holiness. It looked as though the winds of the world had for centuries been blowing odds and ends and worn-out things into this strange room. There were piles of Arabic books that now and then had overbalanced and fallen to the floor. But no one had ever re-erected them. There were glass cases full of scraps of Persian embroidery, modern cigarette cases, Roman glass, Byzantine pottery, all of them covered in dust and lying in rich and riotous confusion. On the floor, stag's antlers, skins of animals and old armour lay about mixed up with Chinese pottery, silver spoons, and bronze pots full of ancient Greek and Roman coins.

An empty cigarette tin full of Egyptian scarabs stood on a Greek tombstone. The walls were hung with strings of beads found in ancient graves, and the ceiling was covered with flintlock muskets, scimitars and Arab embroideries.

The Sheik rose and, after greeting me with dignified formality (knocking down in the process a pot full of coins), settled himself again on his cushion and placed a kettle on a charcoal fire that glowed in front of him. He made Persian tea, picking pinches of spices from various tins lying round him, eventually handing to me a small glass of a sweet, aromatic liquid unlike anything known in the West as tea.

When I expressed surprise at the splendour of his possessions, the Sheik smiled and waved me towards an inner room, which, to my astonishment, was even more hopelessly congested than the first. There were also two floors above, and several rooms round the courtyard, crammed to the roof with the fruit of a long and acquisitive life.

As I went through the protracted process of buying some

Alexandrian tetradrachms, I heard bit by bit the story of the Sheik's life. He was not, as I had supposed, a Syrian Arab, but an Afghan and a British subject. He showed me his passport. It was the first British passport I had ever seen with four wives described in it. The eldest wife was forty-seven and the youngest eighteen. The Sheik was seventy-six and was thinking of becoming a bridegroom again.

Before the War, when Syria was ruled by Turkey, this man was noted for his piety and his pilgrimages to Mecca. When war broke out, Enver Pasha sat where I was sitting and suggested that on the following Friday the Sheik should preach a holy war in the mosque. The Sheik bowed his head.

But when the Friday came, the Sheik mounted the pulpit and said that the friend of the Moslem world was Britain and that its enemy was Turkey. He was at once taken out and flung into prison, charged with sedition. At his trial, he said to his judges:

"I am an old man. I am all alone in this city. You can take me out and kill me. But remember that I am a British subject, and behind me is the whole British army."

At this point in his narrative the Sheik lifted his robe and held up first his right leg, and then his left. Above each ankle was a swelling as big as an apple.

"I was in prison for three years," he said, "and these are the marks of my chains."

This remarkable character turned up in Aleppo again as soon as the War was over, and took up the threads of his life. The news spread across the Syrian desert. From near and far the Bedouin began once more to ride in with rings found in the sand, with glass found in Roman graves, with Greek coins, and with all the odds and ends that the Sheik loves to buy.

I had occasion to visit him again, and this time I saw him sipping his aromatic Persian tea in a circle of men from the desert. He was a changed man. The light of bargain was in

his eyes. He was illumined by the love of barter. With relent-
less courtesy he beat down his opponents and politely tram-
pled their ambitious desires in the dust. Before him in a
twisted rag lay a few bits of broken pottery and some ancient
seals. It did not matter. He treated the trifles as if they were
gold or diamonds. It was this business of bartering that mat-
tered to him.

And I realized, as I watched him, that the fun he gets out of
life is not in selling a few coins or pots to a stranger like myself,
but in accumulating, at his own price, most of the strange
objects brought to him, and thus beating his contemporaries
at their own game.

3

Before the War the only way to get from Aleppo to Antioch
was by horseback, a journey of eighteen hours. Since the
French Mandate, good roads have made an enormous difference to travel in this country and the journey now takes only
two hours and a half by motor-car.

I rose early and set off on the road to Antioch. On a lonely
stretch about five miles or so out of Aleppo, a mounted policeman with a rifle slung across his back spurred forward his
horse and held up his hand. As it was so early in the day, I
knew he was not going to warn me against bandits. I thought
he wished to examine the car for contraband, or for one of
the many mysterious reasons which induce police to hold up
cars in Syria.

He asked the driver if I would be good enough to give his
sister a lift to the next village, where her husband would be
waiting on the roadside. As he spoke, an Arab girl with down-
cast eyes, her broad, unexpressive face disfigured by blue
tattoo marks and her body hidden beneath folds of biblical
draperies, rose from a stone and came forward carrying a
bundle wrapped in cloth.

The contrast between brother and sister was remarkable. They had both come from the same mud village. She had remained an Arab peasant. He, in his smart French uniform, his peaked khaki cap and his air of authority, might have been mistaken by any stranger for a Frenchman. The girl took a seat next to the driver, the brother gave me a smart salute, and off we went.

I noticed that the girl had some difficulty in holding her bundle, so I suggested that she should let me put it on the floor in my part of the car. The driver turned to me with a smile and said:

"Sir, the bundle is a child."

He repeated his remark in Arabic to the woman, who half turned and, looking at me for the first time with enormous black eyes, made larger by a rim of *kohl*, held up for my inspection a small infant wrapped in swaddling bands. He was, she said—carefully accentuating the fact that the child was masculine—eight weeks old.

She passed him over to me as if he were a parcel and I held him with confidence, because he could not suddenly wriggle his arms or legs and fall out of my grasp like a Western baby. The swaddling bands were crossed near his shoulders, and, after firmly pinioning his arms, passed again round his body and came up over his legs. He was like a very small mummy.

Realizing that he was in strange hands, the baby slowly opened his eyes and focused on me a dark and suspicious glance. He drew a deep breath preparatory to a howl, but was too surprised to do anything but lie there watching me with the curious, soft eyes of infancy. His eyelashes were heavily smeared with black *kohl* as a precaution against disease. This black paint, usually made from powdered antimony or burnt almond shells, or from frankincense, was used by the ancient Egyptians and by characters in the Old Testament, and it is still used throughout the East by men as well as women.

An Arab child in Syria to-day is nursed exactly as in Old Testament times. He is bound in swaddling clothes almost as soon as he is born, and remains in them for a year or so. This may be a relic of nomadic times, when a child bound up like this was easier to carry on the day's march. His limbs are rubbed with salt water to harden them, which explains why Ezekiel used the words "Thou wast not salted at all, nor swaddled at all," to denote the birth of an outcast. One can often hear the same remark in Arab countries to-day, when a man wishes to taunt another with softness: "It's easy to see," he will cry, "that you were never salted!"

After travelling for about five miles, we saw a small group beside the road. The husband and various relations were waiting for the arrival of the young mother. They were astonished to see that I was holding the baby.

The husband stepped forward, touched his forehead and breast with his hand and thanked me. After a few complimentary remarks about the baby, I drove off to a chorus of farewells and a row of delighted smiles. Looking back, I saw them, like a picture from the Old Testament, moving slowly through fields of growing wheat to a village in a dip of the hills.

As we went on, we passed several of the curious beehive villages characteristic of the plain of Aleppo. I have seen them nowhere else in Syria, and they do not exist in Palestine. Hundreds of cone-shaped huts stand in regular rows, like the hives of some enormous insects. They are inhabited by ordinary *fellahin* and by packs of savage dogs which run away only when you pretend to pick up a stone. Sometimes a mud wall encloses the whole village.

I went into one village where the patriarchal headman took me into several of the huts. I was astonished to find them as clean as a Devon cottage, a tribute impossible to pay to any other huts I have entered in the East. The women take out the bedding every day and air it in the sunshine.

The huts are well furnished with wooden furniture, and I was surprised to see European beds in some of them instead of the mat on which the Arab usually curls up at night. It seemed to me the standard of living in these beehive villages, which looked so poverty-stricken and primitive from the road, was infinitely higher than in the ordinary Arab village.

I continued my journey through a countryside that St. Paul must have known well in the course of his life in Antioch: a grey, inhospitable land of stony hills, crossed by a Roman road made of large blocks of squared stone. Some miles from Antioch I stopped the car in amazement when I saw this road, a road that Paul may have walked, still crossing the country for several hundred yards. The modern road cuts across it, but the old road plunges on over the hills, deserted now save for a shepherd and his flock of sheep.

I walked over it for about a half a mile, thinking that no relic of Apostolic times that I had so far seen was more eloquent of the age in which St. Paul lived. Here is a fragment of that magnificent road system that linked city to city throughout the Roman world, that crossed desert, mountain, and steppe, that plunged across Asia Minor into Macedonia, changing its name from country to country, purposefully leading, as all roads did in those days, to Rome.

As you stand on this road, it is not difficult to people it again with the traffic of Paul's day: the bands of jugglers and dancing-girls on their way to Antioch—the Paris of the East— cohorts on the march, merchants from Bagdad and Damascus with their silks, spices, and perfumes, itinerant Greek philosophers, gladiators, men with caged beasts for the circus at Antioch, pagan priests begging their way with a god in a tent: and somewhere in that crowd, symbols of the old world and the new, a Roman senator travelling in state on some imperial mission, and, humbly and on foot, a Christian on a greater mission, travelling to the little "church that was in Antioch."

In an hour's time we decended from stony hills into the hot, green valley where the Orontes turns and twists between great mountains to the sea.

There, with the morning sun shining on minarets, I saw Antioch for the first time—the Mother Church of Gentile Christianity.

4

Antioch "the Beautiful and the Golden" still deserves her ancient titles, but her beauty is no longer the splendour of temple and colonnade, and her gold is no longer that of wealth, but of sunshine lying over desolate hillsides.

I thought that never had I seen a town camped in a more lovely place. High mountains shield it; the Orontes, pale-green with melted snow, rushes arch-high beneath the bridge; and the broad shoulder of Mount Silpius towers majestically above a cluster of one-storied Arab houses and a white forest of minarets.

Antioch is less European in appearance than any other town in Syria. It is more or less as the Turks left it after the War and many of the people still speak Turkish. Except for a squadron of colonial cavalry out at exercise, or a Syrian policeman in French khaki drill, there is little to indicate that Antioch is ruled under the French Syrian Mandate. The population to-day is thirty-five thousand Moslems and some seven thousand Latin, Greek, and Armenian Christians.

The main street of Antioch might have come from any of the more prosperous regions of Turkey. It is lined with little open shops in which you can see a number of interesting interiors, especially those of the barbers' shops in which Arabs are being shaved and scented while their tarbushes are renovated on a brass block. Women dressed in black, and veiled from head to foot, saunter through the market, haggling at the little stalls over minute quantities of meat or vegetables. Sleepy drivers of *arabas* suddenly spring to life at the rare sight of a stranger, and urge their reluctant steeds into movement with much whip-cracking. Up and down the lanes, and in the sunny avenues leading from the main street, moves the most gaily dressed native crowd in Syria: the men in coloured Turkish trousers and cone-shaped Phrygian caps, the women in vivid red and blue skirts and richly embroidered jackets.

I did not know that there is an excellent European hotel right in the middle of Antioch, the *Hôtel du Tourisme,* and therefore I drove five miles out to Daphne, where I discovered that the *Hôtel des Cascades* had not yet opened for the season. The Syrian manager, however, apologizing for beds airing in the hall and tables turned upside down elsewhere, immediately offered me a room and was so kind and obliging that I had not the heart to return and find more convenient quarters in Antioch.

I was given a room overlooking the great vale where Daphne, the daughter of the river-god Peneus, on the point of being overtaken by the pursuing Apollo, prayed for aid and was turned into a laurel tree.

There was no sound but the rush of water falling from rock-pool to rock-pool. I could see the dark clumps of laurels which still grow in the once sacred grove. There was another window, looking over the road where shepherds went past with their flocks. Beneath this window every morning came herds of goats moving in a brown mist of dust and to a chiming of bells. When it was dark I would open my windows and see a red fire pricking the night in the hills below, and hear, rising in the stillness, a little endless tune played on a flute, as if someone in the laurels of Daphne were mourning for a lost world.

There was no one in the hotel but the manager, his invisible wife, a six months old pointer called Diana, and a delightful fellow named Georges, a Circassian general factotum, who used to wait on me at dinner dressed in muddy field-boots, a long, torn mackintosh and a black astrakhan fez. In the evening when the air grew cold, Georges would light a brazier of crushed olive stones in my bedroom. The dove-grey powder breathed a gentle heat into the air, and if you blew it there would be a red glow hiding in the grey powder.

I explored the groves of Daphne, climbing the steep rocks at the back and descending beside the waterfalls, noting how earthquakes, which are so frequent in this part of Syria, have deformed and altered the ground. But it is not difficult to imagine this place as it must have been in Paul's time: a ten mile pleasure garden devoted to the orgiastic worship of the river-god. Priestesses dedicated to his worship presided over temples set on the terraced slopes of hills; slave girls of all nationalities, bought by the hundred in the markets of the East, were presented to the grove by pious citizens of Antioch.

Daphnici Mores became a byword, even in a world which witnessed the annual pilgrimages to the groves of the Cyprian Aphrodite at Paphos and could boast that the great Temple of Venus at Corinth possessed a thousand sacred priestesses. Juvenal, hitting at the decay of Roman morals, said that the waters of the Syrian Orontes had flowed into the Tiber, flooding Rome with the decadent superstitions of the East.

It is not surprising that the people of Daphne still are superstitious and do not care to go out alone after sunset, or that mothers will not allow their children to stray from the door unless they are protected by the small blue charm which guards against the wandering spirit of evil.

5

I have sat for hours on the slopes of Mount Silpius, looking down over Antioch. If the traveller is shocked by the disappearance of Tarsus, what are his feelings as he looks at Antioch? Imagine London levelled to the ground, all the bricks and stones carted away, all roads obliterated, and a gipsy encampment between Tottenham Court Road and Charing Cross still calling itself "London": imagine this, and you have a fairly good analogy. Arab Antioch is a small town huddled on a fraction of the ancient area of the city. Antioch once covered the plain on both sides of the Orontes. The four districts that marked the city's development under the various Seleucid rulers were each surrounded by a wall, and were all enclosed by the great city wall of Antioch. Even the steep slopes of Mount Silpius were covered with villas and traversed by roads, and standing up against the sky on the top of this mountain are fragments of the old wall of Antioch, lying now amid miles of desolation.

But where were the race-courses, the famous theatres, the baths, the thousands of marble columns, the countless statues, the fountains, the temples and the market-places? They have disappeared with the world that created them. Sometimes a peasant, digging in a mulberry grove a mile or two from modern Antioch, will come across the relic of a street or the coloured flooring of a bath. If the whole area of ancient Antioch were to be scientifically investigated, the work would employ an archæological expedition for a generation.

When Paul came to Antioch, it was the third largest city in the world. It was wealthy and blatant, and there was a worship of the material achievements of life and the sensory attributes of riches, such as central heating, swimming-pools, plumbing, and flood-lighting, which cannot fail to remind us of our own time.

"In the public baths every stream has the proportion of a river, in the private ones several have the like, and the rest not much less," says the Antiochene writer, Libanius. "He who has the means of laying out a new bath does so without concern about a sufficient flow of water, and has no need to fear that, when ready, it will remain dry. Therefore every district of the city carefully provides for the special elegance of its bathing establishments; these district bathing establishments are so much finer than the general ones, as they are smaller than these are, and the inhabitants of the district strive to surpass one another. . . . With us the public fountains flow for ornament since every one has water within his doors."

As an example of town-planning, ancient Antioch was probably finer than any city in the world to-day. Its main street was a wide corso four and a half miles long—about five times the length of Princes Street, Edinburgh. There was a central passage for horse traffic and chariots, and two covered colonnades for foot-passengers. At right angles to it stretched miles of colonnaded streets paved with marble, laid out on the grid-iron principle in emulation of Alexandria, and on either side of the streets stood public buildings, market-places, temples and triumphal arches. When the sun shone on coloured fountains and gilded statues, on marble colonnades and prancing quadriga, and on the uplifted gold trumpets of Victories, the appearance of Antioch must indeed have been superb.

When night fell, this enormous city was picked out with thousands of lights in order that the business of Antioch, which was enjoyment, might continue as if it were still day. The disbelief in a future life, which makes it imperative hungrily to steal an hour of light from the dark and thus to prolong consciousness, was as prevalent in Antioch as it is to-day in many large cities. "With us," wrote Libanius, "night is distinguished from day only by the difference of the lighting; diligent hands find no difference and forge on, and he who will sings and dances, so that Hephæstos and Aphrodite here share the night between them." This is, I believe, the only reference to street-lighting in the literature of antiquity.

If Alexandria reflected the permanent achievements of the new age, Antioch reflected the transient. It was a city of consumers. It was full of rich aristocrats and *nouveaux riches*, and of wealthy, retired people who sought here one of the finest climates in the world. Something that we associate with Venice in the eighteenth century, with Paris in the nineteenth century, and with Hollywood to-day, with its deification of youth and beauty, distinguished Antioch during the lifetime of Paul. It was up-to-date, amusing, elegant, wicked; and its epigrams could go a long way to make or ruin a reputation. The ridiculous quarrels which centred round the racing stables of Antioch were known throughout the world. The Blue Faction and the Green Faction, which were famous in Paul's time, enlisted even the patronage of the Emperor. Both Caligula and Claudius wore the colours of the Green Faction. In the realm of scurrility and coarse witticism, Antioch stood supreme.

What Mommsen called a "perpetual warfare of sarcasm" went on between the frivolous public of Antioch and any Emperor who spent more than a brief stay with them. The people of Antioch had a genius for coining nicknames, and their scurrility was irrepressible. A taunt similar to the now almost forgotten cry of "Beaver" was aimed with deadly effect by the populace at the Emperor Julian, who in a satirical reply called them "the beard-mockers" of Antioch.

Their passion for the theatre and race-course was proverbial. When they were not watching games, they were talking about the performers. The city was consequently packed with jockeys and tipsters, mediums, dancers, actors and professional athletes. The music-halls and theatres offered a natural start in life to the dancers of Cæsarea, the flute-players of the Lebanon, the actors of Tyre, the wrestlers of Ascalon, and the musicians of Gaza: while the renowned boxers of Castabala, and the jockeys for which Laodicea was famous, were only too happy to make long journeys for the privilege of an audition in a city whose approval was half-way to a career.

In such a city the Jews formed a sombre community. Their colony was one of the most prosperous in the Diaspora. They had many synagogues and possessed not only civil rights, but also self-government by an elected body similar to the Sanhedrin in Jerusalem. They seem to have lived on easier terms with the Gentiles than their fellow-Jews in Alexandria, who existed in an atmosphere of intermittent pogroms. In order to show appreciation for the goodwill existing between Gentile and Jew, Herod the Great paved with marble two and a half miles of Antioch's streets, and erected a covered colonnade beneath which the citizens could seek shelter from sun or rain.

Antioch was a creation of the Hellenistic Age: so was Alexandria, the New York of the ancient world. It was an age that appears surprisingly modern to us, and I have the feeling that a man of the twentieth century would have found himself infinitely more at home in it than in Europe during the Middle Ages.

"The keen and wide-awake intelligence of this wonderful age was everywhere evident," writes Professor Breasted of the Hellenistic Age in his book, *Ancient Times,* "but especially in the application of science to the work and needs of daily life. It was an age of inventions, like our own. An up-to-date man would install an automatic door-opener for the doorkeeper of his house, and a washing machine which delivered water and mineral soap as needed. On his estate olive oil was produced with a press operating with screw pressure. Outside the temples the priests set up automatic dispensers of holy water, while a water sprinkler operating by water pressure reduced the danger of fire. The application of levers, cranks, screws and cog-wheels to daily life brought forth cable roads for use in lowering stone from lofty quarries, or water wheels for drawing water on a large scale. A similar endless-chain apparatus was used for quickly raising heavy stone missiles to be discharged from huge missile-hurling war machines, some of which even operated by air pressure. As we go to see the 'movies' so the people crowded to the market place to view the automatic theatre, in which a clever mechanician presented an old Greek tragedy of the Trojan War in five scenes, displaying shipbuilding, the launch of the fleet, the voyage, with the dolphins playing in the water about the vessels, and finally a storm at sea, with thunder and lightning, amid which the Greek heroes promptly went to the bottom. Housekeepers told stories of the simpler days of their grandmothers, when there was no running water in the house and they actually had to go out and fetch it a long way from the nearest spring."

Antioch, which has so remote a sound, is really much nearer to us than we imagine. After Rome and Alexandria, it was the third largest city in a world which prided itself on its scientific conquests, its material achievements, its emancipation from tradition; a world which worshipped wealth and employed its scientific skill in the invention of new engines of war.

6

Sitting on the slope of Mount Silpius in the afternoon sun, I tried to visualize the life and surroundings of the great missionary during a year in Antioch that is dismissed in the *Acts of the Apostles* in forty-eight words.

It is not always realized how long a time elapsed between Paul's conversion and his arrival as a Christian teacher in Antioch. He went to Jerusalem after his conversion, anxious to testify to his faith, but the Apostles were afraid of him. They could not believe that so fierce an opponent had become a friend.

The man who understood Paul's greatness was Barnabas, and their meeting led to one of the most significant friendships in history. Barnabas vouched for the reality of Paul's conversion, and brought him into personal touch with the Apostles who had known the Lord Jesus. Meanwhile the Hellenistic Jews, and other enemies of Christianity, considered Paul hateful not only as a Christian, but as a turn-coat. Had they not sent him to Damascus to persecute the Christians, and had he not returned a convert to the Faith? What penalty was too severe for such a man?

Fearing that Paul's life was in danger, the Apostles persuaded him to leave Jerusalem. He went to the port of Cæsarea and found a ship that was sailing for his native Tarsus. From that moment until his reappearance in Antioch, a silence of ten or more years descends on Paul. What was he doing during these long years? Of this we have no certain knowledge. It is remarkable that a man of Paul's burning zeal could have been lost for all this time. We can be sure that the years of silence were a period of preparation for his life's work and that during them he grew in spiritual grace.

Those ten years were important in the history of Christianity. The conservative Mother Church in Jerusalem, and the more liberal Daughter Church in Antioch, were moving, each in her own way, towards that liberation from the synagogue which resulted in the spread of Christianity throughout the world. St. Peter had taken the first step by baptizing the Roman centurion, Cornelius, thus anticipating St. Paul and admitting the first Gentile into the Church.

New problems were rising at Antioch. Numerous Gentile proselytes attached to the synagogues were anxious to embrace Christianity. The Church at Jerusalem sent Barnabas to review the situation. He immediately thought of Paul. There was no other man with whom he would more gladly work. Although it was presumably many a year since the two friends had met, Barnabas knew where to find Paul. He therefore went to Seleucia, the port of Antioch, and took ship to the opposite coast of Cilicia. There is, perhaps, a hint—for Luke never wastes a word—that Paul was not immediately forthcoming:

"Then departed Barnabas to Tarsus, for to seek Saul: and *when he had found him,* he brought him unto Antioch."

It is clear that he did not go straight to Paul's house and find him there. He had to look for him. If only a few words had been written by Luke, describing the finding of Paul by Barnabas, and the calling of Paul to the great work of his life, how inestimably precious would they be to us. All we know is that these two great men met, and that Paul journeyed to Antioch with his friend. And in that worldly city on the Orontes the Apostle underwent his missionary training.

What, we ask ourselves, did Paul look like as he walked the streets of Antioch? There is a tradition, based on an apocryphal gospel of the second century, the *Acts of Paul and Thecla*, that he was "a man little of stature, thin-haired upon the head, crooked in the legs, of good state of body, with eyebrows joining and nose somewhat hooked, full of grace: for sometimes he appeared like a man and sometimes he had the face of an angel."

This description is so unflattering and so unlike the ideal portrait one might expect after a lapse of time, that it may be a genuine portrait of the Apostle handed down by those who had seen him.

Again, when Paul and Barnabas were preaching to the heathen, Barnabas was mistaken for Jupiter, king of the gods, while Paul was thought to be Mercury, the messenger of Olympus. This suggests that Barnabas was the more imposing in appearance. In the *Second Epistle to the Corinthians* the writer gives an unflattering self-portrait: "I Paul myself . . . who in presence am base among you, but being absent

am bold toward you"; and he goes on to quote the remark of an
opponent that his "letters are weighty and powerful; but his
bodily presence is weak and his speech contemptible."

From these references it has been inferred that Paul was
not the commanding figure which Raphael set on the steps
of the Areopagus. But we must remember that exaggerated
self-disparagement has always been a polite convention in the
East. "Deign to enter my miserable hovel," the oriental will
say as he waves you towards a palace. "I, who am ugly as sin
and a great stammerer" might, on the same principle, be applied to himself by a handsome and popular orator.

If Paul were small and insignificant in appearance, is it not
strange that the Roman officer Claudius Lysias, who arrested
him in Jerusalem, should have mistaken him for a bold and
dangerous Egyptian agitator, a man who had led a crowd
out of the Mount of Olives, promising them supernatural
wonders?

One thing, however, is certain: that Paul suffered from a
mysterious complaint, his "thorn," or "stake," in the flesh,
that "buffeted" him and caused him grave worry and considerable humiliation. The nature of this complaint has
exercised the ingenuity of scholars of every nation. It has
been suggested the "thorn in the flesh" was either epilepsy,
malaria, headaches, stammering, eye-disease or erysipelas.

The theory of epilepsy has been challenged by Sir William
Ramsay, who, having suffered from malaria in Asia Minor,
recognizes the symptoms of St. Paul's malady in those experienced by himself.

"Now in some constitutions," writes Sir William Ramsay
in *St. Paul the Traveller*, "malaria fever tends to recur in
very distressing and prostrating paroxysms, whenever one's
energies are taxed by a great effort. Such an attack is for the
time absolutely incapacitating: the sufferer can only lie and
feel himself a shaking and helpless weakling, when he ought

to be at work. He feels a contempt and loathing for self, and believes that others feel equal contempt and loathing."

I have seen beggars moaning in the lanes of Eastern cities, trembling all over, their teeth chattering, as they lay in the grip of fever, pitiful to others and humiliating to themselves.

Bishop Lightfoot laid down a list of conditions which any theory of Paul's malady must satisfy:

1. Physical pain of a very acute kind.

2. The malady was humiliating, a set-off against his spiritual privileges and a check to his spiritual pride.

3. It was grievous hindrance to the gospel and a powerful testimony to it when overcome.

4. The affliction seems to have attacked him when he preached, exposing him to possible contempt.

5. The meanness of his personal appearance may be connected with it.

6. The trouble was recurring.

All except No. 5 are fulfilled by one of those distressing attacks of malaria which are sometimes witnessed in the East. The earliest tradition, given by Tertullian, is that Paul suffered from splitting headaches. Headaches can be so severe that they affect the eyes, which would give point to Paul's gratitude to the Galatians because they would have plucked out their own eyes and given them to him, could such a sacrifice have helped him in his illness. Headache, says Sir William Ramsay, is also one of the most trying accompaniments of malaria.

The theory that St. Paul's "thorn in the flesh" was stammering is ingeniously advanced by Dr. W. K. Lowther Clarke in *New Testament Problems*:

"I suggest that St. Paul was a victim to nerves, and that modern men are peculiarly fitted to enter into his experience. Splitting headaches may well have accompanied the attacks, and they could hardly be described more appropriately by the word σκόλοψ, a stake driven into his head. Read 2 Corinthians, and you will see at once that the writer was a mass of nerves, acutely sensitive and a prey to melancholy and depression, which came as the ebb-tide of the mighty incoming tide of exaltation which was the other side of his being. Such was his essential sanity that a cure would probably have been possible if he could have enjoyed a quiet life and sympathetic companionship. But that was always out of his reach. His body was shattered by the experiences described in 2 Cor. 11, 'the care of all the churches' was a terrible mental strain, and the psychic and spiritual side of his life made great demands on his weakened frame. Once his nerves began to go, the conditions of recovery were absent."

The writer cites certain stammerers who have made their mark in literature: Charles Lamb, Charles Kingsley, and Lewis Carroll. He could have included Arnold Bennett.

Interesting as these speculations are, they must be inevitably inconclusive and unsatisfactory, for we shall never solve the mystery of Paul's thorn in the flesh.

More interesting than our speculations about his malady is the interesting side-light that it casts on his character. "It is enough to know," writes Dr. Stalker in Hasting's *Dictionary of the Apostolic Church*, "that the astonishing work done by this man was accomplished not in the robustness of a healthy body or in the self-consciousness of one able at all times to have absolute confidence in himself, but amid weariness and painfulness, shyness and self-distrust."

St. Paul and St. Barnabas arrived in Antioch about 47 A.D. What an interesting time this was in the history of the world. Claudius, the gentle, good-natured man who for three years had ruled the Roman Empire, had earned fame by his invasion of Britain. In the year 43 A.D.—a few years before St. Paul set out on his first mission—the Emperor had sent over an army with instructions that when the enemy were on the run he was to be summoned from Rome to take the credit. He arrived in Britain with the Prætorian Guard and, to over-awe the savage islanders, a phalanx of war elephants. This extraordinary procession marched north through Kent, crossed the Thames and camped with the legions on a hill that is now Colchester. Then Claudius returned to Rome after an absence of six months, of which only sixteen days were spent in Britain.

Standing in a marble street in Antioch, St. Paul may have heard some echo of this adventure. Antioch must have made a joke or a lampoon about it, as the city used to do about every-thing. Perhaps he met a traveller from Rome and heard of the great triumph decreed to Claudius: the processions, the sacri-fices, the captives, the games in the circus. He would hear that in honour of the occasion the Emperor had assumed the name Britannicus, and perhaps some traveller picked from his purse one of the gold coins which were struck to commem-orate the occasion, showing on one side the Emperor and on the other a triumphal arch with "De Britt" inscribed on it.

While St. Paul may have been listening to such stories in Antioch, the first Roman settlers were pegging out their claims on a hill beside the wild marshes of the Thames, a hill that would one day hold St. Paul's Cathedral.

But the event of that period, which was infinitely more interesting to the Jews of Antioch than the inclusion within the Roman Empire of a savage northern race that nobody had ever heard of, was the sudden death of King Agrippa in the circus at Cæsarea.

Agrippa was a character well known in all civilizations: the well-born, clever, penniless friend of princes. He had spent his childhood in Rome and was probably more of a Roman than a Jew. His youth had been employed wander-ing about trying to escape his creditors. Nowadays he would have gone into the City, or sold his name to a board of directors or a newspaper; but in those days it was only possible to make powerful friends—and hope for the best.

When his mad friend Caligula became Emperor, Agrippa's sun began to shine. He was given the estates of the dead Tetrarch Philip, which lay to the north-east of Galilee, and the title of King. The regal return home of this Herodian remittance man so enraged Herodias, mother of Salome and wife of Herod Antipas, the Herod of the Crucifixion, that she compelled her husband to go with her to Rome to ask the Emperor why Agrippa should be a real king while Herod remained a petty Tetrarch. But she was no match for Agrippa. He heard of the deputation and sent messengers ahead to tell Caligula that Herod had packed Galilee with arms; and the result of this family dispute was the banishment of Herod and Herodias and the confiscation of their estates. Agrippa's fortune was then established.

He was in Rome on January 24, 41 A.D., when the body of Caligula fell, stabbed by more than thirty dagger thrusts. As I have mentioned earlier in this book, it was Agrippa who in the confusion that followed, when the revival of the Republic or the continuation of the Monarchy hung on a hair, was mainly responsible for placing on the throne poor, trembling old Claudius.

Agrippa returned to Palestine further enriched by the estates of Judæa and Galilee (the property of the banished Herod Antipas) and well pleased with the knowledge that, having set Cæsar upon the throne, nothing could now stand in his way.

Who knows what dreams he cherished of reviving the glory of the Herodian House? He supported the strict Pharisee party, and this is why he slew St. James and would have slain St. Peter; because, as the *Acts of the Apostles* describes with masterly economy, "He saw it pleased the Jews."

After a reign of three years he entered the circus at Cæsarea with his royal escort. As he rose to address the crowds, the sun glittered on his robe of silver tissue and all the sycophants began to shout that his voice was that of a god and not a man. But he suddenly collapsed with violent internal pains and was carried out. He died five days later. At this time his son, who became Agrippa II. and before whom St. Paul was to make his famous speech on Christianity, was a lad of seventeen in Rome.

St. Paul and his friends must have been dumbfounded by the death of Agrippa. One gains some idea of the immense sensation it caused among Christians by the space given to the event in the *Acts of the Apostles*. Had Agrippa not died, the history of the Apostolic Church might have been very different. Without warning, its most influential adversary had vanished.

I imagine Paul in Antioch a few years after these events, hated by the Pharisees, loved by the proselytes, and endured with a tolerant smile by the Greek and Roman citizens in whose eyes he was merely another of those wandering godmakers. In the glittering, sophisticated city of Antioch what was one more god? The Græco-Roman world loved new gods and Rome's attitude was "the more the merrier," so long as none of them was political. Gibbon put this attitude very well when he said that "the various modes of worship which prevailed in the Roman world were all considered by the people as equally true; by the philosophers as equally false; and by the magistrates as equally useful."

It was in Antioch, the home of catchword and nickname, that the term "Christian" was first used to describe members of the early Church. Who, one wonders, used it for the first time, and what was the occasion?

The word could not have been coined by the Jews, because they used the word Nazarene, and it is unlikely that it was applied by the Christians, for they called themselves "saints," "brethren," and "believers." It follows, therefore, that it was probably a word coined by a Greek, who, knowing something about the new faith, incorporated the name of Jesus Christ with those who believed in Him.

There is a further possibility that the word was used disparagingly by the Roman officials at Antioch, just as the followers of Cæsar were dubbed Cæsariani, of Pompey, Pompeiani, of Herod, Herodiani. If so, we may imagine that the word Christians was possibly first used by a member of the Antioch police force when he was summoned to a street in which Orthodox Jews had attacked the new sect.

"Those Christiani again!" he may have said, unconscious that he had made history.

7

On Friday, the Moslem day of rest, the women of Antioch go out into the fields to gossip under the apricot trees. No man is ever present at these gatherings, and the women gladly lift their veils.

As children play about and pick fistsful of poppies and anemones, the women, sitting in circles, plunge into conversation. At the distant sound of a masculine foot on the hill-path or through the growing wheat, there is a sudden swift movement among the women and in a flash they are a group of black ghosts again, covered from head to foot. No man could hope to see these women unveiled. They are as quick to take alarm as a herd of deer.

When I passed by, I saw a number of black ghosts sitting together on the grass, but when I had climbed a hill that overlooked this group, I saw with amusement that each face was revealed, and I thought that the veil is a great protector of the unlovely. I remembered the remark of a Turk who said to me: "The unveiling of women has been a great shock to all of us."

As I climbed the hills, I carried in my pocket the key of St. Peter's Cave. It had been given to me by the Capuchin monks who tend the souls of a proportion of the seven thousand Christians in Antioch. Their bare little monastery stands near the Orontes; from its terrace one gazes over the flat roofs of the town and over the domes and minarets of mosques to the slopes of Mount Silpius. The monk who gave me the key was a burly father who was followed by an inquisitive and mischievous gazelle.

"Ah, you impertinent!" he cried in a voice of thunder, "you must learn to behave!" and then, in the most gentle and ineffectual manner, he attempted to stop the creature from nibbling his robes.

The gazelle, furious to be stopped, lowered its head and charged the Capuchin, tangling its small horns in the cord that fell from his waist. He aimed a half-hearted kick at it with a sandalled foot, and the creature, tossing its pretty head, ran clattering from the room and out into the sun-steeped garden of the monastery.

"Here is the key. You wish to know the history of the cave? Alas, like all Christian things in Antioch, its origin is obscure. We believe that when the first Christians worshipped in Antioch in the time of St. Peter and St. Paul, this cave was one of their meeting places. It was a church in remote ages, but it has not been used for many centuries. . . ."

The cave lies high on a now deserted mountain side that in Roman times was occupied by streets of houses. Reservoirs in the hills above carried water to the houses through tunnels hewn in the rock. I entered one of these tunnels and walked along it for perhaps fifty yards, led by an Arab youth who pointed out the smooth, water-worn channel. It was unnecessary to bend double except in certain sections. When we had climbed out into the sunshine at the other end, the youth fished from his pocket a handful of green coins.

"*Antika*," he said.

And I looked with interest at the faces of dead emperors. After rain, or in ploughing time, the soil of Antioch gives up these coins as the sea turns up empty shells.

"How did you get these, Mohammed?" I asked.

"I have beautifully quick eyes," he replied. "I can see an *antika* where others see nothing. Look! You did not see. But *I* saw!"

And he picked up a piece of iridescent glass that was lying half-covered with earth.

"Some day," he said, "I shall find a whole man in the earth and then I shall hide him again and tell nobody. You have no idea what thieves and liars live in this town. Then when the time comes I shall sell this man for much money and go away and live in America, or perhaps even in France."

He meant that some day he hoped to find a valuable statue in the fields.

We climbed up to the Cave of St. Peter, which has been faced with masonry and fitted with an iron grille. I unlocked this and entered a damp little rock-cut church in which the Capuchins have erected an altar approached by three steps. Water percolates into the cave from the hills, and there is also a small stream that oozes through the fissures of the rock, falling into a basin in the cave.

I am told that the Christians of Antioch and also many Moslems believe that this water has miraculous healing powers. So in this superstition we may, perhaps, see a lingering memory of the sanctity that was in ancient time associated with the cave.

There is a tradition, repeated from an ancient authority by John of Antioch, who lived in the sixth century, that Paul and Barnabas preached and worked in Singon Street, near the Pantheon, in a district called Epiphania.

We know from ancient literature that behind this district of Epiphania one of the crags of Mount Silpius had been carved into a horrible and colossal head of Charon, the ferryman who in Greek mythology rowed the souls of the dead across the Styx. This had been carved a century and a half before St. Paul's day by the orders of an emperor who hoped to avert plague from the city, presumably by pretending that Death was already its presiding deity. This ghastly head with a gold crown on it was one of the sights of ancient Antioch; a strange one for a city that thought only of the passing hour. If, therefore, this cave is near the legendary site of Paul's ministry, it should also be near the Charonium, as the carved crag was called.

Climbing down the hill, I was surprised to come to a colossal head cut from the rock, and beside it a full-length figure also cut from the mountain. I thought at first that I had found the Charonium, but as I studied the shape of the head, I felt sure that it was not that of Charon, but of a woman.

Charon, no doubt, disappeared in one of the countless earthquakes that have altered the Antioch landscape. But it is significant that gigantic rock carvings still exist in this place, exactly where we should expect them to be if the early Christian tradition about Singon Street were true.

8

During Paul's year at Antioch, the famine mentioned in *Acts* and also by Josephus began in Palestine.

"Then the disciples, every man according to his ability, determined to send relief unto the brethren which dwelt in Judæa: which also they did, and sent it to the elders by the hands of Barnabas and Saul. . . . And Barnabas and Saul returned from Jerusalem, when they had fulfilled their ministry, and took with them John, whose surname was Mark."

It is clear that, when they were in Jerusalem, Paul and Barnabas visited the general meeting-place of the Apostolic Church, the house of Mary, mother of Mark. Mary was related to Barnabas—John Mark was his cousin—and her house was probably a place of some size and consequence. When Peter was released from prison, he went straight there to give the news of his safety. Rhoda, the slave girl, was at first too excited to open the gate, for she recognized Peter's voice on the other side and became astonished and confused. This incident is one of the most vivid in the *Acts*.

John Mark was the author of the *Gospel according to St. Mark*. At the time of Paul's visit to the house of Mary, Mark was a very young man. In later life he was St. Peter's companion and secretary, and it is generally believed that the air of first-hand knowledge which runs through his Gospel is explained by the fact that it embodies the personal recollections of St. Peter.

The association of St. Mark with this house in Jerusalem raises the interesting question: Was the house of Mary also the house of the Last Supper? One curious fact supports this conjecture. In St. Mark's narrative of the arrest of Jesus in the Garden of Gethsemane is a vivid and apparently irrelevant account, found in no other gospel, of a young man who followed in the darkness, having only a linen cloth wound about his body. The soldiers tried to arrest him, but he left the linen cloth in their hands and fled naked.

Was this young man St. Mark? Was he awake in his mother's house on the night of the Last Supper, aware that something terrible was about to happen on the Mount of Olives, and did he, as soon as Jesus and His disciples had left, steal out of bed with a linen sheet around him and follow them down the hill into the Kedron Valley?

If he did, there is some reason to believe that the house of Mary was sacred to every believer in Jerusalem as the scene of the institution of the Holy Eucharist.

Paul and Barnabas returned to Syria, accompanied by the youthful Mark. One night, as the prophets and teachers of the little church at Antioch were at prayer, the Holy Spirit said:

"Separate me Barnabas and Saul for the work whereunto I have called them. And when they had fasted and prayed, and laid their hands on them, they sent them away. So they, being sent forth by the Holy Ghost, departed unto Seleucia; and from thence they sailed to Cyprus."

So Christianity took its first bold stride into the world.

9

The first time I tried to reach Seleucia, I was held up by floods about two miles out of Antioch. The driver, a Syrian Arab, lost his head and ran deeper into the mud than he need have done, and the end of it was that, covered in mud from head to foot, we had to ask a ploughman to unyoke his oxen and pull us out.

It rained during the night and I was told at Daphne that it would be madness to attempt the journey again, because the mud would be worse and the streams higher. However, as I rarely believe anything I am told on such occasions, I insisted on setting off on horse-back in the hope of fording the streams. I rode through the mud easily enough, but found that a narrow tributary of the Orontes was in spate and in one step my unwilling steed was in up to his hocks. I looked at the angry torrent in despair and turned back. After some days I made a third attempt, and this time I succeeded.

I set off on a lovely morning, driven again by the Syrian dandy in his rakish tarbush and shining shoes. I smiled, wondering what muddy misfortune would confront him this time. But, apart from twice getting lost owing to his conceited objection to asking the way, we plunged successfully into a lovely corner of Syria, where men and women still wear brilliantly coloured national costumes every day of the week. I saw an old man in blue, pleated Turkish trousers, an embroidered jacket of deep saffron, and a scarlet tarbush on his head. The women wore long skirts of vivid red or green. They walked with a graceful stride, and their faces were unveiled.

The mountains in this part of Syria are bleak and splintered, but the valleys are full of apricot trees, mulberries and vines. Asphodels grow in pale beauty on the hills, bright oleanders in the marshy places, and hawks sail against the blue sky, gazing earthwards for the poor living that they pick up in such mountains.

We came to a lovely bay, where the pointed peak of Mount Casius towered five thousand feet into the sky. The ruins of Seleucia lie in the northern curve of the bay.

The road petered out in a track, crossed here and there by an irrigation canal. My driver had never driven his car over such obstacles. Every time we came to one of these embankments he invoked the name of Allah, stopped the car, got out and surveyed the land, and then timidly progressed. I was glad when at length we came to a stream which barred all further progress. I left the car and set off on foot.

The ruins of Seleucia lie about a mile from the end of the track. In Paul's time the town was one of the famous ports of the world. It was, however, an inadequate harbour for Antioch. The town was built on the top of a mountain that sloped steeply to the sea, while the port occupied the level ground at the base. Enormous sums of money were spent by emperor after emperor to improve and enlarge this port, but the lie of the land was too difficult for such schemes to be entirely successful. The place was really more like a Syrian Gibraltar than a great commercial port, a fact which must have delighted the rival towns of Tyre and Sidon.

As a passenger port for Cyprus and Asia Minor, Seleucia was perfect. When the missionaries "departed unto Seleucia", they would have arrived in the Upper Town. On a clear day they could see from these heights the distant island of Cyprus, lying like a blue shadow on the horizon.

As I walked on, I was conscious of an intensely blue sea, of golden mountains seen through a screen of fig-leaves, and of mulberry trees lying in the breathless hush of afternoon. I passed some women at a well. They stared at me as if I were a ghost.

I noticed that the buildings of the ancient town have been broken up in the course of centuries, and the ground is strewn for miles with sharp splinters of marble and limestone. The villagers have removed large quantities of these chips from the fields and have piled them on the narrow tracks.

I endured the most uncomfortable half-hour's walk that I have ever experienced. On a hot day these paths of splintered stone, each stone about the size of a pear, are agonizing. However, it was consoling to think that I was going to a place which few travellers have explored.

I found, after a fairly stiff climb up the mountain, that the ruins cover an immense area. They are difficult to see and still more difficult to reconstruct. The whole mountain on which the Upper Town of Seleucia was built is dotted with the foundations of buildings. The steep lower slopes near the sea are honeycombed with enormous caverns which may be the remains of warehouses and suchlike port buildings. There are also many tombs cut high in the cliffs, some of them as large as a big room, containing six to ten loculi with the lids removed, and looking as though they had been rifled only yesterday.

The most remarkable ruin in Seleucia is a gigantic rock tunnel cut in Roman times to divert the waters of a mountain torrent. This extraordinary work is about one thousand, four hundred yards long. It is over twenty feet high and twenty feet wide. Two sections of it are cut through the mountain.

A stream still runs through the tunnel and the walls are worn smooth with rushing water. When Gertrude Bell saw it, she could find only the words "Divus Vespasianus" on an inscription at the entrance, for the rest of the stone was buried in the ground. The whole inscription is now visible, and reads "Divus Vespasianus et Divus Titus," thus proving that this great feat of engineering dates from the Jewish War of 70 A.D. Inside the tunnel are other inscriptions, one of which says that the work was done by men of the IV Syrian Legion and by mariners.

Even more interesting to me were the remains of the port on the foreshore. I climbed down from the hills and examined the site of the harbour, which is clearly marked among the mulberry groves. The mouth of the Orontes, bringing down silt and mud for centuries, has altered the configuration of the land and the sea has retreated. What was once a harbour is now dry land on whose flat, rich acres the natives have gladly planted trees.

Sections of the harbour walls, and what appear to be the foundations of a lighthouse, still stand in these mulberry groves. Beneath a covering of brambles, I saw a flight of harbour steps which led down through the branches of fig trees; it was on such steps—possibly these steps—that Paul, Barnabas, and Mark stepped aboard at the outset of their immortal voyage to Cyprus and Asia Minor.

Not one line of the New Testament had been written. Paul carried the Gospel in his heart, not in his hand. All he knew of Jesus he had learnt in solitary communion with God, and from the lips of St. Peter and the disciples who had known the Lord in life: although the words of Jesus had not yet been preserved in writing, Paul must have known them. As the sail filled with wind, we can imagine the Apostle gazing forward to the distant shores of Asia Minor.

"And ye shall be hated of all men for my name's sake; but he that endureth to the end shall be saved. But when they persecute you in this city, flee ye into another. . . ."

Perhaps Paul heard this Voice crying out in the wind of the sea.

CHAPTER IV

Describes how I sailed to Cyprus in a cargo-boat, how I met a well disguised Pauline student, and visited the ruins of Salamis and the crusading town of Famagusta. I see the Paphian goddess in a museum at Nicosia, spend a night in the mountain monastery of Kykko, and stand amid the ruins of Paphos, where St. Paul addressed the Roman Governor and confounded his astrologer.

1

Two hundred Syrian goats, fattened on the spring pastures of the Orontes Valley, were driven aboard at Alexandretta. They looked remarkably like the annual congress of some learned society.

These creatures filled the ship with a rank pagan smell and a violent life. They leapt on the bulwarks as if about to commit suicide or to deliver a thesis. They sprang nimbly from derrick to companion-way, and succeeded in driving all the third-class passengers forward to the first-class deck. One animal, a malign old red goat, nipped silently into the tiny saloon and stole a lettuce.

As the ship moved slowly to the south, hugging the coast of Syria and passing Sidon and Tyre, our invaders developed a philosophy and stood motionless. When we arrived at Haifa no one regetted their departure, and we watched them pour bleating down the gang-plank to the sunny dock, soothed and encouraged by their herdsmen in the shaggy, throaty language which Pan probably imparted to goatherds when the world was young.

The ship swung for some time off Mount Carmel and then steamed away in the direction of Cyprus. In the dark hatch-

way under the fo'c'sle lay a number of Syrian cows on their
way to Egypt. Hens and turkeys strolled round them and
sometimes ran casually over their bodies. On the deck above,
twelve Arab horses thrust their nervous heads from boxes.
They were going to a trainer in Alexandria.

The ship was an inferno of heat, throbbing engines, and
oil smells. Swarthy Egyptians swabbed the decks, standing
in the iron tunnel outside the cabins, shooting streams from
tin buckets and making a great clatter with their brooms. The
doors of the twelve cabins opened to the intimate domestic
life of a ship. From Cabin 1 there was an admirable view of
the Scottish engineer descending a steel ladder to his rhythmic
engines. Cabin 2 provided an excellent view of the Greek
cook bent with malicious enthusiasm over a greasy stew, and
from Cabin 3 I saw the pantry in which the cook's dusky
assistant prowled, grasping a dead chicken.

Now that the goats had departed, the third-class passengers, chiefly Syrian Arabs, returned to their own quarters aft,
where they lay in distressed attitudes as the ship rose and
fell. A veiled woman would now and then totter to the side
and shamelessly uncover her features to the heaving deep.
And nobody cared. How quickly distress defeats convention!
A husband, who normally would have divorced his wife for
such conduct, lay with closed eyes, moistening his lips from
time to time and restlessly telling the amber beads of his
kombológion.

When I entered the small saloon, I encountered the only
other English passenger. He was drinking a glass of beer,
while the Greek steward hit out at flies with a table-napkin.
He was a large, middle-aged man who had settled in Palestine
since the War.

"I came out and stayed out," he said. "No, I never get
homesick. I like the climate. Dash it all, man, we've a short
enough life. Why should we spend half of it in fog and rain?"

He told me that he was going over to Cyprus to inquire about orange-growing. I asked him why so many Arabs were travelling to Cyprus.

"They're going to Cyprus to buy wives," he replied. "There's a big matrimonial trade between Cyprus and the mainland. Not only are Cypriot women highly esteemed— Cyprus was always famous for love, you know—but wives cost less than in Syria and Palestine."

He then ordered more beer and, mounting his hobby horse, set off at great speed. His obsession was orange-growing; he called an orange a "citrus fruit," a term that grated on me as if I had bitten a lemon.

He continued on the subject of "citrus fruits" for half an hour, and just as I was about to implore him to call them oranges, the steward rattled a little bell and the pungent promise of a Greek soup rollicked playfully round the saloon.

All that afternoon I sat in sunlight on the deck, watching the coast of Palestine fade to a brown line on the horizon.

As I lay with half-shut eyes, I observed, with deep misgiving, the approach of the citrus grower. It was useless to feign sleep.

"Hallo!" he cried, dragging up a deck chair. "I wondered where you'd got to. I say," he continued in an altered voice, "are you a padre?"

"No. Why do you ask?"

"Well," he said, "it isn't everyone who reads the *Acts of the Apostles*, is it?"

"I see. I often read the *Acts*."

"If that isn't the strangest coincidence!" he said, his blue eyes wide open. "Do you know, I once wrote a book about St. Paul?"

This surprised me. It was not easy to connect this citrus enthusiast with the Apostolic Age. He guessed my thoughts.

"Citrus fruit and St. Paul don't seem to go together, do they?" he said. "It was like this. Years ago I was a schoolmaster. Thank heaven I got out of it, for of all the dreary prisons on this earth, schoolmastering is the worst. When the War came, I just jumped at the chance. Have you ever met a man who enjoyed the War? Here's one, at any rate! But I was telling you about my book. St. Paul was my subject. I once wrote a thesis on him and dished it up afterwards as a kind of text-book with maps and diagrams."

As he talked, I grew to like him. I could hardly believe that he was the same man who had bored me with his "citrus fruits." Even after a lapse of years, and a life in which books had not counted very much, he remembered the Epistles and could quote them with effect. What I liked was his appreciation of St. Paul as a human being.

"He is one of the few men in ancient literature who is absolutely modern," he said. "Don't you feel that about him? You would not be surprised to meet him in a wayside pub, drinking a little wine for his stomach's sake. And if you had to borrow a fiver, I think you'd rather ask Paul than anyone else. He was a good mixer and he had knocked about the world. All that comes out in his letters. But Paul is the least understood character in the New Testament. Why? Because no one can really understand his Epistles in the Authorized Version. The language of James I. is fine English, but it's not easy English, and it doesn't express the common Greek, does it? And in the second place, most people have the idea that Paul was a woman-hater. Now in this age, when women rule the world, that's a fatal bar to popularity. It's difficult to explain to modern people what he was up against in the sex-cults of Asia. Paul didn't hate women. The number of women who helped him is proof of that. What Paul hated was the degradation of women in the pagan world. Oh, I'm wrong, am I?"

"No," I told him, "I was smiling to think that all the lampblack has been blown off your studies. You talk as if you'd met Paul last week at Jaffa, or wherever you grow your citrus fruit."

"That's true," he said solemnly. "That's perfectly true. I feel I know Paul much better to-day than I did years ago, when I could have given you chapter and verse in Lewin, Conybeare and Howson, Ramsay, Hausrath, and all the other authorities whose names I've forgotten. But I've been up against it in a foreign country, with precious few friends. I've been nearly broke. And I've got through by hard work and not giving in, which, after all, were two of Paul's chief qualities."

He held out his hands with a broad grin.

"Look at 'em!" he said. "They weren't like that when I was a schoolmaster. You remember how Paul, when he said good-bye to the elders at Miletus, held up his hands and said —what was it? 'Look how these hands have ministered to my necessities!' It seemed to me that sentences like that prove that Paul was never brought up to be an artisan. No workman thinks it's marvellous that his hands have ministered to his necessities. That's what they're for. But *I* do; and so did Paul."

"Do you ever read the Epistles now?"

"I haven't read them since I was at school. But I remember them."

We sat talking about the world of St. Paul until the sun went down.

After dinner I went to my cabin heavy with sleep. As soon as I touched the pillow, three glistening cockroaches ran from under it and disappeared between the bunk and the ship's side. Once cockroaches invade a ship in a hot climate, they can never be driven out unless the ship is torn almost to pieces. I dislike their revolting bent legs, the speed they achieve, and the impression that at any moment they may lift black-brown wings and fly. Therefore, shaking out a couple of blankets, I went up and spent the night on deck.

The moon had gone down, but an intense silver light lay over the sea and there was no sound but the soft hiss of water against the ship. In the middle of the night I awakened to find myself gazing at a sky covered with stars. Our riding-light moved against them like a little moon.

I watched grey light come to the world. The ship swung on a sea the colour of lead, and the stars faded. In this queer half-light I saw a shadow on the sea and knew that it was the long, eastward thrust of Cyprus. More light came, but still the sun did not rise. Then, with a feeling of relief and happiness, I saw the east streaked with uneasy lines of pink that grew stronger second by second until, with a burst of yellow light, the sun jumped out of the sea.

I saw a long, brown and green coast, with tall mountains rising inland, and the little white town of Larnaca.

2

The boat lay in Larnaca Bay, waiting for the shore officials. It was not quite seven o'clock, but the sun was already warmer than on a summer's afternoon at home. I thought Cyprus looked exquisite that morning, with the mists moving like veils from her mountains.

I was content to stand gazing over the rail towards the land where long ago the copper breastplate of Agamemnon was hammered into shape, and where Aphrodite rose from the sea. This island has changed its appearance since classical times. No longer do dense woods cover it, and no longer does the brushwood come to the water's edge. Why, the traveller often asks, have parts of the Mediterranean world, once famous for their trees, become bleak and barren? The answer is: goats. These animals devoured the verdure of the ancient world and no man can exaggerate the damage they have done. The Dalmatian coast once was coveted by the Venetians because of the ship-timber it offered; now it is as bare as a bone. Goats have left their mark on Palestine and Syria. Nothing, except, possibly, earthquakes, has altered the appearance of the ancient world so much as the goat. I do not know if there were any Greek and Roman laws to prevent these animals from nibbling the young shoots of trees and destroying every wave of green vegetation, but the few lines that have been preserved of one of the lost plays of Eupolis happens to be a chorus of goats who, even at that remote period, are heard bleating on the subject of their favourite bushes.

A motor-launch came out to us, flying the British flag. The port doctor and other officials stepped aboard, and the crew lined up on the fo'c'sle. The doctor walked along, examining eyes, throats, chests, and feeling under arms. When he had finished with the crew and the steerage passengers, we were free to go ashore.

I sat in a small rowing-boat. Before the oars cut the water, I looked down into clear, green depths and saw huge, twisted shells lying fathoms deep, and strange fish swimming.

On the hot sea-front of Larnaca a number of carriages converged on me while the drivers, cracking their whips, tried to attract my attention in a bewildering mixture of Greek and English. Although Cyprus has been British for over half a century, I gathered that the English language has not made much progress. One inhabitant, I soon discovered, could speak American.

I went up to a saloon car that stood for hire under a line

of date palms.

"I want to go to Salamis," I said to the driver.

"Sure," he replied. "Step in, boss."

"How far is it?" I asked.

"I guess it's about thirty-five miles."

We ran smoothly out of the town.

"I'm the best driver in Cyprus," he told me.

"Were you in the States for long?"

"Six years, I guess. Saved up enough dough to come here, get married and buy this car."

We went off over a flat road, passing field after field of sweet-scented broadbean flowers. Oxen yoked to ploughs were turning the rich earth. Oxen in the shafts of cumbersome country carts swayed towards us over the road. Now and then we passed through mud-coloured villages where houses with flat roofs and wooden balconies stood huddled in narrow lanes set about with sesame fields and pomegranate and orange groves. For nearly ten miles we ran beside a blue sea, then, turning inland, we mounted into brown hills.

We passed through the ancient, walled town of Famagusta, and after about five miles came to all that is left of Salamis, the port where Paul, Barnabas, and Mark disembarked.

"And when they were at Salamis they proclaimed the word of God in the synagogues of the Jews."

That is all we are told in the *Acts* about the visit to Salamis. But we know from Josephus and other ancient writers that this port was one of the most important in the Mediterranean. It was the commercial capital of Roman Cyprus: Paphos, at the other end of the island, was the Government headquarters.

We may be sure that any town which included more than one synagogue was a thriving commercial centre: the Jews of the first century were never found in poor places. They had settled in Cyprus centuries before Christ, and were engaged in the export of oil, fruit, wine, and copper. They had been there long enough to become rich and powerful.

I left the car and plunged into a dense wood that grows on sandhills near the sea. Presently I found the stump of a marble pillar, and then another. They stood in the shade of acacia and eucalyptus trees. Brambles grew over them. I came to a flight of marble steps half-covered with grass and tamarisks. The whole wood was haunted by the ghost of Salamis.

Then I found the remains of three market-places, three enormous squares which had once been paved with marble pillars and surrounded by marble temples. I found the remains of a splendid Roman house with many bathrooms in it and a complete system of central heating. Here and there in the undergrowth were broken pillars, and scraps of Greek inscriptions on which it was possible to make out that "the City of Salamis" gave this or decreed that. In the largest forum I tore away weeds and exposed some steps on which Paul had probably trodden, for they were in the principal square of the city.

When I looked for the once splendid harbour, I saw nothing but sand-dunes: an earthquake had wrecked both city and harbour and had brought proud Salamis crashing to the ground. I half expected some ghost to step from the shadow of a tree and point and beckon, and my heart was saddened by the utter loneliness of the ruined city and by the ease with which weeds and brambles can conceal the most ambitious works of Man.

A ruin on a hill is stark and sad, but a ruined city in a wood is terrifying. All the way back to Famagusta I was haunted by the ghost of the dead city. I thought of the fallen pillars in the acacia wood and the mournful whisper of wind through trees that had grown out of the bones of Salamis.

3

Cyprus has been compared to a pegged-out deer's skin, the tail being the long, low-lying spit of land running eastward to Cape Andreas. It is the perfect size for an island, not too large for one ever to be unconscious of the sea, yet with inland towns and villages where a fisherman would appear strange and improbable. Mountains are to an island what masts are to a ship. From the mountains of Cyprus you can see northward to the snow-tipped peaks of the Taurus Mountains in Asia Minor, and to the south-east lies the shadowy profile of the Lebanon in Syria. One mountain range runs along the north coast, parallel to the sea, lifting sharp peaks into the sky and standing up like a fence: it is a companion range, but in miniature, of the Taurus Mountains. The other range is grouped on the west side of the island, rising in ever grander heights to the pine-covered slopes of Troödos.

The beauty of Cyprus is a perfect blend of mountain and plain, and of hills that slope to deserted bays half-screened by olive trees. The crisp insistence of the cicada and the sound of the waves make a perpetual duet in the heat.

Scattered over the length and breadth of this island are the relics of two civilizations: the Greek and the Mediæval. There is little left of the Greek civilization except ruins like those of Salamis: but the energy of the Crusaders and of their successors, the Venetians, has planted on mountain tops such castles as the broken crown of St. Hilarion, worn proudly by the peak of Didymus, and has left us the superb gates and walls of Famagusta. If I were obliged to spend the rest of my life out of England, I sometimes think that I should like to live on the magic isle of Delos in the Ægean. But this is an idle thought, for no one except the guardians of the ruins is allowed to live there. My second choice would be Cyprus.

The island is now a British Colony. It is ruled by a Governor, and is garrisoned by a company of infantry provided by one of the regiments stationed at Alexandria. The Union Jack first flew over Cyprus as long ago as 1878, when Disraeli arranged a Convention between Queen Victoria and Sultan Abdul Hamid II., whereby Britain promised to enter into a defensive alliance with Turkey against Russia, and, in order to give us a foothold near the danger zone, Turkey handed over Cyprus to British administration.

On the day the Convention was signed, Vice-Admiral Lord John Hay received a telegram ordering him to take over Cyprus in the name of the Queen. He did it very simply. He drove over in a wagonette to Nicosia, accompanied by two mules loaded with English sixpences to pay off the Sultan's arrears to his officials. The Union Jack was therefore run up with some enthusiasm. In due course the first High Commissioner arrived, Sir Garnet (afterwards Viscount) Wolseley.

This change of rule did not, however, alter the status of the inhabitants, who remained Ottoman subjects, and it did not change the ownership of the island, which technically remained a part of the Ottoman Empire. In fact the Cyprus Government had to pay Turkey £42,000 a year for the privilege of ruling the island. When Turkey entered the last War on the side of Germany, Cyprus was annexed to the British Crown. In 1915, when Bulgaria invaded Serbia, we offered the island to Greece if she would march to the aid of Serbia; but she declined. It was not until 1925 that Cyprus became a British Colony.

The Italian war in Abyssinia emphasized the ease with which Malta could be attacked by air, and there is a possibility that Cyprus may be fortified as a British naval base. Famagusta harbour could be improved, I am told, for a comparatively small sum. Should this project be fulfilled, it would probably mean easier and cheaper transport to Cyprus and the discovery of the island by that large class of Britons who have enough money to escape an English winter. The cost and the trouble of getting to Cyprus are still considerable, so that one of the most beautiful islands in the world remains unknown save to a few discriminating people.

Travellers who visited Cyprus in the nineteenth century describe a wasted island in which neither life nor property was safe. The Christian Greeks were oppressed by the ruling Moslems, and the Moslems were oppressed by their own tax-gatherers. Harbours were inadequate, roads were non-existent, and irrigation had been neglected. One of the most fertile islands of classical times had degenerated into an unproductive waste. In a little over half a century Cyprus has been transformed. The law courts, hospitals, schools, the splendid roads, the agricultural enterprises and the police force, reflect the greatest credit on the handful of British administrators who have ruled the island. If any Cypriots are discontented with British rule, I advise them to read the travel journals published about a century ago.

When William Turner made his tour in the Levant in 1820, he discovered that Cyprus, the prey of a Turkish pasha, had an annually diminishing population and a total trade of only two million piastres. When John Carne arrived there six years later, he discovered the island in the throes of a persecution, and commented that it was "sad to see this large and beautiful island so desolate and ravaged. . . . Large domains of land could be bought for a trifle; and a château, with a garden, together with a small village on the domain, and an extensive tract of land, were offered for a few hundred pounds."

The population of the island is Greek and Turkish. Christian Greeks number about two hundred and forty-seven thousand and Turkish Moslems about sixty thousand. The finest church on the island, the crusading cathedral of St. Nicholas, was turned into a mosque by the Turks, and has remained so ever since.

Now that Kemal Ataturk has abolished the fez and Turkish dress and habits, Cyprus has become the last place in the world where the old Turk can still be seen unaffected by European reform. He wears his fez and his pleated trousers, and sucks his hookah outside a Turkish café. Villages are usually either all Turkish or all Greek, but here and there the population is mixed, although rigidly divided by the barriers of race and religion. The Turks speak a form of Osmanli Turkish, comparatively free from Persian and Arabic words; the Greeks speak modern colloquial Greek. But the country dialect of the Cypriot is a curious language in which are many words of French, Italian, and Turkish origin, a relic of the various foreign occupations of the island.

British rule in Cyprus has been a piece of disinterested colonization, but now that Cyprus is a part of the British Empire, I hope there will be a closer cultural contact between Cypriots and the ruling power. It seems to me strange and unfortunate that so many well-educated, middle-class Cypriots speak atrocious English, although the head of Queen Victoria is on their coinage; when you get into lonely parts of the island, it is often difficult to find a person who can speak one English word, although the Union Jack has been flying over Cyprus for nearly sixty years.

4

The admirable hotel in Famagusta gave me a room in which loomed a bed that seemed to me a weird compromise between a wedding and a funeral. Its hearse-like proportions were contradicted by an immense bridal mosquito-net whose rents were so obvious that even the least experienced mosquito would have treated it as a jest and not as a challenge. But the small Cypriot maid said:

"Oh, sir, it is good. No mosquitoes—yet."

The balcony that ran round two sides of this room gave me a glimpse, through the branches of eucalyptus trees, of the sandy main road. If I had been put down blindfolded in this place, I should have found it difficult to know what part of the world I was in. There is a rich, tropical look about Famagusta.

Through a break in the eucalyptus leaves I saw two of the rare camels of Cyprus walk delicately towards the town, and from the opposite direction came a middle-aged inhabitant in Turkish dress, riding a bicycle. Below the balcony I could hear my Pauline friend of the boat ordering two gin fizzes and, no longer Pauline but entirely citrified, talking in a confident, booming voice about moisture, pests, and square acres.

What a haven of rest! It is the place which women friends instantly declare as the perfect spot for any writer of their acquaintance to "settle in" and produce a book. As I looked at the veranda, the eucalyptus trees and the sunlight, and as I listened, hearing only a mule going past on the road and a bird singing in the trees, I could imagine the sound of those decisive, ringing tones that have plagued many a poor man's soul: "What a lovely place to settle down and write—so quiet, so peaceful, nothing to distract you. . . ." And, flinging myself into the basket chair, I apostrophized the misunderstanding shade: "Madam," I said, "it has been proved time and again that the perfect place for a writer is in the hideous roar of a city, with men making a new road under his window in competition with a barrel organ, and on the mat a man waiting for the rent."

And that is more or less true. The peace of Famagusta is distracting. In the boundless silence the mind swoops and dips and refuses to come to earth. There is nothing to concentrate against; and the only thing to do is to lie at full length gazing into the green fretwork of the spearhead leaves, thinking of all the misdirected effort in the world, all the pointless rush, and of the exquisite beauty of procrastination.

5

I went into Famagusta just before sunset.

I saw a moated high wall of brown stones with squat bastions at the corners, and I saw a splendid fortified gate. Entering the city, I looked round in amazement, for Famagusta is to-day very much as it was when the Turkish guns ceased fire in 1571. I do not think that mediævalists and students of architecture realize how remarkable is the survival of this completely walled city, with its towers, land gates and sea gates, its great Romanesque Cathedral, and its magnificent churches, many of them still bright with frescoes. No description of Famagusta can adequately convey the feeling of surprise with which one walks through the streets of this mediæval Pompeii.

The reason why Famagusta has been spared, and remains more or less as it was over three and a half centuries ago, is because after the siege the Turks swore that no Christians should ever again live there. They accordingly erected flimsy wooden huts among the ruins they had created and, with that lack of energy for which scholarship should be eternally grateful, failed to destroy the ancient churches or the walls, but permitted them gradually to fall down, century by century. And even to-day, when a Christian can, if he likes, live in Famagusta, there is a scared look about the place. There are far more plots of waste land and gardens than there are houses, and above these open spaces rise the high towers of ruined churches, reminding one vividly of shelled towns like Rheims or Ypres, during the War.

Mediæval Famagusta is one of the most remarkable ruins

in the world, and it could be made one of the wonders of the world by one millionaire in search of immortality. Now that Cyprus is a British Colony, we should prohibit building within the walls of Famagusta and we should reconstruct the churches and preserve the frescoes. The preservation of these antiquities is as much our responsibility as the provision of roads, hospitals, and irrigation. Surely it should be possible to found a British School of Archæology at Famagusta. I regret to say that when I remembered Rhodes, and the money that Italy has lavished on the antiquities of that island, I looked at Famagusta with a feeling of shame.

The European occupation of Cyprus began with an English King, Richard Cœur de Lion, who captured the island on his way to the Third Crusade. As he was anxious to get money for his troops, he sold Cyprus to the Knights Templar. The newcomers had a bad time with the natives and were glad to sell the island to Guy de Lusignan, King of Jerusalem, who had been driven out of the Holy Land by Saladin. This collapse of the Latin Kingdom of Jerusalem filled Cyprus with Crusaders and their families, and with religious orders expelled from the shores of Palestine. This new era developed into the golden age of Cyprus. For three hundred years the Lusignan dynasty ruled the island. Wealth poured like a golden river into Cyprus, and Famagusta became one of the richest cities in the world. The splendour of the nobility of Cyprus, and the riches of its merchant princes, became a legend in the East. This was the period that saw the erection of the splendid churches of Famagusta, some of them, like the church of St. Peter and St. Paul, built by the proceeds of a single mercantile adventure.

It was always the dream of the Lusignan kings to reconquer Jerusalem and once more to receive the crown in the Church of the Holy Sepulchre. The Lusignans used to be crowned Kings of Cyprus in the Cathedral at Nicosia, and before the high altar of St. Nicholas in Famagusta they would receive the empty title—King of Jerusalem.

Bloodthirsty quarrels led to a change of rule in Cyprus. The island fell to the Genoese Republic and, later, to the Venetian Republic, which held it for eighty-three years. A victorious Turkish army then won Cyprus for the Ottoman Empire, and so it remained until Disraeli arranged the defensive alliance which I have already mentioned.

I explored about twelve churches, all within a few hundred yards of each other, any one of which would have been the treasured possession of a European city. The most interesting was the great Crusading cathedral of St. Nicholas, now a Turkish mosque. Removing my shoes in the porch, I entered a typical early Gothic church that might have been standing in Lincolnshire, except for the fact that the floor was covered with Turkish rugs. The whole structure had been whitewashed, the stained-glass "images" had long since departed from the windows, and the orientation of the building had been altered to face in the direction of Mecca. The altar has, of course, been removed, but so perfect is the cathedral that it could be made ready for a Christian service in half an hour. I wondered what Richard Cœur de Lion would have said about it.

Outside the cathedral I noticed a stone, now used as a mounting-block. It was the base of a statue and bore the words in Greek: "The City of Salamis offers this statue to the Emperor Trajan. . . ."

A polite Cypriot took me into the Cathedral of the Greeks, which has recently been restored. He called it St. George Ex Orinos. It is the only ancient building in Famagusta now in use as a Christian church.

"It was once a Turkish stable," said my guide. "One day, however, St. George came down from the mountains and was angry to see camels stabled here in his church, so he projected a camel out by the rose window, as a sign of his disapproval."

Wandering round the church, I came to an ikon of St. George which was festooned with votive offerings made of wax. There were wax legs, arms, feet, ears, fingers, and roughly moulded heads of wax. The most remarkable offering was a complete little man made of wax, a figure perhaps two feet in length. It bore the word Mehmet. This puzzled me until I realized that it was a Turkish name.

"Do the Turks also venerate this ikon?" I asked.

"They venerate it indeed," answered the man solemnly, "because St. George is a great healer."

Wax votive offerings are to be seen in Christian churches all over Italy, Greece, and the Near East; but these models in Cyprus looked to me more like the terra-cotta votive offerings that are dug up on the sites of ancient temples than any I had seen.

A few yards away is the Church of St. Peter and St. Paul. I heard the sound of hammering inside, and discovered that this fine old Gothic church is used as a storehouse for oranges, and was piled to the roof with crates and boxes. Even if Great Britain cannot afford to put Famagusta in order, surely she can prevent a firm of orange-growers from using this building as a warehouse?

I made a circuit of the fortifications, so magnificent in their strength and preservation that they give Famagusta a place beside Carcassonne, Ragusa, and Avila, as one of the finest walled cities in the world. The wall is fifty feet high and, in places, twenty-seven feet thick. The Martinengo Bastion is one of the finest sixteenth century fortifications I have ever seen. It is as complete as it was when built in 1550, and in the vaulted casements were holes for the escape of powder-smoke.

In another bastion I saw a place where Venetian blacksmiths used to repair the armour of the knights. The ground is blue with ancient cinders, which have, in the course of centuries, been beaten into the earth. Perhaps one of the most impressive features of the fortifications is the superb Sea Gate built by the Turks. Its great iron-covered door is centuries old, and the spiked portcullis hangs above in a shroud of cobwebs.

Another of the bastions, Djamboulat Bastion, is named after one of the bravest of the Turkish generals in the siege of 1571. The legend is that the Venetians had erected on this bastion a wheel of knives designed to mow down anything that came near the blades. Djamboulat Bey, realizing that this wheel was having a serious effect on the morale of his troops, decided to destroy it, even if he perished in the attempt. He rode his horse straight at the machine. The animal was cut to pieces and the rash but gallant Turk was instantaneously decapitated. But the machine was broken. Until Famagusta fell, so the story goes, the ghost of Djamboulat was observed by his compatriots waving his scimitar in encouragement and holding his head beneath his arm.

Mr. Rupert Gunnis, who tells this story in his book, *Historic Cyprus*, which everyone interested in Cyprus should buy, ends with the delightfully irrelevant fact that to this day childless couples go to eat the fruit of a fig tree that sprang from Djamboulat's grave. "Many of the population of Famagusta," concludes Mr. Gunnis, "owe their being to Djamboulat and his fig tree."

The Venetian hero of the siege was a man whose name is written for ever in the annals of fortitude. Marc Antonio Bragadino, the Venetian commander, suffered one of the most hideous deaths in the history even of a brutal age. When the Turks entered Famagusta, this gallant soldier was brought before the Turkish general, Lala Mustafa, who pretended to execute him. He was forced to bare his neck three times to the executioner's sword, which each time was slowly lowered. Eventually, at a sign from the Turk, his nose and ears were cut off.

"Where is your Christ now?" asked the Pasha. "Why does He not come and help you?"

Those who watched this scene have left accounts in which they tell with what dignity and in what proud silence the tortured man bore himself. For ten days he was forced to carry earth to the ramparts and to kiss the ground each time that he passed the Pasha's tent. Then he was hoisted in a slung seat, with a crown tied at his feet, to the yard-arm of the flagship, and thus exposed to the jeers of the Turkish forces.

At the end of ten days Bragadino was led with drums and trumpets to the great square of Famagusta, stripped, tied to a pillar, and slowly flayed alive by a Jewish executioner. The Pasha looked on and watched his foe die. Bragadino's skin, stuffed with straw, was tied to a cow and, with a red umbrella held over it in mockery, was paraded through the town. The tortured body was cut up like meat and portions hung on the gates of Famagusta. When the Turks sailed for Constantinople, they tied the stuffed skin of Bragadino to the yard-arm and paraded it round the ports of the Mediterranean.

The end of the story further indicates the almost inconceivable character of Mustafa Pasha. He actually bargained with Bragadino's sons, and sold them the skin of his brave foe for a great price.

Whenever I go to Venice, I look forward to the moment when the gondola slides up to a lovely campo where Colleoni, upright in his stirrups, rides proudly into space. Near by, in the church of St. Paul, the skin of the hero of Famagusta lies in an urn. I remember the siege of Famagusta, and feel thankful that some part of this brave man rests at last in the beauty of his own Venice.

6

About four miles from Famagusta is the Monastery of St. Barnabas. The saint was, of course, a Cypriot, and it has been proved time and again by the peasants that no saint in heaven, not excluding the Panagia herself, has a more tender regard for the Cypriot, or a more intimate knowledge of his requirements.

The monastery is a picturesque, many-domed building standing by itself among beanfields, and some distance from the main road. I walked about the little sun-steeped courtyard, but could find no one. The heat of afternoon had closed down on Cyprus, and in the stillness I could almost hear the crops growing.

I went into the cool, white church whose domes are upheld by piers into which are built marble columns from the ancient ruins of Salamis. The gilded *ikonostasis*—which, in Greek churches, takes the place of a rood-screen, and divides sanctuary from nave—groaned beneath the weight of ikons.

The Greek Orthodox Church forbids statues in its buildings, a ban dating from the remote times when sculpture was associated with pagan worship, but it delights in ikons. No matter how poor or small a Greek church may be, it nearly always has a good display of these sacred pictures, to which the country people sometimes attach all manner of miraculous qualities, often piously kissing them to the bare wood.

Coming to a half-open door, I looked inside. A Greek monk was sitting at an easel, painting an ikon. He was so intent that he failed to notice me. He sat there, his knot of hair drawn under a brimless hat, his hand steadied on a bamboo guiding-rod, and his attitude was one of intense concentration as he added little touches of red, blue, and gold to the figure of a saint. When he saw me, he smiled in embarrassment, wiped his hands on his cassock, and came forward.

While we talked about ikons, I discovered that his tech-nique was rooted in the Byzantine Age. He had been taught to mix his colours and to paint by a monk of seventy, who had learnt his art from a monk of seventy; and so on right back to the dim ages of ikonography. Like all people who love the work they do, there was something pleasant and poised about this Greek priest.

"I should like to see the tomb of St. Barnabas," I said.

"Come with me," he replied.

We went out together into the sunlight and down through the beanfield to a little stone building. Inside a flight of steps led underground to the saint's tomb. It was damp and cool in the vault. There were a few rotting ikons on the walls and someone had lit a candle. The monk told me the story of the saint's burial and the finding of the relics.

"Where the body of St. Barnabas was found," he said, "sprang a well of water. And this water cures skin diseases."

We climbed out of the vault and entered a building erected above the well. In a corner was a tin bucket tied to a long rope. The monk let this down into the well and drew it up full of ice-cold water. It is still, he told me, in great demand as a cure for all manner of complaints.

The artist went back to his ikon, and I sat on a wall near the Tomb of St. Barnabas and tried to put together the jig-saw of history and legend.

We know that Barnabas went through Cyprus with Paul and Mark on the first missionary journey, probably in 47 A.D. A second tour was suggested, but Paul refused to allow Mark to accompany him.

So Paul chose Silas and went into Asia Minor, while Barnabas, with his cousin Mark, paid a second visit to Cyprus. Here the clear light of history fades from Barnabas and we see him only in the moonlight of legend.

The Cypriots believe that on his second visit to Cyprus, Barnabas fell foul of Bar-Jesus, the Jewish astrologer in the Governor's household, who had been blinded by Paul on the first missionary journey. This man determined to wreak his vengeance on Barnabas and roused the Jews of Salamis against him, so that they stoned him to death in the hippodrome of that city. Mark stole the body of his friend and buried it secretly at night in a Roman tomb outside Salamis.

So far the legend is possible. It is just the kind of thing that might have happened.

Over four hundred years passed by. Christianity became the official religion of the State. At this time—474–491 A.D.—the Church in Cyprus was engaged in a long dispute with the Church at Antioch. It was a struggle for supremacy. The Church at Antioch declared that Cyprus came under its jurisdiction, but the Church in Cyprus claimed to have been founded by an Apostle and was therefore independent, and also equal in authority with Antioch. However, the dispute was settled in favour of Antioch.

At this critical moment help came from a remarkable quarter. St. Barnabas, appearing in a vision to the Archbishop of Cyprus, revealed the tomb in which he had been placed by St. Mark, and advised him to take the dispute personally to the Emperor Zeno in Constantinople.

The Archbishop, accompanied by his clergy and a great crowd, went on the following day to the spot indicated in the vision and, digging under a carob tree, found the remains of St. Barnabas, lying with the copy of St. Matthew's Gospel which St. Mark had placed on his breast.

The Archbishop at once set out for Constantinople with the relics. The Emperor Zeno was so impressed that he called together a special Synod to discuss the question. It was eventually decided that Cyprus was to be independent of Antioch.

We are now on firm historical ground. So impressed was the Emperor by the discovery of the saint's bones, that he conferred on the Church of Cyprus the privilege of being autocephalous, or of electing its own Head, the Archbishop of Cyprus, a right which this Church still possesses.

The Emperor also conferred on the Archbishop the privilege of signing his name in red ink, a colour used only by Byzantine emperors on their State documents, of wearing a cope of imperial purple, and of carrying a sceptre instead of a pastoral staff.

These privileges, which were granted over one thousand, four hundred and fifty years ago, are closely guarded to-day by the Archbishops of Cyprus. They sign their names in red ink; they wear a purple cope sewn with little bells; and they still carry a sceptre like that of the Byzantine emperors of Constantinople.

7

Looking back on a long vista of queer meals, I think that perhaps the strangest food I have eaten for a long time was given to me in a grocer's shop at Famagusta.

A space was cleared on the table among bars of soap, ramparts of goat's-milk cheese, and baskets of bread. Then my host, breathing heavily and extolling the virtues of the food he was about to place before me, set down a jar of pickled birds, called by the lovely name of *beccaficos*, which means fig-pecker. They are small birds, no larger than a sparrow, but so fat that I wondered how they could ever have flown. I learnt that they find some difficulty in flying, because they gorge themselves on ripe figs until they are ready to drop.

My host, a Cypriot, did not know the English name for these birds, and their trussed appearance gave no clue to it. I think they are blackcaps. I was told that they come over

from Syria in enormous flocks and settle on the fig trees of
Cyprus. The Cypriots salt, spice, and pickle them, and the
effect of this is to harden the flesh and soften the bones, so
that you eat the complete bird, bones and everything.

I cannot describe how excellent are these *beccaficos*. They
are spiced yet sweet, astringent yet oily. But what interested
me about them was the unusual, aromatic flavour, only to be
found in old-fashioned recipes, in dishes of the Elizabethan
age; a flavour of authentic antiquity. And this is as it should
be, because *beccaficos* were first pickled by Crusaders who
came over with Guy de Lusignan.

John Locke, who visited Cyprus in 1553 and wrote a book
about his travels, mentioned these birds.

"They have also in the island," he wrote, "a certaine small
bird much like unto a Wagtaile in fethers and making, these
are so extreme fat that you can perceive nothing else in all
their bodies: these birds are now in season. They take great
quantities of them, and they used to pickle them with vinegar
and salt, and to put them in pots and send them to Venice
and other places of Italy for present of great estimation."

The Abbé Mariti, who travelled in Cyprus in 1760, said
that pickled *beccaficos* would keep for twelve months, and
that every year four hundred little barrels were exported to
England, Holland, France, and Turkey.

My host produced a bottle of amber-coloured wine called
Commanderia, a wine that was made by the Knights of St.
John of Jerusalem and still carries on every bottle a memory
of the title of their Grand Commander.

The wine was first made when the Crusaders came over to
Cyprus in 1294, after the fall of Acre. When the Knights
migrated to Rhodes in 1310, they still maintained their vineyards in the Grand Commandery at Kolossi, and so good was
their wine that casks of it travelled all over the mediæval
world. Our Plantagenet Kings used to warm their hearts with

it in England.

It is a strong, sweet wine, rather like white port, and I can well imagine any man who has drunk too much *Commanderia* in the heat of the day, charging the great gate of Famagusta, waving his stick at the yellow stones and roaring to the archers to draw their bow-strings to the hip.

8

I motored for thirty-seven miles to the ancient town of Nicosia, the capital of Cyprus. It lies in the centre of a hot, flat plain, a town as round as King Arthur's table. I suppose there are other round towns in the world—it was an idea of the later mediæval military engineers—but I cannot remember ever having seen one before.

The wall of Nicosia was built in a panic due to the imminence of a Turkish attack; and it was built none too soon. The Turks attacked Nicosia the year before they besieged Famagusta, and captured it after a siege of seven weeks. It is said that twenty thousand Christians were killed in the street fighting.

"The Turks when they captured Cyprus were particularly bitter against members of the Roman Catholic faith," writes **Mr. Rupert Gunnis** in *Historic Cyprus*, "and especially persecuted them. Therefore such members of the Latin aristocracy as escaped—for the mass of the people were of the Orthodox Church—found it expedient to change their names and their religion, and were gradually absorbed into the Greek Cypriote peasantry. Where, now, is Nores? Where d'Ibelin? Where Giblet? Gone in name, perhaps, but not in blood; somewhere still run these noble strains; diluted and thin they may be, but they are there. The peasant in the village, the policeman in Nicosia, the fisherboy at Paphos, or the priest in the Carpass may, if they but knew it, have bluer blood in their veins than half the aristocracy of Europe, and could boast, perhaps, quarterings that a Howard or a Sackville might envy.

"And of the royal blood itself? The great house of Plantagenet is said to have ended in an illiterate farmhand. The end of the proud house of Lusignan is as sad. For three hundred years kings and queens, their sons had mated with the ruling houses of Europe, while of their daughters five had worn crowns, other had married members of the royal families of Majorca, Naples, Savoy, and Portugal.

"The last descendant of all this glory and wealth of blood and heraldry is said to have been a poor little shrunken old lady, a Miss Eliza de Lusignan, who was a governess in Ceylon in the middle of the last century. She died at a villa in Lower Edmonton, and with her death the last thin, flickering flame was extinguished. Thus ended in a London suburb, the Most Noble House of Lusignan, Kings of Cyprus, Jerusalem and Armenia."

I explored the narrow streets of Nicosia, where Turkish bazaars exhibit a maze of redundant activity. There are the usual streets of small sheds in which men turn out quantities of identical objects in a spirit of brotherly competition. I noticed here, as the traveller notices throughout the East, that once a stranger has made up his mind which shop to patronize, those who a moment before were most forward in trying to lead him in the opposite direction now melt silently away. It is the will of Allah.

I went to the beautifully arranged museum, where I saw the black, cone-shaped stone which is reputed to be the Aphrodite of Paphos. It was found some years ago in a cow-shed at Paphos, and has been erected in the museum in surroundings which reproduce the design of the Temple of Aphrodite as shown on Roman coins of the island.

During the long centuries when Aphrodite of Paphos was one of the most widely-famed cult statues in the world, she never changed her primitive shape. It is curious that the pagan goddess who is associated with physical beauty should, in her original home, have borne no resemblance to the human form. Aphrodite did not become beautiful until she left Cyprus to be reborn in the mind of Greece.

I went next to a fine, thirteenth century cathedral, a lovely church of French pointed Gothic, with three superb doorways and an enormous, whitewashed interior; like its companion cathedral in Famagusta, it is now a Turkish mosque. St. Sophia grew up in the footsteps of St. Louis IX of France, who wintered in Nicosia on his way to the disastrous Fourth Crusade, bringing with him a great train of artificers and architects. Just as St. Nicholas in Famagusta reminded me of England, so St. Sophia in Nicosia reminded me of France. In these two buildings, no longer dedicated to Christ but to Mahomet, the crusading trumpets of England and of France seem to die away in a last salute.

The Greek Orthodox Cathedral in Nicosia is like a jewel-box. There is not one undecorated inch of wall or ceiling. It is covered with elaborate frescoes, with gilded woodwork and with ikons. Crystal chandeliers hang from the roof, and, when a monk switched on the lights, the church sprang into glittering life. The Catholic Church reflects the masculine dignity of the Roman Empire; the Greek Orthodox Church reflects the bizarre, almost feminine, extravagances of Byzantium. A clever woman once said to me: "In England the Catholic Church is regarded as rather extravagant in appearance, but the further East one goes, the simpler it becomes, until a point is reached when the Latin Church looks positively Presbyterian!"

I walked into a courtyard where a flight of steps led to a

gallery. This is the entrance to the Archbishop's Palace. A polite monk, who spoke quite good English, told me that the Archbishop was not in Nicosia, but would I please enter. I was taken to a long, cool room, plainly furnished and decorated with pictures of past archbishops. We indulged in the usual polite compliments until a young monk came in, carrying a tray containing little cups of coffee, saucers of preserved cherries, glasses of water, and a box of cigarettes.

"You may be interested to see the vestments of the Archbishop," suggested the monk. "As you know, these have a connection with the discovery of the body of the holy Barnabas in the reign of the Emperor Zeno. May I show them to you?"

In a few minutes he returned with an armful of brilliantly coloured, embroidered clothes, while another monk walked behind bearing the Archbishop's mitre and his pastoral staff. They were laid reverently on the table for my inspection.

The heavy, domed mitre is inset with enamels and richly decorated with rubies, emeralds, and diamonds. It is similar to the crown worn in Holy Week by the Greek Orthodox Patriarch in Jerusalem. The famous episcopal sceptre, conferred on the Archbishop of Cyprus over fourteen hundred and fifty years ago by the Emperor of Byzantium, is about five feet in length. It is inlaid with mother-of-pearl and ends in a pomegranate-like globe surmounted by a gold cross.

As the monks spread the vestments out on the table, there was a sharp ring of little bells. The Archbishop's chasuble, a richly embroidered red mantle, had twenty bells sewn on it, each one about the size of a cherry; and so had the Stole, or *Epitrachelion,* as the Greeks call it. This custom of sewing bells on priestly vestments goes back far beyond Christian times. Bells are mentioned in *Exodus* among the vestments prescribed for the High Priest, so that their sound might be heard "when he goeth in unto the holy place before the Lord, and when he cometh out." The bells worn by the High Priests of Israel were of pure gold and, according to tradition, had to be seventy-two in number. Similar bells were used in pagan ceremonies and are mentioned in connection with the worship of Dionysius and other pagan gods. I suppose the idea was to drive away evil spirits. The sistrum which was shaken by the priestesses of Isis, and is still shaken by the Abyssinian Christians in Jerusalem, was employed for the same purpose.

After we had admired these fascinating links with Byzantine Christianity, the monk spoke of the saints of Cyprus and of the pre-eminence of the Apostle Barnabas. On the Saint's Day, June 11, an ancient order of Service called *The Akolouthia of the Holy and Illustrious Apostle Barnabas* is sung in the monastery near Salamis. Taking an old book from a shelf, he translated that part of the service which recounted the life of the Apostle. One sentence interested me, because these ancient offices embody traditions that go back far into the ages. This sentence was:

"Aristobulus, who was the first to preach the Gospel in Britain, is said to have been a brother of Barnabas."

Now this is a puzzling and provoking statement. Although Aristobulus was a common name in Apostolic times and was borne by several members of the Herodian House, the only one who at once leaps to mind is the Aristobulus mentioned at the end of the *Epistle to the Romans*. St. Paul salutes "them which are of the household of Aristobulus." This suggests that Aristobulus was a rich Roman or Greek living in Rome, with a household which included certain Christian slaves.

The monk could not say whether this Aristobulus was the man referred to in the ancient office of St. Barnabas. But he was quite definite in his belief, on the authority of the tradition of the Greek Church, that the first evangelist in Britain was called Aristobulus, and that he lived at the same time as St. Paul and St. Barnabas.

9

I left Nicosia one morning with a Cypriot friend who was anxious to show the island to me. We decided to spend the first night at the famous monastery of Kykko, high up in the mountains of Troödos.

My friend was steeped in the early Christian lore of the island and knew the names of more saints than any man I have met. As we motored across the plain, he told me that there is a tradition in the island that St. Paul, St. Barnabas, and St. Mark spent only ten days in Cyprus.

"They landed at the port of Salamis," he said, "and, after meeting members of the synagogues there, went by foot across the island to Paphos. At that time Paphos was the official capital of the island and the seat of the Roman Governor, and Salamis was the commercial capital.

"Barnabas must have known many people in Cyprus, for he was a native of the island, and it is perhaps strange that no legends of his family or his friends have come down to us. It is obvious that no matter what may have been in Paul's mind, the missionaries did not address themselves to the pagans, but went from synagogue to synagogue. Their interview with the Roman Governor at Paphos was not sought by them: it was a royal command from the Governor himself.

"Now the story they tell in Cyprus, and which you will find in no book written about St. Paul, is that the three missionaries walked from Salamis to Citium, which is now Larnaca, and then struck inland to the once thriving town of Tamassos, of which there is nothing left to-day. We are going there now, and you will only see two little villages. It is very likely that this tradition of the route followed is true, because Augustus leased the rich copper mines to Herod the Great, and, as Tamassos was a centre of the mining industry, there would have been a big Jewish community in the district."

As we crossed the hot plain, we passed through groves of the largest olive trees I have ever seen.

"How old are they?" I asked.

"Who knows?" my friend replied. "Does an olive tree ever die? Look how the old tree decays and how another tree grows and spreads out of it. In a village called Salamiou, which lies on the hills behind Paphos, they say that their olive trees, which are even bigger than these, have grown from stones which St. Paul and St. Barnabas threw away as they sat down to eat their food by the wayside."

We turned into a country track that led from the main road to the tiny villages of Politiko and Pera, the site of ancient Tamassos. The word copper, by the way, is a corruption of the name Cyprus. The ancients called the metal *aes cyprium*, which became shortened into *cyprium*, was changed to *cupram*, from which it is only a short step to the English copper, the French *cuivre*, and the German *Kupfer*.

"The hills round about," remarked my friend, "are covered with enormous slag-heaps now hidden by vegetation. They are the refuse of the ancient mines worked in Roman times. At Katydhata, on the north-west of Cyprus, I could show you chain buckets coming down from a mine that was worked by Herod the Great and is now worked by an American Company. . . ."

The road ended in a lush garden of orange trees, where we found one of the most interesting Byzantine churches in Cyprus. It contains the tomb of St. Herakleides, first Bishop of Cyprus, who knew Paul and Barnabas.

The church was locked, and the key was in the pocket of some villager working in the fields. Beside the door was a bell-rope. We pulled this and, as we pulled, the old bronze bell of St. Herakleides boomed out over the olive trees and the corn fields.

It was eventually answered by a villager wearing a shirt and a pair of old trousers tucked into knee boots. His name was Leonidas. I delight in such discoveries. A chamber-maid in Nicosia is called Antigone and a waiter in Famagusta is Themistocles.

Leonidas unlocked the church and we walked into the dark, dusty interior, with its wall of gleaming ikons and its air of decay and neglect. A film of dust had settled on everything. I saw a wooden box on a stool. Inside, lying on old velvet, was a human skull. As I went over to look at it, Leonidas ran forward and gently took the box before I could touch it.

"This," he said, "is the skull of St. Herakleides. Yesterday was a feast day and that is why it has not been put back under the bishop's chair, where we keep it."

He bent down and reverently kissed the glass lid.

My friend then told me the story of the saint.

"We have a legend in Cyprus," he began, "that St. Herakleides was the son of a Greek priest in the temple of Apollo at Tamassos. He met St. Paul and St. Barnabas when they came to Cyprus and was converted, becoming the first bishop of Tamassos. He built churches in Cyprus and could work miracles and cure diseases. But he was burnt at the stake. . . ."

Leonidas unlocked a side chapel that was even older than the church. I stepped into an incredible scene of neglect. This is the mortuary chapel in which St. Herakleides and three other saints were buried. White dust—the dust of centuries—covered everything. Enormous cobwebs hung down from the roof. Rotting ikons, the canvas paintless and bare, lay about in the dust.

When my eyes became used to the gloom, I saw the four

tombs. Someone had broken holes in them to see what was inside. I saw brown earth in the graves, and something grey.

"That is the tomb of St. Theodoros," said Leonidas.

While we were exploring this chamber of dust and decay, an old man with a coloured cloth wrapped about his head stood in the doorway, leaning on a staff. He was the village priest. He came slowly in and pointed with his staff to one of the sarcophagi.

"The grave of St. Mnason," he said.

"Do you mean the Mnason who is mentioned in the *Acts of the Apostles?*" I asked in surprise.

The priest was too old and feeble to understand, but Leonidas did.

"Yes," he replied, "Mnason was a man of Cyprus."

I remembered the verse in the *Acts.*

"There went with us also certain of the disciples of Cæsarea, and brought with them one Mnason, of Cyprus, an old disciple, with whom we should lodge."

The Cyprian legend is that Mnason was baptized by St. John the Divine in Jerusalem. His house was a day's march from Jerusalem, and in it he received Paul and Luke during Paul's last visit to the city.

Among his many miracles was the admirable one when he paralysed the arm of an extortionate moneylender.

10

Mount Troödos dominates the island of Cyprus. It stands up in the west like a green tower lifted towards the cloudless sky. In the autumn it is on the mighty head of Troödos that the first wisp of grey gathers, a sign that rain is about to fall on earth parched since May.

The guide-book says, with unconscious humour, that "Mount Troödos, the ancient Mount Olympus, on whose heights gods and goddesses once met in solemn conclave, is now the summer seat of the Cyprus Government."

This suggests that the gods and goddesses were either officially evicted, or had departed of their own free will as soon as they heard of Queen Victoria and Disraeli. And the words contain, perhaps, a faint note of warning. They seem to warn the traveller that he should not expect to turn a corner and suddenly come upon Persephone playing among the grape hyacinths, but that he should, on the other hand, be prepared at any moment to encounter Mrs. Browne-Jones, whose husband is in the audit department.

As the sun fell towards the west, we climbed up out of the plain through vineyards and past villages clinging like wild bees' nests to the ledges of mountains. We entered a cool world of bracken and hushed woods, where every footfall is silenced on yielding paths of pine needles, and the mind wanders far away to the combes of Bournemouth.

How strange that clear-eyed Athene, that Artemis with her bow and quiver, that the lady Aphrodite herself, should have haunted groves which seem designed by a benevolent providence to prepare the mind of a Government official for retirement to a house called "Pine View." And the strangeness of it grows, for, climbing to the top of the great mountain where Zeus once assembled his thunderbolts, the surprised traveller comes suddenly on hard tennis-courts. Glades once sacred to the escapades of pagan gods are now sacred to the decorous games of His Majesty's Servants.

Towards evening we came in sight of a group of buildings perched like an eagle's nest on the ledge of a mountain. It was strange to see this cluster of chimneys and roofs hanging over an abyss, with the open sky above them.

The Monastery of Kykko, the most famous of all the ancient monasteries of Cyprus, lies 3,800 feet above the sea.

That it should exist on the same mountain with a hard tennis-court is rather like thinking of Thomas à Becket in friendly propinquity with Bunny Austin. But there it is.

The Monastery of Kykko is mediæval and does not want to be anything else. Its appearance, its point of view, and its daily routine, have not altered since the thirteenth century. Kykko has made a habit of being burnt down. The first fire was caused by a villager who was smoking out wild bees' nests in the year 1365. Another fire broke out in 1542, a third in 1751, and a fourth in 1813. But every time the haphazard group of wooden buildings rose again, each new monastery exactly like the one that had been destroyed.

When I saw the great gateway of Kykko in the evening light, with a crowd of muleteers gathered about it and men tying the bridles of their horses to posts and iron staples, I thought that I might be travelling in almost any century but the twentieth. A pungent smell of wood smoke and cooking pervaded the air. Glancing beneath the archway, I saw a file of Greek monks carrying platters; a man crossed the court-yard, driving a mule with a wine-skin slung across its back.

Our arrival caused no surprise, for Kykko has been entertaining strangers since the thirteenth century. Its rambling courtyards are encircled by galleries which contain more than seventy guest-rooms. Pilgrims come to Kykko from every part of the Greek Orthodox world. We had not long to wait. One of the muleteers courteously pulled the bell-rope and a brazen clamour, rising in some interior court, brought forth an old monk with a black beard, who motioned us to enter. We were not immediately shown the rooms which we were to occupy. The old monk led the way along dark stone passages, up and down flights of worn stone stairs. Then, pushing open a heavy wooden door, he waved his hand towards a formal, plush-covered French settee, and motioned us to sit down.

The room was cool and dim. There was a faint aroma of

incense and coffee. Photographs of immensely bearded Greek archbishops, sitting in their finest vestments, gazed down from the walls.

A curtain that was drawn across the room parted to admit a bearded middle-aged priest with a twinkling eye. A gold pectoral cross shone on his dark gown. His clothes were of better quality than those of the ordinary monks, and the hand stretched out in greeting was soft and carefully tended. I knew that he was the Abbot of Kykko, one of the most powerful church dignitaries in Cyprus.

There is an enormous gulf between the monk and the abbot in the Greek Orthodox Church. The traveller who meets only the village priest and the monk might well think that the Church was recruited entirely from rough, unlettered peasants. But the higher orders are different.

The Abbot was a sophisticated churchman. I felt, as we plunged into polite greetings, that the annual balance-sheet of the monastery, the records of the wheat and grape harvest, the sheep and cattle statistics, and so forth, would, no doubt, delight the eye of a chartered accountant. While we talked, the curtains parted again and a young lay brother came forward with a tray of cherry jam and tumblers of water.

The Abbot, with a friendly smile, invited me to take the refreshment that is always offered in a Greek monastery. Sometimes it is preserved quince, sometimes preserved figs or rose-leaf jam, and sometimes sweet, pickled walnuts. I dipped in a spoon, swallowed a mouthful of cherry jam, and sipped the water.

"So you are writing a book about St. Paul," said the Abbot. "Tell me," he asked with his winning smile, "do you think St. Paul was whipped at Paphos?"

Now, this is an old Cyprian legend, and I did not want to offend him. But, taking a plunge, and remembering that you can never get into serious difficulties if you speak the truth, I said: "No, I don't."

"Nor do I," replied the Abbot.

I was immensely relieved.

I discovered that a lay brother, a young man with an immense fuzz of black hair and a black moustache dawning on his upper lip, had been allotted to me as a servant. He was a young lad of Paphos, who had felt a call to dedicate himself to the Church. He led the way up and down the stone stairs and through galleries until he came to a door at the end of a balcony.

He ushered me with a profound bow into an enormous, vaulted apartment in which fifty men could have dined. There was a wash basin, a plush-covered sofa, and in the middle of the floor was a small round table and a few chairs. My friend had been accommodated elsewhere. This apartment was for me alone.

When I went to wash, the young monk rushed to me bearing a pitcher of water and a towel. He did not pour the water into the basin, but waited for me to hold out my hands and poured the water over them. This was always the custom in antiquity.

A flight of stairs in the corner led up to the room where I was to sleep. There were several couches, and near the iron-barred window stood a bed with a mosquito net round it. There were no carpets on the wooden boards and no pictures on the whitewashed walls. Looking out of the window, I could see a pine wood lying several hundred feet below the monastery. Moonlight lay like a silver mist over the branches of the trees.

There is a silence of night so intense that it seems to hypnotize. There was not one sound in the whole of that enormous blue night. The flickering of a bat that came past the window every few seconds, cutting the air without a sound, made the silence seem deeper.

I sat enjoying the hush of darkness for some time and then, going downstairs, I saw that the lay brother was setting the table for dinner. He had lit a paraffin lamp in the centre of the table, but the light hardly touched the corners of the room. My Cypriot friend was, I learnt, dining with a friend in the monastery.

The lad placed red wine before me, made from monastery grapes, and a loaf of bread made from monastery wheat. Then he went out to bring in dinner, and I sat waiting in the large stone room, feeling like a wanderer in some mediæval romance. The first course was a dish of beans and celery. The lay-brother stood beside my chair all the time, with a napkin over his arm, silently anticipating my wishes, cutting bread and offering salt.

He was an odd-looking figure, standing there in the dim lamplight: his enormous bush of hair stuck out at the back of his head, his pot-shaped black hat on top of it, and his meek, round face, smeared with black round the jaws and over the mouth, was like that of a schoolgirl who had corked her face to act Iago.

He shuffled out to return with a dish of pilaf and boiled chicken.

I offered him a cigarette when I had finished, but he shook his head.

I was summoned again into the Abbot's presence. He sat behind a desk, affable and charming. He offered me coffee and strong Macedonian cigarettes. In that strange room, lit with candles, we discussed St. Paul's visit to Cyprus, his conversion of the Roman governor at Paphos, and the few legends of his mission.

One story says that as the Apostles were crossing the island, they came upon a group of young pagans, youths and girls, stripped naked for some race. This so shocked them that they turned back and took some other road. I cannot help feeling, however, that Paul and Barnabas, who had lived in Antioch, must have been used to such sights.

I said good-night to the Abbot and went back to my room. The silence was broken by dogs baying at the moon. I awakened to the sound of a bell and to the rising sun. It was five o'clock. A monk in the bell tower was tugging the rope, sending out a series of triumphant notes over the mountain-sides. It was not the usual, monotonous tolling of a church bell; it was a gay stampede of sound that fell clashing and clanging down the mountain-sides to run gambolling through pine trees to the distant villages beneath.

Noticing that the monks, who were beginning to emerge from their quarters, smiled and nodded to me as they passed, I asked if the wild peals indicated a feast day.

"No," was the reply, "the bells are in honour of you."

I have rarely felt so embarrassed. I was horrified to think that a large portion of Troödos had been awakened so early in my honour.

However, I realized the instant necessity of attending the service, and, dressing at great speed, ran down to the church, where the monks were already standing in their stalls, booming "kyrie eleison" in deep voices.

I was given a front wooden stall facing the *ikonostasis*, which leaned forward as if ready to fall beneath the weight of the ikons framed in it. I had no difficulty in identifying the famous miraculous ikon of Kykko, a painting which has made this monastery famous all over the Greek Orthodox world. It is a painting of the Virgin, and is said to be one of the three existing ikons painted by St. Luke. It is set in an ornate frame and a curtain is kept drawn to hide it from view.

When the service was over, a number of peasants filed into the church, among them two women who prostrated themselves before the ikon. When they rose from their knees, they hung a shirt on a bronze arm that projects from the screen to one side of the ikon. I thought it was a curious gift.

Two young monks drew aside the curtain for me. Several strips of tapestry cover the picture. When a corner was lifted, I saw that the whole ikon, with the exception of a small square about the size of a match-box, was sheeted in embossed silver. A small square of original wood, visible through the opening, reveals a few inches of rather blistered-looking paint.

No one has seen the picture for centuries, and, in fact, disaster is said to descend on anyone who attempts to do so. The last attempt was made by a monk from Rhodes in the year 1776. They still tell at Kykko how he persuaded the Abbot to allow him to spend a night alone in the church; how, consumed with curiosity, he stretched forth his hand to uncover the ikon and how a hot blast struck at him from the picture, leaving him prostrate on the pavement.

The Blessed Virgin of Kykko is revered as a bringer of rain. In the old days the ikon used to be carried in solemn procession, with candles and incense, and lifted towards that corner of the sky from which rain might be expected. And never, I am told, has the Virgin of Kykko refused to bring rain to Cyprus.

"And what is that bronze arm sticking out near the ikon?" I asked.

"That," I was told, "is the arm of a Turk who tried to light his cigarette from a holy taper."

More peasants came in and prostrated themselves before the shrine.

We said good-bye to the hospitable Abbot, to the guest father, and to my attendant lay-brother.

When I reached the gate, the courtyard was in confusion, with mounted men riding off and others dismounting and hitching their bridles to a post. The fuzzy-headed lay-brother came out into the dust of the road to bid me farewell.

"Please," he said, "will you send me the photograph of myself?"

"*Malista.*"

"*Efcharisto!*" he replied with a radiant smile; and when I looked back, he had run to the edge of the bend of the road and was shouting "*chaerete!*"

11

On the way to Paphos we stopped at a wayside coffee-house to get water for the car. While I sat under a vine drinking coffee with my Cypriot friend, the innkeeper came out and talked to us.

He was a remarkable sight. He looked like a brigand in comic opera. Every garment on his body seemed to have its own separate tragedy. He was dressed in strange fragments of clothes. He wore baggy Turkish trousers, an ancient European waistcoat, a striped shirt, a sash, and a pair of sagging striped stockings that looked like the relics of a violent Cup Final. In some odd and inexplicable way the general effect was harmonious.

A man who had been sitting near us, drinking coffee with an ox-wagoner, rose and walked off up the hill path. I thought he was a Turk. He wore Turkish dress and I had noticed that, as he talked, he played with a string of amber beads. But the innkeeper and my friend, after whispering together about him, told me that he belonged to the *Linobambakoi*.

"There are very few of them left now," explained my friend. "In the old days there were many. They are outwardly Moslems, but secretly Christians. It is said that they are descended from Christians who, in order to escape persecution when the Turks conquered Cyprus in 1571, pretended to be converts to Islam.

"But all the time they and their descendants bore secret Christian names, were secretly baptized by the Orthodox priests, observed in secret the feasts of the Greek Church, and received the Sacrament in secret."

We came down to the green vale of Paphos in the heat of the afternoon. A somnolent blue sea lapped the warm rocks of the western shore of Cyprus, and a cloudless sky told of rainless months to come.

It was here, as *Acts* tells us, that Paul addressed the Roman Proconsul, Sergius Paulus, and struck blind the Jewish magician, Elymas. In those days a fair and stately city rose on the seaward thrust of rock, a city that held the administrative headquarters of the Roman Government. Malarial mosquitoes and earthquakes have almost cleared the site. Fishing boats lie at anchor in a shabby little harbour, and on the mole is a ruined Turkish fort in whose shadow barelegged fishermen mend their nets.

Nothing is left of the Roman capital of Cyprus but a series of mounds thick with marble chips, with old pottery, and with fallen pillars. The site is so ruined and desolate that it looks more like a rubble field than the relics of an ancient capital. Near the lighthouse are the scarcely discernible remains of a theatre.

I had not realized that the famous Temple of the Aphrodite of Paphos was some distance away from the ancient city. It lay ten miles to the east of the city. If St. Paul had come down to Paphos from Troödos, it is possible that he never saw this notorious centre of pagan superstition. The temple was built on the coast, and was connected with the port of Paphos by a processional way that lay through bowers of roses and other flowers sacred to the goddess.

We motored to the ruins of the Temple of Aphrodite.

What a disappointing site it is. There are a few stones, mostly the bases of statues, standing on a slight hill some distance from the sea. It is impossible to make anything of them or to gain an idea of the temple that once stood there. An old Turk, who owns a farm near by, took me into a back-yard and, brushing away the dust with a broom, revealed the faint colours of a tessellated pavement, probably the floor of one of the ante-chambers.

The black stone in the Nicosia Museum is believed to be the actual goddess worshipped in Cyprus from remote times. The only beautiful thing about her is the legend of her birth, how she came gently to shore on the sea foam. I am told that in winter, owing to some peculiarity of wind and tide, great masses of white spume are cast up on the beach near the ruins of the temple.

Aphrodite was a barbaric Phœnician or Asiatic goddess and never changed her shape, remaining to the end of her days a truncated black stone. The kings and the people of the earth visited her and consulted the famous oracle. All we know about the appearance of her sanctuary is the assump-tion, from ancient coins of Cyprus, that it was a small, rather Egyptian-looking temple, with two garlanded pylons in front of it and a semi-circular enclosure in the centre of which stood the altar. In the darkness of the temple was the black stone, but whether it was dressed, or otherwise disguised, is un-known.

When Titus was on his way to begin the war that ended with the destruction of Jerusalem and the Temple, he was so full of curiosity that, putting his ship in to Cyprus, he con-sulted the goddess about his future.

"A calm sea and a safe passage were promised," says Tacitus. "He slew a number of victims, and, in terms properly guarded, attempted to pry into his own destiny. The priest, whose name was Sostratus, explored the entrails of various animals, and, finding that the goddess was propitious, an-swered, for the present, in the usual style, but afterwards, at a secret interview, laid open a scene of glory. Titus, with a mind enlarged, and swelling with vast ideas, proceeded on his voyage, and joined his father."

Only male animals were allowed to be sacrificed to Aphrodite, and the best fortunes were always told in the sinews and membranes of kids. Although the altar was in the open-air, no rain was allowed to touch it and it was never stained by blood.

Immense wealth was accumulated in this temple and its fame spread all over the world. Once a year thousands of pilgrims landed in Cyprus and marched the ten miles from Paphos to the shrine of the goddess, where their subsequent conduct was violently condemned by the early Christian Fathers.

12

The next morning we explored the mounds of ancient Paphos, and came to one where several granite pillars were lying half out of the earth. Here again, as at Salamis and Famagusta, is a place crying out to be investigated.

"That is the site of a Roman temple of Venus," said my friend, "and is called by the villagers 'the Hill of the Forty Columns.'"

We examined massive remains of the podium of the temple and of underground passages now choked up. A Turk who years ago committed a murder is said to have sought refuge in these vaults and to have come out a quarter of a mile away, gibbering with fear, saying that he had passed through chambers full of skulls.

A few minutes' walk from this temple is a little Greek church built on the site of what must once have been either a large Roman temple or a market-place. Two granite columns are still standing. There is also a broken Roman pillar surrounded by a whitewashed wall and covered with iron bands to prevent people from chipping off fragments as a cure for malaria. This is called St. Paul's Pillar, and is, by local tradition, said to have been a pillar to which St. Paul was tied and scourged. Nothing is said about this scourging in *Acts*, but we know from *Corinthians* that Paul was thrice beaten with rods, the Roman punishment; once stoned; and on five occasions received the "forty stripes save one," the penalty inflicted by Jewish authorities. Only the stoning at Lystra, in Asia Minor, and the beating with rods at Philippi, are mentioned in *Acts*, and nothing will convince the people of Cyprus that one of the unrecorded scourgings did not occur at Paphos.

In the sad ruins of this once beautiful city of Paphos, I read again the brief account of Paul's appearance before Sergius Paulus the Proconsul, and his first conflict with pagan superstition in the person of the Governor's astrologer, Elymas the Jew. It is a wonderful drama. Every detail is so true to life in Roman times.

Sergius Paulus was an intelligent man. Cicero had been one of his predecessors in office and, like Cicero, he was a man of learning and education. Pliny, who was a contemporary, mentions Paulus as the author of a treatise on Cyprian lore. It was natural that learning of the arrival in his island of two wandering philosophers, he would wish to hear what they had to say. Also, he was on the main line of communication between Palestine and the West. What is more likely than that he already knew of the Crucifixion and had heard of the Resurrection?

Paul and Barnabas were summoned to the Governor's audience hall. Sergius Paulus was clearly stirred by their speech. But behind his chair stood a character who was always in the train of Roman dignitaries, an oriental theosophist and man of science, a "false prophet" or "magician," a Jew who, like Paul, had two names, Bar-Jesus in the Jewish world, and the Greek name of Elymas.

Saul and Bar-Jesus—Paul and Elymas—those two pro-
tagonists, so alike in birth and social status, so unlike in
thought, defied each other in the presence of a man who represented the Roman Empire. How tremendously significant
and symbolic is this first recorded victory of Paul in the mission field. Elymas "withstood them, seeking to turn the deputy
from the faith." Paul, who regarded the magician's qualities
as a gift of the devil, prepared to put forth all the force that
was in him to resist the power of darkness. We learn that
"Saul, who also is called Paul, filled with the Holy Ghost,
set his eyes on him." Those who watched saw with amazement the defeat of the astrologer, who crumbled up like
paper at the withering words which Paul fired at him. All the
time Paul "set his eyes on him."

"And now, behold, the hand of the Lord is upon thee,
and thou shalt be blind, not seeing the sun for a season.
And immediately there fell on him a mist and a darkness;
and he went about seeking some to lead him by the hand.
Then the deputy, when he saw what was done, believed, being astonished at the doctrine of the Lord."

Two remarkable things happened after that audience in
Paphos. Paul is never again called Saul, and for ever after he
leads Barnabas, whom, until that moment, he had followed as
a loyal and devoted friend. Never again do we see the old
order of their names, Barnabas and Saul: in future it is "Paul
and his company."

A number of reasons have been advanced from age to age
to explain Paul's sudden adoption of his Roman name, some
of which are ingenious and others fantastic. Surely the best
suggestion is the simple and obvious one that, as he voiced
Christianity for the first time before a high official of Rome,
he realized that Saul the Jew was a less powerful force in the

world than Paul the Roman citizen, a member of the ruling race. Therefore it was as Paul that he faced the Roman Empire.

From that moment until the end of the great story, Paul became the leading missionary to the Gentiles. At Paphos his power was proved; at Paphos the hand of God was seen to be with him.

Under his direction a ship was found sailing for the shores of Asia Minor. "Paul and his company" embarked. The ship moved northward to Perga.

So Paul took the whole world as his harvest-field.

CHAPTER V

I revisit Turkey, join forces with a Turk, go into the interior
and stay at Iconium (which is now Konya), visit the empty Mosque
of the Dancing Dervishes, hear and see something of the new régime,
and dine in a modern Turkish home.

1

THE three missionaries sailed from Paphos to the shores of
Asia Minor. When the time came for me to follow their steps
back into Turkey, I began to sympathize with John Mark,
who, at that point, turned and went home.

My first visit to Turkey had not been pleasant. Those who
know what it is to live in an atmosphere of suspicion and to
encounter at every turn the ingenious opposition of minor
officials, will be well able to understand with what sinking
feelings I again prepared to be mistaken for a spy. On this
second visit, however, I had provided myself with a wealth
of introductions and with letters from the Turkish Ambas-
sador in London; but, in spite of these precautions, I felt
uneasy as the coasting vessel came within sight of Mersin.

I saw a picturesque little Turkish port lying on a green
plain and backed by the immense, snow-tipped heights of
the Taurus Mountains. The harbour is only large enough for
small fishing-craft, and ships have to anchor a good way out
in the bay, landing their passengers in *caïques*.

Mersin is interesting because it discharges the duties fulfilled in ancient times by Tarsus. It is now the port for the
produce of the Cilician Plain: grain, timber, cotton, and such-
like produce are here shipped to Syria, to Russia, and to other
countries.

The town was soaked in afternoon sun. Men with baskets of freshly plucked oranges stood on the shore near the little Turkish cafés which look so picturesque in sunlight and so bedraggled and squalid in rain. An athletic-looking man of about forty, dressed in a suit of tweed, come up and introduced himself. At first I thought he was English.

"I have come to put myself at your disposal," he said politely. "I am your guide."

As I looked at him, I thought he would be a welcome friend in trouble.

"Shall we go and have some coffee?" I suggested.

"Delighted," he replied, and led the way to a little tin table under a vine.

The waves tumbled on the shingle only a few yards away, and two bootblacks immediately prostrated themselves at our feet and began their ministrations.

I told him that there must be something about me which aroused the worst suspicions of his countrymen, and that it was more by good luck than anything else that I had escaped a prison cell during my first visit to Asia Minor.

He waved his hands airily, as if to dismiss a crowd of inquisitive police, passport officials and common informers.

"Ah," he said, "you will have no such troubles now. *I* shall show you Turkey."

"You speak wonderful English," I said. "Have you been to England?"

"Never," he replied with a smile. "I was an officer of cavalry and was a prisoner of war in Egypt. I was captured on the Suez Canal and learnt English in one of your prisons."

I remembered the commercial traveller of Adana who had also done this.

"I hope," I said gingerly, "that we treated you well."

"No, not very well," he replied, frowning and lighting a cigarette.

"I'm sorry, because now I'm your prisoner, in a sense."

His face lit up with delight, for the Turks love irony.

"War," he said in a loud voice, "is war!"

Then, dramatically, we shook hands and finished our coffee. The two shoeblacks, hearing us talking in a foreign tongue, tried to dun us for more than the regulation five piastres. My friend bent towards them and hissed one word in a low voice, and the men picked up their boxes and fled.

I began to respect him enormously. I hoped he would have the same effect on the police.

In the afternoon we hired a carriage drawn by two little white horses and drove out to the ruins of Soli.

A mile or so out of the town the road deteriorated into a country track full of pot-holes. Camels padded along burdened with enormous bales that took up half the way. Without warning, a hundred soldiers suddenly rose from a field of sugar-cane and ran across the road with their rifles at the ready, flinging themselves down in a ditch.

Hassan, for so I shall call him, watched them with professional interest.

I gathered that, on his release from prison, he had taken part in the military actions that led to the Republic and the Dictatorship. I discovered that he worshipped Kemal Ataturk. To Hassan, everything the Ghazi had done was right. Everything that he proposed to do would inevitably be right.

"At last the Turks have a chance under our Leader to be a great nation in the modern sense," he said. "We have been too long the Sick Man. Now we are healthy. All the old, bad things that held us to our past are going, and we look into a future full of hope."

A file of camels, led by a large man on a small donkey, came down the lane.

"The Turk," said Hassan suddenly and with passion, "is not an Asiatic: he is European."

I thought that he was a good object-lesson, for he might have been English or French, as he sat there in his tweed suit with a soft felt hat pulled down over his eyes.

The ruins of Soli interested me enormously, because they show the kind of town that St. Paul knew so well in the course of his journeys. Like Antioch, Damascus, Jerash, Palmyra, and all the Græco-Roman towns of Syria and Asia Minor, the main street was a long, pillared avenue—a Street called Straight—that ran the length of the city.

In ancient times, the traveller who arrived at the splendid harbour of Soli found himself facing steps that led to the street of columns. There are still twenty-three of these columns standing in a straight line, and many more lie on the ground, overgrown with brushwood. The vegetation covers the ruins of baths, houses, walls, and an amphitheatre.

As I sat with Hassan amid the ruins of this town, I thought what a happy change it was to find an ancient city whose name is written not in blood but in philology; for from Soli we get the word solecism. That is Soli's only claim to fame.

Shortly after Pompey the Great had refounded the town, settling there a number of the Cilician pirates he had captured, the place became notorious for the bad Greek spoken by its citizens. It was so bad that when anyone made atrocious mistakes in grammar and pronunciation, the Greeks said that he must have come from Soli. The Greek term *soloikismos* has become solecism in English and *solécisme* in French.

How curious it is to trace the origin of a word that most of us have used at some time or other to this ruin in Asia Minor, where twenty-three tall columns stalk across the skeleton of a dead town.

"Turkey for the Turks," I heard a voice saying.

"I beg your pardon?"

"I was just saying," remarked Hassan, "that the Turks at last rule Turkey. The Armenians, the Greeks, and the other foreigners who once controlled us are gone. It is Turkey for the Turks!"

"When Lloyd George . . ." I began.

"Ah, that man, that terrible man!" cried Hassan. "He would have given Turkey to the Greeks!"

Then he calmed down and smiled, saying in an almost tender tone of voice:

"We should put up statues to him in all the towns of Turkey. He should, perhaps, stand side by side with Ataturk."

"But why?" I asked, rather puzzled.

"Because he made us fight for Turkey," he cried.

I have no idea what the Turkish national anthem is like, but, with a feeling that he was about to sing it, I rose swiftly and walked back with him across the ruins of Soli.

2

After travelling north from Perga to Pisidian Antioch, Paul and Barnabas preached in Iconium, Lystra, and Derbe. This new mission field suggests to my mind that Paul, with his sure instinct for great commercial cities and highways, had soon realized that Cyprus was, so to speak, "off the map," and would lead them nowhere, and that only by striking north from Perga and preaching in the cities of the great trade route would they spread the seed of Christianity. Thus, at the very outset of his missionary life, Paul gave proof of his sound, practical mind. His action was to prove a fine piece of strategy.

Before they struck northward on their mission, the celebrated dispute took place between Paul and Mark. I call it a dispute because it shook Paul's faith in Mark for many years, although it did not affect the feeling of Barnabas for his young kinsman.

What can this dispute have been about? It may have been that Mark, as a strict Hebrew, disliked and feared the path towards the Gentiles that Paul was so swiftly treading. It may have been that, as a loyal admirer of his relative, Barnabas, he disliked the new tone of leadership which Paul evidently assumed after his interview with the Roman Governor at Paphos. Or was he frightened of the apparently hopeless prospect of converting the world to Christianity? Did he fear the brigands who, despite the police systems inaugurated by Pompey and Augustus, still continued to haunt the Taurus? Was he frightened of the no less terrifying crags and pinnacles of Paul's mind?

There is another possibility. "Mary mother of Mark" is a phrase that occurs frequently in the opening chapters of *Acts*. The two older men had taken this youth from his home and had plunged him suddenly into the rigours of the first Christian Mission. What was "Mary mother of Mark" thinking in her house in Jerusalem? Was she happy to know that her son was plodding through the brigand country and malarial swamps of Asia Minor? If it were a call from home that drew Mark from his duty, we can be sure that it would find no echo of sympathy in the mind of Paul. He could be as tender as a woman. He could weep like any girl. But when it came to spreading the Gospel of Christ, he was inflexible.

There is an ancient tradition that Mark suffered from a deformity. The Greek word is κολοβοδάκτυλος, which means that his fingers were mutilated or stunted, and it has been suggested that this deformity made him nervous. I do not think that much credence can be given to such a theory, for we know with what gallantry people suffering from deformities far worse than this can face the perils of life. I have the feeling that the Abbé Constant Fouard has found the truth when he says that "this disciple of the Jerusalem Church, brought up in the atmosphere of pure Judaism, could not fail to feel some alarm at finding himself associated with the Apostle of the Nations."

The plans of Paul to bring the unspeakable Gentile within the Church and, if necessary, without reference to the Synagogue, must have seemed sheer blasphemy to the orthodox Mark. A man often talks of his projects long before he translates them into action. How many times may Mark have sat in Cyprus and listened with growing fear to the development of Paul's mind?

So Mark returned home; and it was not until many years later, when Paul was an old man and Mark was no longer a young one, that this dispute on the shores of Asia Minor was forgotten.

How did Paul travel? That is a thought which must always occur to anyone bound on a journey such as mine. As we read *Acts*, we cannot fail to be impressed by the ease with which the Apostles planned and carried out journeys that involved years of travelling both by land and sea, and by the regular communication which existed between the early churches. Within a few years of the Crucifixion, the Gospel had spread all over the known world. It had travelled along roads now desolate and into harbours now deserted, for in St. Paul's time Asia Minor occupied the position which Europe occupies to-day.

Alexander's conquest of the East—334–323 B.C.—flung open the gates of the world. Hitherto the only travellers known to us were armies on their way to Troy, Persian hosts on their way to Greece, Phœnician mariners fading into the mists beyond the Pillars of Hercules, and pilgrims on their way to the shrine of some oracle.

Suddenly, in the wake of Alexander's armies, new roads spring up, leading to new cities. Great harbours rise on the sands of the Nile Delta and in the shadow of Syrian cliffs. The Pharos of Alexandria sweeps the darkness of the sea. You can hear the sound of Greek voices, buying, selling, prospecting, and speculating, from the Strymon to the Ganges. Silver pours from the mines of Thasos and Pangæus, and the gold of Persia flows like a red river to the west.

With Paul's age—the Roman Age—the world seems to have become modern. The sea is white with galleys making for Ostia and Rome. Strabo tells us that a hundred and twenty ships sail to Egypt and India in one year. The harbours of the East are piled with luxuries consigned to Rome, and the warehouses at Puteoli and Ostia are heaped with the produce of the earth. The bread baked in Rome is made from corn grown in Egypt, Gaul, Spain, Sardinia, and Sicily. Seneca tells us that when the Egyptian corn ships, with their topsails flying, were sighted off Puteoli, all the populace would rush to the harbour to watch them coming in, an escort of war galleys on either side.

The merchant, the speculator, the profiteer, the middle man, all these familiar characters were on the quays of the ancient world, invoicing, buying and selling. Gums, scents, incense, ivory, silks, Tyrian dyes, and oil, wine and corn from Syria, glassware from Sidon, and other merchandise, were piled in the vast sheds that for a mile lined the banks of the Tiber. "Many a man," wrote Seneca, "through his eagerness as a merchant is led to visit every land and every sea"; and Pliny said that Rome sent over a million sterling a year out to the East in return for cosmetics, scent, and silk, "so much," he added, "our luxuries and our ladies cost us."

Seneca, in his attack on the habits of his day, said:

"May the gods and goddesses bring ruin on those whose lux-ury transcends the bounds of an Empire already perilously wide. They want to have their ostentatious kitchens supplied with game from the other side of the Phasis, and though Rome has not yet obtained satisfaction from the Parthians, are not ashamed to obtain birds from them: they bring together from all regions everything, known or unknown, to tempt their fastidious palate."

Along the new roads, the caravans crossed the world heavy with riches. All the roads on which they travelled led literally to Rome. The Imperial Post, instituted by Augustus, speeded from point to point, changing its horses at post-stations set at intervals on all the great highways of the Empire. Dispatches from generals in the field, instructions to colonial governors, imperial edicts and other official information, crossed mountain and plain at a steady five miles an hour, the average speed of the Imperial messengers.

Ordinary travellers in hired carriages were content to travel from forty to fifty miles a day. Many and varied were the types of carriages that could be hired in Roman times. The huge, luxurious Rolls Royce of antiquity was the *carruca*, which was sometimes fitted as a *carruca dormitoria*, complete with soft beds, and so beautifully painted and decorated that one of them could cost as much as a farm. The *basterna* was a comfortable litter slung on shafts between two mules, one fore and the other aft. The *carpentum* was a smart two-wheeled carriage popular with ladies, and sometimes hooded with silk curtains. The *cisium* was a swift cabriolet, and the *reda* was an ambling four-horse coach. In cities, or for short distances, the old-fashioned litter was used, often carried on the shoulders of eight trained bearers.

That rich and powerful persons travelled in complicated comfort is obvious from references in the classics. Cicero, for instance, relates that he met Vedius in the depths of Asia "with two chariots, a carriage, a litter, horses, numerous slaves, and, besides, a monkey on a little car, and a number of wild asses."

The vehicles in Roman times, more numerous and more varied, perhaps, than at any period of history except in nineteenth-century England, made drastic traffic regulations necessary in Rome. Traffic blocks became so serious that the driving of wheeled vehicles in the city during the first ten hours of the day was forbidden by the Tabula Heracleensis. The only exceptions were carts employed on public work, carriages bearing the Vestal Virgins, the flamens during public sacrifices, or a victorious general in his triumph. The consequence was that as soon as darkness fell, the noise of wheels in Rome became insufferable. "It costs a fortune to be able to sleep in Rome," remarked Juvenal.

Travel by sea was more hazardous than by land. There was a season when the Mediterranean was closed and only those bound on urgent national business would dare to make a voyage. This season was between November 10 and March 10. Even in the sailing season mariners were not fond of the open sea, but preferred to take advantage of the land breezes and coast whenever possible, seeking the shelter of some harbour in the evening and allowing their passengers to sleep on land if they wished.

Paul had a wide experience of travelling by sea, and had every right to give advice during the shipwreck at Malta. He was shipwrecked three times, and on one occasion was adrift for a day and a night on a raft. I wonder if we can see in this the impatient, fiery quality of his temper? Did he sail too often during the closed season, or were his unhappy experiences due merely to bad luck and sudden squalls?

The size of some of the merchant ships in Roman times is surprising. Josephus tells us that one ship, travelling from Judæa to Rome, carried six hundred persons, and even bigger ships were built in Egypt for the transport of corn and of obelisks. If you have read the story of the transport of "Cleopatra's Needle" from Egypt to England in 1878, how it was enclosed in a special cylinder-ship and had to be abandoned in the Bay of Biscay and was very nearly lost for ever, you will feel admiration for the shipbuilders and seamen of the first century, who carried such weighty cargoes safely from Egypt to Rome. Pliny mentions a ship that carried twelve hundred passengers as well as a cargo of papyrus, pepper, linen, and spices. The ship that brought the obelisk now standing in front of St. Peter's in Rome was so enormous that four men with arms outstretched could only just encompass the mast.

When winter closed the seas, it also closed the mountain passes. No one would think of travelling over the Taurus Mountains between November and March. In addition to the snow that blocks the passes, a bitterly cold wind blows across the steppes of Asia Minor and the rain, falling in torrents, can turn the whole land into mud and render movement impossible.

These points are important in attempting to work out the chronology of Paul's travels, because there are certain times when it must have been impossible for him to have moved from one place to another.

The traditional picture of Paul is that of a man with staff in hand, and it is probably accurate. Lack of money may sometimes have forced him to do the fifteen miles a day which is the average mileage a good walker could maintain in that part of the world; but it is surely ridiculous to imagine that he was never offered a lift. I am sure he would readily have accepted a seat in a wagon or a carriage, and would with gladness have ridden a spare mule or a camel.

I can find only one indication that Paul enjoyed walking. When he left Troas at the end of his last journey, his companions took ship and sailed round the peninsula to Assos. But Paul did not go with them. He told them that he would pick up the ship at Assos—"for so had he appointed, minding himself to go afoot."

The journey which he chose to make, when he could easily have stepped aboard the waiting ship, is a tramp of twenty miles.

Hassan, who had been busily going to and from the little station at Mersin, told me in the evening that we could take a train early next morning for Adana, changing there for Konya.

That night we slept in a clean little Turkish hotel run by a Syrian who had been to the United States. For some reason he was convinced that I was American. Every time he came into my room, as he frequently did to ask if I liked his hotel, he would make some flattering reference to New York. He was a nice little man, but I think Hassan looked at him with chauvinistic suspicion because he was not a true born Anatolian.

3

All that day the train pounded across Turkey.

There was an unforgettable three-quarters of an hour after leaving Adana, when we climbed at a snail's pace into the Taurus Mountains. We passed in and out of rock tunnels and cuttings, with a view to our left of savage gorges which, although the sun was shining brilliantly, lay below in partial darkness. We gazed down into desolate ravines reminding me of the Pass of Killiecrankie on a gigantic scale. Far below a small stream tumbled from rock-shelf to rock-shelf, winding its way through a crack in the mountains. Fir-trees and pines climbed the heights.

Colonel Balfour of Dawyck, one of the great authorities on trees, tells me that the trees of Asia Minor have, unlike those in many regions of the Mediterranean, remained unchanged since the time of Paul. Therefore, as the Apostle crossed the Taurus to tell the story of the first Christmas, he would have walked with thousands of little Christmas trees on either side of him, each one a perfect green cone about four feet in height, its branches waiting for candles and toys.

We emerged on a high plateau where the air was colder

than in Tarsus or Mersin; where spring was at least a month later than in Cyprus and on the Cilician Plain; where clouds over the vast slopes of the Sultan Dagh threatened rain. I felt that in climbing up through the Cilician Gates we had climbed in less than an hour out of the East into the West.

I wearied of looking out of the window on the featureless, greenish-brown plains, enlivened only by an occasional horseman or enormous flocks of sheep. The shepherds in their square-shouldered, felt cloaks, would pause to watch the train go past, sometimes waving their sticks. The big white dogs would bare their teeth and stand on the defensive. As they lifted their necks, I could see the massive collars, worn by all sheep-dogs in Asia Minor as a protection against wolves. They are ringed by sharp iron spikes about three inches in length.

Hour succeeded hour, and there was nothing but the same vista receding to distant hills, here and there a poverty-stricken village, but usually only desolate uplands, bleak and wild, on whose unfriendly expanse a band of wandering *yuruks* had the air of explorers.

The sign that we were approaching a town was generally a clumsy four-wheeled cart bumping along a rough track beside the train. Where there was a cart, there must be a track; and all tracks lead to towns. Sure enough in a few minutes we would come to feathery poplar trees, the white finger of a minaret rising above them; and so we would rest with a weary sigh in a station full of ragged loungers who walked two by two along the track, gazing with dull, silent curiosity into the carriages.

Soldiers in loose-fitting, putty-coloured uniforms would patrol the line, rifles slung on their backs. The ubiquitous police, with red tabs on their tunics and red bands round their caps, would come out of the station office and look about with searching eyes.

There is, however, a lighter side to travelling in Turkey.

Every journey is a prolonged picnic. It is only on the trains running from the new capital at Ankara that such luxuries as *wagons lits* and restaurant cars are to be found. On ordinary trains the passenger forages for himself, and the provision of food seems to be the main occupation at some of the poor little wayside halts. Some stations specialize in *kebab*, which is meat cut into slices and grilled on a skewer. Small boys come along selling this, shouting down the corridor. They come into the carriage, put their fingers at the top of the skewer and, withdrawing it, shoot the pieces of roast meat on to a piece of newspaper.

Sometimes there are oranges or apples, or bags of roast chestnuts; and always there are those delicious rings of bread covered with sesame seed, called *simit*, and little cups of hot, sweet coffee, carried rapidly through the corridors by small boys.

But on this journey to Konya I did not need to buy food. Hassan had brought with him a large basket containing a roast chicken, slabs of cheese, and a quantity of bread.

Our fellow-passenger was a model of courtesy and hospitality. He was a young infantry officer returning to his regiment from leave. His luggage was redeemed from the commonplace by a woman's silver fox fur and a bowl containing five gold-fish.

Every now and then he would plunge a tumbler into the bowl and empty out water, which he would throw through the window. Then he would rush to the lavatory at the end of the coach and return with fresh water, which he would pour into the bowl.

His mother had given him enough food to feed the regiment. He had a large tin packed with every kind of Turkish delicacy, including excellent *dolmas* of savoury rice wrapped about with vine leaves. These he handed round to us. We offered him some of our chicken, but he opened another tin and showed us that he also had a cold roast chicken.

He unpacked his bag and brought out a bottle of scented water called "Kemal Lotion," with which he refreshed his hands and his face. He then produced a bottle of the excellent white wine which Turkey is now producing.

So the hours wore on, and the endless brown plains slipped past the window. The sun crossed the sky. . . . The officer removed his tunic and, placing his gold-fish out of the sun, went to sleep. Hassan pillowed his head on an overcoat and also slept.

I looked out of the window, thinking that St. Paul must have had a much easier time travelling across Asia Minor than I had imagined. I had always thought of him trudging through savage mountain passes.

The country westward from the Taurus is rather like Salisbury Plain on a large scale. In Paul's day excellent Roman roads crossed it to all the great centres of population. Towns existed in every place to which water could be brought. Asia Minor was in the first century what Europe became in the Middle Ages: a great country of thriving cities, sharing the same civilization and bound together by the same ties and animated by the same ideas.

Paul walked, or rode, to these cities along wide, firm roads. His peril of robbers was, probably, not so great as long as he kept to the main roads of Asia Minor, for on such roads he would not often have been alone. He would find himself with caravans of merchants, bodies of Roman troops and local militia, bands of travelling jugglers and actors, wandering priests, itinerant philosophers, and schools of gladiators touring the theatres of the province. Only when he left the main roads would he have been a lonely traveller, in danger from floods and from robbers.

In the whole course of his travels there is only one mention of an inn—the "Three Taverns" on the Appian Way—and there is no indication that Paul ever stayed in one. Yet he must have rested in these road-houses and inns on countless occasions, and I believe that his "peril of robbers" referred not to highwaymen and brigands so much as to the inn thieves who were a notorious feature of wayfaring life in Roman times.

The innkeeper of antiquity had a bad reputation, and the cities were full of low-class taverns. On lonely roads, the poorer class of inn was probably no better than the modern *khan*: a cheerless resting place for man and beast, where neither food nor furniture are provided, so that the traveller curls up in his own blankets and cooks his own food over a communal fire.

I suppose locks were not more numerous in those days than in ours, and no doubt many an inn had its own particular band of thieves, or a villainous proprietor who, waiting until the travellers had sunk into the coma of exhaustion, stole silently upstairs to rob and murder.

Cicero tells a gruesome story of two Arcadian friends who retired to rest in an inn. One of them awakened, thinking that he heard his friend in another room imploring help because the innkeeper was murdering him. But he turned over and went to sleep again. He was awakened again by the ghost of his friend, who begged him, although he had failed to aid him when alive, not to allow his death to go unavenged. The ghost told his companion that the innkeeper had slain him and hidden his body in a dung cart, and it urged him to go to the city gate in the morning and intercept the cart on its way to the fields. This he did, the dead body was discovered, and the innkeeper was convicted.

Luxurious places of entertainment were to be found in the cities, often built by municipalities to entertain distinguished and official visitors. Epictetus mentions hotels so comfortable that they encouraged an unnecessarily long stay, and Strabo, writing of the inns beside the Alexandria–Canopus canal, says, "Men and women dance, totally unembarrassed, with the utmost licentiousness, some on the ships, others in the inns on the side of the canal, which seem to be made for such riotous and voluptuous proceedings."

That description might have been written by a Puritan of our own day who has not become accustomed to the surprising sight of emancipated youth dancing round the swimming-pool of a road-house.

Paul must have encountered customs officers at various stages of his journey. The system of road taxes, local and Imperial customs and frontier dues, must have been as irritating in his time as it is in ours. The delightful Apollonius of Tyana—educated at Tarsus in the first century—travelled all over the world, even to India, and must be the only traveller who has ever really scored off a customs official:

"And as they fared on into Mesopotamia, the tax-gatherer who presided over the Bridge (Zeugma) led them into the registry and asked them what they were taking out of the country with them. And Apollonius replied: 'I am taking with me temperance, justice, virtue, continence, valour, discipline.' And in this way he strung together a number of feminine nouns or names. The other, already scenting his own perquisites, said, 'You must then write down in the register these female slaves.' Apollonius answered: 'Impossible, for they are not female slaves that I am taking out with me, but ladies of quality.' "

4

Hassan had been in Konya some years before, in command of a squadron of Republican cavalry. He was eager, as the train approached the town, to see again the scenes of his exploits.

"Look!" he cried excitedly, pointing towards a belt of trees, "that is where I burnt a farm to the ground! Rebels were hiding in it. I burnt it over their heads, and they ran out in the smoke right into the arms of my men."

He looked again, and seemed disappointed to find that the place had been rebuilt.

I looked with curiosity at the town, once the Iconium of the New Testament, which I had come so far to see.

The train approached miles of feathery trees and bright green gardens, a welcome contrast to the brown, stone-scattered Lycaonian Plain which we had endured since morning. Wherever I looked, there were blue mountains rising on the horizon like islands from a sea; only to the north did the flat plain vanish in brown distance.

Above the tops of trees I saw the roofs of single story buildings, with here and there the minaret of a mosque. I saw a file of camels slowly padding along a track on the outskirts of the town. I saw an old Ford car, full of Turks, trying to race the train on a fairly good road that had sprung up from somewhere and went beside the track for a few miles. As I looked at Konya and tried to imagine what Roman Iconium once looked like, I realized that Paul must inevitably have compared it with Damascus.

Both cities lie in a sudden burst of green due to the presence of water. Just as the Abana, gushing through the limestone rocks of the Anti-Lebanon, has created Damascus, so water flowing from the mountains of Pisidia irrigates the plain of Konya. Both Konya and Damascus are high above sea level, and in Paul's time both towns were commercial stations on the great caravan routes of the world.

When the train stopped, we jumped down to the track and found ourselves in the motley crowd which gathers at Turkish stations. Weary-looking men in shirt-sleeves leaned down from the windows of the coaches and bought skewers of *kebab*.

bottles of water, and oranges. Turkish officers gazed out from the windows of first-class carriages, looking rather British in their khaki tunics, but German when they were wearing their high-waisted coats of field-grey.

In the station yard were waiting about thirty shaky old carriages, each one drawn by two lively, well-matched little horses. The box-seats were occupied by whip-waving and whip-cracking drivers, who in pre-Republican days would have worn Turkish dress, but are now obliged to wear the European reach-me-down. Their caps were so old and their suits so ancient and patched that they would create despair in the Flea Market of Paris.

"I know they look shabby," said Hassan, "but that matters not. These clothes represent a change of mind and a break with tradition."

We selected an *araba* and set off with much whip-cracking for the town, which is some distance from the station. On the outskirts I saw a newly-erected statue of the President in military uniform, standing on a decorative plinth in the middle of a small public garden. The statue is redeemed from the commonplace because the Ghazi's hand rests, not on the hilt of his sword, but on a tall stalk of ripe barley. This statue is the work of a Turkish sculptor, and its dignity and symbolism are admirable.

We clattered over a paved road into Konya, which, as befits the largest town between Smyrna and the Taurus, has a spaciousness about its new streets in strange contrast to the narrow, winding labyrinth of the old bazaars.

Side by side with the new houses and shops of Konya are ruined Seljuk buildings which date from the eleventh century, crumbling town walls of the same period, and miles of narrow shops, open to the street, where traders make and sell their goods.

Above this strange confusion of old and new rise the slender minarets of many a fine mosque and the stumpy candle-snuffer cone, covered with sage-green tiles, that marks the ancient headquarters of the now expelled Order of the Mevlevi Dancing Dervishes.

We caused great interest in Konya, where visitors—one of them obviously a foreigner—are not seen every day. Whenever I saw a policeman's eye on me, I thought with contentment of Hassan, ready always to present my credentials.

We had some difficulty about an hotel. The first one we tried had a gramophone which blared out Turkish dance music incessantly and did not look at all inviting. Eventually we discovered a modest-looking hotel, the *Seljuk Palace*, standing some way from the road in a little garden. I was told that it was owned by Russians.

The people were charming. They hastened to carry our bags up the uncarpeted staircase. They rushed to take posession of my passport, and no doubt they rushed it to the police.

I was given a small bedroom containing a wardrobe, a chair and a bed. Two worn rugs covered the scrupulously clean floor-boards. The window-curtains had shrunk at both top and bottom so that complete privacy was impossible. The most important object, as I was to learn later, was a stove standing almost in the middle of the room, with a big black pipe that spouted up to the ceiling and traversed the room on its way to a chimney outside. Konya, lying over half the height of Ben Nevis above sea-level, can experience hot days, but during the night the temperature may be a little above freezing point. When a wood-fire is lit in these Russian stoves, a room hitherto near freezing point is warm in about ten minutes.

At dinner that night a smiling, collarless waiter placed before me a roughly-hewn scrap of meat and potatoes which had been painfully cut into thin slices and then subjected, before a slight heating, to a bath in one of the more revolting oils. From the expression of eager expectancy on the faces of waiter, proprietor and proprietor's wife, I gathered that this was either a speciality or a death verdict. Sawing off a portion, I took an apprehensive mouthful, whereupon the waiter bowed, grinning all over his face, and the proprietor came forward and, also bowing, pointed to my plate, and said with some difficulty:

"Beef-roast!"

Then I realized that in this far-off place the pathetic sweetness of the human heart, that transcends all barriers of race, had devised a little compliment to England. I rose and told them in sign language that the meat was superb. They laughed and bowed with delight. And when the room was empty for a moment, a little hungry dog that had slipped beneath the table was a friend in need and—in deed!

Silence had descended on Konya when I went to bed. Then, suddenly, the quiet night was cut by a mournful whistle, and another, farther off, and another. It was as though many owls had chosen the same minute to hoot all over Konya. There came a whistle almost beneath my window. I tiptoed over and looked out. I saw a bulky figure emerge from the shadow of a wall opposite and walk slowly away in the starlight.

He was wearing a fur cap and a huge sheepskin coat with the fleece outside. He carried a thick staff, a revolver was belted to his fleecy waist, and every now and then he would pause and lift a whistle to his lips, uttering a long, melancholy call. There would come an answering whistle; and he would move on, a queer, barbaric figure who might have come from the camp-fires of Genghis Khan.

That was my first sight of the whistling watchmen who come out at nightfall in Konya.

5

I spent the following day in a vain attempt to find something in Konya that might have been there in the time of Paul and Barnabas. Not one relic of Greek or Roman Iconium has survived the centuries. I was taken into the cellar of a private house in which a number of heavy spiders, with bodies the size of a half-crown, were lurking in a tulle-like festoon of web; but it was, I think, part of the crypt of a Byzantine church, and had nothing to do with the Iconium of the Apostolic Age.

At much the same time that William the Conqueror was invading England, the ferocious Seljuk Sultans were sweeping westward, building an Empire that eventually extended from Afghanistan to the shores of the Mediterranean. Their capital was Iconium, and the finest things in Konya are the few relics of this age: a gateway or two, a fragment of wall, the ruins of a few mosques. But in a country which until now has never possessed any sense of history or antiquity, these buildings have been allowed to decay and fall.

The life in the network of narrow, intersecting streets fascinated me. The redundant little shops in the bazaars, each one presided over by a languid Turk, contained chiefly the necessities of life. The most attractive speciality of Konya is a large, gourd-shaped water-bottle of glazed pottery. The potters of Konya must have derived their craft in unbroken descent from Byzantium, for the colours and the thick yellow glaze used on these bottles are identical with those of the common pottery of the Byzantine world.

Near the maze of bazaars is a square where camel caravans set off across the plain. Wild tribesmen, wearing goathair coats with the skin inside and the rough pelt outside, their baggy trousers tucked into the ends of top boots, moved about among the roped camels, adjusting a burden here and tightening a rope there. With a series of reproachful grunts, first one camel, then another, arched his back and, bubbling with rage, rose to pad softly through the narrow streets on some long journey to the Taurus. Horsemen from the plain came in covered with dust, their faces tanned like brown leather, and, as they swung from the saddle, their dark, hooked-nosed faces, reminded me of Hittite monuments.

The police system of Turkey must be as efficient in the remote deserts and hills as it is in the towns, for not one of these tribesmen was wearing the forbidden fez. The weird assortment of felt cones, cloths, shapeless caps, and other slices of skin and fabric which bore no resemblance to any known type of head covering, proved that the word had gone forth to the utmost confines of the land. Into the middle of this wild-looking, dust-covered, braying, neighing and grunting tangle of tribesmen, donkeys, camels and hill ponies, came the figure of a young Government official, dressed in striped trousers, black coat, waistcoat, and bowler hat.

I called on the Governor of Konya, whose office is in a large building in the main square. There is a big courtyard like a *khan*, with a gallery running round it. Sitting on divans were the usual crowd of suitors, and, crouched on the floor, more humble suppliants.

A policeman showed me at once into the room where the Deputy-Governor—for the Governor happened to be away—was sitting behind a desk. He immediately gave me permission to photograph anything that was not of a military nature. Coffee and cigarettes appeared. Ringing a bell, he gave an order that would have been impossible in old Turkey. He wished me to meet his daughter, who was shortly going to England to finish her education. A girl of about eighteen entered. She was dressed like any English girl. She shook hands shyly and, urged by her father, said "How do you do," which was almost the extent of her English.

My interview over, I passed through the bazaars and visited the most interesting building in Konya, the famous Mosque of the Dancing Dervishes. This used to be a holy spot in pre-Republican days, and no Christian was ever allowed to enter the room where the sarcophagi of Jelal-ed-din, the founder of the Order, and his father, lie beneath immense embroidered cloths. The building is distinguished by a picturesque group of domes and minarets, including a broad-based cone covered with glazed, green tiles. There is a lovely little garden with a fountain in the centre, and I thought it the most attractive place I had seen in Turkey. A caretaker in a brown uniform and a peaked cap replaced the dancing dervish who used to be on duty at the gate, a sign that the mosque is now a museum.

All religious communities have been suppressed in Turkey, Christian and Moslem. If Catholic monks or nuns wish to remain in the country, they are obliged to wear ordinary clothes and find lodgings, for community life is not allowed. I have heard that there are nuns who wear ordinary coats and skirts and have let their hair grow, but, generally speaking, missionaries have naturally left a country in which religious instruction is no longer allowed.

The confiscation of mosques and lands belonging to Moslem orders, and the suppression of these orders, sent a profound shock through Turkey in 1925. It was announced that the Monastic orders were reactionary and a source of danger to the young Republic. With one stroke of his pen, the amazing Ataturk calmly seized their property and turned many of the mosques into museums.

I believe there are about a hundred dervish orders in existence in the East. They are distinguished by their costume and by allegiance to various holy men, their founders. Some dervishes are incredibly old and dirty and appear to be mad. They will stop and beg in the most arrogant and insulting manner. The older, the dirtier and the madder they are, the deeper seems the veneration of the peasants and country people. Insanity in the East has always entitled the sufferer to respect.

Most of the dervish orders practise some art which, resulting in a state of trance or ecstasy, is said to release the soul from the body.

I have seen the disgusting hypnotic performances of the Howling Dervishes. They work themselves into a frenzy by repeating the name of Allah, beating tom-toms, clashing cymbals, rising, swaying, and shouting, until foam gathers at the corners of their mouths. When they reach a certain pitch of ecstasy, they become so insensible to physical pain that they can stick red-hot pins into their bodies. I have often thought that these dervishes are in direct descent from the priests of Baal, who "cried aloud, and cut themselves after their manner with knives and lancets, till the blood gushed out upon them."

The Dancing Dervishes, who originated in Konya and have establishments all over the East, are, however, as interesting and attractive as the howlers are revolting. In the old days the head of the order was one of the most important men in Turkey. It was his duty to gird every new Sultan with the sword of Osman.

The founder of the order was Jelal-ed-din Mevlana, the great Sufic poet of Persia, who was born in Asia Minor in 1207 and died in Konya in 1273. In Konya he won a great reputation for piety and for the beauty of his mystical poetry. He evolved a number of moral and ethical precepts, the most famous of which are the *Spiritual Mathnawi*, in forty thousand double-rhymed verses. His idea of eternity was expressed as follows:

"You say the sea and its waves; but in so saying you do not mean two different things, for the sea, in its rising and falling, makes waves, and the waves, when they have fallen, return to the sea. So it is with men, who are the waves of God; they are absorbed after death into him."

Jelal-ed-din was passionately fond of music, and he devised a devotional dance to the sound of flutes.

When I saw this ceremony in Damascus, I thought it was impressive and beautiful. The usual term Dancing Dervishes does not really describe the movement. It would be more accurate to call them Turning Dervishes.

The ceremony is solemn and dignified. After prayers, a band of either nine, eleven, or thirteen dervishes stands out on the empty floor, and a band composed of eight musicians, playing old-fashioned instruments such as a dulcimer, a tabor, and a one-stringed violin, strikes up a rhythmic and attractive tune.

The dancers are dressed in long, high-waisted, pleated gowns that fall to the ground. They wear tall, brown felt cones on their heads. Each one, as he begins to turn, stretches his right arm straight up, the palm held upwards to the roof, while the left arm is held stiffly down with the palm towards the earth. The head is slightly inclined to the right shoulder. I asked a dervish if there were any meaning attached to this posture, and he replied:

"The dance symbolizes the revolution of the spheres, and the hands symbolize the reception of a blessing from above, and its dispensation to the earth below."

Entering the mosque, I found myself in a dim, white building which has been kept exactly as the dervishes left it. Their enormous turbans and cone-shaped hats are to be seen in glass cases side by side with their ceremonial vestments, their musical instruments and their exquisitely illuminated manuscripts.

Costly Persian and Arabian rugs lie on the floor and decorate the walls. To the left is the room where the ceremony of

Turning once took place, and opposite, in a railed enclosure, are several immense sarcophagi lying beneath clusters of hanging lamps: the tombs of Mevlana and his followers. At the head of each tomb is an unwieldy, dusty turban.

It is the fashion for the modern Turk to scoff at the superstitions and traditions of his fathers, and therefore the caretaker smiled in a superior manner as he showed me round. But I detected a note of reverence when we came to that mysterious dim place in the mosque where the barrel-shaped tombs of Jelal-ed-din and his father lie under embroidered cloths. The founder is regarded throughout Islam as a great saint.

When they buried the son, they had to make room for his immense sarcophagus by placing the father's sarcophagus in an upright position. But this explanation is too prosaic.

"When the great saint was carried in," said the caretaker, "behold, the tomb of his father rose up and bowed in reverence. So it has remained."

I was taken to the domestic quarters, where the dervishes lived in a whitewashed, vaulted building with a kitchen like that of an Elizabethan manor house. Their admirable library still remains, every book in its place on the shelves.

An extraordinary feature are the splendid English eighteenth-century grandfather clocks which still tick away in corners. I noted two majestic specimens, one made by "W. Jourdain, London," and the other by "George Prior, London." The latter announced proudly on the clock-face that it could play "Hornpipe-Air-Song-Dance." It is curious to think of these mahogany relics of Georgian England standing like dignified flunkeys round the tombs of dervish saints.

Sir William Ramsay, who knows this part of Asia Minor and its bearing on Pauline history and archæology better than any man, has indulged in some fascinating conjectures about the Mevlevi Dervishes. In his book, *Cities of St. Paul*, he suggests that the foundation may have had a Christian origin.

"The holy colour of the Mevlevi," he notes, "is not the Moslem green, but the Christian blue. They do not regard themselves as debarred from drinking the juice of the grape, but openly and publicly offer and drink wine."

In his *Historical Commentary on the Galatians*, Sir William makes the still more interesting suggestion that the remarkable dance-tune of the Mevlevi Dervishes may be a survival of the pagan worship of Cybele.

"Almost the only inventions attributed to the Phrygians were in music: various kinds of cymbals, and similar instruments, the flute, the trigonon, perhaps the syrinx, were considered Phrygian: a musical mode said to be of melancholy yet of emotional and exciting character was called the Phrygian: certain tunes, the Lityerses or harvest song, the harmateion or carriage song, etc., were of Phrygian origin. There was also a Phrygian dance. These are all creations and accompaniments of the Phrygian religion.

"Associations connected with the Phrygian worship, passing under various names in different parts of Asia Minor, such as the *Herdsmen*, the *Korybants*, the *Hymn-Singers*, the *Satyroi*, survived even in Rome time, and have thus become known to us. They are still represented by the Mevlevi or dancing dervishes of modern Turkey, with their strange, yet most impressive music and dance, which have probably been preserved in essential characteristics from the worship of Cybele."

If Sir William Ramsay is correct in his assumption, then the music of the Mevlevi dance is the oldest in the world. I have therefore gone to some trouble to print a few bars of this strange tune. I learnt in Konya that there was a Turkish gramophone record of the dance, and after some difficulty I obtained the disc from which the following version is adapted.

Mr. Becket Williams, who was kind enough to transcribe the air for me, sent his manuscript with this note:

"To give an idea of this wild dance on the piano is very difficult. The tone-colour of the reed pipes is absent, and the fact that they are blown frequently off the note (or 'out of tune,' as the phrase is) adds an atmosphere of barbarity which is absent from the domestic keyboard. Then there is the question of accompaniment. In early music the general opinion is that that accompaniment (harmony, if you like) was absent, or at the most confined to a drone bass, like the bagpipes, or one's neighbour picking out the latest illumination from the geniuses of Tin-Pan Alley. To give the proper primitive effect, I suggest the following to be played *all the way through* with the left hand:

Bass

"To the musician the tune is interesting because of the progressions. The tonality, or key, is mostly, I think, in the Mixo-Lydian mode, but it frequently breaks out of this. I think you will find the transcription correct, however strange it may look.

"What often puzzles the pundits about old music, and causes monographs, is purely and simply a wrong note! We are all liable to make them, more especially primitive musicians."

The only account known to me of the ceremony at Konya is one written in 1918 by Walter A. Hawley in his book, *Asia Minor*:

"After the beating of drums and a barbaric chant that had all the plaintiveness of a dirge," writes Mr. Hawley, "nineteen dervishes, some still with the flesh of youth, others with wan, ascetic faces, marched with funereal tread several times

THE DANCE OF THE MEVLEVI DERVISHES

about the room, paying homage before the tombs of their departed chiefs, before the Chelebi and before each elder. Then, separating, they turned, at first slowly, with a look of vacancy in their eyes, as if their minds were sunk in profound repose. But soon they turned faster and faster, until they whirled like spinning tops, passing and repassing one another in their revolutions, but never colliding; while through their midst glided an old past-master, keenly watching every movement, and stamping disapproval, first at one, then at another.

Each had sombre-looking garments except one with a white fluted skirt, who moved with almost the grace of a woman. Yet even he failed to escape the censure of their preceptor. But soon they appeared to pass beyond the realm of communion into an abstraction leading to complete ecstasy.

"The day without was shortened by the heavy clouds that covered the sky; the light within grew dimmer, till at length the dervishes seemed like shadows from some other world flitting across the floor; but the elders and the Chelebi sat motionless and in perfect silence like those in reverie, seemingly only partly conscious of the fading splendour of the hall, the weird music, the phantom forms; and as if their own minds and wills were completely dominated by those forces that were symbolized before them."

6

Leaving the Mosque of the Mevlevi Dervishes, I passed through a narrow market where I saw a bent old man buying bread. A ragged brown coat wrapped his body and flapped about his scarecrow limbs. Even a comic little hat, such as small boys wear at the seaside, could not disguise his air of hungry tragedy. And I thought that eyes followed him with interest as his tall, thin body, with its flapping brown coat, moved from stall to stall. I was told he used to be one of the Dancing Dervishes.

"How does he live?" I asked Hassan.

"Who knows?"

"Is he allowed to beg?"

"No."

"Do people give him things for the sake of old times?"

"Who knows?"

I had to leave it at that. But I have an idea that in a town which for centuries has been the headquarters of this extraordinary cult, there must be a few kindly hands ready to thrust a crust of bread towards an old dervish who cannot escape to one of the many Mevlevi monasteries outside Turkey.

We went on through the bazaar, where I stopped to look at a pile of felt hats stacked on the pavement. They had just been made and were drying in the sun. I smiled to think that I had discovered one source of Ataturk's hat supply.

The door of the shop opened and a man, who had evidently been watching me from inside, came out smiling and invited me to enter. I have found that nearly every Turk, unless he is dressed as a policeman, is charming and good-natured and, above everything, loves a joke. He could see that I was amused by his pile of hats and I believe that he also thought them rather funny, for, as he led the way into his shop, he looked back at them and laughed.

I was in a Turkish hat factory. Two hatters sat cross-legged on the floor—the only indication that they were Turks. I noticed that in an excess of loyalty they wore fine new undented specimens of the best European pattern.

They rubbed and pummelled the felt, while the owner of the shop, delighted by my interest, exhibited his primitive blocking and steaming devices.

"So this is an industry of new Turkey?" I inquired.

"Oh, no," replied Hassan. "This is the shop which once made the tall felt hats for the Dancing Dervishes. But when the Dancing Dervishes were expelled, what were these men to do? They said to themselves: 'We can make good hats for the dervishes; why should we not alter the shape and make good hats for the farmers, now that the fez is no longer to be worn?' "

They told me that the cone-shaped hat of the dervishes, which was about a foot high, was called a *kulah*. The Mevlevis say that before the world was created, a world of the spirit

existed in which the soul of Mahomet was present in the form
of light. The Creator took Mahomet's soul and placed it in
a vase, also of light, in the shape of a *kulah*.

The hatter laughed merrily and shook his head when I
asked him if he, as a maker of many a *kulah*, believed the
story. "We cannot know such things," he replied, smiling.

I asked him if it is easier to make hats for the dervishes or
for Kemal's loyal subjects. He said there was no comparison.
A dervish cap was a difficult thing to make, but an ordinary
felt hat was easy. He could turn them out by the hundred.
And he waved his hand in proof towards the display on the
pavement.

"Is it more profitable?" I asked.

And the hatter nodded his head, smiling as if to say that
all was well with the world.

As we walked away, I asked Hassan what has happened to
the fezzes of old Turkey.

"They have been destroyed," he said grimly.

He would not listen to the story that many an old Turk
still keeps his fez carefully hidden, and wears it behind locked
doors to remind him of the good old days when Turkey was
Turkey and a harem was a harem.

"If it were so," he said, "we should make laws against it."

"But, honestly now, do you really like wearing a hat better
than a fez?"

"We like wearing what Kemal Ataturk tells us to wear,"
he replied, drawing himself to attention and listening to that
inaudible national anthem which accompanies all mention of
the President.

"Did not the Chinese cut off their pigtails in 1911?" asked
Hassan. "The fez was to a progressive Turk what the pigtail
was to a progressive Chinaman—a sign of his bondage to the
past. He cut off his pigtail: we threw away the fez . . . we
have an old legend which says that not until the Turks leave

the Bosphorus and return to Anatolia will they be a great nation. Constantinople, which is now Istanbul, smothered and debased us. Now that we have made our capital at Ankara, our fortunes will change. We are Turks again!"

7

Anyone who knew Turkey in the old days would be astonished by modern Konya. Women who used to be veiled from head to foot now wear Western clothes, and even stop in the street to talk to their men acquaintances. They read fashion papers and do their best to copy the modes of Paris.

The old-fashioned, monumental woman, stuffed fat on sweets and idleness, is now merely a survival. The modern Turk claims to admire slim women, and I notice that his advertisements for cigarettes, and any other product which affords an excuse for the picture of a pretty girl, show a slender figure dressed in the latest fashion, often smoking a cigarette with a dashing air of emancipation.

The most significant sight, as I look out of my window, is the large elementary school opposite, the finest new building in the town. About half an hour before the janitor unlocks the school gate, a hundred noisy little boys and girls gather there with books under their arms, eagerly waiting to be let in. As soon as the gates open, I see children running from every corner, tearing across the playground and disappearing into the building. At the same time groups of young Turkish girls, aged about eighteen, walk sedately past, carrying portfolios or attaché cases. They wear dark blue coats and skirts and rakish peaked caps bound with gold braid. These are pupil-teachers on their way to an academy. Before the Republic they would have been closely veiled and in a harem.

The more I see of Turkey the greater is my admiration for the achievements of the Ghazi and his band of staff officers at Ankara. Given ten years of peace, the world will see a new and remarkable Turkey.

The present rulers of Turkey took over a country that was riddled with inefficiency and nepotism, bound by tradition and custom, bankrupt and apparently hopeless. They have modernized it, flung over tradition, turned out the foreigner, and got the wheels to work again.

Kemal Ataturk is not unlike Alfred the Great. He has driven the Danes out of his kingdom and now, his sword cast aside, he is making new laws for his people.

The soul of Kemalist Turkey is a Sinn Fein movement. The Turk has for centuries been submerged by Greeks, Armenians, Jews, and other foreigners, in whose hands the whole commerce of the country was gathered. His language and religion has been invaded by Arabic words and beliefs. The Ghazi is creating a Turkish Turkey and, in order to do so, he has had to smash a thousand idols. Everything foreign must go.

I am amazed by the apparent placidity with which the nation has seen the overthrow of tradition, the disappearance of Sultan and Caliph, the change in social custom, the freedom of women, the abolition of national dress, and the virtual abolition of religion.

Even those who view with cynical amusement the model he has taken of cocktail-drinking, fox-trotting, bowler-hatted Europe, cannot fail to admire the tremendous drive and courage of the Ghazi in his determination to give Turkey a European status. He is even rewriting the history of the Turk in order to give his people a European outlook.

Of all his achievements perhaps the most interesting is the new system of education.

When I told Hassan that I wanted to see the big elementary school in Konya, he said, to my astonishment:

"I think I shall let you go alone; if I come with you, I may disgrace myself and cry."

I looked at him in amazement. Was this the man who boasted of burning down farms, slaying rebels, and charging with drawn swords on Greeks and royalists?

"You don't understand," he cried. "You come from a country where education is easy, where there is nothing remarkable about a school. But think! When I was a boy, I sat on the floor in a grimy building outside a mosque while an old man, who did not care whether we listened or not, read the Koran to us. That was Turkey in my youth. But now it is different. Every young Turk, boy and girl, can get knowledge free. Learning is like water in your country. It is free. Everywhere—free! I tell you, you cannot understand. When I see these children—I, I feel it here. . . ."

And Hassan, the cavalry officer, gave himself a great blow over the heart.

However, we went together to the school, a light, airy building constructed on modern lines. There was a bust of Ataturk in the entrance hall.

The headmaster told me that all classes are mixed. The teachers are men and women. The old Arabic alphabet is taboo. Every word written or spoken in the school is the new Turkish language, written in Latin characters. Religion is not allowed to be taught.

We went into a classroom. The fifty little Turkish boys and girls stood instantly to attention. The classroom might have been that of any London County Council school. Each child had a desk of his own. There was a blackboard on which a young woman teacher had been writing. At the back of the room was a large tray of sand, perhaps six by three feet in size. The smaller children are taught the alphabet in a pleasant and original manner. They fill small funnels with sand and, rather as a cook ices a cake, spell letters in sand, controlling the flow by placing a finger across the hole in the funnel.

When the master asked the class if any boy or girl would like to stand forward and write a sentence on the board, every hand shot out. A small boy with a close-cropped head was chosen. He walked out without the slightest embarrassment and took the chalk. In a sure and efficient way he wrote a sentence on the board, bowed to the headmaster, and went back to his desk.

"What has he written?" I asked.

"He has written," said the headmaster, " 'When I grow up, I shall be of service to my country.' "

Looking round to say something to Hassan, I was just in time to see him disappearing through the door with his handkerchief to his eyes.

I was taken into classroom after classroom. I was impressed by two things: the solemn intelligence of the children and the fact that girls and boys worked together in perfect equality. For centuries the Turk has been brought up to regard woman as an inferior being. A son is the god of a house, but a daughter is the servant. One might think that this feeling, existing century after century, would have had some effect on the atmosphere of a mixed class of girls and boys. But the atmosphere of the harem and the subjection of woman has had no effect on this generation.

Suddenly the play-time bell rang through the school. There was a crash of feet all over the building as children stood to attention. They marched out two by two, singing a patriotic song.

Hassan wiped his eyes again and coughed, blowing his nose violently.

"You see the new Turkey," he whispered. "Is it not wonderful?"

The headmaster stood beaming in the hall as the long files

of singing children marched out into the sunlight.

"These are the teachers, the doctors, the architects of new Turkey!" cried Hassan, his voice charged with emotion and pride as the little dark-eyed and the little blue-eyed Turks passed, singing under the bust of Kemal Ataturk.

8

As I talked to Hassan in the evenings, I began to share his enthusiasm for the Ghazi. This man has not merely rallied his people and given them a focus for self-esteem: he has given them a new spiritual life. He has turned their backs on the past and has set their feet on a new road that may lead—who knows?—to a great and splendid future.

Hassan described to me one of the most important moves in the national regeneration of Turkey.

"When I told you that we Turks should set up a monument to Lloyd George, you smiled," he said. "I said this to you at Soli. You remember? But it is true, and I say it again. The statesmen of Europe who permitted Venizelos to have his way in 1920 and 1921, when we were weakened and smashed after the War, roused our courage, put new blood into our veins, made us a nation again, more truly a nation than we have been since we captured Constantinople in the Middle Ages. Beaten as we were, we combined to fight the Greeks and we won our fight under the Ghazi. It was at the conference table at Lausanne that the new Turkey was born. From that moment, Turkey was to be Turkish. Foreigners must go.

"How may Greeks and Armenians do you see in Turkey to-day? Not many. There are fewer Greeks in Turkey than there have been since the days of Alexander the Great. It was arranged at Lausanne that Greeks in Turkey should go, and that Turks in Macedonia and Greece should come here in exchange. Between 1921 and 1927 more than one million, three hundred and fifty thousand Greeks left Turkey, and nearly five hundred thousand Turks came here from Greece. The economists in Europe laughed at us. They said, 'How is it possible for this foolish country to progress if it turns out its commercial men?' But they did not know that the Greeks and the Armenians were the middlemen. They sold us goods from Europe which we can buy just as well ourselves. We have not suffered.

"The next move of the Ghazi was to expel the Khalif. 'What is this?' asked Europe. 'Has this country, which once dreamed of Pan-Islamism, gone mad?' For just that reason we expelled the Khalif. Islam is static. No progress can take place within its boundaries. Republican Turkey knew that if she wished to become a modern state she must throw off those traditions which bound her to the past."

Hassan took out a paper and a pencil and sketched for me a brief outline of Turkey's economic regeneration. Railway construction is going on at great speed year by year. New coal-mines are being opened up. By-products such as benzol, tar and gas are to be produced. Copper-mining is soon to be started. Sulphur beds are being worked at Keciburly. A silk factory has opened at Broussa; a factory for woollen goods at Ankara; a glass factory at Pasabahce, on the Bosphorus, will soon turn out five thousand tons of moulded glass annually; a sugar refinery has been opened at Alpullu, and others are being built at Usak, Eskisehir and Turhal.

"Is this progress, or is it not?" asked Hassan, his eyes sparkling.

"And all the money left over from these developments goes into the army and in State education?" I asked.

"Naturally," said Hassan. "We must keep our country safe, and we must educate our children to inherit the new Turkey."

"Has it ever occurred to you, Hassan, that the new Turkey which you are so proud of is the result of Christianity?"

He looked astonished, and told me that religion in Turkey was a matter of personal opinion.

"You don't quite understand. Europe is the result of centuries of Christianity. All the things you are striving for to-day are the result of Christian culture. You even observe the Christian Sunday and not the Moslem Friday. Perhaps someday you will become logical and accept Christmas."

9

We were invited out to dinner in Konya. The house was that of a municipal official with whom I had had some dealings, a quiet, agreeable man who always wore a black jacket and striped trousers, like any London clerk.

The house stood in a dark, narrow street where the pavements were still unmade. It rose up with a sinister air that, in spite of its present occupants, spoke of harems and old Turkey. Once inside, however, we were very definitely in modern Turkey.

The wife, a woman of about thirty, greeted us in the hall, and in the background—after the usual European custom—was the husband! He came forward and shook hands, leading us into a room in which everything was self-consciously Western. The walls had been distempered grey and were decorated with framed pictures of our host in military uniform. A suite of fumed oak, upholstered with snuff-coloured velvet, occupied the room, and a table was set for dinner. A tremendous rebuff to the spirit of old Turkey was delivered by a small metal figure of a gilded and painted ballet-girl, such as one sees in the windows of French second-hand furniture shops. She stood pirouetting on the mantelpiece, a queer little household god, suggestive of cabarets and dress suits.

Our host offered us *raki* served in little glasses, and as we sipped it, his vivacious wife superintended the arrival of a lavish dinner.

It was all rather strange. I thought that had I come to this house in 1920, I should not have seen the wife, I should not have seen a dinner-table and a fumed oak suite: I might have been sitting cross-legged on a divan, exchanging courtesies with an outwardly different host.

How, I asked myself, do Turkish families in the middle of Asia Minor know how to furnish their houses in European fashion? If a London family had to turn their dining-room into a Turkish apartment, they would be hopelessly at sea. Then I realized that the French and German illustrated papers tell them all they wish to know. Those interiors of houses in Paris and Berlin, those pictures of women at Long-champs, have a destiny far beyond the dreams of their origi-nators.

Our menu was composed of thick soup, red caviare, a pilaf made of wheat, and home-made baklava, the sticky pastry made with honey that is a speciality of Tarsus. Eloquent of new Turkey was the bottle of white wine with a grey wolf on the label. It is an excellent wine and, could it be exported at a moderate price, might become popular in Europe.

I was interested in my hostess, who was typical of the modern emancipated Turkish woman. She spoke quite good English, learned at the American College in Tarsus, and her enthusiasm for the Republic and the new life it offered the women of Turkey was apparent in everything she said. Her maidservant, she told me, was a peasant girl from a neigh-bouring village, and very old-fashioned and wrong-headed. It was difficult to make some of these ignorant people learn new ideas. It was all a matter of education. For instance, the girl's husband had just been called up to the army. When he had left to do his military training, the maid had come to live in, bringing also her newly born child.

"She has strange, wrong ideas from the old days," said my hostess with a frown. "For instance, she does not think it right to wash her baby until it is six months old. She thinks that water would kill it. But when she goes out, she does not know that I rush to her baby and wash it all over. Hygiene is one of the important things; do you not think so?"

After dinner my hostess gave me an ash-tray of lalique glass in the form of a flying nymph with trailing hair, an object that would have horrified her mother and would have had an effect on her grandmother which I find it difficult to imagine. While Hassan and the husband played a game of tric-trac, the wife sat beside me on the fumed oak settee, turning over the pages of a photograph album which revealed her husband in various stages of infancy. Strange as it may seem, it was an instructive social and political survey. I saw him first as a fat little Turk wearing the now forbidden fez, standing hand in hand with an ancient man in the costume of old Turkey.

"That is his grandfather," said the wife with a laugh; for it is the privilege of modern Turkey to laugh at its grandfathers.

As she turned the pages, I noticed that our host was becoming more and more European, his military *kalpak* **of astrakhan** merged into a peaked service cap, and then, as the years advanced towards the Republic, we saw him at last in the full glory of bowler hat, striped trousers and black coat.

The game of tric-trac over, I listened to the two men discussing the question of inheritance in Moslem countries. Turkey has, among her many reforms, abolished the absurdities of this system. In the old days it was not possible for a man to will his possessions to any one individual: they were automatically split up among his immediate family. Thus it frequently happened that after a man's death, his house became the property of perhaps fifteen or more people, each of whom was entitled to move in with his wife and family. Even cattle and horses, and other indivisible objects, can have a plurality of owners in the East. It is no uncommon thing to hear of a man who has a tenth share in a cow or a fifth share in an olive tree.

This, of course, explains in a great measure the horrible squalor of an Eastern town. Not only are many of its houses owned by twenty or thirty quarrelsome relatives, but property very naturally falls into ruin because these owners cannot come to an agreement about the sale of it.

Now that Turkey has adopted the Swiss Code, there will perhaps be greater incentive for a man to hand on to a single inheritor property which that descendant will keep in repair. Possibly that is why modern Turkey is building in stone, whereas old Turkey built in the cheapest kind of wood.

Two visitors arrived in the course of the evening. The husband was a shy young man who spoke only Turkish; his wife was a pleasant, chattering little creature who reminded me of a full-blown tuberose. Like so many girls of adequate dimensions, her manner was kittenish, and I watched with admiration how she bounced neatly among the nicknacks with agility and success. This Turkish girl also had been educated at the American College, but she had not managed to absorb as much English as my hostess and I was soon to learn that her grasp of the language had not advanced beyond the kindergarten.

"Do you speak English, madam?" I asked. She nodded her head vigorously and, folding her hands, fixed her large dark eyes on me, saying, slowly and solemnly:

"Pusey-cart, pusey cart, where haf you been? I haf been to

Lon-don to see the Queen. Pusey-cart, pusey-cart, what saw you there? I saw a leetle mouse under the Queen's chair."

As I was applauding her, and, perhaps pedantically, correcting the last line, I noticed that the others had stopped talking and were listening with interest.

"But would such a thing be possible?" inquired Hassan, gravely. "Could there be a mouse under the throne?"

"It is unlikely," I replied.

He nodded his head, reassured.

"I thought so," he said, "but it is nice to know."

I had enriched the vocabulary of the tuberose with a rhyme, which she rendered with charming solemnity as: "Twankle-twankle, leetle stair," when the time came to say good-night. Our host grasped a stout stick and said that he would escort us to the hotel. We begged him not to do so. He insisted, because, he said, the dogs were sometimes savage after dark. Bidding farewell to his wife, we followed him through the streets.

Konya looked very lovely that night, with moonlight spilling itself over old walls, half the narrow streets washed in green light and half in darkness. As we turned a corner, there was a piercing whistle and one of the burly guardians of the night moved out of the shadows in his sheepskin coat, his hand on the butt of his revolver.

CHAPTER VI

In which I describe the sites of Pisidian Antioch, Lystra and Derbe, travel into the mountains, where I see a lost city, and across the plain, where I find men leading a ram garlanded for sacrifice. In the silence of Iconium I read a letter to the Galatians.

1

THE city of Pisidian Antioch had been a Roman colony for about fifty years when St. Paul and St. Barnabas went there to preach the Gospel. It was one of six colonies established by Augustus to bring Roman law and order to the bandit infested highlands of Southern Galatia.

Like all Roman colonies, it was a city where ex-soldiers were given important civic privileges. These settlers of Antioch were veterans of the Alauda Legion—"the Lark"—a legion raised in Gaul by Julius Cæsar, which bore on its standards the regimental badge of a skylark.

The Romans took over a city that had had a long and interesting history as one of the sixteen Antiochs which Seleucus Nicator had dotted about the Hellenistic world and had named in honour of his father, Antiochus. A magnificent site had been chosen for Antioch in Pisidia: a hill overlooking the plain of the Anthius and backed by the immense pinnacles of the Sultan Dagh, in whose corries the snow sometimes lies until midsummer.

As soon as the city became a colony, its history as a democratic Greek city came to an end and it developed as a Roman city modelled as far as possible on Rome. The leading citizens were old soldiers who, no matter what their racial origin, were probably determined to be more Roman than the Romans. They issued proclamations in Latin and conducted their municipal business on the Roman plan. Probably the intellectual section of the populace was Greek. The usual Jewish trading colony, perhaps originally a settlement from Hellenistic times, proved the truth of the old adage that trade follows the flag. The slaves were probably native Anatolians.

This city, the military capital of the Roman Province of Galatia, stood within its wall, a strong, thriving child of Rome. When he came to Antioch along the mountain road from Perga, Paul must have looked at the Latin inscriptions on the public buildings and on the statues with the feeling that he was nearer Rome than he had ever been before. He had preached the Gospel in Syria, in Cilicia and in Cyprus. But he had not yet preached it in a Roman colony. When he went to bed in Pisidian Antioch he would hear the night-watch give their commands in Latin; and he would think that on this hillside in Asia Minor had been flung a reflection of the capital of the world.

Paul and Barnabas addressed themselves to the Jews of Pisidian Antioch, and were welcomed in the local synagogue. They spoke there on two Sabbaths and their message was at first well received, until the Orthodox Jews opposed them and rejected the Gospel. Then the Apostles made a pronounce-ment that has rightly been called one of the most important ever spoken:

"It was necessary that the word of God should first have been spoken to you: but seeing ye put it from you, and judge yourselves unworthy of everlasting life, *lo, we turn to the Gentiles.*"

In that moment Paul and Barnabas gave the remote hill town of Pisidian Antioch a position among those places in which the major events of Christianity have occurred. See how the chain has developed since the Crucifixion: Jerusalem, where St. Stephen, the first martyr, died; Damascus, where

IN THE STEPS OF ST. PAUL

Paul was baptized; Jaffa, where St. Peter baptized the first Gentile; Syrian Antioch, where the first missionary church was founded; and now in Pisidian Antioch came the pronouncement that flung wide the door of Christianity to the world. *"Lo, we turn to the Gentiles."* It was no longer necessary for a Christian to stoop through the narrow door of the synagogue. In this little patch of Rome the two missionaries "waxed bold" and proclaimed the universal Christian Church.

If Michael Angelo had painted this scene, I think that in the clouds above Pisidian Antioch he would have traced the outline of St. Peter's.

In the *Acts of the Apostles*, the last three verses of chapter thirteen and the first six verses of chapter fourteen describe the flight of Paul and Barnabas from Pisidian Antioch and from the next city which they visited, Iconium. It will be noticed that the methods employed by the Orthodox Jews to stir up trouble against the Apostles varies in each of these two cities.

When the Jews of Antioch wished to expel the Apostles, we read that "they stirred up the devout and honourable women." Now, why did they do this? The reason is that they were living in a Roman colony and did not dare to take the matter into their own hands. These "devout and honourable women" were the proselytes who gathered about every synagogue. They were often influential women, the wives and daughters of the ruling caste in the city. The Jews knew perfectly well that if they applied to the Roman magistrates for a summons against Paul and Barnabas, they would receive no satisfaction.

"Have these men broken the law?" would be the question. And the Jews would have been compelled to say, no.

The indirect approach, however, was effective. Each woman pestered her husband to get rid of the "blasphemous visitors."

The rabbi, who was such a good man and such a friend of the Roman State, had told them how dangerous the preachers were, how disloyal to the cult of the Emperor, and what an insult to the Cæsar was this new creed of a king who would some day rule the world! Very cleverly, and with no fuss, the Jews achieved their ends.

But what happened in Iconium, a city only sixty miles away? The Jews there behaved differently. There was no whispering to "devout and honourable women." There was no oblique approach to the city fathers. Instead, we see violent crowds in the streets and something like a riot. But the city was divided. "Part held with the Jews and part with the Apostles." The end of it was that Paul and Barnabas, learning of a plot to stone them, considered it prudent to escape to Lystra, a Roman colony eighteen miles away.

What is the explanation of this? Why should the attitude of the Jews have been different in these two cities? The reason is that Iconium was not a Roman colony: it was a democratic Greek city where the populace held the power. The most effective way to expel the Apostles was obviously to create a public argument, to rouse the whole city against them, and then sit back and allow democracy to do its worst.

I think these few verses of *Acts* are a good example of the meticulous accuracy of Luke, and of the deeper meaning that is to be read into his words. Even if coins did not tell us that, in the time of Paul, Antioch was a Roman colony and Iconium a Greek democracy, the action of the Jews in these two cities would indicate their origin as clearly as any inscription in Latin or Greek.

2

Sixty miles to the west of Konya, near a Turkish town called Yalovach, the broken arches of a Roman aqueduct stand on a bleak hill. There is little else to show that Pisidian Antioch once stood there, except that the rocks bear the signs of having been flattened and shaped, not by the imperious sweep of ice or the tempestuous strokes of fire, but slowly and painfully with the picks and axes of men.

In ancient times the aqueduct marched over hill and hollow to the foothills of the Sultan Dagh, where it received water from a rock tunnel and bore it arch-high to the city of Pisidian Antioch.

The more I explored the ruined cities of Asia Minor, the more truly I realized that the history of man in this country was writ literally in water. Sometimes, after travelling far to reach a certain place, I have come to it through mountain gorges where even the eagle and the hawk find it difficult to live, and on some slope or summit I have seen evidence that men had once built libraries of marble in that place and had sat in a half-circle on the hill, listening to the words of Æschylus. Travelling across a burning plain, I have come to a mound covered with little stones which whiten the ground for miles. I pick one up and see that it is a chip of marble that had come long ago in a ship from Greece; another stone is red, a chip of porphyry from Egypt. They are the only signs that centuries ago philosophers argued beneath the columns of a marketplace, that sculptors strove to create beauty there, that merchants unloaded spices, perfumes and gold for the adornment of fastidious, painted women.

How is it possible that such desolate clefts in the hills and such cruel deserts could have supported the life of the classical world? The answer is, of course, water. It may not be visible there to-day. The stream may have dried up, or it may be running to waste on the wrong side of the hill. But wherever you encounter a ruin in an inhospitable and uninhabited part of Asia Minor, you may be sure that the Greeks or the Romans had once built an aqueduct that bore a sparkling stream from a neighbouring mountain into the heart of the city.

A civilization built on aqueducts is a perilous one. Unless you are strong enough to defend your life-giving archway, one barbarian with a pick-axe can turn your city into a parched desert. Once the aqueduct is broken, the life of the city is ended. Asphodels will grow in the cracks of the *agora*, the roofs will fall, crushing the marble shelves of libraries, birds will nest in the dry cups of the public fountains, and the jackal will nurse her young in the temple court.

And this has happened to the shining cities of the Hellenistic Age. The barbarians allowed the water to spill itself into the earth. They pitched their tents near the break in the aqueduct so that they could scoop up the water in their hands. So century by century the walls of the cities have fallen. The marble streets have been rent asunder to provide stones for sheep-folds. Shining pillars, brought in ships from Greece and from Egypt, have been pulled down to be inserted horizontally into walls. Graves have been rifled for hidden gold and for marble coffins: the carved sarcophagus, in which a Roman was laid to rest, makes, after all, a perfect drinking-trough for goats.

Therefore, in the broken aqueduct of Pisidian Antioch you can read the tragic history of the downfall of Ephesus, of Miletus, of Pergamum, of Hierapolis, and of other proud cities of Asia Minor, which in ancient times shone among the great names of the world.

3

Nothing could more vividly illustrate the darkness that descended on Asia Minor after the Turkish conquest than the fact that the site of Pisidian Antioch was lost until a century ago, that Lystra was unknown until 1885, and Derbe until 1888.

The first of the three cities to be discovered was Pisidian Antioch. It was found in 1833 by a Cornish clergyman, Francis Vyvyan Jago Arundell, British chaplain at Smyrna, in the course of a journey into the interior of Turkey. This man, who added so much to the knowledge of New Testament geography, is buried in the churchyard of Landulph, in Cornwall, where the river Tamar, flowing westward, forms a wide stretch of water called Kingsmere Lake. In the little church is also buried Theodore Palæologus, a descendant of the last Emperor of the East, to whom Arundell was in some remote way related, for he belonged to a family that numbered among its more exotic memories intermarriage with this last of the Byzantine Imperial family.

Theodore was fourth in descent from Thomas, brother of Constantine XIII, who died defending the walls of Constantinople against the Turk. Seeking exile in England, Theodore married the daughter of William Balls of Hadleigh, in Suffolk, and one of their daughters married an Arundell of Landulph. It was while on a visit to Cornwall in 1636 that Theodore Palæologus died and was buried in the little Cornish church.

So the winds of fate, that blow so strangely, have placed the man who discovered Pisidian Antioch side by side in Cornish earth with the man whose imperial ancestor died in defending Christianity against Islam. The beginning and the end of Christianity in Asia Minor may be said to be linked together in this unlikely spot.

While living in Smyrna, Arundell found his natural tastes for archæology and oriental studies sharpened by contact with the Morier family. James Morier was a distinguished diplomat and traveller, the author of two admirable books on Persia and of that gem of Eastern life and psychology, *Adventures of Hajji Baba of Ispahan.* Arundell married James Morier's sister.

His discovery of Pisidian Antioch greatly assisted the identification of various other sites, for once the site of Antioch was established, other ruins in the neighbourhood fell naturally into their places on the map.

Arundell set off in search of Lystra and Derbe, but, as the winter rains were expected at any moment and he feared that the consequent seas of mud would prevent his return to Smyrna, he was reluctantly obliged, when only one day's march from Konya, to abandon his quest.

Driven out of Pisidian Antioch, Paul and Barnabas decided to seek safety in Iconium, sixty miles away to the south-east. They stayed in that city for a long time. The intellectually curious Greeks, ever anxious to hear some new thing, flocked to hear them. The Word fell upon good ground and on bad. Five short verses in the *Acts* describe their missionary activities in Iconium, but there is not one word about the conversion of the ardent and noble virgin, Thecla.

This remarkable and charming story is told in the apocryphal *Acts of Paul and Thecla,* written probably in the second century by an unknown presbyter of Asia. The story gained enormous popularity in the early world and St. Thecla became one of the most famous of all Greek saints. Justinian built a church in her honour near the Julian Gate at Constantinople, and there was also a Church of St. Thecla on the Via Ostiensis, not far from St. Paul's-without-the-Wall at Rome. Thanks largely to the researches of Sir William Ramsay, scholars are now willing to see in the story of Paul and Thecla either an account of something that actually happened in Iconium, or a story which accurately reflects not only the atmosphere of Apostolic times, but also the lasting impression which Paul's preaching created in Asia Minor.

The story begins with Paul's flight from Pisidian Antioch. A certain man of Iconium, called Onesiphorus, knowing that Paul was on his way to that city, went out along the "Royal Road" in order to intercept him and offer hospitality. Onesiphorus had never seen Paul, but he had been given a description of him. Therefore he stood where the road branched to Lystra, scanning the faces of the travellers who came past.

"And he saw Paul coming, a man little of stature, thin-haired upon the head, crooked in the legs, of good state of body, with eyebrows joining, and nose somewhat hooked, full of grace: for sometimes he appeared like a man, and sometimes he had the face of an angel."

After greeting the Apostle, Onesiphorus walked with him to Iconium, and "when Paul entered into the house of Onesiphorus, there was great joy, and bowing of knees and breaking of bread." Now this house was overlooked by one of the mansions of Iconium in which lived a rich woman, Theocleia, and her eighteen years old daughter, Thecla. Like the houses of Pompeii and Herculaneum, these dwellings were separated by a road only a few feet in width, and it was therefore possible for anyone at a window of Thecla's house to hear a voice raised in the courtyard of the house near by. As Thecla sat at her window, she could hear the voice of Paul preaching in defence of chastity: "and she stirred not from the window, but was led onward by faith rejoicing exceedingly: and further, when she saw many women and virgins entering in to Paul, she also earnestly desired to be accounted worthy to stand before Paul's face and to hear the word of Christ; for she had not yet seen the appearance of Paul, but only heard his speech."

Her mother was alarmed and worried by the change in Thecla. So was the girl's sweetheart, a young Greek named Thamyris.

"For three days and three nights Thecla ariseth not from the window," said the mother to the young man, "neither to eat nor to drink, but looking earnestly as it were upon a joyful spectacle, she so attendeth to a stranger who teachest deceitful and various words, that I wonder how the great modesty of the maiden is so hardly beset. . . ."

They both went up to the window, where the girl sat as if enchanted.

"Thecla, my betrothed," cried Thamyris, "why sittest thou thus? and what passion is it that holdeth thee in amaze?"

The girl did not seem to hear.

"Thecla," cried the mother, "why sittest thou thus looking downward and answering nothing, but as one stricken?"

But Thecla continued to sit in her enchantment, listening for the sound of Paul's voice.

Thamyris then plotted to bring Paul before the governor. The Apostle was charged and flung into prison. When Thecla heard of it, she came out of her dream and became a resolute, self-willed young woman. She stole out at night, bribing the door-keeper of her mother's house with a valuable bracelet and clutching to her breast a silver mirror with which she bribed her way into the prison.

"And so went in to Paul and sat by his feet and heard the wonderful works of God. And Paul feared not at all but walked in the confidence of God: and her faith also was increased as she kissed his chains."

When they found the girl in the morning, they took her with Paul before the governor. Paul was scourged and expelled from the city, and Thecla was ordered to be burnt as an example to the women of Iconium.

"Now the boys and the maidens brought wood and hay to burn Thecla: and when she was brought in naked, the governor wept and marvelled at the power that was in her. And they laid the wood, and the executioner bade her mount upon the pyre: and she, making the sign of the cross, went up upon the wood. And they lighted it, and though a great fire blazed forth, the fire took no hold on her; for God had compassion on her, and caused a sound under the earth, and a cloud overshadowed her above, full of rain and hail, and all the vessels of it was poured out so that many were in peril of death and the fire was quenched and Thecla was preserved."

Sir William Ramsay, who has analyzed the story of Thecla in his book *The Church in the Roman Empire,* states that the whole incident of the trial and burning at Iconium must be a later interpolation. There was no Roman governor in Iconium at that period. The judges would have been Greek city magistrates. But an analysis of the work leads Sir William Ramsay to the conclusion that the groundwork is a genuine first century story which later scribes have touched up and re-written. He cites the unreality of the burning incident, which I have quoted, with the realistic and vivid description that follows of Thecla's adventures in the arena at Pisidian Antioch.

The story resumes with Paul, who was hiding in a disused tomb in some solitary place on the outskirts of Iconium, in company with Onesiphorus and his family. Paul had mourned Thecla as dead, believing her to have perished in Iconium. But she was searching everywhere for him and happening to encounter the son of Onesiphorus, who was out buying bread for the fugitives, she was led to Paul's hiding-place. She said to him:

"I will cut my hair round about and follow thee withersoever thou goest."

But Paul would not hear of this.

Onesiphorus and his family returned to Iconium, while Paul and Thecla went together to Pisidian Antioch. They approached the city on the eve of a festival. There were to be shows of wild beasts in the amphitheatre. As they entered Antioch, they encountered a great procession in which was a "certain Syriarch" named Alexander, an important high-priest. This man, struck by Thecla's beauty, stopped and embraced her and, it seems, tried to purchase her from Paul. Then occurred what Sir William Ramsay rightly calls "the detestable incident of Paul's denial and desertion of Thecla," in which he sees again the hand of a later editor of the story.

"I know not the woman of whom thou speakest, neither is she mine," Paul is made to say as he disappears in the crowd. In the earlier versions of the story, says Sir William Ramsay, Paul was not present; Thecla in her trouble called on his name, "and the dull wit of a later time thought that this implied his bodily presence."

However, Thecla, finding herself in Alexander's embrace, "rent his cloak and took the wreath from his head and made him a mocking-stock." The offence was serious. She had assaulted the high priest while he was wearing his priestly vestments. She had committed sacrilege, and was condemned to exposure in the arena during the forthcoming festival.

A remarkable touch of realism is the fury which this decision creates among the women of Pisidian Antioch. The city was at this period one of the newly-founded Roman colonies and was, perhaps, unaccustomed to the brutal sport of the arena, which was never popular among the Greeks. Another good touch is the presence in the city of Queen Tryphæna, with whom Thecla is lodged. This woman was Queen of Pontus in the time of Paul, and would have been nearly sixty years old when the Apostle made his first missionary journey. We learn that she became deeply attached to the unfortunate Thecla, and bewailed that "so great beauty was to be cast unto the beasts."

The scene in the arena is extraordinarily vivid, with its suggestion of noise, shouting, and the roar of animals. Some spectators shout, "Bring in the sacrilegious one!", while the women scream: "Away with the city for this unlawful deed! Away with us all, thou pro-consul! It is a bitter sight, an evil judgment!"

"But Thecla, being taken out of the hand of Tryphæna, was stripped and a girdle put upon her, and was cast into the stadium: and lions and bears were set against her. And a fierce lioness running to her lay down at her feet, and the press of women cried aloud. And a bear ran upon her; but the lioness ran and met him and tore the bear in sunder. And again a lion, trained against men, which was Alexander's, ran upon her, and the lioness wrestled with him and was slain along with him. And the women bewailed yet more, seeing that the lioness also that succoured her was dead. Then did they put in many beasts, while she stood and stretched forth her hands and prayed."

Her prayer is not given in the Greek version from which I am quoting—as translated by M. R. James in *The Apocryphal New Testament*—but it is given in the Syriac version. It is a lovely and touching prayer:

" 'My Lord and my God, the Father of our Lord Jesus, the Messiah, Thou art the helper of the persecuted, and thou art the companion of the poor; behold Thy handmaiden, for lo, the shame of women is uncovered in me, and I stand in the midst of all this people. My Lord and my God, remember Thy handmaiden in this hour.'

"And when she had ended her prayer, she saw a great tank full of water, and said: 'Now is it time that I should wash myself.' And she cast herself in, saying: 'In the name of Jesus Christ do I baptize myself on the last day.' And all the women seeing it, and all the people wept, saying: 'Cast not thyself into the water': so that even the governor wept that so great beauty should be devoured by seals. So, then, she cast herself into the water in the name of Jesus Christ; and the seals, seeing the light of a flash of fire, floated dead on the top of the water. And there was about her a cloud so that neither did the beasts touch her, nor was she seen to be naked.

"Now the women, when other more fearful beasts were put in, shrieked aloud, and some cast leaves, and others nard, others cassia, and some balsam, so that there was a multitude of odours; and all the beasts that were struck thereby were held as it were in sleep and touched her not; so that Alexander said to the governor: 'I have some bulls exceeding fearful, let us bind the criminal to them.' And the governor, frowning, allowed it, saying: 'Do that thou wilt.' And they bound her by the feet between the bulls, and put hot irons under their bellies that they might be the more enraged and kill her. They then leapt forward; but the flame that burned about her, burned through the ropes, and she was as one not bound."

That was the last of her ordeals. The governor called her and asked:

"Who art thou?"

"I am the handmaid of the living God," she replied.

He ordered garments to be brought and said:

"Put on these garments."

"He that clad me when I was naked among the beasts the same in the day of judgment will clothe me with salvation," replied Thecla.

She took the garments and put them on; and, as the governor released her, the women of Pisidian Antioch shouted "as with one mouth" until all the city shook.

Thecla then dressed herself as a boy and went in search of Paul. After long wandering she found him at Myra, and her greeting is, I think, the loveliest thing in all this naïve story:

"I have received the washing, O Paul," she said, "for He that hath worked together with thee in the Gospel hath worked with me also in my baptizing."

Paul departed on his mission and Thecla returned to her

native town to teach the word of God. Legend became busy with her history, first at Seleucia of Isauria and, later, in Rome.

It is impossible to say how much history is contained in this curious and simple romance. But I think anyone who reads the *Acts of Paul and Thecla* will agree that whoever wrote it had sat in the amphitheatres and had witnessed the Roman games.

I am sure that most of us will be content to accept the story of Thecla as a legend of great beauty which may have some historic foundation, a story so early that its sweetness and simplicity carry us back to the fresh dawn of Christianity.

4

Every morning my friends in Konya would arrive in my room while I was still in bed. Coffee would appear on little trays, my friends would sit on the bed, and I would hold a motley levee while they spread out my maps and proposed expeditions to places I had no intention of exploring. I began to like these Turks. They were simple and curiously child-like, and pleasantly free from the Levantine vices of procrastination, untruthfulness, and avarice.

I wished that I could speak Turkish, if only to enter into the wild archæological enthusiasms of an elderly ex-school-master who was never far from my doorstep. He was the only archæologist in Konya, and there was a common bond of brotherhood between us, despite the fact that we could never hope to exchange a thought save through an interpreter. He bore the name of Gaffar Totaysalgir. I shall never forget Gaffar in his old brown coat, gentle brown eyes in a lined face, and his air of meek patience that always suffered a brilliant transformation at mention of the word "Hittite."

On three occasions Hassan, Gaffar and I tried to motor to

Lystra, but every time a sudden cloud-burst defeated us. These cloud-bursts, which often break without any warning over Asia Minor, bear a notable resemblance to the miraculous interventions in the apocryphal gospels. At one moment the sun is shining, and at the next you are cowering beneath the lash of a storm that soaks a square mile and leaves the rest of the country as dry as a bone.

I was anxious to follow the steps of the Apostles from Konya to Lystra. Although only about twenty-five miles away, this is a journey of considerable difficulty until summer has dried and baked the earth.

I was fortunate in the services of an excellent driver, a large, collarless Turk, animated, it seemed to me, by an overwhelming desire to take me wherever I wanted to go in the excellent little American saloon car that he had somehow managed to acquire.

The towns in this part of Turkey possess roads which start convincingly enough in various directions, but suddenly give up and dwindle into mule-paths and camel-tracks. Such difficulties served only to inspire my driver. He would give a shout of joy and, driving his gallant car over rocks and along the edges of ploughed land, would neatly dodge intervening boulders and plunge with a mighty splash into some mountain stream. The smell of burning brakes only made him laugh. When we came down heavily on the back springs, he would rub his head with rueful amusement after it had cracked against the roof. I was ashamed to pay him at the end of the day because I was sure that we had taken more out of the car in solid damage than I had paid for the day's hire.

It is really absurd to make these motoring journeys in Turkey; yet if I had demanded a horse or a mule, which is still the only sensible way to visit remote places, I should have been regarded as eccentric. Motor salesmanship has entered Turkey well in advance of the motoring road, and, as the aver-

age Turkish driver has never seen a real road, he has no idea
that every day he performs with the greatest nonchalance feats
which would turn a trophy driver pale with horror.

However, the morning came which my rough-riding motorist and my various friends and advisers considered propitious;
and so off we set. The road runs due south over the plain,
with a magnificent view of the twin peaks of St. Philip and
St. Thecla lifting themselves about five miles away to the
southwest.

We made the inevitable departure from the road and began
to bump over a rough mule-path leading over a hill. As we
topped a rise of ground, we saw, lying to the far south, the
most impressive mountain barrier I have seen in any part of
the world. Blue in the distance, their mighty crests white with
snow, this screen of heights stood up with clouds massed upon
them. I was looking at the Taurus Mountains from the north.
I had seen them from the south at Tarsus, and they were the
mountains that I had seen from Cyprus across sixty miles of
sea. From the slopes of Mount Troödos these mountains had
looked like icebergs floating on the distant horizon.

We made our way painfully across open country, edging
round ploughland, striking off over stony hills, and coming
at length to a fairly good track. At this pleasant moment we
discovered that we were on the wrong road.

Gaffar was delighted! He knew of a wonderful village in
the mountains about six miles farther on, where we should see
amazing ruins . . . simply amazing. It was really good fortune, he said, that had led us from the road. There was little
to see at Lystra; but at the place he would take me were many,
many wonderful things. Only six miles to the foot of the
mountains, and he knew a man in a village who would give
us horses or mules; for we should then have to leave the car,
because there was no good road like this one. His hat fell off
as his head struck the roof of the car; and on we plunged.

Ascending a steep track into which water had been diverted from a stream, so that the path was indistinguishable from a mountain torrent, the car stopped, the wheels revolved, and we were stuck. The car was covered with mud. The wheels sank heavily in the water. We got out and piled brushwood in front of them. We carried stones and flung them in the bed of the torrent. At last the driver went to the back of the car, where, I discovered, he kept a spade as a spare part. He dug two new wheel-tracks. We then piled more thorn and dry wood in the water, and weighted them with stones. Settling himself at the wheel, he reversed the car, struck the two tracks, and swung out above the banks of the stream. It was a fine bit of obstacle-driving.

In another half-hour or so we descended into a green and lovely gorge. The hills on either side were of friable rock that had crumbled away, exposing a pillar-like formation that ran for mile after mile at a uniform height on the hills. At the end of the ravine we saw an isolated mountain of this grey rock, facing the gorge in a most impressive way. From a distance it bore a resemblance to some stupendous crusading town. It appeared to have mighty walls which enclosed a tight mass of crowded streets, turrets, church spires and crenellated battlements. As we drew nearer, we saw that this impression was created by the columnar formation of the rock. The entire hill was volcanic tufa which had somehow resisted the disintegrating process that had carved the valley. The grey rock was partly covered with a dark green lichen, giving the hill a queerly spotted appearance. There was a Turkish village on the top whose mud walls made it almost invisible until we were within a mile or two. From this distance we saw that the tall cones of tufa were honey-combed with small black holes, the entrances to ancient dwellings, some of them hundreds of feet up on apparently sheer walls of rock.

We left the car and started to climb a path up this extraor-

dinary hill. Gaffar said that the name of the village was Kilistra. I believe that Sir Charles Wilson and Sir William Ramsay
visited the place in 1883, and there are seven lines describing
it in Professor Sterritt's *Wolfe Expedition to Asia Minor*;
there is, so far as I know, nothing else written about it.

As we climbed about the hill, we discovered that the rocks
had been carved into cave-like dwellings and into small Byzantine churches, several of them with Greek crosses carved
over the porches and interiors which bear traces of frescoes.
The most remarkable is a miniature church beautifully carved
from one detached column of tufa. It is a tiny cruciform building which could hold perhaps twenty people. The central
tower is square, so are the east and west ends of the building,
but the transeptal arms are rounded. We had to crawl inside
because the building was more than half full of accumulated
leaves and bracken. Apart from its curiosity as a building
carved from one block of stone, the church has a curious air
of being in miniature. Its proportions are admirable and the
design, as I say, suggests a building a hundred times the size.

At first I thought that these churches and cave-dwellings
must have been the retreat of anchorites, but on the other side
of the hill I discovered a long, sloping ramp leading down to
the plain and commanded on either side by two watch-towers
cut from the solid rock. If the Christians who carved these
churches were monks, they must have belonged to a militant
order, for the only weak spot in their fastness was defended
with consummate skill.

Churches and rock-cuttings similar to those of Kilistra exist
also in Cappadocia, round the district of Urgub. A friend of
mine, who visited them from Syria, has sent me recently a
number of photographs in which the resemblance is obvious.
The rock formation is the same soft, volcanic tufa, and the
architectural style is similar. I do not know if these churches
have ever been dated. It is clear that the people who once

lived there were either driven from more comfortable surroundings, or took refuge in this remote spot in order to
isolate themselves from their fellows.

The little Turkish village of Kilistra is some way back on
the crest of the hill. The villagers were more primitive than
any I had yet seen in Turkey. European dress had not been
very successful, although I did see a few young boys wearing
the peaked cap that proclaims an elementary school. All the
girls, and most of the women, wore old-fashioned baggy Turkish trousers and home-made moccasins of skin with slightly
up-turned toes. The men were, as usual, ruined in appearance
by cloth caps.

Behind the village rose a dark, dome-shaped mountain
called Ali Sumasü Dagh. Beyond it, stretched the snow-fields
of the Taurus. I discovered that Ali Sumasü Dagh was the
mountain which the optimistic Gaffar intended to climb on
mule-back. One glance at it told me that if we attempted to
do this, we should spend the night in the open; and, to my
astonishment, he agreed. We left the queer, stalagmite village
and made sure, this time, of the right road to Lystra.

5

The site of Lystra was unknown until 1885, when an American, Professor J. R. Sitlington Sterrett, had the good fortune
to discover in its original position an inscribed altar which
gave the name and the colonial status of the town.

One of the most picturesque incidents recorded in the *Acts*
took place in Lystra. Paul and Barnabas had prudently retreated from the storm which the Jews in Iconium had worked
up against them. The Roman colony of Lystra would not have
had much sympathy for the prejudices of its Greek neighbour,
and was an obvious and sensible place of retreat.

As the Apostles walked the streets of Lystra, they saw a sight which is still so common in the East: a man who had been crippled from birth and had never walked. He was one of those poor creatures who drag themselves about in the dust of Eastern cities and sit stretching out their hands at the gates. Paul, "steadfastly beholding him," saw that he had faith to be healed. He commanded the cripple to stand upright, and he did so. The people were amazed. They believed that the gods had come down to earth in the likeness of men.

They thought that Barnabas was Jupiter, King of Gods, and that Paul, the more talkative, was Mercury, the messenger of the gods. It was natural that the peasantry of Lystra should have believed this, for the story of Philemon and Baucis was localized in the neighbourhood. No doubt every man, woman and child who saw the Apostles knew this story by heart: how Jupiter and Mercury came down to earth disguised as poor mortals and were turned away by all men save an old couple called Philemon and Baucis. Ovid tells the story in the *Metamorphoses*:

> *A pool stands near, once habitable land,*
> *And now the haunt of wild fowl of the mere,*
> *Divers and coots. Here once in mortal shape*
> *Came Jupiter and his son Mercury,*
> *Lord of the wand, but of his wings bereft.*
> *House after house they tried, in search of rest;*
> *House after house was barred; save one alone,*
> *A tiny cottage thatched with reeds and straw.*

* * * * *

> *Now when the heavenly pair drew nigh the house,*
> *And stooped their heads to pass the lintel low,*
> *The old man set a seat, and bade them rest;*
> *And Baucis, careful housewife, on the seat*
> *Spread some rude covering from her humble store.*

The end of the story would commend itself to the peasants of Lystra, for, so the legend goes, shortly after the appearance of the gods a flood submerged the plain and all those who had turned Jupiter and Mercury from their doors perished, while the old couple, Philemon and Baucis, were not only carried into safety, but their humble dwelling was transformed into a splendid temple of which they became the priests.

Therefore, how natural it was for these superstitious peasants to imagine, as they saw the cripple leap and walk, that once again Jupiter and Mercury had descended from Olympus. On this occasion they were determined to recognize the gods.

"The gods have come down to us in the likeness of men!" they shouted "in the speech of Lycaonia." This is the only time that Paul and Barnabas are mentioned among the native-speaking tribes of Asia Minor. All their other contacts were with Greek-speaking city folk. But these people of Lystra were the native Lycaonians, the rabble of the Roman colony.

With surprise and dismay the Apostles watch the crowd rush shouting to the Temple of Jupiter, and their intention becomes clear only when the priest is seen advancing with oxen garlanded for sacrifice. This destroys the last vestige of self-composure and both Paul and Barnabas rend their garments and rush among the people, crying at the top of their voices: "Sirs, why do ye these things? We also are men of like passions with you!"

Only with difficulty do they restrain the eager, simple Lycaonians from doing sacrifice in their honour.

The end of their stay in Lystra came suddenly. Jews from Iconium pursued them, and found it easy to influence the populace of Lystra. The very people who were ready to hail the Apostles as gods now picked up stones to fling at them. Paul was stoned and left for dead outside the town. But the

disciples rescued and healed him, and on the following day
he went with Barnabas to Derbe.

We came down from the hills into quiet, pastoral country.
There were groups of slender poplar trees. The fields were
green with growing wheat. A company of storks stood in a
marshy place, fishing for frogs. We came to a stream spanned
by a tumble-down bridge of seven arches; every large stone
in it had come from some ancient city. There were big,
squared stones that had been part of some large and imposing
building of Roman or Byzantine date, and I saw several sculptured tombstones inserted upside down. Soon after crossing
the bridge, we came to the mud-walled village of Khatyn
Serai. A pack of dogs surrounded us, baying in a circle, while
the children of the village formed an equally excited outer
group.

The head man drove away the dogs, and each time one of
us turned round, we unconsciously drove away the children.
They would creep up like a herd of deer, slowly, step by step,
but as soon as they saw our eyes on them, they would turn and
dash for cover and we would see small ragged bundles and
bare feet in hasty retreat to the nearest wall.

A villager offered to guide us to the site of Lystra, which was
about a mile away. We saw a long, low hill covered with stones
and minute fragments of ancient pottery. I scraped with my
stick and unearthed the rim and the base of a red bowl. There
was not one ancient building left, yet the earth had that uneasy look which suggests that something is concealed beneath
it. There was a sheepfold on the side of the hill whose walls
were built of large brown stones, some of them three or four
feet in length. The thatched roof was upheld by a central
roof-tree. From the inside I counted over fifty large squared
stones which must have come either from the city wall of

Lystra or from some notable building of ancient date.

The only object of interest on this desolate site is the altar, still standing on the hill in the position where Professor Sterrett found it in 1885. It was an extraordinarily interesting relic to me, because it must have been there when Paul came to Lystra. It is a massive, carved stone about three and a half feet high and twelve inches thick, much damaged and cracked, but still bearing in clear-cut Latin characters the following inscription:

DIV AUG (ustum)

COL (onia) IUL (ia) FE-

LIX GEMINA

LUSTRA

CONSE-

CRAVIT

D (ecreto) D (ecurionum).

A literal translation would be: "Gemina Lustra, the Fortunate, being a Julian colony, dedicated Augustus Cæsar as a god: [the altar] being decreed by the Urban Council."

It is interesting that this last surviving relic of Lystra should preserve the Roman spelling of the name, Lustra, for so it also appears on the few known coins of the colony. Lystra is the Greek form of a possibly native Anatolian word—such as Kilistra or Ilistra—and the Romans preferred to call it the colony Lustra, to give it, suggests Sir William Ramsay, an apparent connection with the Latin *Lustrum*.

The hill has never been excavated. The city that once stood there has been allowed to fall into ruin, while all the large stones remaining above ground have been gradually carted away to build the neighbouring villages. The capital of a massive marble column, projecting from the earth, fires the imagination with thoughts of the discoveries that may some-day be made here.

In the village of Khatyn Serai the word had gone forth that a stone-gazing foreigner had come again to those parts. With the utmost politeness I was conducted into backyards and to the walls of sheep-folds and cow-sheds, while inscribed stones were eagerly pointed out to me by the elders the women and the children standing on the roofs and gazing solemnly down from a distance.

Darkness overtook us, as I feared it would, on the return journey to Konya. A cloud-burst turned the narrow track to a glutinous red porridge in which we crawled sideways, our headlights revealing two bright beams of descending rain. The car skidded up a bank and, in some miraculous way, hung there. We were at first afraid to get out in case we upset the balance and flung the car on its side. When we finally clambered out, we stepped ankle-deep in mud and one glance told us that it was useless to attempt to put our shoulders to the wheel.

Gaffar said we were six miles from the nearest building, an abandoned khan. We counted our food: two hard-boiled eggs, a piece of bread, and three oranges. While we stood in the shower-bath of rain, the burly figure of the driver was seen busily digging a new road. He shouted to us to find stones. We filled the two miniature streams which he had dug with anything that was likely to give the tires a grip on the earth; then we waited with bated breath while that amazing driver gently eased his car forward, until one more inch seemed to threaten an instant overthrow, and performed what had seemed impossible.

In an hour's time we saw the lights of the town. Konya, which once had seemed to me so primitive, so far away, so sundered from the world, now took on the character of a metropolis.

As we held our dripping garments to the stove, the mournful Gaffar said that perhaps it was a good thing we had not climbed Ali Sumasü Dagh. The driver tossed back a glass of *raki*, wrung his cap out in the wood-box, and asked if I should want him in the morning. As a study in composure, I place the Turk somewhere between the Scot and the Chinaman.

6

Next morning the sun shone over the Lycaonian Plain as we motored to the south-east to find the site of Derbe.

I had already crossed this plain in the train. Closer contact with it, however, the feel of the cold wind, the sight of the track winding away among stones and the fear that rain might fall and maroon us in miles of mud, gave me a more intimate feeling of its bareness and its size.

Once again I thought what a strange experience it was to leave the luxuriant, semi-tropical coast of Asia Minor and to climb to this savage land where bare mountains stand sentinel over a barren plain lifted four thousand feet above sea level.

Kara Dagh, which rose on our left, is the mountain of "the thousand and one churches," a picturesque local term for the ruined Byzantine churches which cover it. It is an ominous and romantic mountain, lifting its graceful curves from the brown plain. Clouds were anchored on its summits; owing to some peculiarity of the light, the whole mass was blue-black in colour and I knew why the Turks call it Kara Dagh, the Black Mountain.

I shall always regret that I had no time to explore Kara Dagh. Its Byzantine ruins are among the most remarkable in the world, dating from the fifth to the eleventh centuries, and nowhere else is it possible to study in one place the development of six centuries of Christian architecture.

We travelled for many a mile with this dark mountain on our left, until to the south enormous mountains shouldered the sky, with mud villages like nomad encampments on their lower slopes, crouched thirstily in the path of the snow-water.

The only signs of life on this plain are slow-moving flocks of sheep which wander heads down to the iron-hard earth. They are guarded by ferocious white dogs nearly as big as Great Danes. These creatures, observing the unusual sight of a car bumping its way across the solitude, would detach themselves from the flock and rush at us with a deep-throated baying, leaping ahead and baring their white teeth to our wheels.

They wore collars fitted with four-inch iron spikes as a protection against wolves, who always go for their throats. This spiked collar was once common throughout Europe, and the brass studs on the collars of our bull-dogs are a survival of spikes and a link with days before the last wolf was slain in England.

Most travellers in Asia Minor have commented on the ferocity of the sheep dogs, but few have praised their splendid bodies and magnificent heads. They are creamy white, with two bars of dark brown running down the muzzle below the eyes and a shading of lighter brown from the eyes upward to the ears. In middle age they develop a mastiff-like jowl and an intellectual wrinkle of fur over the eyes. Their speed when running is astonishing for such heavy animals. They are absolutely fearless and will tackle, single-jawed, two or three wolves. I am told that the wolves in Asia Minor never hunt in packs. Panthers are occasionally found in the Taurus, and so are bears, but the wolf is found everywhere and is the great enemy of the sheep-dog.

In infancy the sheep-dog is an amusing and delightful little fellow. He exhibits the most touching astonishment when picked up and made a fuss of; for such things do not usually happen to puppies in Asia Minor. His muzzle in puppy-hood is a uniform blackish-brown, just as if he had pushed his nose into a bag of soot.

7

On the edge of the plain, and backed by a snow-dusted mountain called Haji Baba—Pilgrim Father—we came to all that remains of the city of Derbe. As at Lystra, there is nothing left but a huge mound called Gudelisin, strewn with fragments of broken pottery.

Walking over the hill, I picked up pieces of granite, marble, and porphyry, evidence of the splendid temples and statues that had once stood there. Again, like Lystra, the spade of the excavator has never turned this soil. I hope that some day this mound may increase our knowledge of New Testament times.

Derbe was one of the towns that received the Gospel with thankfulness, and Paul was never persecuted there. It was also the last town on his missionary journey. Instead of pressing on to the south-east, along the trade road that would have taken them through the Cilician Gates into Tarsus, the Apostles turned back from Derbe and with great courage went again through the territory where they had been stoned and persecuted. They retraced their steps to Perga and travelled to Attaleia, on the coast, where they took ship for Antioch in Syria.

That was the conclusion of the first Christian Mission to the Gentiles.

Some three miles farther on from this barren site I came to a Turkish village called Zosta. From the hill above we looked down on the usual ragged mass of low roofs, stone and mud walls; in the centre was a domed mosque which I discovered later to be Seljuk.

The villagers came out to drive off the dogs and to greet us. One of them told us that the name of the village had recently been changed to Akar Kuey, which means "white village." As we went towards it, a crowd of men strolled out, full of curiosity; women peeped from behind stone walls, and children ran inquisitively all round us. In the middle of the crowd I saw an astonishing sight.

A group of men were leading a suspicious and indignant-looking ram. A wreath of hill flowers was set round his horns. There were coins hanging in the fleece. Across his back was hung a strip of vivid cloth.

"Ah, it is a wedding!" cried Hassan. "They are going to sacrifice the animal to bring good luck to the bride and bridegroom."

Although I knew that in remote places in Turkey peasants still observe all kinds of strange customs and superstitions dating from Greek and Roman times, I was astonished suddenly to come on an animal garlanded for sacrifice. It was only a few miles away, at Lystra, that Paul and Barnabas had looked on a similar sight.

And here I was, in the year 1936, watching the descendants of the people mentioned in the New Testament bringing a ram and garlands unto the gates. We joined the crowd that poured between the stone walls. A peasant approached and invited us to follow him up a flight of steps to the room of a house.

"Will you please enter?" said Hassan. "They wish to invite you to the wedding celebrations."

I saw a small door leading into a room. Bending down, I took off my shoes and stepped inside. Striped camel rugs were set against the walls, leaving a vacant space in the centre. The room was about five yards long and four yards wide, and there must have been at least fifty men squatting on the rugs.

With the reserved temperament of the Turk, which is so different from that of the excitable Arab, the elders of the village stood with outstretched hands, bidding us welcome.

We managed to insinuate ourselves into the assembly, and, squatting down, plunged into the usual polite greetings.

"Of what nationality is the pasha?" Hassan was asked.

"Of England," he replied.

The grave old men, who probably could neither read nor write and had never before, I imagine, come into contact with anyone English, nodded their heads solemnly as if the arrival of guests from England were an everyday occurrence in the village.

The Turk has many qualities that remind me of the Englishman. One is his placid acceptance of the unusual and his reluctance to admit that he is, or could be, surprised. And as I looked round at this picturesque gathering in a mud hut in the middle of Asia Minor, I was struck by a remarkable thing. Half the men in the room were fair-haired and blue-eyed, and, except for their pitiful rags and tatters and their wild air, might have been Englishmen.

A young Turk entered, bearing the little cups of coffee that appear, as if by magic, even in the desert. As we sipped the coffee, three musicians, squatting in a corner, began to thrum on a guitar, a one-stringed fiddle, and a drum. Those sitting in the middle of the room edged away to the side as a remarkable figure bounded into the vacant circle.

At first I thought it was a woman, but a second glance at the flat flanks and the hollow chest revealed a young Turk dressed in a woman's red silk dress. His eyes had been blacked with *kohl* and his cheeks brightened with rouge. He was as fierce as a wild cat.

He began to posture to the sound of the tom-tom and the thin, discordant wail of the violin. He shook and shivered and stamped his feet, slowly turning, his eyes half shut, and tossing back a hank of black hair that kept falling over his forehead. Yet he was not ridiculous. I could not smile at him. He was too fierce and primitive, like some wild animal dressed up for a circus.

As he quickened his steps, his eyes blazed, his colour heightened, and his breath came in gasps. Every time he twirled round, his skirt flew out and exposed a pair of knee-high Russian boots splashed with mud. Grey knitted stockings were folded down over the tops of his boots and into them were tucked the ends of his trousers. As he continued to turn and stamp, I thought that in just this manner the wild horsemen of Genghis Khan must have amused themselves in the light of camp fires.

Oriental audiences always interest me. They exhibit the unblinking, uncompromising scrutiny of a cat. They rarely show approval or disapproval; they just stare. The men in the room gazed at this savage young dancer in a cold, aloof manner, tapping the ash of their cigarettes on the floor, almost over his feet. When he had finished, someone shouted out a request.

"They are asking for the knife-dance," whispered Hassan to me. "If he comes at you with knives, show no surprise."

I soon discovered that the first dance had been merely an introduction to the knife-dance. The dancer, flourishing two thin daggers about a foot in length, began clashing the blades together, crouching and leaping, stabbing the air, and, in the intensity of the drama he was acting, muttering guttural words as the steel flashed in the uncomfortably small room.

The musicians thrummed a monotonous, rather hypnotic rhythm—the same theme repeated over and over again—and as they played, the dancer stamped until dust was breast-high in the room. His muddy boots and his whirling red skirt moved in a cloud like smoke; but his head, his grotesque face with its parted lips, and the moving flash of the knives, were in the clear air above the dust. It was a savage sight, for he now began to act the part of a man stabbing a victim.

He would single out some member of the audience and

springing at him suddenly, and crouching before him, would slash the knives together within an inch of his throat and draw them with terrifying closeness before his eyes. The man selected for this ordeal would show no fear, gazing back at the dancer as if unconscious that the knives had nearly carried off his nose or his eyebrows.

I understood why Hassan had warned me. I expected to be put to the test and was ready. I thought they would be interested to see how the stranger would behave. But with the innate politeness of these people, he left me out of it, feeling, perhaps, that he ought not to subject a guest to such an ordeal.

When the dancer had finished, he flung the knives to a man in the crowd and make a clumsy exit.

"Who on earth is he?" I asked Hassan.

"Only a man of the village, who is a good dancer."

The appearance of the bridegroom brought the proceedings to an end. He was a shy young fellow who might have been a Norfolk farm labourer. He shook hands with me and, when I wished him happiness and many sons, blushed and said it was all in the competent hands of Allah.

We then rose and put on our shoes at the door. It was good to breathe fresh air again. The head man said that as the pasha was from Europe, he was doubtless interested in all ancient stones. Would he, therefore, care to see the old stones built into the wall of the mosque and into various houses in the village.

I replied that nothing would delight me more, and so we set off, a motley throng, through the muddy little lanes, between stone walls, and into backyards where children lined the roofs to watch us. They showed me Greek stones with weathered inscriptions, fragments of Greek altars and suchlike relics of the great city that had once stood on the hill near by, stones which had perhaps stood in the streets when

Paul preached the Faith in Derbe.

The whole village saw us off. The women stood afar and gazed curiously. Somewhere was the house on whose doorstep the blood of the ram had been sprinkled in deference to the old gods of Anatolia, the gods who were worshipped when Paul passed by, who are still alive in the hearts of these superstitious people.

I returned to Konya over the wide, featureless plain, thinking that nowhere could a stranger have received greater kindness, nowhere could he have met with better manners.

8

The silence of night lay upon Konya. Only the shrill call of the watchmen's whistle awakened echoes in the dark town.

I had finished the first stage of my task. I had visited those places in Galatia which first heard the Gospel of Christ; and now, by candlelight, I read the *Epistle* which St. Paul addressed to the people who lived in this town eighteen centuries ago.

Galatia was a great territory in the heart of Asia Minor, and in the time of St. Paul had recently become a province of the Roman Empire. It took its name from the Gauls who invaded Phrygia in the third century before Christ.

The Celtic tribes passed eastwards in their thousands, raiding across Macedonia and entering Asia Minor. They were rough, savage warriors, who fought half-naked, with a basket shield for armour: great fighters, great drinkers, big, blue-eyed men with yellow hair. They settled in Phrygia, living in tribal state in fortified towns and villages. One of their chief towns was Ankara, which Kemal has chosen to be the capital of modern Turkey.

There is no indication that St. Paul came into close contact with these Gauls. He visited Roman and Greek cities. He met Romans, Greeks, Jews, Lycaonians, and Phrygians. If he ever met the Gauls of Galatia, they would have been men and women who had wandered from their tribes into the towns. It has often been asked why Paul addressed his converts as "Galatians." But is there any other word that could have described so mixed a crowd? Even had these converts been confined to the native Phrygians and Lycaonians, he could not have used these terms. Phrygia was famous for its slaves—so famous that the name Phryx denoted a slave all over the Empire—and Lycaonia was notorious for bandits and thieves. To use such words would have been equivalent to calling his audience "slaves and robbers." But "Galatians," a term that was politically correct, embraced everyone under Roman rule, from the aristocrat in Antioch to the little slave girl in Iconium.

Paul's letter was written when he was far away from Galatia and had been absent for some time from his converts. It is an indignant letter, in which anger, pain, astonishment and tenderness are blended together. Since he had visited Galatia, the Church had become involved in its first controversy: the old Judaizing Party had opposed the Apostle's attitude to the Gentiles. They wished to keep Christianity within the synagogue and thus to retain it as a branch of the Jewish faith. They had sent cunning advocates among Paul's Gentile converts in Galatia, telling them that Paul was not a genuine Apostle and that his attitude towards Christianity was false. It seems that they appealed cleverly to the Gentiles. Under Roman law all Jews were protected. In all the foreign cities throughout the Empire they were recognized "as the kingdom of the Jews within the city." St. Jerome says that all circumcised people were treated as Jews by the Romans, and were thus entitled to receive the protection which the State allowed. But Paul's Gentile Christians were neither Jew nor pagan: they were a midway people. Therefore, Paul's opponents appear to have argued, how much wiser it would be to accept circumcision and the Mosaic Code, and belong to a protected and authorized society. And in proof, these Judaizers could point to the chief Apostles in Judæa, who believed in Christ, yet still observed the Law of Moses.

That, in brief, was the situation which called forth St. Paul's *Epistle to the Galatians*. This letter is his reply to the slanders of his foes. It is also the great Christian declaration of Liberty.

In order to appreciate its vigour of expression and its breadth of thought, we must think of the epoch in which it was written; and we must read it in Greek or in a modern English translation. Every one who wishes to understand the New Testament should possess Dr. Moffatt's parallel edition, and all extracts from the Epistles in this book are in his rendering.

"It is probable that not one in a thousand of the ordinary congregations of our Churches could say in a few words what any one of the epistles is really about," writes the Rev. R. H. Malden in *Problems of the New Testament To-day*. "It is to be feared that many of those who attend Public Worship understand very little of many of the New Testament lessons which they hear read."

The reason is that letters written eighteen centuries ago in the fire of the moment, couched in easy, vigorous colloquial Greek, have come to us heavily draped in the austere embroideries of Jacobean English. The Authorized Version is very lovely, very decorative, but it conveys to the minds of twentieth century Englishmen nothing of the sparkling vigour of the common speech in which St. Paul wrote to his various converts. Therefore, in order not only to understand the issues involved, but also to appreciate the idiom in which Paul wrote, we should read his letters in modern speech.

And when we read St. Paul's epistles, we must remember that he wrote them before the Gospels were written. Every time he mentioned Jesus, he was drawing on his own knowledge of Him or on something which he had been told by those who had followed our Lord. He did not write his letters as doctrinal theology. He was not primarily a theologian: he was a lonely missionary finding his way through the darkness of paganism with no light of the recorded Gospel to help and guide him. But he did not require such guidance. He had the unwritten Gospels in his heart. . . . "Not I, but Christ in me." Those six words are the clue to Paul's life, as, indeed, they are the clue to the lives of all good Christians.

He begins his letter to the Galatians with an autobiography, in order to confute those opponents who had belittled his authority. He describes his conversion on the road to Damascus. It is a letter dictated in the heat of dismay and pained surprise. See how he plunges into the very heart of the matter in his first words:

"Paul an apostle—not appointed by men nor commissioned by any man but by Jesus Christ and God the Father who raised him from the dead—with all the brothers who are beside me, to the Churches of Galatia. . . . I am astonished you are hastily shifting like this, deserting Him who called you by Christ's grace and going over to another gospel. It simply means that certain individuals are unsettling you; they want to distort the gospel of Christ. Now even though it were myself or some angel from heaven, whoever preaches a gospel that contradicts the gospel I preached to you, God's curse be on him! I have said it before and I now repeat it: whoever preaches a gospel to you that contradicts the gospel you have already received, God's curse be on him!"

In the fury and emphasis of this opening we can visualize a man walking about and dictating. We can sense the atmosphere of a man thinking and speaking quickly, and this feeling runs right through the letter.

Paul's fury is the anger of a great man who sees the supremacy of Christ threatened. The question at issue is nothing less than the survival or the disappearance of the Gentile Church. Is this fine, true thing that he is trying to create for the whole world to be bent down and narrowed into the porch of a synagogue? Who must come first, Christ or Moses?

"I have been crucified with Christ," he cries, "and it is no longer I who live, Christ lives in me; the life I now live in the flesh I live by faith in the Son of God who loved me and gave Himself up for me. I do not annul God's grace; but if righteousness comes by way of the Law, then indeed Christ's death was useless."

And at this point Paul's fury goes from him and he melts in love and compassion for his "churches of Galatia."

"O senseless Galatians," he pleads, "who has bewitched you—you who had Jesus Christ the crucified placarded before your very eyes? I simply want to ask you one thing: did you receive the Spirit by doing what the Law commanded or by believing the gospel message? Are you such fools? Did you begin with the Spirit only to end now with the flesh? Have you had all that experience for nothing (if it has really gone for nothing)?"

Then again the tenderness that always underlies his stern and autocratic nature wells up in a great burst of fondness, and he cries out to his distant converts:

"O my dear children, you with whom I am in travail over again till Christ be formed within you, would that I could be with you at this moment, and alter my tone, for I am at my wit's end about you! . . .

"Brothers, you were called to be free; only, do not make your freedom an opening for the flesh, but serve one another in love. For the entire Law is summed up in one word, in *you must love your neighbour as yourself* (whereas if you snap at each other, and prey upon each other, take care in case you destroy one another), I mean, lead the life of the Spirit; then you will never satisfy the passions of the flesh. . . . Now the deeds of the flesh are quite obvious, such as sexual vice, impurity, sensuality, idolatry, magic, quarrels, dissension, jealousy, temper, rivalry, factions, party-spirit, envy, (murder), drinking bouts, revelry, and the like; I tell you beforehand as I have told you already, that people who indulge in such practices will never inherit the Realm of God. But the harvest of the Spirit is love, joy, peace, good temper, kindliness, generosity, fidelity, gentleness, self-control: there is no law against those who practise such things. . . . Never let us grow tired of doing what is right, for if we do not faint we shall reap our harvest at the opportune season. So then, as we have opportunity, let us do good to all men and in particular to the household of the faith."

And this, I think, was to have been the end of the letter. Paul stopped dictating. Then he came over and took the reed pen from his amanuensis, dipped it in the ink and wrote these words:

"See what big letters I make when I write you in my own hand!"

But he was unable to finish. Like many a man whose emotions are worked up, he feels that he has not, after all, done himself justice in written words. If only he could be speaking it all.

"Take this down!" he says, and strides about the room again. And that, I think, is why the last six verses of *St. Paul's Epistle to the Galatians* are pure repetition, and add nothing to the force of his message.

What a world of conjecture has been built up on those few words: "See what big letters I make, when I write you in my own hand," a sentence whose meaning is lost in the mistaken translation of the Authorized Version: "Ye see how large a letter I have written unto you with mine own hand."

It has been suggested—wrongly, I think—that Paul added an illiterate scrawl and that his writing was the clumsy hand of a manual worker. It has been suggested that the Apostle's eyesight was bad and that he could not see the letters he was forming. Perhaps the most sensible suggestion is that Paul wished to end on a note of emphasis and wrote, as many of us do to-day, a few final words in unnecessarily large letters.

It was the custom in Paul's time for people of rank and wealth to dictate their letters to a secretary and add a final salutation in their own hand. That is the method which St. Paul employed in "writing" his epistles.

There are two references to writing materials in the letters. In the *Second Epistle to the Corinthians*, chapter three, verse three, St. Paul mentions ink, which was at that period a mixture of pine-soot and glue; and in the *Second Epistle to Timothy*, chapter four, verse thirteen, he asks that parchments may be sent to him.

Papyrus as thin as the finest modern paper was in use in Paul's time, as well as a thicker kind of parchment. Quintilian states that in his day it was impossible to write with ease on parchment because the surface was bad and made it necessary to write in large letters. Is this yet another conjecture? Was Paul writing on this rough parchment when he made his large letters? "See what large letters I am making when I write to you in my own hand (because I am not accustomed to write on this rough parchment)." Is that what Paul meant?

I put down this letter with the knowledge that once again a man had heard Paul's voice in Galatia. The candle was burning low. The awful solitude of the central plains pressed down upon Konya in the silence of the night. Before I fell asleep, I heard the watchmen's whistles shrilling over the town. Then silence, deeper than before, closed down upon Iconium.

CHAPTER VII

Describes a journey to Izmir, a voyage to Mitylene and to the coast of Macedonia. I see the place where St. Paul stepped ashore in Europe, I go over the hills to walk among the ruins of Philippi and I see the stream in which Lydia was baptized. In Salonica I see a strange funeral, and in Berœa, which is now called Verria, I am told something about St. Paul.

1

ABOUT eighteen months had passed since Paul, Barnabas and Mark had sailed to Cyprus: a time of glad service in the cause of Christ, but a time also of physical stress and peril.

No sooner were the Apostles back in Antioch than the first church crisis was created by certain Judaists who demanded that all Gentile converts should first become circumcised Jews. This was Paul's first open fight with his life-long enemies. These men were to dog his steps across the world, to speak against him and to strive with all their power to chain Christianity to Judaism. Paul fought them with all his strength. He saw that only by freeing Christianity from bondage to Judaism could it ever become a world faith.

Divine guidance led him to submit this question to the Church at Jerusalem, where, during the first Council of the Church, St. Peter supported St. Paul. St. Peter testified to the Divine command that had led him to baptize Cornelius, the Roman centurion, and thus open the Church to the uncircumcised.

Fresh from this victory, Paul planned another missionary tour. His thoughts turned towards his beloved Galatians. How were they getting on in his absence? It has been said that the love of a missionary for his converts is like no other love on earth; and it was this love that filled the soul of St. Paul from the moment of his first mission until his martyrdom in Rome.

"Let us return now," he said to Barnabas, "and visit the brethren in every church wherein we have proclaimed the word of the Lord, and see how they fare."

Barnabas also was anxious to begin another journey, and suggested that Mark should accompany them. How clearly this infers the period of remorse that Mark had suffered. How anxious he was to establish himself again in the favour of Paul and to atone for that moment of weakness or distrust which caused him to return home from Perga. One can almost hear Mark's voice pleading with Barnabas: "Ask him if I can come this time. Say I am sorry. He loves you and will do this for your sake." But Paul was not willing to overlook what he regarded for a long time as Mark's desertion. He refused to accept the young man as a companion on the Second Missionary Journey and, sad to say, the great companions parted: Barnabas and Mark for Cyprus, and Paul, with a new associate, Silas, for Asia Minor.

Silas was a Jew, and a leading member of the primitive church in Jerusalem. It has been suggested, but on slight evidence, that, like his leader, he enjoyed the privilege of Roman citizenship. The short, Greek form of his name is used in *Acts*, and the long, Roman form, Silvanus, is used in the Epistles.

Setting out together, the missionaries revisited the territory of the first journey: Derbe, Lystra, Iconium and Pisidian Antioch. It was at Lystra or Derbe that a young man, Timothy, joined them. The son of a Greek father and a Jewish mother, Timothy was to play a great part in the subsequent development of Christianity.

Paul and his two followers now embarked on a journey which has been called the most remarkable in *Acts*. At one moment the missionaries are in the centre of Asia Minor;

at the next they are far away on the sea-shore, facing the Ægean and—Europe. There is no indication of their route, but we are told that Paul was guided by the Spirit and was "forbidden of the Holy Ghost" to speak the Word in Asia. When he wished to pass into Bithynia, the "Spirit of Jesus" prevented him. So Paul was guided here and there on a journey that avoided all the great centres of population in which, so one imagines, he was anxious to preach.

Why, we ask ourselves, was he shepherded so carefully from Ephesus, which would have seemed his logical destination? Rackham's theory is suggestive: "What is obvious to man is not always the choice of God, and St. Paul's plans were overruled. He was to reach Ephesus—but not this way. As 'Asia' was now the great centre of Hellenism, it seemed as if the Apostle needed a preliminary training in pure Greek life, just as Ephesus itself with its cosmopolitan elements was a preparation for Rome."

Therefore, accompanied by Silas and Timothy, St. Paul was guided to the sea-coast where the Roman colony of Alexandria Troas faced westward over the Ægean Sea. But were there only three missionaries? Was there not a fourth with them, and had he not been with them for some time, modestly concealing his identity? It is at this point in the narrative that St. Luke, the author, slips naturally into the first "we-passage," thus indicating that he had joined St. Paul. If St. Luke were a man of Macedonia, as it is often thought, it is significant that he should choose this point in the story to emphasize his presence, for Macedonia was to be their next mission field. St. Paul received a vision of a man, who, perhaps from his speech, was recognizable as a Macedonian. He stood begging the messengers of Christ to cross over into Europe.

"And a vision appeared to Paul in the night; there was a man of Macedonia standing, beseeching him, and saying, 'Come over to Macedonia and help us.' "

He told his companions of this vision in the morning, and they concluded that it was a call from God. Going down to the docks at Troas, they found a ship about to sail for the coast of Macedonia. Thus, St. Paul, St. Luke, Silas and Timothy crossed into Europe.

2

I found that it was impossible to make for Alexandria Troas for several reasons, the most cogent being that it was a Turkish military zone. I therefore decided to go to Smyrna, or Izmir as the town is now called, and cross from there to the Macedonian coast. The journey by train from Konya to Izmir takes twenty-four hours.

All that long day I sat looking out at the bare plains and the hills. The one feature which enlivened the landscape for me were the storks. Wherever there was a field of turned earth or a marshy place, these sleek visitors, whom I had seen high in the air above the Cilician Gates, would stand reflectively above an unfortunate frog, or tread priggishly with nodding head through the high crops. The black and white of these birds, and their red legs and long red bills, make them objects of extraordinary beauty in the green-and-brown landscape of Asia Minor. Some of those who come regularly in the spring to build their nests on the chimneys of Turkey have migrated from India and Cape Colony. Those that fly north over Palestine follow the line of the Jordan, where I have seen them in the spring flying at so great a height that only the flicker of the sun on their white feathers drew my eye to them.

The stork is seen at his best in the fields. He has no fear of man. He follows the ploughman with stately step, with an air not of rendering assistance but of inspecting with critical approval each newly turned patch of soil. He will stand for hours in an attitude of meditation, like the president of some learned society who is wondering where he has left his top-hat. For a silk hat is all these birds need to complete their air of old-fashioned dignity.

Hassan told me that the stork is a sign of good luck in Turkey.

"Sometimes the country people go out to meet them because they believe, very foolishly, for they are ignorant people, that these storks bring the spring," said Hassan. "The peasants are proud when storks build nests on their houses. Happy is the man, they say, who has a stork's nest on his chimney. Storks give a good example of family life, too. I remember when I was farming—oh, yes, I have been a farmer—some boys took away the stork's eggs for fun and put hens' eggs into the nest. And in time the chickens were hatched. When the—how do you say it?—the man-stork came, he looked at these things that were not storks, and he called his wife, and was very, very angry. Then up he flew into the air, and called his friends to see this awful thing that had been done to him! And they flew down and attacked the—how do you say?—the female bird. . . . Yes, the storks give a good example of family life. They love little storks, but not little chickens."

Hassan thought this was very amusing. He was alarmed when I told him that, as a new Turk, he should be a more ardent feminist.

I have already described how sociable a railway journey in Turkey can be; how the traveller is always offering a hard-boiled egg to a fellow passenger and receiving, in friendly return, a piece of cold chicken or a home-made *dolma*.

This journey contained, as usual, every element of acute indigestion. As we drew into each station, ragged little children besieged us with refreshment, old men and boys walked the length of the train selling *simit*, and poor, tattered little girls stood woefully extending a hard-boiled egg in each hand.

With pathetic eagerness their thin little fingers would seize on a few piastres; for this daily train, with its stop of ten minutes, was their only chance of making money.

I accumulated in the course of the first eight hours a brown jar of spring water, a bag of apples, a bag of roast chestnuts, two circles of *simit*, a piece of newspaper full of scraps of grilled mutton, a sticky bag of *halva*, and six hard-boiled eggs.

At one of the stations a small, plump, hook-nosed man entered the carriage. He turned out to be that new character in Turkey, a Turkish business man. I gave him an egg and he gave me an orange.

"I talk much bad English," he said.

"If I could speak Turkish as well as you talk English, I should be very proud," I said.

"You are much kind," he replied, rising and bowing.

He told us that his task in life was selling motor-cars. I suggested that roads should come before cars, and he thought this was a good, though novel, idea. He mentioned that he had been in England, and I asked him how he liked it.

"Berlin is better," he said. "London I no like."

While we argued about the respective merits of London and Berlin, the wide, central plains of Asia Minor rolled past, and we left behind the province that in Paul's day was called Galatia, and entered that which once was Phrygia.

Dusk invaded the plain. At a lonely station backed by immense hills, we drank cups of scalding sweet coffee in a little café on the platform. The room was full of big-boned, impassive mountaineers crouched over tric-trac boards, gazing round, as they shook the dice, with the placidity of the true Turk, while their friends sat watching the game, sucking reflectively at their hookahs.

There was a stove in the centre of the room, and the walls were decorated with highly coloured lithographs showing men in fur caps taking aim, from the shelter of pine trees, at bears which advanced threateningly on their hind legs.

Peasant women crouched in corners, nursing their children. Infantrymen on leave pulled their kit-bags out of the way of customers and, munching food wrapped in brown paper which they brought from their pockets, washed it down with sips of hot coffee in tiny cups, curiously feminine-looking in their big, brown hands.

The bell warned us that the train was about to go, and we ran back to our carriage. Night had now come. We pulled out over the long plain between featureless hills, and gradually our conversation wilted and, one by one, we fell asleep. Hassan curled up in an orderly manner and slept as if he were in a cavalry bivouac with a sword beside him; the little motor salesman became a swarthy, rather stupid little boy of about eight. His mouth was half open and his air of acute dealing had gone from him. But it is unfair to look at people who are asleep. I withdrew my fascinated eyes from my companions and, punching my overcoat into a hideously uncomfortable pillow, closed my eyes.

When I opened them I was conscious that something was different. A cold light filled the carriage. The windows were spattered with the grime and back-flung mud of a long night-journey, but the salesman's luggage had gone from the rack and the little man had departed. Hassan emerged from sleep like a diver coming up out of deep water, and was instantly awake.

"Ah," he said, "our friend had to leave us at Alashehr. He said good-bye to you . . ."

Poor little fellow! Fancy trying to sell a motor-car in Alashehr.

We were coming down to the coastal plain. The air was warmer. The brown land had given place to green. There were miles of growing crops, fig trees, fruit trees of all kinds, and the sun poured down on a richer, more kindly, landscape. Through this opulent, warm country we came to Izmir and to the sea.

3

My impressions of Izmir are of steamship offices; of drives here, there, and everywhere in a two-horse *araba* over rough cobbled roads; of cup after cup of coffee; and of a photographer who took my photograph and delivered the result in thirty minutes, thus enabling me to enrich the police records with the eight portraits demanded from departing visitors.

The situation of Izmir is magnificent. It is spread out at the foot of Mount Pagus. Hills march down to the sea all round. On the still blue water of the harbour ride ships from the Ægean, and they sail out into the very eye of the sunset, onwards to Rhodes, to the Piræus, to Salonica, to all the old heroic places.

But of the commercial magnificence of Izmir of which I always read, I saw nothing. After the War, the Allies handed Izmir to the Greeks as a colony. The Turks captured it in 1922, and in the confusion of a night of terror the city was burnt to the ground under the eyes of the Allied Fleet. I have heard men in the Navy describe the sounds and the smells of that night: how the whole water-front was a hideous tapestry of flame against which thousands of black figures were seen fighting, struggling and dying, while over-burdened boats rowed frantically towards the battleships.

Izmir has not yet recovered from that night. It has grown up again, it is true, but it is a different city: a city drained of its wealth and of commercial aristocracy. The Greeks, the Armenians, and the Jews have gone. The European commercial communities, once so opulent and so powerful, have dwindled to a suspected and unprivileged minority who strive in an atmosphere of espionage to pull together the tattered ends of their lost fortunes.

Over cups of coffee someone told me that the game of Bridge originated in Izmir. It developed, I was told, from a card game called "Khedive," which migrated to the London clubs towards the end of the nineteenth century as "Biritch" or "Russian Whist." In Izmir Hassan said good-bye to me.

"You will come back some day," he said, "and we shall make an expedition to Miletus and Halicarnassus."

"I hope so with all my heart."

Then I drove, as I had been recommended to do, to a house near the station called the English Pension. My business had taken all afternoon, and it was now dark. I was so weary that I went straight to bed. I entered a room that might have been that of an English schoolgirl twenty years ago. The furniture was white-enamelled. There were occasional wicker-work tables. Dante was meeting Beatrice on one wall; Psyche was at her bath on another; and Sir Lawrence Alma Tadema had contributed his picture, "The Question."

I had encountered nothing like this in all my travels. I told myself with an effort that I was in Izmir, with Mount Pagus lifting itself into the night above the Ægean. From its slopes, no doubt, could be seen the lights of Mitylene. Behind it lay the mountains rising to the great central plateau of Asia Minor. On one of the occasional tables I found a copy of the *Bystander*, eight weeks old, bearing the marks of having been folded and sent through the post from England.

In fact, the whole room was improbable: it was just as if someone had transplanted a portion of his youth to Turkey, where it had refused to grow up. There was nothing later than Alma Tadema or Lord Leighton. It was a curious little piece of mid-Victorianism to discover in this recently bloodsoaked town.

At seven in the morning there was a tap on the door, and a brown arm held out a tray containing a pot of tea and a plate of biscuits. The teaspoon bore a coat-of-arms on the handle and one word—"Skegness."

As I was having a hurried English breakfast in a room downstairs, for I had to catch a boat that was sailing for Mitylene, a small, precise Englishwoman of middle age entered the room.

"Good morning," she said. "I am Sister Grace. I am sorry you are going so soon."

She was dressed in black, and she wore a brooch formed of three Roman denarii—three Cæsars side by side. She was the kind of middle-aged Englishwoman who would create a nice, antiseptic hospital in a desert or a swamp, and who would walk deliberately through a riot or a revolution with an unrolled umbrella, trying to restore order with a series of sharp raps. No other nation in the world breeds this type. No matter how intimately they may know a foreign language or how deeply they may plumb the mystery of foreign psychology, they never for an instant lose their Englishness, but stride an alien world, introducing into distant places a little touch of Tunbridge Wells or Eastbourne.

Sister Grace told me that the house had been built by Arthur Hichens, brother of Robert Hichens, the novelist. Arthur Hichens had been British chaplain in Izmir before the War. I asked her if she had been in Izmir during the massacre. Oh yes; she had been there. She had seen the old world go crashing down in flame. It had been necessary to fly with other residents to the safety of the *Iron Duke*, leaving behind the body of an Englishman who had died in the house. It was terrible to have been forced to do that. After several years she had returned. The house was just the same, but very dirty. The Turks had not touched anything, which was very good of them.

"Well, good-bye," she said. "Write to me and tell me how you get on. You won't forget, will you?"

How could one forget this kindly Englishwoman, who wears three Cæsars at her neck?

The small boat moved from the Gulf of Izmir and steered to the north, where Mitylene towers from the sea. I cannot exaggerate the happiness with which I looked forward to the countries that lay ahead of me: Macedonia and Greece. Soon, I told myself, I should be walking the ruined streets of Philippi; I should see Thessalonica and Berœa; I should see Athens and Corinth. As the little boat lifted gently on a smooth sea over which summer had already cast its spell. I would not have changed my adventure for any other in the world.

We came into Castro in the forenoon, a town grouped in exquisite beauty at the foot of high hills. The little harbour was stacked with oil-barrels and the air reeked of soap-making. The splendour of Castro melted on closer acquaintance into a series of narrow streets clustered round about the harbour, Turkish in their atmosphere in spite of the crowds of voluble, swarthy Greeks which filled them. How different were these quick, talkative folk from the self-contained Turk.

Behind a rampart of barrels I discovered the office of a shipping agent. The clerk, a dark little garlic-smelling man, told me that I was lucky. I should not have to spend three days in that God-forsaken island—he was a Greek from Athens —because a boat that was fifteen hours late would leave that very evening for Kavalla and Salonica. So we went together to the little *Kapheneion* under the trees near the harbour and drank coffee and smoked Macedonian cigarettes. The little Athenian launched into a long and tedious account of the political situation in Greece.

Mitylene is, of course, the Lesbos of antiquity, but he was not interested in antiquity and had never heard of Sappho. He knew a lot about olive oil: in the old days the island grew grapes, but now it is an island of olive trees. They are more profitable.

I did not like to go far from the town in case the ship came in and sailed off without me. When a Greek cargo-boat is only fifteen hours late, you never know what she may do. I climbed the hill to the empty shell of the Genoese castle, and looked across ten miles of water to the hills of Asia Minor. They rose up round Pergamum, pink with the setting sun, and a few clouds in the evening sky drifted towards them, to lie there during the night and melt in the morning. I felt summer in the air, the wonderful settled summer of the Mediterranean world; I felt the nearness of those long weeks of cloudless days, a blue sky curving overhead, brown islands lifting their sharp outlines in sunlight from a blue sea.

The ship left in the dark. The moon was almost full. The cabin reeked of a thousand smells and so I lay on deck in a rug, watching the light on the copper-coloured sea. It may have been on a night like this that Paul, with Luke, Silas, and Timothy, set sail from Troas to Kavalla, which in those days was called Neapolis.

"Setting sail from Troas *we* made a straight course to Samothrace, and the day following to Neapolis; and from thence to Philippi, which is a city of Macedonia, the first of the district, a Roman colony: and *we* were in this city tarrying certain days. . . ."

It has been suggested that Luke was a native of Philippi, because his account of that place is not only vivid but also reflects local pride. If so, we can imagine how he would instruct St. Paul in local history and personalities, and tell him of the many things which a missionary about to enter a new sphere of work would like to know.

The ship in which they sailed was similar to that in which I was making the same voyage. It was one of the little coasting vessels that linked the Ægean islands together, picking up and

putting down cargoes in a dozen little harbours, just as these
ships do to-day. As Paul and his companions set sail from
Troas, they would leave the dark mass of Tenedos on the
port bow, cross the mouth of the Dardanelles and breast the
strong current that flows southward from Cape Helles. Imbros would lie before them; beyond Imbros the high mountains of Samothrace would rise like towers from the waves.
Cities like Lystra and Derbe have fallen into ruin, or, like
Syrian Antioch and Iconium, have changed their character;
but the traveller who sails the Ægean knows that the coastline
has not altered since Paul and his missionaries passed that
way in the first century.

I watched the moon-path grow faint on the sea; I listened
to the rhythmic hiss of water against the ship; and I watched
the hills grow dim round the Gulf of Adramyttium as we made
for Lemnos.

4

It was early morning and the sun was already warm. The
ship rode at anchor on a sea like green glass. Looking shore-
ward, I saw a town of exquisite beauty clustered at the foot of
a mountain. A high rock jutted out to sea, with houses rising
in narrowing terraces to a summit crowned with the towers
and walls of an ancient castle. This sea-girt rock was linked
to the hills at the back by a Roman aqueduct of double arches.

Such is Kavalla, the Neapolis of St. Paul's time, in whose
little harbour the Apostle first set foot in Europe. This moment is one of the most significant and dramatic in the mission of St. Paul. Christianity had at last come from the East to
the West. But we are, perhaps, apt to forget that St. Paul himself had no such feeling as he stepped ashore in Macedonia.
He did not think of Europe and Asia as we do. He had merely
crossed from one Roman province to another. He had come
from Roman troas to Roman Neapolis. The Via Egnatia, ly-

ing before him, did not lead to a new and different continent, but to the same kind of Roman colonies and Hellenistic cities that he had left behind on the great Asiatic trade routes. The energy and commercial wealth of the world lay behind him in Egypt and Syria; the great cities, the great libraries, the great temples lay behind him in Asia Minor: in front of him lay weary Athens, living on the glories of its past, and Rome, vital and powerful master of the world. Westward of Rome was a vague land of Germans and Gauls and, farther still, an unknown savage little island called Britain, which Claudius had just added to the Empire.

Neapolis, as Paul saw it, was a small roadstead in the shadow of a hill, almost an island, on whose crest was a temple modelled after the Parthenon at Athens. It held the statue of the Venus of Neapolis. The fleet of Brutus and Cassius had anchored in the bay during the Battle of Philippi, and it was to the lovely little island of Thasos, lying a few miles south of Kavalla, that Brutus had sent the body of Cassius for burial, so that his funeral would not disturb the morale of the army.

The Neapolis that Paul saw, as the ship from Troas came in with a following wind, must have been very like the Kavalla that I saw on that still, bright morning. The temple has disappeared from the top of the hill and a Byzantine-Turkish citadel takes its place, but the square white houses, dazzling in the sunlight, each house with a roof of red tiles, must have grouped themselves round the hill, tier above tier, the lowest reflected in the water, just as they do to-day.

The skyline is the same. The wild mountains of Macedonia have not changed. They rise from a sea of emerald green, lifting themselves, mountain against mountain, to the north, where only thirty miles away they meet the frontier of Bulgaria. Far to the west, almost lost in the heat haze, is the long, mountainous silhouette of Mount Athos. . . .

No departure has such an air of finality as that by rowing-boat. When the traveller sees his suit-cases flung downward to the arms of boatmen standing far below in the shadow of a ship's side, and when he prepares to descend the suicidal ladders which are lowered at such moments, he has the feeling that the solid world is about to recede, and there comes over him a loneliness which has been shared by all those who have been marooned.

The two boatmen sang as their oars cut into the smooth water. I could not catch one word of their chant. Though the words were Greek, I was sure that the tune was Turkish. Stepping ashore on a little half-moon of sand packed with men and donkeys, I watched brown, barelegged porters running up and down planks flung from the sterns of sailing-ships, bearing on their backs bundles of firewood from Thasos and sacks of charcoal from Mount Athos. These were loaded on donkeys and taken into the town.

A few yards away was the fish-market, evidently a centre of importance. I can never resist a fish-market in a remote part of the world. It is fascinating to see the kind of fish which men take from strange waters. There were fish in this market whose destination should have been an aquarium and not a kitchen: queer, flat, coloured fish, and long, thin, silver fish. There were trays full of the black and green octopi which is relished all over the Ægean and the Mediterranean, and there were calamare, or ink-fish, flaccid and horrible in death. Most sinister of all were red oysters in huge gnarled shells. Noticing my interest in these, a polite fishmonger deliberately picked out one of the most deadly-looking and offered it to me with a charming bow. But my courage failed me, whereon, with the boastful air of a man performing a conjuring trick, he snicked the oyster with his knife and defiantly swallowed it.

I discovered that Kavalla, like many a coast-town in this part of the world, does not live up to its appearance from the sea. It proved to be a place without civic grandeur or plan, a new town full of big, stone warehouses on the water-front, and an old town winding round the citadel hill, a warren of un-made roads and narrow streets.

I was fortunate enough to make the acquaintance of a young archæologist, George Bakalakis, whose enthusiasm for Ne-apolis warmed my heart. How dreary the world would be without fiery young men who would pull down ten town halls to find one ancient inscription. He took me into a dusty shed where all that is left of the marble city of Paul's time lies about among the dust and the rats.

As we walked through the town, my companion told me that it is the centre of the Macedonian tobacco industry. The tobacco leaf is stored in the large warehouses which lie close to the harbour. Some of the best tobacco, still known as "Turk-ish," is grown in the district, and the tobacco workers are the only electors in Greece who send communist members to Parliament.

A war memorial stands in the centre of a little public gar-den. It is not an inspired memorial, and the usual lion ram-pages on a stone cenotaph: but what interested me was the Greek inscription; "To those who died 1912–1922."

Our own war memorials, with 1914–1918 inscribed on them, cover a long period of suffering, but Macedonia knew ten years of war. When the first Balkan War broke out in 1912, the country was Turkish: when the Turks were driven out, Bulgarians occupied Kavalla: then came the second Bal-kan War, at the end of which the town became Greek. During the European War the Bulgarians again swooped down, com-mitting frightful atrocities during their occupation. In 1918 the Greeks resumed possession, and in 1921 plunged into war with Turkey.

We climbed the citadel hill, but I was disappointed to find that the castle, which looks so splendid from the sea, is just a hollow shell. On the top of the hill, on a terrace overlooking the open sea and the isle of Thasos, is the shrouded statue of a man on a horse. It is carefully concealed from view, and has been so for many a year. It is an equestrian statue of the great Mehemet Ali. The late King Fuad of Egypt promised to unveil it, but never managed to do so.

The only show-place in Kavalla is the home in which Mehemet Ali was born in 1769. It is now the property of the Egyptian Government, which maintains a caretaker in a fez. It is an interesting old Turkish house, with latticed harem windows and floorboards which creak ominously. I had never realized that Mehemet Ali, who became Viceroy of Egypt, was, until the age of thirty or so, a humble tobacco-merchant of Kavalla.

Descending the hill, we went to the little square near the harbour where, beneath matting stretched on poles, the male population of Kavalla not engaged in packing tobacco, unloading charcoal, or selling fish, was drinking coffee and proclaiming its Turkish traditions by playing tric-trac. To sit at a little table under the matting was, I discovered, to invite the attentions of small boys who cried shrilly, "*Loostro verneeki!*", and, hitting a shoe-brush against a tray of polishes slung round their necks, flung themselves with violence on my feet. The number of young Greeks who begin life as *loostro-verneeki* boys must be prodigious.

Not far from the quay is a Greek church which has a curious history. It was once dedicated to St. Paul, then became a Turkish mosque, and has now become a church again, but dedicated to St. Nicholas.

The priest, a big, square-bearded Greek like a Hebrew prophet, sparkled up at once when I told him that it was a disgrace to Kavalla that his church should not be dedicated to St. Paul.

"Ah," he cried. "You are right. In the old days it used to be so. The holy Apostle Paul stepped ashore at this place, which in ancient times was the quay-side; for the sea has gone back at this point. Come with me."

He led me round to the back of the church where, at the entrance to a little alley, is a round mark in the pavement.

"You are looking at the place where the Apostle Paul landed from the shores of Asia Minor. A big plane tree once marked the spot."

His voice shook with indignation as he added:

"The Bulgarians cut it down."

"But you say that the church was once dedicated to St. Paul. Why is it now dedicated to St. Nicholas?"

He told me that when the Turks evacuated Kavalla, it was necessary to spend some money on the mosque in order to turn it again into a place of Christian worship. The fishermen agreed to find the money, but they would not hear of the re-dedication of the building to St. Paul. The continuity of the Christian tradition had, of course, been broken by centuries of Moslem occupation, and St. Paul meant little to the local fishermen, who, like all Greek sailors, placed their faith in St. Nicholas, their patron saint.

Therefore the church which Byzantine tradition linked with St. Paul's first step on Western soil is now the Church of St. Nicholas.

St. Nicholas, by the way, in addition to protecting sailors, children, travellers, and merchants, is also the patron saint of pawnbrokers. The story goes that a nobleman of the saint's native town, Parara in Asia Minor, had lost all his money, and did not know how he could endow his three beautiful daughters. St. Nicholas, hearing of his trouble, went by night and flung through the window three bags of gold with which the nobleman was able to provide handsome dowries. These three bags are shown in all early ikons as three gold apples, and the gold apples of St. Nicholas are the origin of the pawnbroker's sign.

5

I hired an old car with torn celluloid side-screens and set off over the hills for Philippi, nine miles away.

The road leaps suddenly into the bleak fastness of Mount Symbolum, which stands like a barrier between the Plain of Philippi and the sea. This mountain is a continuation of the Pangæan range, famous in antiquity for its silver mines. The road twists to the summit, a height of 1670 feet, and then slides down to an immense plain, green with crops and brown with marshland, as flat as an inland sea. The road was deep in dust. Every horseman, every ox-cart, every shepherd, moved in a little puff of brown cloud.

On these wide plains, and among these treacherous marshes, the Roman Republic came to an end forty-one years before Christ was born. It was here that the legions of Antony and young Octavius defeated the forces of Brutus and Cassius, and, to celebrate the victory, founded the colony of Philippi on the death-bed of the Republic.

I am sure that anyone who in his schooldays has played the part of Brutus in Shakespeare's *Julius Cæsar* must look at the Plain of Philippi with more than usual interest. This, then, I told myself, was the reality behind the little platform in the governor's room at the end of term, this wide and desolate place so like my conception of it; and it was on these marshy levels that the real actors in one of the world's greatest dramas suffered and died. As I went on across the plain, I seemed to hear again the sepulchral voice of that Cæsar who was to die so soon in France, warning me from a patch of erratic limelight that I should see him again at Philippi. . . .

After travelling for about eight miles I came to an inn on the right of the road, remarkable only because a Roman monument is built into the wall. It is a gigantic sepulchral stone about twelve feet in height, and set on a plinth. It bears the name and titles of a Roman officer named C. Vibius. As I was looking at it, a peasant came out of the inn and, seeing my interest, began to show off the monument and to point out a better vantage point. I had read in Mr. G. F. Abbot's *Macedonian Folklore* that the name of Alexander the Great is still remembered by the peasants, but I did not expect to receive such a swift confirmation of this.

"What is this monument?" I asked.

"We call it the feeding-place of Bucephalus," he replied.

"And who was Bucephalus?" I asked, to see if he were merely repeating a name parrot-like.

"Bucephalus," he replied at once, "was the horse of King Alexander."

I asked him if he could tell me any stories of "King Alexander," but he became suspicious and shook his head, thinking, perhaps, that I was making fun of him.

In another mile or so I approached a conical hill with an ancient tower on the top of it, and, almost before I was aware of it, I found myself among the ruins of Philippi. The modern road follows the line of the old Via Egnatia and runs right through Philippi. The ruins lie ten or fifteen feet below the modern level, and I walked down from the road into the forum, where the bases of marble columns, rain-gutters, and paving stones, cover acres of ground recently excavated by French archæologists.

The only modern building is a watchman's hut on the side of the road: otherwise the city, which St. Luke described with pride as "a city of Macedonia, the first of the district," is now desolate in the plain, its white bones shining wherever ten feet of soil have been removed.

The watchman came from his hut and took me through the dead city. Its most spectacular features are the piers and gateway of a Byzantine basilica. Before the French archæologists began to dig, this church was the only ruin above the ground.

It stood in the fields, a landmark on the flat plain, and was wrongly described by the few writers who passed this way as a triumphal archway. It was a Greek cathedral dedicated, no doubt, to St. Paul. The caretaker told me that the local people have always called it "the palace of Alexander the Great."

What, I wonder, is the history of this church? Was it built on the site of the prison of St. Paul, or was it built on the site of the house of Lydia, in which St. Paul stayed? Its size and splendour indicate that it was a church of great importance, and I looked at its mighty ruins with emotion.

I explored the market-place with intense interest. The whole area of the central meeting-place of Philippi—a place St. Paul must have walked—has been excavated. The ground plan is perfect. The stone rain-gutters that drained it in Roman times are so well preserved that they still carry off water in the wet season. Steps lead from the forum to higher levels, where marble floors and the bases of columns indicate the fine public buildings and temples that once lined the square.

Many inscriptions are lying about, just as they were taken from the earth. One, which was difficult to decipher, seems to describe the dedication of a temple, but others of a more personal character suggest that people did not live to a very great age in Philippi. Lying together in a room off the forum are two tombstones, one recording the deaths of Cassia Gemella and Antonius Alexander at the age of twenty-five, and the other commemorating Velleius Plato, who died aged thirty-six, after having made a tomb for himself and a relative, evidently a doctor.

The most interesting inscription is on the base of a statue; thirteen lines of Latin as clear cut as they were when they left the stonemason's hand centuries ago. They state that the statue was erected by soldiers under the command of L. Tatinius, who had begun his military career as a private in the footguards and had risen to the rank of centurion.

From the air of secrecy with which the caretaker led me to a certain ruined house, I gathered that he was about to show me the most precious relic of Philippi. He took a broom and swept away several inches of sand, revealing a beautiful pavement made of small red, white, and black tesseræ.

"The walls of Philippi!" he said dramatically, and looking down as he swept away the sand, I saw that the sunlight was falling on a pictorial diagram of square fortified towers, arched gateways, and a machicolated wall.

I remembered the touch of local pride which seems to inspire St. Luke's mention of Philippi—"the first of the district." And here again was something of the same pride: the finest thing with which this long dead citizen of Philippi could decorate the pavement of his room were the walls and towers of his native town.

The caretaker asked my permission to cover the pavement, and when I consented, he stood with his broom sweeping the brown sand on the little coloured stones; it required little imagination to transform his broom into a scythe and himself into Father Time.

The Via Egnatia runs almost beneath the modern road, at a depth of ten to fifteen feet. This stretch of the famous Roman highway is made of enormous stones, some of them six inches in thickness, scored to the depth of three and four inches with the marks of wagon and chariot wheels. The Via Egnatia came straight across Mount Symbolum from Neapolis, skirted the west side of the hill, on which the old town of Philippi was built, and ran the whole length of the forum, so that travellers arriving in Philippi would find themselves at once in the centre of the town. On one of these stones, scratched possibly by soldiers in a guard-house, is a pavement game played with stones and dice. It is a circle divided into nine segments, five of which are marked by semi-circles drawn on the broad end of the segments.

As I sat in these lonely ruins, I was able to build a picture of the Philippi that St. Paul, St. Luke, Silas, and Timothy saw when they came along the Via Egnatia from Neapolis. The old town which Philip of Macedon, Alexander's father, had founded, climbed the acropolis hill; its streets were steep, its houses were old and Greek-looking, its temples, flashing in the sun, were a shining landmark for miles. On the flat land at the foot of the hill was the new Roman colony which Augustus had founded, very Roman, very official, very proud, full of old soldiers, or the sons and grandsons of old soldiers.

It was in Philippi that Augustus had settled the veterans of the battle in which he defeated the forces of Brutus. Ten years later, after the Battle of Actium, he settled there other veterans who had helped to defeat Antony and Cleopatra. That was eighty years before the Apostolic visit. The grandsons of these veterans were then the middle-aged fathers of Philippi.

There were fewer Jews in Philippi than in any other town visited by St. Paul, except Lystra, which also was a Roman colony. These military towns did not attract Jews until they assumed a commercial importance, and that is why there was no synagogue in Philippi and why the Apostles went forth on the Sabbath by a river-side, "where we supposed there was a place of prayer." The "river-side" still exists, about a mile north of the ruined city, where a clear, swift-flowing but shallow river about ten to twelve yards wide flows across the plain. It is the only stream of any size for miles.

The four missionaries found a number of women gathered by the banks of the stream, among them a native of Thyatira, in Lydia, a woman of some wealth and position, who sold the expensive purple fabrics for which her native city was famous. This Lydia—for so she was called after her native district—became the first Christian convert in Europe. She and her household with her were baptized in the little stream that still runs through the desolate plain, and, in gratitude, Lydia begged the Apostles to stay in her house. So the first Christian church was formed in Europe.

Then occurred that perfect little cameo of ancient life: the incident of the wandering prophetess. As the Apostles were on their way to the place of prayer, they encountered a group frequently met with on the roads and in the cities of the ancient world. A half-witted slave-girl credited with the gift of divination was being led about, probably by a master and a mistress who interpreted her ravings in return for a small fee. Such Pythones, Eurykleidai, or Sternomanteis, were the lowest grade of the oracular profession. At the head of the cult was the Delphic Oracle, with its mysterious priestess whose utterances were famous throughout antiquity, whose advice helped to found the colonies of Greece and to whose rocky shrines the great ones of the earth made pilgrimage. At the other end of the scale were these poor girls, who tramped the roads in charge of persons who pretended to discern a meaning or a message in their ravings.

The girl followed Paul and his companions day after day, crying: "These men are servants of the Most High God, which proclaim unto you the way of salvation. And Paul, being sore troubled, turned and said to the spirit, I charge thee in the name of Jesus Christ to come out of her. And it came out at that very hour."

The girl's master, finding that she no longer raved and that his livelihood had gone, took Paul and Silas (Luke and Timothy were evidently elsewhere) and "dragged them into the market-place before the rulers"—the very market-place whose stones lie beside the road to-day—and charged them with being Jews who were spreading doctrines unlawful for Romans to receive or observe. The suggestion was that the worship of Jesus Christ was a treasonable heresy that endangered the cult-worship of the reigning Emperor. As all colonies felt that they upheld the dignity and the honour of Rome among a welter of lesser breeds, this was quite enough to condemn the Apostles. And for some reason which is not clear, Paul and Silas allowed the lictors to perform the unlawful act of stripping them and beating them with rods of elm wood. Either Paul and Silas preferred to remain silent, or, as is more likely in the light of their future conduct, their cries of "Civis Romanus sum!" were drowned by the furious crowd. Or is it possible that Paul only was a Roman citizen, and scorned to claim an immunity which would not be extended to his friend? However that may be, both of them were whipped and flung into prison.

Paul and Silas were put in the stocks in an underground cell. During the night their hymns and prayers roused the other prisoners, who listened with astonishment and wonder: "and suddenly there was a great earthquake, so that the foundations of the prison house were shaken: and immediately all the doors were opened and every one's bands were loosed."

"Anyone that has seen a Turkish prison," writes Sir William Ramsay, "will not wonder that the doors were thrown open; each door was merely closed by a bar, and the earthquake, as it passed along the ground, forced the doorposts apart from each other, so that the bar slipped from its hold and the door swung open. The prisoners were fastened to the wall or in wooden stocks; and the chains and stocks were detached from the wall, which was shaken so that spaces gaped between the stones."

The jailer, leaping from his bed and believing that he would be held responsible for the escape of the prisoners, was about to prove himself true to the traditions of Philippi when he heard Paul's voice crying, "Do thyself no harm: for we are all here!"

The jailer and his family were converted, and a touching and beautiful conclusion to the incident was the washing of the Apostle's stripes by the jailer; and the little feast of thanksgiving that followed was proof that although this man could not have received much Christian instruction, the seed had been sown in good ground.

On the following morning, the lictors brought an order of release from the magistrates. These self-important officials had by this time realized how serious a breach of the law they had committed. They had lowered the dignity of Roman citizens, and it was a matter that might land them into trouble with higher authorities. Paul knew this too. He was not going to allow them to insult him and then dismiss him with no further word. He refused to leave prison until the magistrates came in person and apologized. This they readily did. They "besought them" and "asked them to go away from the city." It was, therefore, with dignity that Paul and Silas bade farewell to the members of the infant church at Philippi, and, leaving Luke and Timothy behind, took the road to Thessalonica.

6

I walked along the road to the stream on whose banks Lydia was baptized. The watchman told me that the modern Turkish name for it is Bounarbashi, which means headstream.

As I sat on the banks watching a herd of buffaloes wade in among the watercress, a bare-legged, massive girl came down to the stream with a knife. She tucked up her skirts and waded into the water, where she began to cut the cress. I was about to take a photograph of her when, seeing me, she threw down the watercress and stampeded out of the water in terror. In lonely places there are still people who hate the idea that some stranger may take away an image of them in a little black box; and I am not sure that I blame them.

In rage, Lydia was charming. I had no idea that such a

sturdy, muscular creature could be so girlish. She stamped her bare foot and made pettish movements with the knife. I sent the watchman over to try and soothe her, but she became even more temperamental, stamping her bare feet and waving her knife. When, however, I took out a book and began to read, she regained confidence and forgot all about me.

St. Paul's *Epistle to the Philippians* was written to the Christians of Philippi who were baptized beside this stream in the year 50 A.D.

It was written some years after St. Paul's visit to Philippi; and it was composed in prison. The general belief is that it was written in Rome when St. Paul was awaiting the result of his appeal to Cæsar, but a few critics think that it may have been written during an unrecorded imprisonment in Ephesus. The object of the letter is to thank the Christians of Philippi for gifts of money sent by them to help the Apostle in his misfortune. These gifts had been carried by a man of Philippi called Epaphroditus, who cheered St. Paul in his prison. Epaphroditus fell seriously ill during his mission, but returned safely to Macedonia, bearing the *Epistle to the Philippians*.

"I thank my God for all your remembrance of me," wrote Paul; "in all my prayers for you I always pray with a sense of joy for what you have contributed to the gospel from the very first day down to this moment. . . . It is only natural for me to be thinking of you all in this way, for alike in my prison and as I defend and vindicate the gospel, I bear in mind how you all share with me in the grace divine. God is my witness that I yearn for you all with the affection of Christ Jesus Himself. . . .

"I would have you understand, my brothers, that my affairs have really tended to advance the gospel; throughout the

whole prætorian guard and everywhere else it is recognized
that I am imprisoned on account of my connection with
Christ, and my imprisonment has given the majority of the
brotherhood greater confidence in the Lord to venture on
speaking the word of God without being afraid."

A note of weariness creeps into his letter. Paul was no longer
a young man. He had endured years of mental and physical
hardship, and as he lay in his prison he longed, at last, for rest.

"The outcome of all this, I know, will be my release . . .
my eager desire and hope being that I may never feel ashamed,
but that now as ever I may do honour to Christ in my own
person by fearless courage. Whether that means life or death,
no matter! As life means Christ to me, so death means gain.
But then, if it is to be life here below, that means faithful
work. So—well, I cannot tell which to choose; I am in a
dilemma between the two. My strong desire is to depart and
be with Christ, for that is far the best. But for your sakes it is
necessary I should live on here below. I am sure it is, and so
I know I shall remain alive and serve you all by forwarding
your progress and fostering the joy of your faith. Thus you
will have ample cause to glory in Christ Jesus over me—
over my return to you.

"Only do lead a life that is worthy of the gospel of Christ.
Whether I come to see you or only hear of you in absence, let
me know you are standing firm in a common spirit, fighting
side by side like one man for the faith of the Gospel. Never
be scared for a second by your opponents; your fearlessness is
a clear omen of ruin for them and of your own salvation—at
the hands of God. For on behalf of Christ you have the favour
of suffering no less than of believing in him, by waging the
same conflict that, as once you saw and now you hear, I wage
myself."

He tells them that Timothy, his beloved companion, is

with him. He reminds them that Timothy has "served with me in the gospel, like a son helping his father," and he says that he hopes to send Timothy to Philippi as soon as he knows the outcome of his trial, in order that he may receive more news of the Church there, adding, "though I am confident in the Lord that I shall be coming myself before long."

The warmth of affection which Paul felt for his Philippians lights up the last chapter of this letter. He calls them "his joy and crown." He gives them advice which rings down the centuries with undiminished beauty:

"Finally, brothers, keep in mind whatever is true, whatever is worthy, whatever is just, whatever is pure, whatever is attractive, whatever is high-toned, all excellence, all merit. Practise also what you have learned and received from me, what you heard me say and what you saw me do; then the God of peace will be with you."

Paul then concludes his letter in dignified gratitude for the financial help which the Philippian church has rendered to him. It is an extraordinarily interesting sidelight on the saint himself.

"It was a great joy to me in the Lord that your care for me could revive again; for what you lacked was never the care but the chance of showing it. Not that I complain of want, for I have learned how to be content wherever I am. I know how to live humbly; I also know how to live in prosperity. I have been initiated into the secret for all sorts and conditions of life, for plenty and for hunger, for prosperity and for privations. In him who strengthens me I am able for anything. But you were kind enough to take your share in my trouble.

"You Philippians are well aware that in the early days of the gospel, when I had left Macedonia, no church but yourselves had any financial dealings with me; even when I was in Thessalonica, you sent money more than once for my needs.

It is not the money I am anxious for; what I am anxious for is the interest that accumulates in this way to your divine credit! Your debt to me is fully paid and more than paid! I am amply supplied with what you have sent by Epaphroditus, a fragrant perfume, the sort of sacrifice that God approves and welcomes. . . ."

So, with dignity, gratitude, love, and words of Christian counsel, St. Paul spoke from his prison to the first and possibly his best-loved Christian community in Europe.

I took a farewell glance at the ruins lying in the shelter of the hill. Generations of men had grown up and had been harvested like corn and, like corn, had left no trace but this furrow on the plain that once had been the Roman colony of Philippi. But the words of Paul to this city were as warm and as full of life as they were when the wagons creaked along the Via Egnatia; when streets, now lying cold and open to the sky, rang to the sounds of men. . . .

I drove on to the rail-head at Drama. This dusty Macedonian town looked to me like the world's end. There were a few soldiers returning from leave, sitting under the roof of the station café while a patient Armenian tried to sell them a carpet.

I sat down with them and waited two hours for the train to Salonica, drinking cup after cup of Turkish coffee and eating Turkish delight speared on little sticks. The village idiot, a youth whose hair grew right down his neck at the back, a horrible phenomenon which I had never before seen, kept sidling up, touching me softly on the arm and bursting into fits of silent laughter. I became quite used to him.

The mountains changed colour, the dust swirled up under the hoofs of approaching horsemen, and at last a bedraggled train puffed into the little station.

7

Salonica is about seventy miles from Philippi as the crow flies. St. Paul reached it in three days, travelling along the Via Egnatia, which went through Amphipolis and Apollonia, two cities which have now disappeared from the map. The train, winding between the mountains west of Drama, covers something like a hundred and fifty miles on its journey to Salonica. The track bends and twists in the valleys, making an immense détour in order to avoid the great mountain mass of Beshik Dagh, whose topmost summit wears snow until midsummer and is known locally as Pilaf Tepe from its fancied resemblance to a plate of rice.

Traversing the Struma Valley, the train runs for miles along the foot of the Bulgarian Mountains and almost enters Yugoslavia at Lake Doiran, where the frontier line between Macedonia and Yugoslavia passes across the water, dividing the lake between the two countries. For more than two years our troops held the Doiran Sector, fighting uphill all the time in every sense of the word. There is many a walled war cemetery on these lonely hills.

In Salonica I was given a room and a bath, which at that moment seemed to me the very apex of luxury. And there was a little balcony from which I could see, through a tangle of telegraph cables, the ships anchored in the harbour.

The charm of my surroundings was heightened by the fact that water actually ran from the bath-taps, that someone answered the bell, that there was a connexion between the light-switch and the light and between the blind and its cord.

When I explored Salonica in the morning I saw a city that in ancient times must have been exquisite to look upon, lying, as it does, on a hill at the head of a blue gulf, mountains piled behind it, and to the far south the snow-covered summit of Thessalian Olympus rising from the sea. Modern

Salonica is a rather shabby reflection of two worlds. There is the new town built to European standards on the low ground which was swept by the great fire of 1917, and there is the old Turkish town which escaped the fire and climbs the hill, lying in picturesque disarray behind mighty Byzantine walls complete with square towers and gateways. The only features of interest in the new town are the Arch of Galerius, which spans the main street, and the Byzantine churches whose architecture and mosaics make Salonica as interesting as Istanbul to the student of this period. The main street covers a stretch of the Via Egnatia.

The most interesting of these churches, dedicated to St. Demetrius, the patron and guardian of Salonica, was gutted by the fire, although happily some of the finest mosaics were undamaged. A fourth century crypt was discovered in 1919 at the east end of this church. It contains a round, marble baptismal font upheld by columns; and in graves near by were discovered the bodies of four bishops, sitting fully clothed in their state vestments. Unfortunately the bodies fell to dust when the tombs were opened. A workman led me to a contractor's hut in which all that is left of the metal decorations is lying among potsherds. I looked at a belt buckle and other fragments of Byzantine enamel, which, unless they are placed in a museum, may soon find their way into the pocket of some visitor.

The old town is a maze of narrow, crooked streets, unexpected trees, courtyards, and mosques disused since the Turks were expatriated under the Lausanne Treaty, leaving Salonica a city of Greeks, Armenians and Spanish Jews. When the sun shines and the roads are dry, old Salonica exhibits the eccentric charm of intense individualism; but once the sun goes in, or, worse still, if rain falls, the old city is revealed as a squalid collection of ill-built and insanitary shanties.

In one of the little streets leading steeply to the old city,

I read a plaque on the wall of a humble little house over a potter's shop. It states that here Ghazi Mustapha Kemal first saw the light of day. The inscription is in French, Greek, and Turkish. A little higher up this street, I encountered a remarkable funeral. It came swaying from side to side down the steep, cobbled lane, led by two Greek priests, solemnly chanting. A man walked in front, holding the lid of the coffin; behind came a black hearse containing the coffin, and inside it, gruesomely exposed to every passer-by, was the body of a young woman. It was a distressing sight, but no one seemed to think anything of it. The children stopped playing and a few men took off their caps as the coffin went past.

I had heard that the custom of taking the exposed corpse to the cemetery is still observed in country places in Greece, but I was surprised to see it in such a big city as Salonica. The origin of this custom goes back to the Turkish occupation and to the days before Greece won her independence. The Turks, learning that Greeks were holding mock funerals in order to smuggle in arms and ammunition, brought in a law forbidding bodies to be buried in closed coffins.

A young student whom I met in Salonica gave me some details about Greek funeral customs. A candle is kept alight in the room of the departed for three days, because it is believed that the soul is sometimes lost for three days and returns to the place of its earthly associations.

"There is a special cake also put beside the candle," he said, "a cake spread with honey."

I thought of the honey jars which were placed on the pyre of Patroclus. No doubt many of these funeral rites go back to remote antiquity.

When three years have expired, the ceremony of "taking up the remains" is performed, an intensely gruesome ceremony to my mind, but one to which the Greeks attach great importance. They approach it also with a certain fear. Incorruptibility, which in the West has always been considered a proof of holiness, rouses in Greece the utmost horror and repugnance. It means that the dead person has been under a curse, or has become a vampire; and the evil spirit must be solemnly exorcised and the body destroyed. This, fortunately, does not often occur. The ceremony of "taking up the remains" is one in which members of the family go to the cemetery, bearing wine with which they wash the bones of the departed and pack them away in a small wooden box. Every Greek cemetery has a special building for these boxes of bones. The priest is present at this ceremony ready, in case the body has not disintegrated, to release the dead from the curse under which it is believed to lie.

A feature of Salonica that impresses the visitor are newspapers and advertisements printed in Hebrew characters. There is an enormous Jewish colony in the port, but I am told that it has decreased since the Greek occupation. In Turkish times Salonica was often called a Jewish city. These Jews, however, are a different race from the Jews who were present in New Testament times. They are Separdic Jews, who speak a corrupt variety of Spanish called Ladino, and they settled in Salonica when the Jews were expelled from Spain under Ferdinand and Isabella.

I looked everywhere in Salonica for some memory of St. Paul. There is a street leading up to the old town which is called in common speech the "street of St. Paul." At the top of the hill is an attractive little Greek monastery, in a clump of cypress trees, called the Monastery of Vlatadon, which seems to have some connexion with the Apostolic visit. There is a tradition that when Paul came from Philippi to Thessalonica, he visited a house in this part of the old city and knelt in the courtyard to pray. The spot is marked by a circular marble from Thessaly, a dark stone forming the centre of a white cross. I do not know whether this is an early tradition.

The monastery is not very old, and I could find no one who could tell me whether it was built on the site of an early church. The founders of the monastery were two Cretan brothers called Vlata, who lived in the thirteenth century. Their monastery was the only one respected by the Turks after the conquest of 1430, because the monks offered to show the Turks how to capture Salonica if they would promise to protect them and respect their rights when the city was taken. They informed the besieging army that the only way to subdue Salonica was to cut the water-pipes that supplied the whole city with water from Mount Hortiati. This advice was followed, and Salonica was forced to capitulate. So great was the rage of the populace, however, that the traitor monks had to be protected, and the Sultan stationed a Chaoush, a Turkish officer, in the monastery for this purpose. Since that time the place has been called locally the Chaoush Monastery.

Behind the municipal hospital is a small chapel dedicated to St. Paul. The legend is that when the Apostle was driven from Thessalonica he spent the night in this place, outside the walls of the ancient city, and that from the tears shed by Paul on that occasion sprang a stream of holy water.

8

Paul came to Thessalonica with Silas and Timothy. The three missionaries lodged with the Jewish Colony, which was naturally prominent in such a large commercial city.

At this time Thessalonica was a free Greek city, a privilege conferred after the battle of Philippi in recognition of its prudent support of Antony and Octavius. It was the capital of one of the four divisions of Macedonia, and was ruled by magistrates, named politarchs, and by its own popular assembly. During the days of destructive Biblical criticism, when some authorities believed that the *Acts* was a second century forgery, the word "politarch" was cited as a stumbling-block. It was believed that the author had given himself away badly, for such a word was unknown in ancient literature. Recently, however, the word has been discovered on a Greek inscription in Salonica and also on one of the Oxyrhynchus papyri, thus helping to confirm, as, in fact, the researches of scholars have continued to confirm, the minute historical accuracy of Luke.

Paul, with Silas and Timothy, lodged at the house of Jason, their fellow-countryman, and spoke in the synagogue on the Sabbath, converting many Gentile proselytes and many of the Macedonian women. I think the supplementary information contained in the first *Epistle to the Thessalonians* and in *Philippians* proves that the Apostle stayed much longer in Thessalonica than one might imagine from the narrative of *Acts*. Paul settled down at his trade of tent-maker, the first time that we hear of him earning money in order to support himself, and more than once he received grateful contributions from the little Christian community at Philippi. This argues a longer stay than the three weeks suggested in *Acts*. Also, the amount of instruction imparted to the Thessalonians would seem to indicate a long visit.

The success of Christianity in Thessalonica stirred up the Orthodox Jews exactly as it had previously done in Pisidian Antioch and in Iconium; and their methods were as cunning, as oblique, and as successful. They stirred up "certain lewd fellows of the baser sort," who haunted the agora of Thessalonica—corner boys is an eloquent modern name for them—and, with these agitators running here, there, and everywhere, public opinion was soon turned against the preachers in a sly and adroit manner.

It should be noted that Jewish opponents of Christianity

have always been extremely clever in appealing to self-interest and fear. In the same way that they threatened Pilate by suggesting that if he acquitted our Lord he was not "Cæsar's friend," these Jews in Thessalonica played on the servile fears of a city which owed its privileges to the capricious favour of Rome. They insinuated that Rome would not view with any favour the emissaries of an "emperor" called Jesus. The very whisper of *læsa maiestas* was enough to create panic in any of these cities: in fact, Tacitus points out that in the reign of Tiberius a charge of treason was the universal resource in accusations, and Pliny tells us that nothing enriched the exchequer more handsomely than such charges. Therefore the politarchs of Thessalonica, no matter how futile and untrue they felt this charge to be, were obliged to pay attention to it.

Paul and his companions were evidently not in the house of Jason when the Macedonian police came to arrest them. But taking Jason and other Christians, they charged them with actions contrary to the decrees of Cæsar, by "saying that there is another king, one Jesus." Jason and his friends were ordered to keep the peace and were then discharged. "And the brethren immediately sent away Paul and Silas by night unto Berœa. . . ."

Timothy, it seems, was not a target for the wrath of the Jews. Perhaps he had remained in the background.

He stayed in Thessalonica, probably on instructions from Paul, while the Apostle and his companion Silas made their way to the town of Berœa, about forty miles to the west.

The first letter to the Thessalonians was probably written from Corinth, within a few months of his flight from Thessalonica. It was sent in order to refute Jewish slanders, to strengthen the affectionate links which bound Paul to his converts in the city, and to give instruction on a subject which was agitating them: the Second Coming of Christ. I believe that this epistle is an answer to letters sent by the Thessalonians to Paul and delivered to the Apostle by Timothy. The second epistle, designed to correct certain misconceptions, seems to have followed soon after.

Reading between the lines, it seems that Timothy came to Paul with information that the Thessalonian Christians were loyal to the Faith and wished to see him again; that enemy Jews had charged him with self-interest and had in other ways impugned his motives; that certain converts were liable to slip back into their old ways; that some were using the imminence of the Second Coming as an excuse for idleness and that others, who had lost friends and relatives by death, were anxious to know if these would share the Resurrection.

Those, I think, were some of the questions which Paul set out to answer when he dictated his first *Epistle to the Thessalonians*.

This epistle gives us the picture of a loving pastor anxious for the spiritual welfare of his flock, and is infinitely touching. Paul reminds his followers how hard he had worked while in their company:

"Brothers, you recollect our hard labour and toil, how we worked at our trade night and day, when we preached the gospel to you, so as not to be a burden to any of you . . ." And the missionaries strove collectively and individually with their converts "encouraging you, and charging you to lead a life worthy of the God who called you to his own realm and glory."

The personality and personal example of Paul must have been tremendous. He left behind him in the various cities little self-governing brotherhoods bound together by the good news of the Christian message, as yet without the organization of a priestly hierarchy but held together by the Spirit of Christ and by the memory of the Apostle's teaching and example.

Nothing like St. Paul and his Christian communities had been seen in the world. And how near his converts were to paganism, or to a relapse into paganism, is clear from his earnest exhortations:

"Finally, brothers, we beg and beseech you in the Lord Jesus to follow our instructions about the way you are to live so as to satisfy God; you are leading that life, but you are to excel in it still further. You remember the instructions we gave you on the authority of the Lord Jesus. It is God's will that you should be consecrated, that you abstain from sexual vice, that each of you should learn to take a wife for himself chastely and honourably, not to gratify sexual passion like the Gentiles in their ignorance of God—no one is to defraud or overreach his brother in this matter, for the Lord avenges all these sins, as we told you already in our solemn protest against them."

What a picture such words give us of the Apostle, his hands weary with work, sitting down in the evening among a circle of his converts and speaking to them with earnest simplicity as a teacher speaks to his children. The gentleness, the tenderness, and the charm which Paul, a man capable of so much nervous temper, expended on these simple converts is one of the most beautiful things in ancient literature.

The subject which above all others agitated the people of Thessalonica was the End of the World. It is a subject which has recurred time and again in history, and will no doubt continue to do so. "It seems to appeal most to minds whose natural stability is not very great, and the effect is always bad," writes the Rev. R. H. Malden, in *Problems of the New Testament To-day*. There was, however, a special reason why Paul's converts should have been worried and alarmed. During the closing years of the reign of Claudius a fear that the world was coming to an end was spreading not only among the Jews, but also among the Gentiles. Just as the Christians looked for the Second Coming of Christ, and as the Jews looked for the arrival of the Messiah, so the Gentile world, appalled by the excesses of Imperial madmen and imbeciles, and the rule of such women as Messalina and Agrippina, believed that the time was coming when the gods would wreak vengeance on the infamy of men. Signs and portents were written in the sky. Dreams and omens were given to men. "It was one of those moments," says Hausrath, "when the nations stand in breathless expectation of what the next hour will bring forth. The *Epistle to the Thessalonians* on a small scale mirrors forth what was disturbing the world at large."

In his second *Epistle*, Paul returns to this subject. Perhaps other messages had been delivered to him from the community at Thessalonica, asking for direction and stressing the fact that in expectation of the Second Coming, many Christians had stopped work and were accepting charity from the others. Therefore Paul warns them in his second letter not to be shaken in mind, or to be deceived by any forged letters written to them in his name—a vivid sidelight on the malevolence of his enemies.

Reading the concluding sentences in this second letter, it seems to me that the centuries fall away and we are admitted into the little workshops and the weaving sheds of Thessalonica in the first century.

"Brothers," writes St. Paul, "we charge you in the name of the Lord Jesus Christ to shun any brother who is loafing, instead of following the rule you got from me. For you know quite well how to copy us; we did not loaf in your midst, we did not take free meals from anyone; no, toiling hard at our trade, we worked night and day, so as not to be a burden to any of you. Not that we have no right to such support; it was simply to give you a pattern to copy. We used to charge you even when we were with you, 'If a man will not work, he shall not eat.' But we are informed that some of your number are loafing, busybodies instead of busy. Now in the Lord Jesus Christ we charge and exhort such persons to keep quiet, to do their work and earn their own living. As for yourselves, brothers, never grow tired of doing what is right. Only, if any one shall not obey our orders in this letter, mark that man, do not associate with him—that will make him feel ashamed! You are not to treat him as an enemy, but to put him under discipline as a brother. . . ."

Then, as his habit was, Paul took the reed-pen from his amanuensis and wrote:

"The salutation is in mine own hand, Paul's; that is a mark in every letter of mine. This is how I write. 'The Grace of our Lord Jesus Christ be with you all.' "

9

Berœa, to which Paul and Silas retired by night, lies about forty miles south-west of Salonica. It took this name from its founder, Pheres, but the Macedonians had some difficulty in pronouncing "ph," and they transformed Pherœa into Berœa. It is interesting that modern Greeks should have reverted to something like the ancient Greek pronunciation, for the name of the town to-day is Verria.

I motored out to Verria one morning with a young man who lives in Salonica and studies Byzantine history. He was anxious to show me a number of "hidden" churches in Verria which, he assured me, I should never discover by myself.

The road led across a wide plain where shepherds in black, hooded cloaks guard their flocks, leaning on long sticks and calling vainly after their dogs as they galloped baying at the car. The sheep-folds are made of plaited rushes. Slow herds of oxen moved across the plain, duck rose from the marshes, and hawks hovered in the sky. Sixteen miles or so from Salonica we crossed the Vardar river, which flows from the

Yugoslav mountains through marshes to the sea.

Ahead to the west rose an enormous barrier of heights, where the mountains of Macedonia met the mountains of Yugoslavia and Albania.

Verria is a quiet little agricultural town sitting on a flat ledge of Mount Bermius, six hundred feet above the marshy plain. Streams pour down from hills at the back of the town, filling the streets and the gardens with their melody and nourishing a rich vegetation notable for a wealth of pomegranates, fig-trees and vines. The houses are pure Macedonian in style and bear a close resemblance to our own Elizabethan black-and-white houses. The upper stories project two or three yards above the lower, and in narrow streets nod together like friendly gossips, as they do in York.

The interior design, however, is different. A semi-circular gate in a stone wall usually leads to a courtyard from which a flight of wooden steps ascends to the first floor of the house. While we were looking at one of these courtyards, an elderly woman came out on the balcony and smilingly invited us to enter her dwelling. Like most of the elderly women of Verria, she was dressed like a Rembrandt portrait. She wore a skull-cap on her white hair, a bunchy black skirt, and a little jacket edged with fur. The younger women wear their hair in long plaits.

We climbed the stairs into a bright little sitting-room. The old lady came in carrying a tray containing saucers of crystallized oranges and small glasses of *ouzo*, a favourite Greek apéritif. As she sat watching us, her hands on her lap, she was like a thousand women in England, Scotland, Ireland, or Wales.

"Ah," she said, shaking her head, "every time I see a stranger, it is like seeing my own son."

From the happy expression with which she regarded us, I gathered that her son was alive and well, and I asked where he was. Oh, she replied, he is in a far land, and she had not seen him for three years.

I asked if he were in America.

"No," she replied, with a sigh, "he is in Drama."

As the crow flies, Drama is only about a hundred miles from Verria. . . .

We talked about the hidden churches of Verria, and the old lady told us that one was in her back garden. She led the way down the wooden stairs towards a stone building attractively roofed with old red tiles. It looked like a small barn and there was nothing about it to suggest a church. When we entered, we discovered that the outer walls were camouflage. They had been built to conceal the building within them, a diminutive Byzantine church, probably of the fourteenth century, with an *ikonostasis* rocking beneath the weight of ancient ikons. Dust lay thickly over everything. Admirable frescoes covered walls and dome, and the church when full might have held forty persons.

"There are more than twenty churches hidden away in Verria," said my acquaintance. "They are Byzantine churches which were concealed from the Turks."

We said good-bye to our hostess and entered one after another of these churches, some larger, some as small as the first, but all dark, empty, dusty, concealed by outer walls and built behind houses. There are churches dedicated to St. Christ, St. Photini, St. Kyrikos, St. Stephen, St. George, St. Nicholas, St. Paraskevi, and to the Apostles. My friend was right. No stranger could possibly find these churches for himself.

When Paul came to Verria with Silas, he was received by the only Jewish colony which did not persecute him. The Jews of Berœa heard the Gospel with gladness, so also did the Greeks, both men and women. While the Apostle was teaching in Berœa, Timothy arrived, doubtless to inform Paul that his enemies were on his track. Leaving Silas and Timothy in Berœa, Paul was guided by some of his Berœan converts to the coast and conducted to Athens.

It is delightful to discover that the love and affection which distinguished ancient Berœa in its dealings with St. Paul still animate the modern inhabitants. While the memory of St. Paul has almost vanished from its larger and more famous neighbour, Salonica, little Berœa is intensely proud of its connexion with the Apostle. Any small child in Verria can lead you to a railed-off enclosure in the school playground and point out a flight of four massive steps, from which, he will tell you, the Apostle preached. On the top step it is just possible to trace the word "Pavlos" in Greek letters.

We called on the Bishop of Verria, for the little town is one of the historic bishoprics of Apostolic Christianity, and after a time we were received in a gaunt, bare house by a square-bearded prelate wearing a black cassock over a violet gown. He had been educated at Istanbul, and expressed a keen interest in the legends of his small town. After a servant had carried round crystallized oranges, coffee, and brandy, the Metropolitan discussed St. Paul's connexion with Berœa.

"It is known, of course," he said, "that the first convert of Berœa was Sosipatros, who is a saint in the Greek Orthodox Church."

This Sosipatros is called Sopater in the Authorized Version of the New Testament. He was with Paul at Corinth when the Epistle to the Romans was written, for his name appears in that letter, spelt Sosipater.

I told the Metropolitan that discussion has been waging for years on the question: did St. Paul leave Macedonia by boat, or by land through Thessaly? He told me that local tradition, handed down in the Greek Church in Berœa, is quite definite that the Apostle went by sea.

"We have a strong tradition," said the Metropolitan, "that

when St. Paul was hurried away from Berœa, he was first taken to Colyndros, whose ancient name was Æginion, and then to the coast village of Eleutherochori, once called Methoni. There he found a boat sailing for Athens."

Reluctantly I tore myself away from the gentle, cultured Polycarpos and from his attractive little town, for I had to hurry back to Salonica, where I caught the boat for Athens as they were about to pull up the gangway.

CHAPTER VIII

I stay in Athens and meet a man called Sophocles and another called Byron. On the Acropolis and on the Areopagus I encounter the Athens of St. Paul. My friends introduce me to the life of modern Athens and, in the heat of afternoon, I bathe at Phaleron.

1

IN the summer heat the ship moved past the coast of Thessaly. I saw the head of Mount Olympus lying against the sky; thirty miles south was Ossa, and in another thirty miles came Pelion, whose tall trees made the *Argo*.

The ship was so close to land at times that I could smell the wild thyme and the mint, and I could hear dogs barking in the folds far up on the scented hillsides. The sun dropped behind the mountains and a mist like a band of copper edged the sea, as if Priam's chariots had raised the dust again upon the fields of Troy. Then darkness with a host of stars swooped down upon the world.

In the early morning we came into a narrow channel stagnant as a village pond, lying between two ranges of hills. There was not a ripple on the water. It was like green oil. Its surface was covered with countless yellow jelly-fish, which propelled themselves in a sinister and rather repellent way by sucking in and blowing out the water. Such was the Gulf of Lamia, in which we lay for some hours. There was a wooden jetty piled with barrels, the harbour of a small town called Stylis.

I went ashore, and was driven to Thermopylæ in an old car which I found on the quayside. Summer had leapt on

Greece like a conqueror. The heat was terrible. Men lay as if dead, asleep in the shadow of olive trees; and the beasts in the field and the goats on the hill stood mournfully courting the shade of walls, waiting for the sun to set. The green hills had turned brown. The flowers had died. The earth was cracking in the heat. Over burning gullies of white stones strode high, pointless bridges, and above the helpless earth lay a sky across which, it seemed, no cloud would ever sail again.

Thermopylæ looked like a salt desert in Arizona. The sun flickered over a plain dotted with hummocks of tough grass. It is now difficult to recognize the famous pass which Leonidas with his three hundred Spartans and seven hundred Thespians defended against the Persian army. Perhaps I might have been able to do so on a spring day, but the task was quite beyond me on this tropical forenoon. Earthquakes have changed the lie of the land, and silt brought down by the river Spercheius has built up a wide plain between the mountains and the sea. There is certainly nothing at Thermopylæ to-day which a battalion of Highlanders could not defeat in half an hour. But it was worth the journey, if only to wonder where that famous hillock stood on which Leonidas and his heroes fell one by one, pierced by the arrows of the Medes; if only to say to myself in after-years that I had stood upon the ground where Dienekes spoke a sentence that flew straight into immortality:

"The number of the barbarians is so great," he was told, "that when they shoot their arrows the sun will be darkened."

And Dienekes replied:

"So much the better, we shall then fight in the shade."

I walked to the sulphur springs which gave Thermopylæ its name. The day was so hot that no steam rose from them. They were warm and green and stank like parts of Harrogate. Under a burnt-up awning of vine boughs, I drank wine with a company of villagers who thought I was mad. Then summoning up my courage, I faced the heat again and went back to Stylis and the ship.

Night fell as we steamed through the narrow channel between the mainland and the island of Eubœa. Early in the morning we came quite close to Marathon.

I saw a little bay with flat land lying back to the hills. Somewhere there was the low mound beneath which, buried on the field of battle, lay the Athenians who died under the rain of Persian arrows. From the hills at the back, ten thousand Athenians marched against the host of Darius, driving them sea-ward to their ships. In that same bay Cynægirus, the brother of Æschylus, held on to a galley with his right hand; when it was severed by a Persian scimitar, he held on with his left; and when that hand, too, was severed, he continued to hold on with his teeth. In the last century the mound of Marathon was opened and men saw the charred bones, and the pottery and other objects placed with the dead over two thousand four hundred years ago.

The ship passed Marathon and approached the rocky headland of Sunium. Behind that majestic cliff were the mines of Laurium, whose silver built the fleet that smashed the Persians at Salamis. Then, as we rounded the point, I saw a sight that remains in my mind for ever as one of the loveliest memories of Greece.

High on the crest of a cape stands the ruin of a white temple. It is all that is left of the Temple of Poseidon at Sunium, the most southerly point of Attica. In the old days, mariners coming from Asia Minor or from Egypt kept a look out for the flash of sunlight on the temple at Sunium. It was built in remote ages to propitiate Poseidon, god of the sea, who was believed to have evil designs on all ships passing the cape. It was while passing Sunium that Phrontis, son of Onetor, who excelled all men of his day in navigation, fell dead at the steering-oar of the galley that was bringing Menelaus back from Troy.

When the ship had passed the Temple of Poseidon, the sailors would look along the hills for the first sign of Athens; and they would see the sunlight flashing from the gilded point of the spear which Athene held high above the Acropolis.

St. Paul's ship came this way, and he too would have looked for that flash of light on the hills; he would have listened to the sailors who crowded forward to explain to each new voyager that they were looking for the spearhead of the great Athena Promachos, whose helmet rose seventy feet above her sandals. And this mighty statue was standing there long after the glory of Athens had been humbled to the dust. Alaric the Goth saw it four centuries after Christ, and at the sight of it, they said, he turned his pirate ship and fled in terror.

There are no words to express the first sight of Athens as a ship moves across Phaleron Bay towards the Piræus. It is one of the supreme moments in travel.

The sun was sinking behind the island of Ægina. The last warm light was shining full on the slopes of Mount Hymettus. Five miles from the sea, and on ground that rose only slightly, I saw a large city of brown-and-white houses. From the centre of the city, rising as abruptly as the rock of Stirling Castle springs from the Links of Forth, was a brown hill: and I knew that I was looking at the Acropolis. I could see the white pillars of the Parthenon in the clear light. And I was so happy at that moment, watching the last light of day fade from the city of Athens, that I felt happiness must be a prolongation of such a moment to the end of life.

It did not matter now if Athens were to disappoint me; if she turned out to be a poor thing hiding behind a mighty name; for I had seen her in the light of evening as I had always imagined her to be; proud, splendid, and old.

As soon as I stepped ashore in the morning and moved from the protective barrier of the dock gates, a dark-visaged crowd of men swooped down on me. Some held out brown sponges, others boxes of Turkish Delight; some imagined me to be the kind of man who wanted a doll dressed as an *efzone*, others offered me post-cards of the Acropolis and horrid little plaster replicas of the Venus de Milo. They all talked at the top of their voices, reducing their wares from fifty drachmæ to forty and thirty and twenty without any encouragement on my part; and those who were not trying to sell something offered to guide me through Athens and to find the best car to take me there.

I looked at these men, if not with pleasure at least with appreciation. In an age that cheerfully accepts every kind of fake, they seemed to be delightfully authentic. They might have been a crowd out of Aristophanes.

Standing in the middle of this crowd, feeling rather like a bone that is being pulled to pieces by a pack of hungry dogs, I had sufficient detachment left to wonder if Sir Alma-Tadema's well-washed, well-laundered and pleated Greece ever really existed outside the imagination of Victorian romanticists who saw in Periclean Athens everything that Victorian Sheffield was not. I have an idea that landing in Greece must always have been like this. I remembered how Lycinus, in the *Amores* of Lucian, says that as soon as he stepped ashore on the island of Rhodes "two or three people immediately hurried up, eager to tell me the history for a small fee. . . ."

Shaking myself free from the guides, I leapt into the nearest car and told the driver to take me to Athens. We soon left the Piræus behind us, and rounding Phaleron Bay, on whose waters rested an Imperial Airways seaplane, we entered the straight, five-mile motor road to Athens. This road is built on the site of the northern Long Wall of Themistocles, which, with its companion wall to the south, was in ancient times compared to a cable anchoring Athens to the coast. When we were within a mile or so of the city, I caught a fleeting glimpse of the Acropolis rising in a blaze of morning sunshine, one of the grandest sights in the world.

We plunged into the broad, straight streets of a modern European city, with good shops, green tram-cars, murderous green motor-omnibuses, a press of noisy cars, hundreds of cafés, whose tables overflowed to the pavement, newspaper kiosks, public gardens full of exotic trees (and German nurse-maids); and a great central place, the focus of modern Athens, Constitution Square, beneath whose pepper trees the modern Athenian gathers to discuss, with that passionate fervour which has always been a characteristic of the Greek, the latest political rumour.

The roof of my hotel was flat and accessible. From its height I looked over Athens. I saw the high, oblong rock of the Acropolis rising above the city, and I saw the wooded peak of Mount Lycabettus, the tame, domesticated volcano of Athens. The size of Athens surprised me, for this big city is the creation of only a hundred years.

How strange it is to realize that Athens, so famous in antiquity and so vigorous to-day, disappeared from history from the time of Pausanias, in the second century, until comparatively modern days. Practically nothing is known of Byzantine Athens, Latin Athens, or of Turkish Athens. It disappeared as a mighty, but dying, classical city, to emerge in 1675 as a Turkish village.

The first Englishman who expressed a wish to see Athens was John Milton, but his wish was unsatisfied. As he was about to cross into Greece, the Civil War broke out in England and he returned, because he "considered it base that, while my fellow-countrymen were fighting at home for liberty, I should be travelling abroad at ease for intellectual culture."

The first Englishman actually to explore the site of ancient Athens, and to give some measurements of the Parthenon, was Francis Vernon, a Londoner. He was born in 1637 and was afflicted with "an insatiable desire of seeing," which curiosity caused him on one occasion to be captured and sold by pirates and eventually, at the age of forty, to be murdered by Arabs in Persia, during a quarrel about a pen-knife. Vernon's notes on Athens are embodied in a letter to a friend in England and they are still, I believe, in the possession of the Royal Society. So far as I know, they have never been published.

The earliest published account in English is that of Sir George Wheler, who in 1675 spent a month in Turkish Athens. His book, *A Journey Into Greece*, was printed in 1682. It is a delightful and valuable book, for the author was an observant classical scholar and he was also able to relate with charm a journey through a country which at that time was unknown and unexplored. Wheler discovered that the Parthenon had become a Turkish mosque, with a minaret built beside it, to the top of which he climbed. Gunpowder was stored in the exquisite Temple of the Wingless Victory, and he was not able to get into the Erechtheum "because the Turk that lives in it hath made it his *Seraglio* for his Women."

Athens at that time was a town of about eight to ten thousand inhabitants, three parts of them Christians, the rest Turks. There were no walls, but the outermost houses were built close together and thus served as a wall, the approaches being closed at night with gates: for even at that time pirates were such regular visitors that the garrison patrolled the walls of the Acropolis all night, "making a great hallowing and noise to signify their watchfulness."

The Turks, contrary to the general conception of the race, have always been a tolerant, easy-going people, and Wheler counted about two hundred churches, fifty of which had regular priests in attendance.

He was shocked by the amount of paint used by the Greek women, who "looked very graceful in their manner of dress, but so horribly painted, that it was hard to conjecture what their natural complexion was by reason of the thick Vizard of Paint they had on." Again he noted that: "When a Virgin is to be married, she is brought to the church as richly attired as the fortunes of her relatives will bear, but her face is so be-daubed with gross paint that it is not easy to determine whether she be flesh and blood or a statue made of plaster. She returns home from the church to the house of her hus-band with a great crown of gilded metal on her head, accom-panied by all the guests and her near relations with pipes and hand-drums and the best music they can make: whilst she in the meantime is conducted at so slow a pace that it is scarcely perceivable that she moveth. And so soon as she is entered into the house of her spouse they throw sugar-plums out of the windows upon the people, who are crowded and throng'd at the door."

The painted women of Athens invariably impressed the early travellers, and the fashion is, I think, of interest, be-cause it may have been a survival from classical and Byzan-tine times. The classics are full of references to the eye-paint, the rouge and the coats of white lead used by the women of Athens.

There is a big gap between the explorations of Wheler and the scientific travellers of the eighteenth century, who, begin-ning with Stuart and Revett in 1751, unconsciously pre-pared classical scholars in England to champion the cause of Greek Independence in the following century by caus-ing them to identify modern Greeks with the heroes of their schooldays. Stuart and Revett's four mighty tomes, the *An-tiquities of Athens*, give a splendid idea of the city as it used to be under Turkish rule.

The Acropolis was a warren of labyrinthine Turkish streets

and gardens. Turbaned Turks in flowing draperies practised archery and exercised their horses in the shadow of the rock. When Wheler saw the Parthenon, the roof was still intact. But in 1687 the shells of the Venetian fleet fell on the building, igniting the powder stored there and killing three hundred Turks: the roof was blown off and many columns were destroyed. Characteristically, the Turks did not restore the Parthenon, but built a mosque and houses inside it. The Erechtheum, no longer a Turkish harem as in Wheler's time, was a roofless ruin with one of the Caryatides missing. An engraving of this building shows that the accumulation of earth on the Acropolis was so deep that the level of the roadway was about two feet below the Caryatides, so that nearly half this temple was below the ground.

In the following century it became the fashion to visit Athens. Byron first saw Greece in 1809—more than ten years before the War of Independence began—when, as a young man of twenty-two, he travelled across Europe with his Cambridge friend, John Cam Hobhouse, who afterwards became Lord Broughton. Hobhouse left a record of this tour in the form of a large volume entitled *A Journey through Albania and other Provinces of Turkey in Europe and Asia.* Byron recorded his impressions in the Second Canto of *Childe Harold.* The two friends saw everything that the early travellers had seen; but, to Byron's rage, they also saw Lord Elgin's agents sensibly engaged in taking down the metopes from the Parthenon and packing them for shipment to England. A lot of unkind things are said, perhaps naturally, about Lord Elgin in Greece, but anyone who compares the two series of casts in the British Museum of those figures still in position on the Parthenon—one series taken by Lord Elgin and the other fifty years later—will realize that even in that time the frieze has suffered severe deterioration. Also, had Lord Elgin not taken the marbles, someone else certainly would have done so.

The Greek War of Independence began eleven years after Byron's visit, but it was not until 1833 that the Turkish garrison left Athens. In 1834 it was decided to create Athens the capital of the independent Kingdom of Greece.

A German architect, Schaubert, was employed to plan the wide streets, the squares, the boulevards: and so Athens, which in 1834 was a village of five thousand inhabitants, has become in 1936 a city of over four hundred and fifty thousand people.

2

I could sit for hours in Constitution Square—the agora of modern Athens—watching the Greek talking his eternal politics. The race has been diluted by all kinds of Balkan blood, but some of the chief characteristics of the classical Greek remain. Was it not Demosthenes who pictured the Greeks bustling about the agora, asking, "Is there anything new?" or "What is the latest news?" If you sit at a café table under the pepper trees in Constitution Square to-day, you will hear each man, as he sits down at a neighbouring table, say to his friends:

"Well, and what is the latest news? Is there a recent development?"

Heads in black felt hats are obscured by one of the numerous newspapers, which is immediately flung aside when a boy comes along crying, so truly and delightfully, *"Ephemerides!"* with the latest crop of political discussion under his arm.

One side of the square is occupied by the huge yellow monstrosity of the old Palace of King Otho, now the Parliament House. The guard of tall *efzones* in their Albanian costumes —stiff white kilts, embroidered jackets, woollen tights, red upturned shoes with pompons on the toes—leans picturesquely on its rifles beside the Grave of the Unknown Warrior. Now and then a tourist steals up to take a photograph, and these good-looking young men instinctively adopt an heroic pose, because, like the Life Guards of Whitehall, they are used to it.

One of the first things the visitor notices about Athens is the clarity of the atmosphere. Plutarch somewhere speaks of air like spun-silk; and it is this silk-like air that covers Athens, creating in the mind a state of exhilaration and a sense of well-being. There is a sparkle and a happiness in the air of Athens which drive away ill-humour and depression.

The language of Aristophanes—let us not be pedantic about this—has kept abreast of the times. I look round at the hoardings and see that chocolate, cigarettes and Dunlop Tires are the best advertised objects . . . ΣΟΚΟΛΑΤΑ . . . ΣΙΓΑΡΕΤΤΑ . . . ΕΛΑΣΤΙΚΑ DUNLOP.

I see, inscribed above a door, the word tooth-doctor, ΟΔΟΝΤΙΑΤΡΟΣ, and, opening an Athens newspaper, I discover that the disciples of Æsculapius, unlike their British colleagues, by no means deny themselves the pleasure of self-praise and advertisement. The cinema announcements, too, prove that Greece has been enriched by many new heroes. After a moment of indecision, I translate ΜΑΡΛΕΝ ΝΤΗΤΡΙΧ into Marlene Dietrich. Greta Garbo is not, perhaps, any easier—ΓΚΡΕΤΑ ΓΚΑΡΜΗΟ; but it takes me some time to believe that ΚΛΑΡΚ ΓΚΕΪΜΛΛ is Clark Gable. High on a board, with the air of a battered and returned Odysseus, shines the word gramophone—ΓΡΑΜΜΟΦΟΝΑ.

It is good to sit among the eager, chattering crowds in this sunny place and to watch and listen. There is sometimes no need to listen, for the Greeks have a complete vocabulary of gesture. It is known to everyone. What can be more significant than the gesture of distrust or dislike, a gesture also of warning? A man will lightly grasp the right-hand lapel of his coat with the first finger and thumb of his right hand and quietly, almost secretly, move the cloth back and forwards, saying at the same time, "Pup-pup-pup-pup." Or the gesture that denotes something fine and splendid and rare? The right hand is lifted shoulder high, first finger and thumb together, fingers curved, the palm of the hand towards the face of the gesturer, and the hand is brought down through the air several times in a very sharp, definite manner, only the hand and the forearm moving. Then there is the gesture inferring riches and splendour. The open right hand scoops the air in a luxurious way, as if shovelling invisible gold into the face of the speaker. Leisure and vitality describe Parliament Square as, I imagine, they would describe the agora of Athens in the time of Pericles.

There are no titles in Greece, except a few old Venetian ones used locally in the Ionian Islands, and there is no feeling of social caste. It seems to me that rich and poor rub shoulders more intimately in Greece than in any other country I know. The little boot-black, whose sharp rap of brush against his boot-box is one of the characteristic sounds of Athens, will glance up from polishing the shoes of a politician or an officer and, as equal to equal, give the usual Greek greeting:

"And what do you think of the political situation?"

The politician and the officer may smile with amusement, but they will answer gravely enough, as if to their own son.

There can be few countries where members of the Government are more readily accessible to every sort of suppliant and time-waster. In other countries secretaries and undersecretaries bar the way to Cabinet Ministers, but this would not work in Greece. Everyone, if he has a grievance, regards it as his right personally to see the man who can remove it. Whether this innate sense of democracy is a legacy from ancient Greece I do not know, but it was one of the first things that impressed me. It is surprising to be told that when a man pushing a barrow of melons threatens to go and see the Prime

Minister, he is probably making no idle boast. George I, grandfather of the present King, understood this side of the Greek character. He would often walk in the streets and talk to anyone. Once, meeting a fiery Republican, George I asked him:

"And do you still persist in wishing to hang me?"

"Certainly, Your Majesty," replied the deputy, "as long as you remain on the throne. If you abdicate and become a Republican, I should become your closest friend."

Naturally the Greeks have a word for it. It is *automismós*—individuality. Every Greek, no matter how humble, prizes *automismós* as his dearest possession. This makes the country a difficult one to rule, but the free and independent expression of opinion, and the complete absence of any servility or feeling of inferiority between rich and poor, make the little country of Greece a stimulating and sometimes incomprehensible place to visit.

The ambition of every Greek is to live in Athens. When a man makes money in England, his first act is generally to build or buy a house in the country. In Greece his first act is to live in Athens.

There is, consequently, no country life in Greece as we know it in England. There is a splendid peasantry, but few landed proprietors. There are no country houses such as those of England, or the châteaux of France, or the estates which once existed in Spain.

The dream of the average Greek is to sit in the cafés of Athens, reading the newspapers as they pour from the press. It has been said that every Greek reads ten newspapers a day. This may be true of Athens, and I am sure it would be true of the rest of Greece if ten different newspapers were obtainable.

"Why is your political news so bad over the wireless?" a Greek asked me. "Whenever I manage to get London, what do I hear? Cricket! Football! Do you think of nothing else? If I want British political news, I must get Berlin or Rome."

"Well, you must understand that cricket and football occupy much the same position in my country that politics do in yours," I told him. "We have test matches and cup finals; and so do you. But *you* call them revolutions."

At first sight it would seem that every vestige of Turkish Athens has vanished; but this is not so. At the foot of the Acropolis are a number of narrow lanes full of rickety old Turkish shops, owned, of course, by Greeks. The ambitious visitor can go to this place—the name is Shoe Lane—and buy as many fake tanagra figures, fake Greek vases, newly-coined tetradrachms, and such-like, as he can afford; and they will not be cheap.

In these lanes lives the last of Turkish Athens. You will see an old man in European clothes turning over and over in his hand a string of amber beads, the *kombológion*, or rosary of the Orient; and, glancing inside a café, you will see a Greek sucking at the mouthpiece of a *narghilé*, like any Turk or Syrian. In the markets where peasants bring their fruits and vegetables, you will notice round the neck of mules and donkeys the little string of blue beads which Moslems believe to be a charm against the evil eye.

This faint flavour of the Orient, a note struck again by the date palms in the public gardens, by the presence of pilaf on the restaurant menu, by the little glasses of *ouzo*, which is like the *arak* of Syria and Palestine, and by the vivid gestures of the Greeks, explains in some measure the peculiar charm of Athens.

3

I paid my ten drachmæ to the man in the little green office on the side of the Acropolis, and began to mount the steps to the Propylæa. We have all been familiar with pictures of the Acropolis and the Parthenon since we were children. We have seen them in books, in the vicar's study, in steamship offices; and we have received them on post-cards from every friend who has gone on a Hellenic cruise.

I had been warned by Professor Mahaffy not to expect too much. This is what he says, in *Rambles and Studies in Greece*:

"There is no ruin, all the world over, that combines so much striking beauty, so distinct a type, so vast a volume of history, so great a pageant of immortal memories. There is, in fact, no building on earth which can sustain the burden of such greatness, and so the first visit to the Acropolis is and must be disappointing. When the traveller reflects how all the Old World's culture culminated in Greece—all Greece in Athens—all Athens in its Acropolis—all the Acropolis in the Parthenon—so much crowds upon the mind confusedly that we look for some enduring monument whereupon we can fasten our thoughts, and from which we can pass as from a visible starting-point into all this history and all this greatness. And at first we look in vain. The shattered pillars and the torn pediments will not bear so great a strain; and the traveller feels forced to admit a sense of disappointment, sore against his will."

With this warning fresh in my mind, I mounted the steps leading to the Propylæa; and the sun blazed so violently over the pillars of that exquisite entrance hall that my eyes ached as I looked. The ancient Athenians were so proud of this lovely building that, says a comedian of the period, "they are always belauding four things: their myrtle berries, their honey, the Propylæa, and their figs."

As I passed through the Propylæa, I saw before me a great space of rough rock rising upward, and on the summit of this rock the Parthenon stood against the blue sky.

I thought that never in my life had I seen anything so

beautiful. I was almost afraid to go any nearer in case I was wrong. How Dr. Mahaffy could have written so strangely of the Parthenon puzzled and amazed me; for if there is one sight that seems to me to exceed the most ardent expectation, it is the Parthenon. Lifted high above Athens, with nothing behind it but the blue sky of summer, far larger than I had ever imagined it to be, yet looking queerly weightless, the Parthenon, even in ruin, looks as if it has just alighted from heaven upon the summit of the Acropolis.

As I drew near to this inspired building, I said to myself: "I have seen the Pyramids, Karnak, Abu-Simbel, Baalbec, Timgad, and a hundred other remains of the ancient world, but you are the most lovely thing I have ever seen; you are the only ruin on earth that a man would care to see again, again, and again; and I would like to climb this hill to see you every year until the end of my life."

As I stood in the presence of the Parthenon, I realized that my ascent of the Acropolis, and my approach through the Propylæa, was a preparation for this moment: and I remembered the words of Socrates, that a temple should be difficult of access so that men would approach it in purity of heart. You cannot come suddenly on the Parthenon: you must ascend to it.

Why can no picture or photograph ever succeed in portraying the Parthenon? It is not an easy question to answer. There is something about the balance of this temple, something purely Greek in its rejection of the unnecessary, which is almost impossible to convey on canvas, because it appeals not so much to the eye as to the mind. I can best describe it by saying that to me the Parthenon has a quality of life which suggests a bird alighting from the air, in that brief moment as it closes its wings and is still poised and balanced.

Those tall pillars of Pentelic marble have yellowed with time, because of the oxide of iron in them. The colour has been described as gold or brown; but it is neither; it is a curious milky gold, the colour of crust on Devonshire cream.

I felt an enormous sense of gratitude to the Turk for turning the Parthenon into a mosque, for propping up the various buildings with walls, and for generally preserving everything that stands on the Acropolis to-day. A more energetic and meddlesome race would have torn the whole building to the earth. Although the Turks never took the trouble to put up anything once it had fallen down, they also rarely pulled down anything as long as it would stand up.

How different the Parthenon and its temples must have looked as they left the hands of their creators fifteen centuries ago. Instead of the cream-coloured marble now worn and weathered by the years, many of the statues and much of the architecture shone with gold and with colour.

The Greeks loved colour and brilliance. Their statues were often painted and gilded: hair was painted red, and draperies were green, blue, or red. Spears, sandals, crowns, horse bridles and chains, were of bronze or of gilded bronze. In the gloom of the Parthenon stood the forty feet high statue for whom all this splendour was devised, the great wooden figure of Athena, helmeted, standing with her left hand touching her shield, and in her right hand a figure of Winged Victory.

This statue by Pheidias was one of the most remarkable works of antiquity. Although made of wood; because it was the traditional material for statues, not an inch of wood was visible. The face and hands were plates of ivory. The eyes were of precious stones, and tresses of gold hair fell from a gold helmet.

Even in times when men could combine to make so perfect a thing as the Parthenon and all that it contained, envy was at work, and human nature was not always noble. Pericles, knowing that the time would come when Pheidias might be in trouble with the citizens, insisted that all the gold plates on his statue, weighing forty talents, should be removable.

Sure enough the time came when enemies charged Pheidias with stealing part of the gold which the State had entrusted to him. The artist was able to detach the plates and order them to be weighed. The charge was at once proved false. But his enemies persisted and eventually succeeded in driving a genius to his death in a disease-laden prison.

The Erechtheum is a wonderful contrast to the austere Parthenon. It is amusing to reflect that an unhappy copy of this lovely building, smoke-blackened and grimed by London soot, stands in the Euston-road, incorporated inappropriately in the church of St. Pancras.

Anyone who has been to Athens will agree with me that the abiding memory is the Parthenon, high above the modern city, the blue sea seen far off between the columns, and sunlight touching the creamy marble.

No men in all the world found a more exquisite stage for their genius; and no stage was ever more fortunate in its artists.

4

Descending from the Acropolis, I saw on the right a high outcrop of rock. It is separated from the Acropolis by a narrow path, and an ancient staircase of about fifteen or sixteen steps leads to the top, where the rock bears trace of having been artificially levelled. This is the Areopagus, the ancient meeting-place of the famous assembly before whom St. Paul delivered his speech to the Athenians.

Some people believe that the rock of the Areopagus is the spot from which the Apostle spoke, while others consider it more probable that he addressed the assembly from some other place, possibly the agora or the King's Stoa. If the first are correct, St. Paul must have ascended these rock-cut steps, he must have stood on this commanding crag, and, as he told his listeners that God "dwelleth not in temples made with hands," he must have pointed towards the Acropolis, rising a few paces from him, crowded with marble temples and dominated by the colossal Athena whose gold spear-tip was visible to mariners at Sunium.

During the summer the Areopagus is one of the loneliest places in Athens. Few people care to visit that unshaded rock. It is haunted only by a melancholy man in a black hat, who sidles up to the visitor and says: "Mister, I will show you where St. Paul made his speech."

Finding it less irritating in the long run to indulge guides who, having good memories, ever after leave one in peace, I allowed him to lead me to a certain portion of the flat rock, where he delivered his stilted little speech in a pathetic atmosphere of anti-climax. From that time onwards, when I went there early in the morning or in the cool of the evening, he would rise and touch his black hat to me; and we became quite friendly. On one occasion he introduced his little boy to me, a lad who, from the look of him now, will grow up to be a terror to tourists in twenty years time. So in this easy way I purchased the freedom of the Areopagus. I rarely met a soul when I went there to sit and watch the Propylæa change colour in the setting sun.

When St. Paul came to Athens, the city had fallen from its ancient splendour. The great days of Hellas were as distant from the Apostle as the Tudor Age is from ourselves. Marathon and Thermopylæ were as remote to him as Bosworth Field is to a modern Englishman.

I have no idea whether St. Paul had ever read Homer, Thucydides or Herodotus, or whether he took any interest in the history of the race whose language he spoke; but surely, as a liberal-minded Hellenist and the child of a great Hellenistic university town, he must have felt his pulse quicken when he approached Athens.

As he walked beside the Long Walls and saw the Acropolis rising from the plain, the Voice of Jesus may have sounded in his ears, in words like those recorded by St. John:

"And other sheep I have, which are not of this fold: them also I must bring, and they shall hear my voice; and there shall be one flock and one shepherd."

In preaching the Gospel in Athens, for the first time in his life, the Apostle stood alone in a world-renowned city of the West. It is true that he had turned to the Gentiles at Pisidian Antioch, but he had approached them through the synagogue. He had journeyed among the Jews of the Dispersion through Asia Minor and Macedonia; but in Athens that world was behind him and he stood alone, the first Christian missionary in the intellectual stronghold of the Roman world. I think there are few moments in the history of early Christianity more dramatic, or in their sequel more notable, than the moment when the eyes of St. Paul first saw the Acropolis.

Athens at that time was not even the capital of the Roman senatorial province of Achaia. The Piræus had silted up, and the commercial life of Greece had moved to the new Roman colonies of Patras, Nicopolis, and, above all, to the capital of the province, Corinth, a city almost as rich and dissolute as Syrian Antioch. But Athens, although no longer powerful commercially or politically, was still the most famous city in Greece. She survived by virtue of her past glory. The Romans were the first Philhellenes, and in their sometimes contemptuous affection they pardoned Athens deeds that would have brought destruction on any other city in the Empire. In the afterglow of creation, the once-splendid city of Pericles and Plato was content to be the university of the Roman world. She gave herself all the airs of greatness, but she no longer created anything: she merely criticized. She no longer did anything: she read history instead. Her academies and her

streets were filled with the arguments of Platonists, Peripa-
tetics, Stoics and Epicureans.

At this period the moral and intellectual decline of Athens
appeared complete. From Theomnestus, Curator of the Academy in 44 B.C., to the time of Plutarch's teacher, Ammonius
Alexandreus, who taught in the last decade of the first century, no man of first-rate importance was produced by Athens.
It is only fair to remember, of course, that intellectual centres
had developed at Rome, Alexandria, Antioch, and Tarsus, and
perhaps a share of the intellect, that would in ancient times
have blossomed in the shadow of the Acropolis, was at this
period spread about the world.

Outwardly Athens was, perhaps, more brilliant than ever.
Her streets were thronged with the rich youth of the world.
Philosophers and teachers were never more numerous. Distinguished men banished from other lands could always find
a happy retreat in a city that, in spite of its mental and moral
decline, was still a great intellectual force. Tourists on their
way to visit the ruined temples of Egypt, and to write their
names on the base of the Colossi at Thebes, would break
their voyage at Athens. These first Hellenic travellers, led by
their voluble guides, would visit the famous relics of the past,
inspecting the statues and the works of art, standing in awe
on the Acropolis, where the temples, blazing with gold and
colour, stood among their crowded votive-offerings much as
they did in the time of Pericles. Athena Promachos rose above
them, grasping her golden spear.

Although Athens had begun to decline, she preserved her
antiquities and monuments, for on them her existence de-
pended. She multiplied the number of her festivals. The sacrifices offered at her temples, and the succession of great occasions which attracted pilgrims from every part of the world,
never failed to astonish those who visited the city. In addition
to the Dionysia, the Panathenia, and the annual mysteries at

Eleusis, historical events, such as the Battle of Marathon and the birthdays of men like Plato and Socrates, were religiously commemorated, giving to the present a vivid beauty and excitement.

At the time of St. Paul's visit to Athens, another wayfarer, in whom many a modern reader must have detected a first-century Bernard Shaw, was making the same journey. This was Apollonius of Tyana, whose encounter with the customs official I have already quoted. Like St. Paul, Apollonius noted the fact that at Athens "altars are set up in honour even of unknown gods," and the sights that met this philosopher, as he walked to Athens from the Piræus, were the same as those which must have met the eyes of the Apostle. Philostratus, who wrote the life of the sage of Tyana, gives us an intimate glimpse of his journey to Athens.

"Having sailed into the Piræus at the season of the mysteries, when the Athenians keep the most crowded of Hellenic festivals," writes Philostratus, "he went post-haste up from the ship into the city; but as he went forward, he fell in with quite a number of students of philosophy on their way down to Phaleron. Some of them were stripped and underwent the heat, for in autumn the sun is hot upon the Athenians; and others were studying books, and some were rehearsing their speeches, and others were disputing. But no one passed him by, for they all guessed that it was Apollonius, and they turned and thronged around him and welcomed him warmly; and ten youths in a body met him and holding up their hands towards the Acropolis they cried: 'By Athene yonder, we were on the point of going down to the Piræus there to take ship to Ionia in order to visit you.' And he welcomed them and said how much he congratulated them on their study of philosophy."

The experiences of Apollonius in Athens are interesting to the student of Paul's time because they reflect the scenes in which the Apostle moved. When he reached Athens, one of the first actions of the philosopher was to present himself for initiation into the Eleusinian Mysteries; but he was refused, because, said the hierophant, he had dabbled in magic. Whereupon Apollonius remarked in a blunt and Shavian manner: "You have not yet mentioned the chief of my offence, which is that, knowing, as I do, more about the initiatory rite than you do yourself, I have nevertheless come for initiation to you, as if you were wiser than I am."

The degeneracy of the Athens of St. Paul's time is mirrored in the magnificent denunciation which Apollonius flung at certain dancers at the festival of Dionysius:

"Stop dancing away the reputation of the victors of Salamis, as well as of many other good men departed this life," was his splendid opening. "For if indeed this were a Lacedæmonian form of dance, I would say 'Bravo, soldiers; for you are training yourselves for war, and I would join in your dance'; but as it is a soft dance and one of effeminate tendency, what am I to say of your national trophies? . . . You are softer than the women of Xerxes' day, and you are dressing yourselves up to your own despite, old and young and tender youth alike, you who of old flocked to the temple of Agraulus in order to swear to die in battle on behalf of the fatherland. And now it seems the same people are ready to swear to become bacchants and don the thyrsus in behalf of their country; and no one bears a helmet, but disguised as female harlequins, to use the phrase of Euripides, they shine in shame alone. Nay more, I hear that you turn yourselves into winds, and wave your skirts and pretend that you are ships bellying their sails aloft. But surely you might have at least some respect for the winds that were your allies and once blew mightily to protect you, instead of turning Boreas who was your patron, and who of all the winds is the most masculine, into a woman; for Boreas would never have become the lover of Oreithya if he had seen her executing, like you, a skirt dance."

While one cannot help feeling that the sage was rubbing it in rather hard, for Athens at this period made no pretence at heroism, one is grateful for this glimpse of the frivolity of a city and the effect it had on an ascetic of the old school.

What effect it had on the mind of St. Paul can easily be conjectured. Some writers have imagined the Apostle walking in amazed horror between lines of Athenian statues. I do not believe this. Neither the life nor the religion of Athens could amaze St. Paul. Had he not lived in Syrian Antioch? Graven images were to him an abomination, but he had seen them every day of his life.

I believe that St. Paul joined the crowds of tourists in Athens and visited all the show places with them. He would have entered the Parthenon and looked on the famous Athena of ivory and gold, gleaming in the shaded light, her sandals on the level with a man's eyes and her helmet-plumes almost touching the roof. He would have seen the Temple of Nike Apteros, the Erechtheum, and the Cave of Pan. I believe that he must have studied, with no pleasure it is true, the great host of statues, Greek and foreign, which stood on pedestals in street and temple.

"Now while Paul waited for them at Athens, his spirit was stirred in him, when he saw the city wholly given to idolatry. Therefore disputed he in the synagogue with the Jews, and with the devout persons, and in the market daily with them met with him. Then certain philosophers of the Epicureans, and of the Stoicks, encountered him. And some said, What will this babbler say? other some, He seemeth to be a setter forth of strange gods: because he preached unto them Jesus and the resurrection.

"And they took him, and brought him unto Areopagus, saying, May we know what this new doctrine, whereof thou speakest is? For thou bringest certain strange things to our ears: we would know therefore what these things mean. (For all the Athenians and strangers which were there spent their time in nothing else, but to tell, or hear some new thing.)"

How true is this description in *Acts* of the curiosity and mental restlessness of the Athenians. It is mentioned by Plato, Euthyphron, Phædo, Protagoras, Demosthenes, and by Plutarch, who commented on the Athenian restlessness, subtlety, love of noise, and novelty. Curiosity mingled with mental arrogance describes the Athenian attitude to St. Paul. The word translated as "babbler" in *Acts* is σπερμολόγος—*spermológos*—an Athenian slang term, which means "seed-picker," and was applied to people who loafed about the agora and the quay-sides, picking up odds and ends. In modern life a *spermológos* would be a tramp, or one of those who contrive to make a poor living by picking up cigarette-ends and by exploring dust-bins in the morning. As the Athenians applied it to St. Paul, it conveyed contempt. The philosophers believed the Apostle to be a snapper-up of unconsidered theological and philosophical trifles.

Conscious of the contempt with which these arrogant philosophers regarded him, St. Paul nevertheless eagerly agreed to address them. And his address, couched in terms of polite irony, proves that although he may have explored Athens as earnestly as any tourist from Rome or Alexandria, he was unmoved by the sights that impressed other visitors because his mind was wholly occupied with the salvation of Mankind through Jesus Christ. The only things that impressed him in Athens were connected with this mission. Everything else was purely trivial and secondary. So, scorning to flatter the Athenians, as many a philosopher making his first speech must have done, by some graceful reference to the beauty of the city or its ancient fame, St. Paul springs at once to the only thing that impressed him as he wandered the streets of Athens: the multiplicity of altars.

Standing either on the rock of the Areopagus, or among the members of the Court of the Areopagus, he began:

"Ye men of Athens, in all things I perceive that ye are somewhat superstitious," or as Dr. Moffatt has translated the speech: "Men of Athens, I observe at every turn that you are a most religious people. Why, as I passed along, and scanned your objects of worship, I actually came upon an altar with an inscription TO AN UNKNOWN GOD."

It was an excellent beginning. It had the local touch, the right note of something surprising to follow. To everyone who listened to St. Paul, the altars inscribed TO AN UNKNOWN GOD were, of course, a commonplace. Everyone knew the story of the plague that visited Athens in the sixth century before Christ; and how, after sacrifices had been made to every known god and the plague continued, the services of the Cretan prophet, Epimenides, were requested. He drove a flock of black and white sheep to the Areopagus and allowed them to stray from there as they liked, waiting until they rested of their own free will: and on those spots were the sheep sacrificed "to the fitting god." The plague ceased, and it became the custom, not in Athens alone, to erect altars to unknown deities.

St. Paul, having arrested the attention of his audience, then built up his argument:

"God that made the world and all things therein, seeing that he is Lord of heaven and earth, dwelleth not in temples made with hands; neither is worshipped with men's hands, as though he needed anything, seeing he giveth to all life, and breath, and all things; and hath made of one blood all nations of men for to dwell on all the face of the earth. . . ."

St. Paul developed his message with masterly skill and tact. Clever, as always, to suit his words to his audience, he made no mention of the Hebrew scriptures, which would have conveyed nothing to the Greeks, but dealt briefly with fundamental facts of religion.

The Greeks listened carefully to the sermon until the speaker proclaimed the coming Judgment of the World and the Resurrection of Jesus, when they cut him short with the words: "We will hear thee concerning this yet again." So ended in an atmosphere of contemptuous mockery St. Paul's address to the Athenians.

The apparent failure of his speech, the lofty scorn, the haughty air of amused tolerance with which the Greeks had listened, weighed on the sensitive nature of the Apostle. He was companionless in this strange, vain-glorious city; like his Master, he was despised and rejected of men. And into *Acts* creeps something of Paul's sadness as he paced the streets of Athens.

Yet history has shown that Christianity has never been more triumphant than in apparent failure. The seeds had been sown. Paul could not know, as he gazed up at the temples on the Acropolis, that the day would come when the mighty Parthenon would be consecrated as a Christian Church dedicated to the Mother of God.

All he saw was that, despite the scorn that had been thrown on him, two human beings had come to him with open hearts, only two from all the thousands in Athens. They were Dionysius, a member of the Areopagus, and a woman named Damaris.

Nothing further is known of Damaris, but legend has been busy with the name of Dionysius. According to Eusebius, he became the first Bishop of Athens; but another account says that he went with St. Paul to Rome, stayed with the Apostle until his martyrdom, and then was sent by St. Clement, Bishop of Rome, to preach the Gospel in France. Settling on a little island in the Seine, he made many converts and became Bishop of Paris. He suffered martyrdom under Domitian on the Hill of Martyrs (Montmartre), and so became St. Dionysius, or St. Denys, patron saint of France.

As I sat one evening on the Areopagus, watching the sunlight fade from the brown slopes of the Acropolis, I thought that Athens contains more buildings that Paul must have seen than any site I had visited in Palestine, Syria, Asia Minor, or Macedonia.

He saw the Acropolis and the buildings whose ruins crown it still: the Propylæa, the Parthenon, the Erechtheum, and the Temple of the Wingless Victory. He saw the Asklepieion, whose ruins are still cut in the side of the Acropolis, and he saw the lovely theatre of Dionysus at the foot of the hill. He saw the Theseum, which to-day is the most perfectly preserved Greek temple in the world, and he must have seen the Tower of the Winds and the circular Monument of Lysikrates. All these monuments of Paul's day have defied the chilling touch of time.

5

I had not been in Athens more than a week before I began to call a number of friendly Greeks by their improbable Christian names. There was Sophocles, there was Demetrius, and there were the two Vyrons, which is, of course, Byron, one of the most popular masculine names in Greece.

I think it was one of the Vyrons—or it may have been Sophocles—who introduced me on many occasions as an ardent Philhellene. The description made me smile. It was as though someone had used the word "beau" or "rake" in dead earnest. I had no idea it was still current. I soon discovered that one of the most touching things about Greece is her abiding gratitude for the help given by Great Britain during the Greek War of Independence, especially for the championship of "Lordos Vyronos," to whom a statue is erected not only in the Zappeion Gardens, but also in countless Greek hearts.

The Englishman in Greece realizes, almost with a feeling of

astonishment, that Byron was a very great man. We who place him on the shelves among the unread poets are apt to forget his tremendous European reputation. Every time he wrote a poem, a flood of translations poured across the world. There were nine German translations of *Manfred*, four Russian translations, three Spanish, three Hungarian, three Italian, two Polish, two French, two Dutch, two Danish, in addition to Romaic, Roumanian and Bohemian editions. No living writer has an audience like that. Therefore, when the greatest literary figure of his day, and an English "milord," decided to assist in freeing the Greeks from the Turks, the fact that he died tragically in Greece, although he had not heard a shot fired in battle, was worth more to the cause than a whole series of Turkish atrocities. No matter how cynically the modern biographer may regard Byron's Philhellenism, the fact remains that he died as truly for Greece as if he had died on the field of battle, and the Greeks, to their credit, will never forget that he died with the words "Forward. Follow my example . . ." on his lips.

The Greeks of Byron's age were not interested in classical Greece: it was of Byzantine Greece they were thinking when they raised the flag of freedom, a Greece that had been kept alive by every little Greek church in the land. Ever since Catherine II of Russia had christened her grandson Constantine and had sent agents among the Greek subjects of the Sultan, the idea of a revival of the Byzantine Empire, with a Christian Emperor on the throne at Constantinople and an orthodox priest resuming the interrupted mass in St. Sophia, had been firmly planted in the Ægean. It was Constantinople, not Athens, St. Sophia, not the Parthenon, that always seemed important to the Greek.

This Byzantinism is natural and instinctive. As recently as the last War, the theatres in Athens used to stage a Tableau which showed an actor, dressed as King Constantine, enthroned in Byzantine state like a king on an ikon. This expression of something deep down in the superstitious nature of the Greek, far more genuine than any Philhellenism, always, I am told by those who witnessed it, drew forth thunders of applause.

Thoughts such as these are bound to run through the puzzled mind of the visitor who finds himself called a Philhellene; and they are followed by the thought that no Greek seen in the streets or shops of Athens bears the slightest resemblance to the work of Pheidias or Praxiteles. How much of the blood of ancient Hellas runs in the veins of the modern Greek?

This is an enormous subject. Fallmerayer's sweeping statement in 1829 that the Greek race had been exterminated, and that not a single family had ancestors who were not either Albanians, Francs, Lombards, or Asiatic settlers, has been revised by more generous observers. As the folk-lore of the Palestinian Arab suggests that he is the Canaanite whose customs and beliefs colour the Old Testament, so the folk-lore of modern Greece, as well as the personal characteristics of the people, suggest that there is a link between the Greeks of to-day and the Greeks of classical antiquity.

That they have lost their good looks is obvious to any observer; that is, if the models chosen by Greek sculptors were not exceptional persons. I never saw the bridgeless nose of classical sculpture, in spite of the fact that countless peasant women, I was told, always pinch up the flesh on the nose of a newly-born child to build up the bridge. I have looked long and earnestly for an Apollo or an Aphrodite among the modern Greeks—I must have scanned the faces of thousands—and I did not discover one. It is distressing to admit that one could easily discover more convincing representatives of ancient Greek beauty during a walk down Regent Street, or among the crews of the Oxford and Cambridge boats, than in the streets of Athens.

6

"I have noticed in Athens," I said, "many eating-places tucked away in side streets. There is generally an old vine growing over trellis-work, and through the open door you see a yard where a man in shirt-sleeves is always drawing wine from a barrel. Let us go and dine in one of these taverns."

"As you wish," replied Sophocles.

It was about 9 p.m., the hour that Athens dines. The heat of the day still lay over the city, but the ghost of a sea wind was beginning to blow from Phaleron.

We left the brightly-lit main street and dived into one of the many dark side roads where the big wine carts and empty market wagons were trundling over the stones. We passed through an open door into a paved courtyard piled with barrels.

A cheerful individual in shirt-sleeves, trousers and carpet slippers, was sitting beside a wire fence, feeding a pet sheep with herbs while a small dog sat up and begged for attention.

The courtyard was roofed, like most Greek taverns, with vine-covered trellis-work, in spring a welcome green shade, but in summer burnt by the sun into a roof of crackling brown. Round the courtyard were three or four simple little white-washed rooms with tables and chairs set ready for dinner. An appetizing odour of food came from the opposite end of the courtyard, where, through glass windows, I could see the cook busy over an enormous fire.

"You will eat here?" asked the proprietor, who shook hands with me in the friendly Greek fashion. "Come and choose your dinner."

He led the way into the kitchen.

It is the admirable custom in Greek taverns to inspect the food you order before it is cooked. The kitchen was full of wine, meat, fish, and vegetables. There were langoustes, there were red mullet, which they call *barbouni*, and there were the horrid ink-fish which are eaten stewed in oil.

After we had ordered our meal, the proprietor, followed by his pet sheep and his dog, led the way into one of the alcoves, where the three of us sat down together. The sheep nibbled our trousers and had to be turned out, much to the delight of the dog.

Little glasses of *ouzo* were produced, accompanied by the assortment of hors d'œuvre which generally comes with it, for the Greeks never drink without eating. There were squares of bread covered with red caviare, crisp potatoes, pistachio nuts, and slices of cucumber.

The proprietor lifted his glass, said how much he admired England and the English, and how complimented he was that a stranger should have decided to dine in his tavern: then, rising, he went out to superintend the dinner.

"The Government," began Sophocles, "is said to have decided . . ."

"Do you mind, Sophocles," I said gently, "not talking politics to-night? Talk about food instead. It is so much healthier. Tell me what the Greeks eat. . . ."

As he described the favourite dishes, I realized that the food of Greece is a legacy from the Turkish occupation. There is scarcely a Greek dish that is not Turkish in its origin. Whether the Turks borrowed the Byzantine *cuisine*, as they borrowed so many things, I am not prepared to say. The names are Turkish, with the addition of a Greek affix. *Pilaf* becomes *pilafi*, *dolma* becomes *dolmades*. Nearly all the sweets of Greece are the well-known Turkish sweets and pastries.

The proprietor entered, bearing slices of red melon.

"Where does this come from?" I asked.

"It comes from Larissa, the capital of Thessaly," he said.

I remembered the great hills of Thessaly, piled up round Mount Olympus, that I had seen from the ship; and Larissa I thought, was the town that centuries ago placed on its silver coins a copy of the lovely head of Kimon's Arethusa.

"All the best red melons come from Larissa," continued the proprietor, "and all the best yellow melons from Argos."

He placed on the table a jug of resinated wine.

"This is in your honour," he said to me with a bow. "It is made from my own grapes."

Resinated wine, called *retsinata* or *retsina*, is the *vin ordinaire* of Greece. The majority of strangers, I am told, dislike it, and compare the taste to that of turpentine. When the wine is young, resin tapped from pine trees is placed in it as a preservative; and this has been the method of making wine in Greece from remote ages. There is probably no more authentic relic of antiquity in the life of modern Greece. The wand which Dionysus carries in a thousand statues and reliefs, and on a thousand vases, is the *thyrsus*, a sceptre surmounted by a pine-cone.

"Good health."

We all touched glasses and drank. The Greek is always flattered and delighted when a foreigner drinks *retsinata* without a shudder.

When we had finished our Thessalian melon, we were given langouste cut into slices and covered with a vinaigrette sauce. This shell-fish, I was told, had come that morning from Oropos, which faces the island of Euboea. We then ate veal, and a salad of tomato and cucumber.

While Sophocles and I sat talking over the ruins of this romantic meal, the door opened to admit a thin, cadaverous man who had not shaved for some time. He regarded us with burning eyes. Silently he advanced into the room, half closed his eyes, and, stretching out an arm dramatically, began to declaim in a high, sing-song voice.

"Who is he?" I asked.

"He is a wandering poet," whispered Sophocles. "He goes from tavern to tavern."

"I cannot understand him. What is he saying?"

"It is a poem he has made about the political situation. It is very clever. It suits both sides, so that no one can take offence at it."

"He cannot be a Greek, then."

"Oh yes, he is," said Sophocles earnestly. "I can tell from his accent that he is an Athenian."

The poet finished, and asked me for a cigarette. He lit it and recited a poem in which life was compared to the smoke of a cigarette. He apostrophized the cigarette, blew clouds of smoke into the air, and at the end, with a terrific gesture of finality, he stamped the cigarette beneath his feet and ground the life out of it on the stone flags.

When the oration ended, the poet came up to our table and accepted a glass of wine. A crowd of workmen and artisans, each one with his evening paper, came in and ordered wine. They plunged into violent political argument.

When they had drunk their wine, Sophocles asked them to share our enormous jug of *retsinata*. They gathered round and each one, before he drank his glass, toasted me—"the stranger" —coupled with the United States of America. Neither Italians nor Greeks can tell the difference between an American and an Englishman. When I corrected them, they rose to their feet and toasted England. America, they said, "very nice," but England—ah, England!

Then followed such a series of varied toasts, first one and then another rising and proposing something, that I felt the situation contained all the germs of a violent political discussion. I was rather glad when one man rose to his feet and asked us to drink to the health of "Vyron."

How Byron would have delighted in the sight of us standing under the scorched vine that hot night, dramatically drinking his health as the saviour of modern Greece.

"Vee-ron!" they cried, lifting their glasses in the air.

I could think of no Greek statesman whose name would have been received with unanimous approval, therefore I weakly sought refuge in Philhellenism:

"To Pericles," I cried.

"What does he say?" I could hear them asking.

When it was explained, they rose out of sheer politeness and emptied their glasses.

The door opened to admit three musicians, who sang a series of songs in a curiously high-pitched tone.

"Let us escape now," said Sophocles, "or we shall be here all night."

"Are all Greeks as friendly?" I asked him. "Have all Greeks the same flood of talk? Do you all know the recipe for a happy Greece?"

"That is the curse of my country," said Sophocles. "We all know. We all think we could do so much better than the people in charge. We all believe that if we were in control of the country everything would be all right. Every Greek rules Greece in his own mind."

The proprietor stood at the door of the tavern, accompanied by his dog and his sheep. He poured out a glass of *retsinata*.

"This," he said, "is something particularly good. Will you please taste?"

I lifted my glass.

"Long live England," said the proprietor.

"Thank you," I replied, "and long live Greece."

And with a last handshake we plunged into the side-streets of Athens.

7

I have indicated that it is hot in Athens during the summer. It is, in fact, so hot that sleep descends on the city from noon until about four o'clock in the afternoon. Between these hours the shops are shut, the cafés are deserted, and most people go to bed.

I cannot do this. I dislike the siesta as a scandalous waste of time. Therefore, after eating a slice of red melon, which is all a man needs at noon in hot countries, I go down to swim in the Bay of Phaleron.

The sea is still and blue and warm. I can see the white, firm floor of sand, with the sun ripples moving over it. The little bathing place is deserted, for the Greeks are not enthusiastic swimmers. They have a curious superstition that it is unwise to bathe until the melons are ripe and consequently they keep away from the sea during April and May, when the sun is stronger than it is with us during an August heat wave. By the time the real furnace-heat begins, they have put off the plunge so long that they presumably forget all about it.

It is pleasant to have the Bay of Phaleron to myself. The sand is unbearable to the naked feet, and I race down to the edge of the sea and wade out into water that is too warm to be stimulating.

The isle of Ægina lies to the south, blue in the heat-mist, and to the west I see the rocky coast-line running towards Corinth. As I float on my back in the blue water, it is Hymettus that enchants me, rising behind Phaleron and lifting its great shoulders against a blue sky. The mountain is the haunt of shepherds with their pipes, as it used to be in ancient times. The bees still gather honey from the wild thyme: and although all honey in Athens is called "Hymettus," you can, if you know where to go, get the real scented combs from hives in the shadow of the mountain.

During my last bathe, I thought of my weeks in Athens with intense happiness. I had been to Marathon, to the temple of Poseidon at Sunium, and to the ancient mines at Laurium. I had no desire to leave Athens. It will always remain in my memory as one of the few entirely lovely places on this earth.

CHAPTER IX

I follow the steps of St. Paul from Athens to Corinth, where American archæologists are revealing the city in which the Apostle preached. I climb to the summit of Acro-Corinth, meet a Greek who tells me something about peasant superstition and, journeying to Cenchreæ, find that the once famous port is now a deserted bay.

1

I SET off for Corinth about six o'clock one morning, hoping to get there before the sun made travelling too uncomfortable. In less than an hour we were running down to an unruffled bay looking like an inland lake, for the isle of Salamis—as blue that morning as a bunch of hot-house grapes—seems to close the outlet to the sea. Far off, shining in the morning light, I saw the little town of Eleusis lying on the edge of the water. The road from Athens to Eleusis follows the route taken in ancient times by the great crowds who went by torchlight to become initiated into the Mysteries. The ruins which cover a large area of ground at the foot of a hill were hidden beneath the town until fifty years ago. Now, however, hundreds of broken marble columns and pavements are seen in bewildering profusion.

St. Paul was in Athens during the summer or autumn, just about the time that the city would be full of those who had come to participate in the Greater Mysteries. The Lesser Mysteries, or the Mysteries of Agra, which were a preparation for full initiation, used to be held in the spring in Athens, in a temple dedicated to Demeter and Cora. On both occasions heralds proclaimed a sacred truce throughout Greece, which lasted for two months.

It seems hardly possible that St. Paul could have stayed in Athens during the summer without coming into contact with this famous religious festival, which sought to satisfy the pagan hunger for a better life. He may have seen the great procession from Eleusis to Athens on the fourteenth day of the month of Boedromion, when at full moon, the priests of Eleusis, nobly escorted, brought the Sacred Objects to the foot of the Acropolis. On the following day a proclamation was made forbidding barbarians and murderers to take part in the Initiation. Then came purification by bathing in the sea, the sacrifice of pigs and, finally, the great procession at nightfall to Eleusis.

I walked into the ruins, which are at first confusing. The Great Hall of the Mysteries is, however, unmistakable, and is one of the most remarkable ruins in Greece. It is the only Greek temple built to house a congregation, for the ceremonies of the Eleusinian Mysteries, unlike all other Greek religious celebrations, took place behind locked doors.

The Great Hall is really a covered theatre built to hold about three thousand people, and the ordeals experienced by the initiates must have occurred in full view of all who attended the Mysteries. What were these Mysteries? It was once thought that the Initiates were led by a priest through underground passages in which symbolic apparitions were encountered, ending with the appearance of the terrified candidate into the clear light of day. But when archæologists uncovered the ruins of Eleusis, they found no trace of underground tunnels or of the elaborate machinery which, it was once believed, the priests must have employed to stage their terrors. Eleusis has guarded its secret as faithfully as its initiates used to do.

There were scoffers and sceptics in classical times, and many an indiscreet satirist like Lucian. But not one has betrayed the vows of secrecy and not one has left an account of the scene that took place at night in the Hall of Mysteries.

Many Greek philosophers, including Plato, professed a reverence and respect for a ceremony which, in the words of Cicero, taught men "not only to live happily, but to die with a fairer hope."

2

When the road to Corinth leaves Eleusis, it mounts into hot hills where olive trees cast pools of shade on the burning rocks. Then it sweeps down to an exquisite bay in whose smooth waters fishermen stand with poised spears like figures from an Attic *kylix*. The only town on this road is midway between Athens and Corinth, the ancient town of Megara, whose people pride themselves on the purity of their Greek ancestry.

Beyond Megara the road plunges into the hills and runs up and down in a hair-raising manner on the edge of the Scironian rocks, with a sheer drop down to the sea.

The timid motorist, or one who does not trust another's skill at the wheel, gives a sigh of relief when the road descends from the rocks and, straightening out at last, runs on to Corinth beside the Gulf of Ægina, where woods of dwarf pine-trees march down to the blue water.

We came to the Corinth Canal, where I got out of the car and walked along the frail-looking, iron bridge. The Canal runs straight as a knife-cut through the four miles of grey clay which used to join the Peloponnesus to Attica. Before this Canal was cut, ships sailing between these seas were forced to make a détour of two hundred miles, round the Morea with its dangerous and feared Cape Malea—the Cape of Good Hope of antiquity.

The bridge crosses the Canal in the middle, and is a hundred and seventy feet above the water. I looked east along a deep cutting of two miles to the Gulf of Ægina, and westward along a similar cutting to the Gulf of Corinth.

Although the utility of such a canal was recognized in ancient days, it was not until 1893 that the Corinth Canal was completed. The reason for this is curious. Every time an attempt was made to cut through the isthmus, it was superstitiously abandoned. There was a legend that the earth spouted blood whenever an attempt was made to link the Gulf of Corinth with the Gulf of Ægina. Alexander the Great, Julius Cæsar, and many other men of antiquity, wished to cut the canal, but all were obliged to abandon the scheme.

Nero made an attempt in the autumn of 66 A.D., only two years before his suicide. On an appointed day the Emperor left Corinth at the head of a brilliant gathering and, reaching the site of the canal, snatched up a lyre and sang an ode in honour of Neptune and Amphitrite. He was then handed a golden spade. To the sound of music, he thrust the spade into the earth and collected the sods in a basket which he slung on his back. He then made a speech to the assembled labourers, among whom were six thousand young Jews recently captured by Vespasian in the lake-side villages of Galilee, where the Jewish War had begun. It is strange to think that the work of digging the Corinth Canal was begun by Jewish prisoners of war whose fathers and grandfathers had no doubt heard our Lord preaching on the Sea of Galilee.

Nero's attempt, like all others, was soon abandoned, and a number of reasons have been given to explain his failure. Among them was the strange theory, quoted by Philostratus, that the level of the Gulf of Corinth was higher than that of the Gulf of Ægina, and that if the two seas were connected the water would rush down and swamp the island of Ægina. But throughout Roman times, although there was no canal, the famous *diolkos*, a structure on which ships were moved across the isthmus on rollers, was in use. In 1881 a French company resumed work at the exact place where Nero's workmen had given up.

While I was leaning over the bridge, a cargo-boat from the

Gulf of Ægina moved slowly through the Canal. Even a small boat must go with extreme care, because the Canal is only twenty-six feet in depth and the wash from the deep seas at each end, combined with winds and currents, keep the skippers on the bridge all the time. Large ships squeeze through the narrow slit with wooden bumpers tied to their sides, in order to protect their paint and also the sides of the Canal.

Modern Corinth, a town of about nine thousand people, stands on the edge of the Gulf of Corinth as if waiting for the next earthquake, but quite unable to tear itself away from the paradise of green waters and blue hills among which its dangerous life is set. I cannot understand the gallant fatalism which induces people to continue to live on the slopes of volcanoes and in earthquake zones. Surely life is already sufficiently dangerous? Yet the people of Corinth look remarkably cheerful, and even express local pride in a place which may at any moment begin to shiver and tremble.

Corinth reminds me of those Middle West towns so familiar to us in the days of the silent film, towns fated to exist in a state of arrested architectural development. Corinth has ambitious wide streets, but they lead nowhere and there are sinister gaps in them, as if two or three houses had experienced a private little earthquake that had swallowed them up quietly during the night. The houses are made of soft, mud bricks which absorb the shocks and, in the event of real trouble, cause fewer casualties than stone.

The reward for having the courage to live in Corinth is the view of the mighty blue mountains rising all round the Gulf, and the green water, clear as glass near the shore and deepening into the dark blue of the summer sky.

All round Corinth in the summer, wherever there is a space of level ground, the raisins and currants are spread out to dry in the sun. They lie in various shades of sunburn, through the variations of brown and burnt sienna to the rich purple of complete dehydration.

Ever since I was a child I have loved a fistful of currants, and the kindly folk, who camp out all summer beside their drying grapes, generously offered me their finest fruit. I discovered that there is nothing more delicious than a grape which has been sun-bathing at Corinth for two days, just long enough to warm and swell up the fruit, but not long enough to dry it. The word currant, is by the way, a corruption of Corinth, or rather, a form of the old pronunciation, Corauntz.

Until 1858 modern Corinth was built on top of the Roman city, but in that year a terrible earthquake occurred and those who survived decided to build a new town nearer the Gulf. In 1928 this town was also destroyed, but it is now nearly all rebuilt. Ancient Corinth lies about three and a half miles away, and the road leading to the ruins is surely the dustiest in all Greece. The clay of Corinth powders to a flour-like dust, and in ten minutes my car was covered with it. In ancient times the Corinthian potters made charming and characteristic pottery from this clay, and their little bottles, which probably contained oil or scent, are found all over the Ægean, Asia Minor, Italy, and Sicily.

I turned off towards the sea to discover if there was anything left of that ancient eastern port, Lechæum, which used to be joined to Corinth by a double wall two miles in length. The waves of the Gulf lapped a broad sweep of sand that has been blown into significant dunes and hummocks which looked as though they might hide masonry. The great port, in which the merchant fleets of Italy and Spain once gathered so thickly that their masts were like a pine-forest against the sky, is now a lonely sweep of shore without a single boat to relieve the desolation.

As I continued towards ancient Corinth, I noticed that the land rises gradually from the sea in the form of two terraces.

The top terrace, on which ancient Corinth stood, is a long, undulating plateau dominated by a stupendous mountain—Acro-Corinth. This mountain, the colour of a lion's skin, rises straight into the blue sky and has the same strength, the same precipitousness, and the same bleak and uncompromising grandeur as Gibraltar. It rises for nearly two thousand feet—much higher than Gibraltar—and its massive sides are scored by corries and fretted with countless pinnacles that catch the light and vary in shade from pale pink at morning to the deepest blue at sunset. In the shadow of this majestic guardian lay Roman Corinth, a city six miles in extent, with a wall all round and the two-mile double wall connecting it with the docks and harbour of Lechæum.

At first I could see only seven Doric columns, the remains of the peristyle of a temple, which stand up dramatically from the plateau, and I thought how strange it was that although nearly every modern city can show a rich variety of Corinthian columns in its public buildings, ancient Corinth cannot show one.

Walking over the uneven ground, I came to the discoveries which the American School of Classical Studies at Athens has made since it began to excavate Corinth in 1896. A pleasant little guide appeared from somewhere and, after greeting me, assumed his official voice and led me through the ruins.

The area uncovered is only a fraction of the ancient city, but it is the most important portion. Streets, temples, baths, fountains, public squares, the line of porticoes, foundations of shops, an odeum, and an amphitheatre, have already been discovered, and the entire circuit of the wall has been traced.

A stretch of the Lechæum road has been excavated: it is forty feet in width and is paved with rows of paving-stones, eight to a row. The rain gutters which caught the water from the roofs of a now-vanished colonnade are in perfect condition, and the pavement stones bear no trace of wheeled traffic, for the Lechæum road descended by flights of steps to the harbour. St. Paul may have walked these very stones, which belong to the Imperial period of ancient Corinth.

Another interesting discovery is the Fountain of Pirene, so famous throughout antiquity that Corinth was often referred to by the poets, and in the ambiguous utterances of the Delphic Oracle, as "the city of Pirene." The guide hoisted himself over a ruined wall and disappeared into a series of caves faced with masonry, into which I followed him. In the time of St. Paul, Pirene was an attractive, open-air marble basin about twenty by thirty feet in size, filled with water and with a marble walk all round on which people could stand to fill their water-jars. The water came from a spring in the rock which towers above the marble basin, and the entrance to the spring was an elaborate façade of six arches, once covered with marble, leading to four long tunnels, or rather reservoirs, cut back into the rock. The guide told me that the supply of these reservoirs was a hundred thousand gallons, which seemed to me enormous.

My energetic little companion then took me to a dank, underground chamber. Before we descended the stone steps, he lifted one finger dramatically and lowered his voice.

"We are going to see," he said, "a fountain. It was hidden by the Greeks centuries before the Romans built Corinth, and was hidden because the water had dried up. It must have been a very holy fountain, for it was walled up so carefully that the Romans built their streets on top and never knew that it was there. Think!", and again he lifted his finger, "we are going to see something in Corinth that even the Romans did not know of; even St. Paul, when he was here, did not know. . . ."

He lit match after match to illuminate the damp little stone chamber in which we stood, and I could see a fountain made probably five centuries before Christ; the two bronze lions· heads, from whose open mouths the water once dripped, were still in position on the wall.

The place is a mystery. The water must have been considered holy, but the supply can never have been more than an occasional drip. The lions' mouths are hardly worn at all. There is a place on the ground for jars to stand while the precious drops fell into them, and there is no provision for an overflow. When the supply of water failed, the priests evidently sealed the fountain and built another immediately on top, fed by water from a different source; thus suggesting that it was essential for some reason to have a fountain of water at this precise spot. How weird it is to emerge in the sunlight of the twentieth century, having gazed on a fountain that was unknown to the Corinthians of St. Paul's time.

There is another mystery not far away. This is a secret passage and a water channel, both leading to the ruins of a small shrine. It has been suggested that these may have been the means by which the priests of Dionysus performed their celebrated "miracle" of turning water into wine.

3

A number of peasants were setting off on mules for the top of Acro-Corinth. As nothing in Greece has a fixed price, except, perhaps, cigarettes, railway tickets and patent medicines, I bargained briskly with them for a spare mule, and, having terminated what to an onlooker must have seemed like a bitter quarrel, sat sideways on a pack-saddle following my companions up the mountain track.

As the tawny hill enfolded us, the heat came from all sides so that it was like riding into the mouth of a furnace. In an hour's time we approached the enormous, ruined Byzantine–Venetian–Turkish castle which crowns the mountaintop and commands the whole of southern Greece.

I said good-bye to the peasants and climbed to the first

of the three great gate-houses leading into the now ruined and desolate stronghold. A fortified wall runs up and down the crags, encircling about a mile and a half of the summit. Within this enclosure was once a mediæval town which was inhabited until the end of the Turkish occupation; but to-day not a soul lives there.

The strength of this mountain fastness almost defies description. It is approachable only from the west, and the cliffs elsewhere drop straight down to the plain nearly two thousand feet below. In Greek times it was regarded as so strong a fortress, says Plutarch, that it was garrisoned by only four hundred men and fifty dogs. Philip of Macedon was told that if he wanted to capture the Morea, the mountain of Acro-Corinth was one of the horns he must seize in order to secure the heifer.

It took me half an hour to walk from the first gate to the mountain-top, and from this point I looked down on one of the grandest views in the world. Spread below like a map were the vineyards of the isthmus, the blue waters of the Saronic Gulf lying to the south, dotted with the islands of the Cyclades, and the blue waters of the Corinthian Gulf to the north-east. I looked beyond the Corinthian Gulf to the mountains of Boeotia, which rose range against range in all shades of blue and grey, mightiest of them all the immense flanks and peak of Parnassus lifting themselves behind the high ravines of Delphi. To the south-west, the blue mountains of the Peloponnesus faded into the distant hills of Arcadia. A heat mist closed the view over Attica, but I believe that on a clear day it is possible to see the Acropolis of Athens forty miles away, shining through a gap in the mountains of Salamis.

Half an hour on the summit of Acro-Corinth teaches more Greek geography than months of work with books and a map, and it also illustrates vividly why Corinth in the time of St. Paul was one of the chief commercial cities in the world. It was the half-way house between Italy and the East, and between Egypt and Asia Minor and the West. It must have been an extraordinary sight in St. Paul's time: a city built on a narrow neck of land, with its eastern harbour full of Egyptian, Asiatic, and Phœnician galleys, while the western harbour was full of the cargo-boats of Italy, Spain, and the Adriatic. Wagons must have been constantly crossing the few miles from Cenchreæ with the goods of Egypt, Asia Minor, and Syria for transhipment to the west at Lechæum; and a reverse line of wagons from Lechæum must have carried western merchandise to Cenchreæ for transhipment to the Orient. No wonder that Corinth, situated between two such ports, developed a cosmopolitanism tinged with the vices of the foreign nations whose ships lay in her harbours.

When St. Paul came from Athens to Corinth, he encountered the sharpest contrast in Greece. He had left an old, intellectual Greek city for one that was new, materialistic and, officially, Roman. Corinth's streets were thronged with merchants and industrialists, Romans, Greeks, Jews, Syrians, and Egyptians, drawn together by the hope of money.

The city was not a hundred years old when St. Paul saw it, yet already it was as large as Athens. It grew with speed as soon as the quick-witted Greeks, Syrians, and Jews realized that its revival meant the concentration at the Isthmus of all the trade of East and West. Descendants of the old Corinthian merchant families, who had fled to the island of Delos when the city was destroyed in 146 B.C., now came flooding back with money for new commercial ventures.

With no aristocracy but that of wealth, and no tradition but that of making money, Corinth had become a byword for every vice in the short space of a century. The pleasures of Corinth and the expense of living there were notorious throughout the ancient world. The word "Corinthianise" was coined to describe an evil life. The notorious Laïs practised at Corinth, and Pausanius, who saw her tomb, says that it was surmounted appropriately by an effigy of a lioness clutching her prey. On the summit of Acro-Corinth was a temple of Aphrodite served by a thousand priestesses. It is necessary to realize the immorality of Corinth if we are to understand the meaning of St. Paul's letters to the Corinthians.

I looked down from the mountain-top to the site of the city and saw, in imagination, that busy and beautiful place in which St. Paul spent a year and a half of his life. It was a city crowded with statues, some of them gilded, their faces painted red, others made of the finest marble, and others of wood, with hands, faces, and feet of stone. The triumphal archway that led to the Lechæum Road was surmounted by two four-horsed chariots of gilded bronze, bearing Helios, the Sun God, and his son Phæthon. There were marble squares, fountains, trees, covered colonnades upheld by pillars of marble, temples, baths, and two exquisite theatres, situated so that the audience would look out over the still waters of the Gulf towards the mountains that culminate in Parnassus, who wears his cap of snow sometimes until June.

Although I had spent nearly four hours exploring Acro-Corinth, I discovered that the man who had hired his mule to me was still waiting, although he knew that I had expected to walk down. He was fast asleep in the shadow of a wall. All his friends had gone hours since down to the plain, but he had stayed on out of kindliness and courtesy and with a complete disregard for time. I was so touched by this thoughtfulness that I gave him a whole packet of English cigarettes; and you can give a Greek no more welcome gift. They have a passion for Virginia tobacco which can never be satisfied because of high import duties.

He was so happy that he sang weird, stirring songs all the way down to Corinth.

4

A plump little Greek like an over-fed gnome came to stay in the hotel. He was a curious little man with original table manners. He seemed to be melting away in the heat without becoming any thinner. As we were the only people in the hotel, we gradually got nearer and nearer until one day we had dinner at the same table. He was elaborately courtly, in fact he treated me as a wicked old marquis might treat a beautiful ingénue in a melodrama. He would never sit down until I was seated, and the business of offering salt and pepper became a deferential and irritating ritual.

I had put him down as a currant merchant, but I found out that he earned his living by guiding tourists through Greece. He disliked the word "guide" and preferred to be called a courier. He had just come from Delphi, where he had "couriered" an apparently fabulously rich American family. Every time he mentioned them, he blew out his cheeks and shovelled imaginary gold in the air with one hand. His English was amazingly fluent, but his pronunciation was so original that it was often impossible to understand him.

When he got to know me better, his air of showing off vanished and he became easier to live with. He was, like all his countrymen, quick-witted and intelligent. He was peasant-born, and was a perfect mine of country stories and customs. He got it into his head that I was writing a book on Greek folk-lore and he courteously set himself out to give me information, often beginning his remarks with "Now write this down," and looking earnestly over my shoulder to see that I had the spelling right.

He told me that in certain parts of Greece the shepherds

throw out corn three times a year to placate "the monster" who has designs on their sheep.

"And what is the monster like?" I asked him.

"He is Pan," replied the little man. "He has the feet of a goat."

He told me that the Nereids and Naiads of classical fable still live in the superstitions of the modern peasant. There are trees and caves all over the country which are said to be haunted by them. The Nereids are beautiful white women, taller sometimes than an ordinary human being, and they can frequently be seen in the evening in olive groves. Those who see them cross themselves and get away as quickly as possible. Sparta is a great place for Nereids. There is a notorious band who dance on the summit of Mount Taygetus and have feet like donkeys.

The Greek peasants tell many stories about Nereids who have married men. Apparently many a Greek villager is pointed out as a man who had a Nereid great-grandmother. Like the seal-wives of Hebridean folk-lore, these Nereid wives invariably disappear to the freedom of the hills, returning now and then to look at their children. The Naiads are always found near water. In some parts the people call them "the thirsty ones." They are quick at kidnapping and in some Naiad-haunted districts it is considered dangerous to send children to the spring at dusk.

I suspected that my little friend was by no means too sophisticated to believe in these stories himself. After telling him solemnly that in an old country like Greece such apparitions were not surprising, I suddenly asked him:

"Have *you* ever seen a Nereid?"

The sophisticated little courier fought a moment with the peasant, and then he admitted with considerable uneasiness:

"One evening in Sparta I saw some strange thing among the olive trees. I think—well, it may have been."

This confession brought us closer together.

Listening to the stories he told, I realized, as I had never realized before, that the superstitions of the Greek peasant are entirely classical. The gods, the nymphs and the satyrs of yesterday have become the ogres and bogies of to-day. The hundreds of queer Greek saints, whose shrines stand on lonely mountain slopes or beside springs, are either converted sprites or are Christian influences placed there to counteract the malign pagan influence in such places.

One night my little friend told me that he had been cured of a disease at the miracle-working shrine on the isle of Tenos.

"Look at me now!", he cried hitting his chest, "am I not strong? Would you say that I was ever pale and thin? But I was! I was dying. Then I went to Tenos and—I was cured."

I was fascinated by this story, because the miracle-working ikon of Tenos is famous throughout Greece. It is well known that during the change over from paganism to Christianity in Greece, many purely pagan customs were incorporated in the new Faith and are still observed to-day. Perhaps the most notable example is the annual pilgrimage to Tenos in March, when thousands of poor cripples and blind and diseased persons sleep in the crypt of the church, thus perpetuating to-day the famous temple-sleep of classical antiquity. Such dream cures were well known throughout the ancient world and were a regular feature of the treatment at such places as Epidaurus. I asked my friend to tell me what happened to him at Tenos.

"I was so ill that I could hardly walk," he said. "There were thousands of people going up the hill to the church, some on their hands and knees. They had come from all over Greece. There were many blind, and some had lost an arm or a leg. Others were carried in chairs. The night before the service I slept in the caves under the church where the ikon was found. They were crowded with people. We had all taken our beds with us. We drank the holy water in the spring that rises there and tried to sleep. In the morning we went up to the church and kissed the holy ikon. It is quite small and covered with silver. It was then that I felt good health coming back to me. I cannot tell you how happy I was. That is many years ago and I have been well since then. . . ."

In a few days the courier left Corinth to meet a party of visitors in Athens. I saw him once again. He was standing with some English visitors in the ruins of Corinth, reeling off a list of dates in a loud, unnatural voice. I waved my hand to him and he, once more the courtier, removed his hat and gave me a profound bow.

5

When St. Paul was in Corinth, he must have seen many of the buildings whose ruins have been excavated. He must have seen the Fountain of Pirene, the Lechæum Road, many of the first-century streets whose foundations are exposed, and the seven remaining columns of the great Temple of Apollo.

There are, however, two other relics which may have a close and intimate association with him. One is a fragmentary Greek inscription on a stone which is believed to have come from the entrance to a Jewish synagogue, and the other is the ground-plan of the basilica in which it is almost certain the Roman Proconsul, Gallio, held his court. This hall was enlarged at a later period, but excavations have revealed the outline of the building as it was at the time of St. Paul's stay in Corinth.

I went there one morning to read the *Epistles to the Corinthians*, and sat on a wall with the capital of a marble column as a back-rest; below me were the grass-grown ruins of the audience hall, where green lizards come out to lie in the sun. I was probably sitting not more than five minutes walk from the houses of those Corinthians to whom Paul's letters were addressed.

St. Paul came to Corinth, a man in middle age, hardened by years of travel and privation, the marks of the rods of the Philippian lictors still on his body, the memory of the Thessalonian persecution still in his mind, and in his ears the mocking laughter of the Athenian philosophers. He came, as he confessed, "in weakness, in fear, and in much trembling."

He did not intend to stay long in Corinth. That is evident from verses seventeen and eighteen in chapter two of the *First Epistle to the Thessalonians*, which was written from Corinth. He came to the city longing to go north again to Macedonia, waiting anxiously for Silas and Timothy to come, so that he could make plans to return with them and resume in Thessalonica the work which had been so violently interrupted by his Jewish enemies. Perhaps St. Paul still felt himself bound by the Divine command to go into Macedonia, and he may have blamed himself for allowing his faithful friends in Berœa to hurry him south to Athens out of danger.

St. Paul may have associated Corinth with Jerusalem, for the Beautiful Gate of the Temple of Herod, the Gate where St. Peter and St. John found the lame man—the Gate which St. Paul must have seen so often—was made of the celebrated Corinthian bronze. Josephus describes it as "the brazen gate, which was that Gate of the Inner Temple that looked towards the sun-rising" (or the Mount of Olives), and he tells us that it was so heavy that the strength of twenty men were required to close it.

Corinthian bronze in such quantity was an unheard-of

thing, and the Beautiful Gate was more costly than if Herod had studded it with gold and silver. I like to imagine that as the Apostle walked in Corinth for the first time, he may have remembered the link between that city and the distant city of his fathers, set high among the olive groves and vines of Judæa. If this did not help to lift the sadness from his heart, his life was soon to be enriched by one of the most beautiful and fruitful friendships in the history of Apostolic Christianity.

It was in Corinth that St. Paul met a man and wife, Aquila and Priscilla, who had recently come to Corinth from Rome. Aquila was a Jew, "a man of Pontus by race," but it is not known whether Priscilla was a Jewess. Some scholars, among them Sir William Ramsay, believe that she was a Roman woman of birth and influence.

We are told in *Acts* that these two had left Rome "because Claudius had commanded all the Jews to depart from Rome." The Roman historians tell us that the expulsion was ordered because the Jews were always rioting "through some agitator called Chrestus." It is tempting to think that this may be the first reference to Christianity in Rome.

Somewhere on the plain of Corinth to-day, perhaps in a vineyard or beneath the courtyard of a whitewashed farm building, is the site of the house where Paul, Aquila and Priscilla settled down to make money for their daily needs; for Aquila also was a tent-maker. As the summer ended with the first rains and as winter drew near, the tent-makers of Corinth, who were also sail-makers, would have almost more work than they could execute. With both harbours full of ships laid up for the winter and anxious to refit while the seas were shut, the ships' chandlers of Lechæum and Cenchreæ must have had work for almost any man who could stitch a length of sail-cloth.

Sewing is work which encourages thought and conversation. It must have been of Rome that Paul and Aquila talked as they sat side by side, stitching sails that in spring-time would take some proud ship over the western sea. For the first time in his life, Paul was brought into long and intimate contact with a fellow Jew who had lived in Rome and could answer all his questions about the Imperial city. No doubt Rome had always been in Paul's mind as the focus of the Christian Faith: but it seems that in Corinth he longed for the first time to visit Rome. How many times he must have gone down to the western port of Lechæum to watch some galley from Rome come into the harbour, and how often must he have stood amid the exciting bustle of departure, watching the gang-planks drawn up, the sail hoisted, and the ship putting out to sea, standing there like one of the idle watchers in all great harbours, whose hearts go onward with the ships.

Aquila would have told him of the Church in Rome and, perhaps, of St. Peter's work there, for the tradition that St. Peter had been in Rome in the reign of Claudius is a strong one. Monseigneur Barnes believes that St. Peter may have been expelled from Rome with Aquila and Priscilla during the Claudian expulsion, and that he may even have come to Corinth with them; but this would have been just before St. Paul arrived there.

On the Sabbath eve Paul and Aquila would put away their needles and thread and would light the Sabbath lamp. In the morning St. Paul would go to the synagogue to preach the Gospel of Christ. Then with a new week would begin another stretch of toil.

How naturally the materialistic spirit of Corinth underlies the narrative. Had Paul been "weak and in fear and much trembling" in Philippi or in Galatia, we cannot imagine that his kind-hearted Philippians or Galatians would have allowed him to waste his eye-sight in order to earn a few miserable sestertii for his daily needs. They would generously have shared their money and food with him; and he would have returned their affection by accepting their kindness. But not in Corinth nor in Thessalonica. In those two hard trading communities Paul accepted nothing and chose to work for every sestertius. Paul was in the richest city in which he had ever lived, with the exception of Syrian Antioch, yet he had never been poorer. He knew that to ask for help, or to accept proffered help, would be to set these money-grubbers muttering among themselves. How true this is to life. It is rarely from his wealthy friends that a man accepts financial help; if he does so, he must first put his pride in his pocket. Paul's pride was magnificent: it was the pride of a rich man who has become poor.

Another reason for Paul's financial scruples has been well expressed by Dr. G. S. Duncan in St. Paul's Ephesian Ministry: "Paul would take nothing that might look like payment from those among whom he worked, but he was willing for the gospel's sake to accept support from churches which he left. Behind this principle we may trace the apostle's high conception of the missionary vocation: into every city that he entered he came as one who had been 'sent,' and such support as was required ought, he felt, to come from those who joined in sending him rather than from those to whom he came. And in the Gentile world there was a special necessity for the adoption of such a principle. There a familiar figure was the philosophical or religious teacher who gathered around him his own pupils and lived by the fees they paid him. And had Paul not been careful, this is how he too would have been regarded; and indeed part of the trouble which he had to face later at Corinth was that some of the brethren there, so far from understanding the principles of the Church of God, separated themselves into coteries as they found Paul or Apollos the more attractive teacher."

Throughout that winter he worked and preached, still dreaming of Macedonia, still restlessly waiting for Silas and Timothy, yet held a prisoner in Corinth by the closing of mountain passes and the shutting of the seas. He preached regularly in the synagogue and made some converts whom, in the absence of Timothy, he baptized with his own hands, a practise that he usually avoided in case his enemies charged him with baptizing in his own name.

When eventually Silas and Timothy arrived in the spring, they found their leader living, as usual, in an atmosphere of mental and spiritual energy. He was "constrained by the word," preaching with tremendous zeal, and his success had again stirred up the Jews against him. Their animosity culminated in a terrible scene. During an argument in the synagogue, the Jews cursed Christ. The Jews of Pisidian Antioch had uttered a similar blasphemy years before, and on that occasion Paul and Barnabas had turned to the Gentiles. Now the horrible scene was repeated. The Jews of Corinth, in their rage and hate, evidently flung at Paul the old taunt that every man who died upon a tree was accursed, and to shrieks of "Anathema Iesus!" Paul rose in anger and performed the symbolic gesture of repudiation which Nehemiah had made in ancient times: he "shook out his raiment," and crying, "Your blood be upon your own heads; I am clean: from henceforth I will go unto the Gentiles," he left the synagogue never to enter it again.

The Christians of Corinth then met in the house of a Roman colonist, Titus Justus, who was evidently a well-off and hospitable member of the new faith. As so frequently happens in such a situation, the members of the synagogue were now obliged to take sides. St. Paul had left them and they had either to forsake him or to go over to him wholeheartedly. Among the great number of converts who decided to follow him was Crispus, the ruler of the synagogue, whom

Paul baptized with his own hands as he had baptized Gaius.

From that moment the history of the Church at Corinth took on a new importance, and as if to set the Apostle's lingering thoughts of Macedonia at rest, he received one of the visions that guided him in all the critical moments of his life. "The Lord said unto Paul in the night by a vision, Be not afraid, but speak, and hold not thy peace: for I am with thee, and no man shall set on thee to harm thee: for I have much people in this city."

St. Luke, with a brevity which leaves so much to the imagination, simply says in *Acts*: "And he dwelt there a year and six months, teaching the word of God among them."

This was the longest period that St. Paul had settled in any one place since he had started out on his missionary journeys. His life in Corinth was full of effort. Silas and Timothy had brought back news from Macedonia which inspired the two *Epistles to the Thessalonians*. They were written at Corinth to recall the Thessalonians to a sense of duty and to correct their fears about the end of the world.

These may be the first epistles written by St. Paul, but some scholars believe that *Galatians* had already been written. It is interesting, I think, to realize that although such letters are the first of their kind ever written, in so far as they are the loving, helpful instructions of a pastor who is concerned for the moral and spiritual welfare of his flock, they have a precedent in the circular letters sent out to the scattered synagogues of the Dispersion from the central authority, the Sanhedrin at Jerusalem. In this way the million of Jews living in every part of the world were kept informed of the calendar of festivals, the decisions of the legislature, and other important news which bound the scattered race with its theocratic headquarters.

At the end of eighteen months the Church at Corinth had grown enormously in numbers. R. B. Rackham, in his commentary on *Acts*, says: "The number of converts was very large, and they received the word with extraordinary enthusiasm. There was a great display, or we might say outburst, of spiritual gifts, of prophesy and speaking with tongues. The Church was an organism whose intense vitality found expression in a variety of highly diversified ministries: there were apostles, prophets, teachers, miracle-workers, healers, helps, 'governments,' speakers with tongues. The excess of enthusiasm gave rise to actual disorder in the assemblies of the brethren. This almost too exuberant growth of the vine of the Church was partly due, no doubt, to immunity from the pruning and chastening hand of persecution."

The Jews, however, were biding their time. Their long silence meant only that they were waiting for the right moment to wreck the infant church and to drive forth the Apostle. This moment seemed to have arrived when a new Proconsul was appointed to Achaia, Junius Annæus Novatus Gallio. This man, who is so briefly mentioned in *Acts*, was noted for the sweetness and the amiability of his nature. He sprang from a remarkable family. He was born in Cordova, Spain, the eldest son of Lucius Annæus Seneca and his wife Helvia. He had two brothers, L. Annæus Seneca, the great philosopher and tutor of Nero, and Annæus Mela, the father of the poet Lucan. The reason why the first son was known as Gallio is because he was adopted by his father's friend, Junius Gallio, the rhetorician, and took his name. There are several references to him in classical literature. Seneca dedicated *De Ira* and *De Vita Beata* to him, and speaks of his charming disposition, a quality praised also by the poet Statius, who calls him "sweet Gallio."

This was the man who, no sooner had he taken over the

supreme office of Proconsul of Achaia, found himself involved in what he regarded as a singularly foolish Jewish dispute. The technique of Paul's Jewish enemies always varied from place to place, adapting itself to the form of government in power. We have seen how in a Roman Colony the Jews were strictly legal in their accusations, and how in a Greek city state they became demagogues. In Corinth their genius for creating trouble took a slightly different turn, which, unless one reads the text very closely, is easy to miss. They realized that they had no hope of impressing the new Proconsul if they merely charged Paul with assailing the protected Jewish religion. Something more dramatic was necessary, something which would be likely to impress, or perhaps even frighten, a governor new to his task. Therefore they "with one accord rose up against Paul." This means that by agreement the whole Jewish quarter organized a demonstration in order to attract attention, and then produced Paul before the *bema,* or judgment-seat, in the Basilica, crying "This man persuadeth men to worship God contrary to the law."

This meant that as Judaism, or, as they expressed it, the act of worshipping God, was everywhere protected by the Roman Law, Paul had been guilty of some offence against a lawful religion. It was a typical piece of Jewish hairsplitting, enormously helped, no doubt, by the stage setting of a crowd of injured Jews. The technique was similar to that of the shouting crowd which bullied Pontius Pilate.

Gallio, however, looked on the scene calmly; and what a scene it must have been. Seneca's brother, in a white toga, seated on his chair of state, the marble columns framing on one side a picture of the Lechæum Road with its shady porticoes, and, on the other, the gaunt mass of Acro-Corinth; sunlight touching the bronze helmets of the Roman guard; the lictors, rods on shoulder; and St. Paul standing on a floor of coloured marble. One can imagine the Jewish clamour that would be silenced by the lifting of Gallio's finger. Then, having heard the Jews, Gallio would not even permit Paul to open his mouth in defence, but, turning to his accusers, declared that had it been a matter of wrong, or villainy, he would have heard them, but as it was a matter of words and persons and the Jewish Law, they could deal with it themselves.

"I will be no judge of such matters," he said.

The lictors were then ordered to clear the court, but the verdict of the Proconsul was so much to the liking of the assembled Gentiles that they set upon the leader of the synagogue, Sosthenes, and gave this representative of the unloved race a beating in the judgment-hall. The Proconsul affected not to see what was going on: "Gallio cared for none of these things."

That immortal sentence has been twisted by Christian writers into a variety of meanings, many of them, it seems to me, unjustifiable. It is unfair that his name should be synonymous with lack of interest in higher things. Gallio was a cultured, well-mannered Roman aristocrat. He had wasted his time by listening to a trivial, trumped-up charge that should never have been brought to him. The crowd agreed with him. If they cared to beat the vindictive rabbi, the spokesman of a malicious and unruly rabble—well, why not? It served him right.

"For Gallio cared for none of these things."

St. Paul had now finished his work at Corinth. Eighteen months had passed since first he came there, and a large and flourishing church has been founded. It was time to go. Waiting a few days, and taking with him his beloved Aquila and Priscilla, he found a ship going to Syria that called on the way at Ephesus.

So Paul bade farewell to Corinth.

6

The *First Epistle to the Corinthians* was written by St. Paul from Ephesus about three years or so after he had left Corinth. The second letter was written a year or so later, as he passed through Macedonia before paying a final visit to Corinth.

Reading between the lines of these letters, we have a remarkable glimpse into a primitive Christian community. The names of the Corinthian converts might at first suggest a citizen roll in an Italian city rather than in a city on Greek soil, but that is natural, because St. Paul had turned to the Gentiles, who were either Roman colonists or Greek traders. There were Titus Justus, Gaius, Crispus, Quartus, Fortunatus, Tertius (a good penman, who later, took down to St. Paul's dictation the *Epistle to the Romans*), and added to these were three Jews, Lucius, Jason, and Sosipater, as well as a man probably of some influence, Erastus, who has been identified with the city treasurer of Corinth. Generally speaking, however, the members of the church were humble working people, "not many mighty, not many noble," who, when their day's work was over, went at nightfall to the house of Justus to pray and to eat the Lord's Supper.

We know that this house was near the synagogue, and as we also know that synagogues were often built beside running water, some writers have suggested that the house of Justus may have stood on the slopes of Acro-Corinth. I have examined the lie of the land and I do not think so. I think that the house of Justus was not in the heart and centre of Corinth but in the industrial district called "the Potter's Quarter," which the American archæologists have recently discovered on the edge of the plateau. Here are to be seen a maze of foundation walls, all that is left of a busy industrial district where the famous Corinthian ware was manufactured.

The beds of grey clay are there, so are the sites of the ovens and dumps from which the excavators took hundreds of thousands of trial pieces, imperfect and discarded specimens, as well as moulds for making figurines and other shaped objects. Is it too much to see in Titus Justus a member of the famous potter family of Corinth, the Titii, whose work, mentioned by Strabo, was sent to every part of the world?

This would explain his position of wealth and influence and would make it almost certain that his house was probably in the Potter's Quarter, in industrial Corinth, and the most likely place, incidentally, in which to look for the synagogue.

It is not difficult, as one stands on the stones Paul trod, to imagine Corinth on some Sunday night long ago. From here and there in the great city, men and women would leave the crowds and the lights to pass hurriedly through the streets in whose taverns the seamen of Tyre, Alexandria and Carthage fought the seamen of Ostia, Syracuse and Gades. They would hurry across the moonlit squares where the stone faces of god and emperor smiled in the light of braziers, and leaving behind them the brooding shadow of that height on whose summit the Asiatic Aphrodite offered the unholy darkness of her groves, they would pass through the narrow streets to the Potter's Quarter and the house of Justus.

Paul would be there to greet them. Silas and Timothy would be there, the companions of his wandering; also Aquila and Priscilla. Paul would teach them. They would sing a hymn. The meeting would conclude with the observance of the Lord's Supper, at which rich and poor would sit down together. But for a single reference to the sanctity of the Lord's Supper in the first letter to Corinth, we might not have known that so early in primitive Christianity this rite was a feature of worship, as it apparently was, in all the Pauline churches.

A citizen of Corinth, passing the house of Justus one night and hearing the sound of voices, may have glanced in and have seen a man standing in the feeble lamplight telling the story of Someone Who said "Do this in memory of me." How could such an eavesdropper have foreseen that gatherings like this, multiplied and again multiplied in the cities of the world, would one day bring the temples and the bronze and marble gods crashing to earth?

Unfortunately the early Christians of Corinth were not all of them like the saintly early Christians in *The Sign of the Cross*. They were ordinary men and women striving to live a different life in the midst of pagan society. Some of them had been gathered in the highways and byways and had been redeemed from a life of sin. "Nor thieves, nor covetous, nor drunkards, nor revilers, nor extortioners, shall inherit the kingdom of God. And such were some of you," wrote Paul to the members of this church. Once the amazing personality of Paul no longer dominated them, jealousies, immoralities, and irregularities crept in among them. It was to correct these that he wrote his *First Epistle to the Corinthians*.

What a glimpse into the life of a pagan city, and what an insight into the difficulty of living the new Christian life in such surroundings, is given in this letter. During the brief time of Paul's absence, schisms, law-suits, gross immorality, gluttony, drunkenness, and even irreverence at the Lord's Supper, have invaded the community. The little church is swinging back into paganism. The Lord's Supper is in danger of becoming a temple feast at which men and women get drunk. The little community has not been strong enough to withstand the luxury and immorality of Corinth. In revolt against this invasion of paganism, a few members have gone to one extreme of asceticism, while others have swung round to *antinomianism*, which is the sinful theory that no moral impurity can stain the soul.

The more devout members were troubled by problems which to-day we find it difficult to envisage. Should they, as good Christians, eat meat offered to idols? That seems to us a strange and fantastic problem, but it was one which affected many a Christian in the cities of the pagan world. In antiquity, the priests were the butchers. They were given a portion of the sacrificed animal, which they sold in the common market. In fact the ancient Greeks had no word to describe meat: the word they employed meant a sacrificial victim. It was natural that the first Christians should have asked St. Paul a problem that faced them every day: was it right to eat meat that had already been dedicated to a pagan god? There were social difficulties too. Suppose a pagan invited them to dinner, should they ask whether the meat had come from a temple?

There were also problems concerning women, which prove, incidentally, how numerous women were among the early converts; and other problems concerning marriage, which became acute because Christians of the first century expected the Second Coming of our Lord in their lifetime.

Nothing, perhaps, in the wide range of Paul's letters has caused greater misunderstanding than his advice to the unmarried, which is bluntly interpreted in the Authorized Version as "better to marry than to burn." When St. Paul wrote these words, he had, of course, no thought of hell fire in his mind. A more accurate translation of this advice reads: "it is better to marry than be aflame with passion."

Again, his words on the veiling of women have puzzled many people. He says that a woman should cover her head at public worship, or "have power on her head" or—as the Revised Version puts it—"a sign of authority on her head." This mysterious statement is explained by Sir William Ramsay in *The Cities of St. Paul.*

"In Oriental lands the veil is the power and the honour and the dignity of the woman. With the veil on her head, she can go anywhere in security and profound respect. She is not seen; it is the mark of thoroughly bad manners to observe a veiled woman in the street. She is alone. The rest of the people around are non-existent to her, as she is to them. She is supreme in the crowd. She passes at her own free choice, and a space must be left for her. The man who did anything to annoy or molest her would have a bad time in an Oriental town and might easily lose his life. A man's house is his castle, in so far as a lady is understood to be there; without her it is free to any stranger to enter as guest and temporary lord.

"But without the veil the woman is a thing of nought, whom any one may insult. The true Oriental, if uneducated in Western ways, seems to be inclined naturally to treat with rudeness, to push and ill-treat a European lady in the street. A woman's authority and dignity vanish along with the all-covering veil that she discards. That is the Oriental view, which Paul learned in Tarsus."

In this *First Epistle to the Corinthians*, St. Paul, in reply to a disagreement on the Resurrection of the dead, wrote words whose calm beauty has soothed the ache of parting wherever the English Burial Service has been read. . . . "Now is Christ risen from the dead, and become the first-fruits of them that slept. . . . There is one glory of the sun, and another glory of the moon, and another glory of the stars; for one star differeth from another star in glory. . . . So when this corruptible shall have put on incorruption, and this mortal shall have put on immortality; then shall be brought to pass the saying that is written, Death is swallowed up in victory. O death, where is thy sting? O grave, where is thy victory?"

It is also in this letter that we find the exquisite little hymn on Charity—or Love, as the Revised Version has it—which is often read during the Marriage Service.

"If I speak with the tongues of men and angels, but have not love, I am become sounding brass, or a clanging cymbal. . . . Love suffereth long, and is kind; love envieth not; love vaunteth not itself, is not puffed up, doth not behave itself unseemly, seeketh not its own, is not provoked, taketh not account of evil; rejoiceth not in unrighteousness, but rejoiceth with the truth; beareth all things, believeth all things, hopeth all things, endureth all things. . . . But now abideth faith, hope, love, these three; and the greatest of these is love."

Between the writing of this letter and the letter known to us as the *Second Epistle to the Corinthians*, St. Paul seems to have paid a brief visit to Corinth—the sea journey from Ephesus is a short and easy one—and this visit gave him great pain. We do not know what happened on this occasion. It seems possible that his authority was being undermined by a rival mission of Jewish Christians who were contradicting his teaching and belittling his motives and his character. There is a suggestion that one of his Corinthian converts had insulted him.

When he returned, broken-hearted, to Asia, he wrote a "stern letter" to Corinth, which has been lost, although some critics believe that a portion of it has become incorporated in the *Second Epistle to the Corinthians*—an easy error in days before printing and after centuries of copying—and is to be found in chapters ten to thirteen.

However, when the riot of the silversmiths at Ephesus marked the end of Paul's long stay in that city, he set off on a journey which took him to Corinth for the third time. It was while he was on his way to Corinth that he addressed the letter known to us as the *Second Epistle to the Corinthians*. It was probably written from Macedonia. In this letter the spirit of Paul alternates between happiness and stern reproof. He lashes out at the "super-Apostles" who have belittled him in Corinth, expresses his love for his converts and his desire to see them again, and deals with the question of a collection which the churches were making for the poor Christians of Jerusalem.

Soon after this letter had been delivered, St. Paul himself must have arrived in Corinth, where he spent some months.

7

I was awakened one night by a commotion which I thought must be an earthquake. Doors and windows were banging. Sheets of rain were drumming on the roof. Leaping out to draw the shutters, which were being wrenched from their staples, I saw that the thirsty earth was baked so hard that it was unable to absorb the first rain of the autumn. Streams of water were running down the ill-made roads.

In the morning I set off for Cenchreæ, which is only about five miles from Corinth. The road, however, is an ordinary country cart track and the rain had turned its surface into a slippery porridge. After skidding along for a mile or so, the car became bogged. While it was being pulled out by a villager and a couple of mules, I thought that I had better try to approach Cenchreæ some other way. I went back to Corinth and rang up a friend in Athens, who promised to use his influence to get the Canal Company to lend me a motor-boat. This he was able to do, and the next morning I motored to the offices at Kalamaki.

I stood on the little stone pier at the eastern end of the Canal, waiting for the boat that came exploding towards me, breaking the oil-like stillness of the sea with its wide wash. A young Greek who might have sat for Praxiteles held the tiller. The boat was called, in English lettering, the *Narcissus*, and the mystery was explained by a brass plate with an English shipbuilder's name and "Maidenhead" upon it.

It was a lovely day, but future rain hung over the mountains in huge gold clouds. We sped across the water, keeping close to the rocky shore. The Bay of Cenchreæ, which lay about three miles off, was for a time hidden by intervening hills. As we drew nearer, the young Apollo pointed to a tall mountain which rises above Cenchreæ and told me that in a cave near the summit lives a hermit who had left his monastery because he did not agree with such new fangled notions as the reform of the Greek Church calender.

"Is he a very holy man?" I asked.

His eyes widened and, pursing up his lips, he gave several backward nods to his head, at the same time shovelling the sunlit air with the open palm of his hand: that eloquent Greek sign language that begins where superlatives end.

Cenchreæ surprised me. I had expected at least a small village on the shores of a bay which had once held a harbour famous all over the world: but there was nothing save one white-washed cabin on the shore that might have been taken bodily from any of the bays in Connemara. The mountains rise all round Cenchreæ, but where the valley goes north to Corinth is an opening in the hills, in the centre of which rises the big, blue dome of Acro-Corinth.

Two guardians of olive groves and an ancient dame, who seemed to be the only inhabitants of Cenchreæ, crowded to the shore, excited by the arrival of the Company's motor-boat. Think of that, you who are given to moralizing on the pointlessness of human effort! Where once the proudest navies of the world let down their sails, there is nothing now but one old woman and two old men, full of curiosity when a little boat comes into the bay. But no; I had underestimated the population of Cenchreæ. There was another old man, standing almost to his waist in the water, spearing fish.

Below the waters of the bay are the ruins of the harbour from which St. Paul sailed to Ephesus. An earthquake has shovelled them into the sea. I saw the harbour walls lying below the green water, and near the shore are several Roman walls twisted fantastically as an earthquake had tilted them. If I had not known that a great port once stood here, it would have been difficult to have believed it. As Paul saw it, there was a semi-circular basin sheltered by hills, with a temple of Aphrodite on one arm of the promontory and a temple to Æsculapius and Isis on the other. In the centre of the bay, rising from the water, was a colossal statue of Poseidon, a dolphin in one hand and a trident in the other. Behind the harbour rose the warehouses and the town.

I walked some way into the valley, where olives and corn are grown. The hummocks look as though they hide remains of the ancient city, and on a hillside just above the ruined harbour are the walls and floor of an ancient chapel, still covered with plaster and the crudely drawn outlines of several fish. Whether this symbol of Christianity identifies this building as an early church or not, I cannot say. There was a church at Cenchreæ in St. Paul's time, presumably founded from Corinth, and possibly during the Apostle's long stay there. A woman called Phœbe "our sister, which is a servant of the church which is at Cenchreæ," who has been "a succourer of many and of mine own self," is mentioned in the *Epistle to the Romans*.

As I looked across the lovely bay, gazing south towards the mountains of Argolis, I might have been in some deserted corner of the Hebrides. Here it was that St. Paul shaved his head because he had made a vow. How many reams have been written by scholars on the problem: was it Paul or his companion, Aquila, who had made the vow? The Ethiopic versions say that both did so. It was a common custom in antiquity, among Jews and pagans alike, to dedicate the hair to a god, often in thankfulness for escape from danger. Homer speaks of parents who dedicated their children's hair to a god, and Nero, when he first cut his beard, placed it in a golden box and dedicated it to Jupiter Capitolinus. St. Paul's vow may have been the ordinary Nazarite vow, which consisted in shaving the head, abstaining from wine and grapes, and, after the passing of thirty days, offering the hair that had grown again at the altar in Jerusalem.

This is what St. Paul may very well have intended. He was returning to attend the feast of Pentecost in Jerusalem, probably in a pilgrim ship which called first at Ephesus and then went south to Syria. We know that he spent at least the Sabbath in Ephesus, where he spoke in the synagogue; but he could not be persuaded to stay there. Perhaps his vow drew him to Jerusalem. Leaving Aquila and Priscilla behind in Ephesus to form the first germ of the Christian Church, he went aboard and in due course landed at Cæsarea.

In that brief visit to the greatest city in Asia Minor, he had seen the next scene of his missionary life. Ephesus was to rank even higher than Corinth as the scene of his ministry. St. Paul may have arrived in Syria in the spring of 53 A.D. He left it again in the summer of the same year to begin his Third Missionary Journey. Visiting his Galatians again, he came at length to Ephesus, where he was to spend three years in teaching the Gospel of Christ.

My plans to follow in the steps of the Apostle to Ephesus were now interrupted by the rains, which began to fall every other day, sometimes with tropical ferocity. It would be the same, or worse, in Asia Minor. Therefore I returned to England, and it was not until six months later that I saw Ephesus.

CHAPTER X

Describes a journey to Ephesus, the site of the Temple of Diana, and the theatre in which the silversmiths demonstrated against St. Paul. I voyage to Palestine, stay with Carmelite Fathers, and visit Cæsarea. I then take ship to Malta, where I see the bay of the shipwreck, travel on to Naples, and reach Rome. My journey ends at the tomb of St. Paul.

1

THE ship's captain was a big, gentle Hebridean, whose blue eyes, having gazed for so long into the night and into mist, had taken on a mystical, almost trance-like, stare. He was so accustomed to look at something beyond the immediate range of his vision that he would rarely turn to address his remarks to you. He spoke in a soft, low-pitched voice, as if he were thinking aloud.

When the ship was passing between the southern shore of the Troad and the north coast of Mitylene, he sent a messenger to invite me to go up on the bridge. I found him levelling binoculars at the land. Without removing them, he spoke to me.

"What does that put you in mind of?" he asked quietly, as he continued to examine Cape Baba and the hills running down to the Gulf of Adramyttium.

The ship was lifting in a heavy sea. It was one of those gusty days in March when the turquoise-blue of the Ægean turns to the colour of lead-piping; when thunder-laden clouds hang on the mountain-tops; when veils of grey suddenly obliterate an island, or form a barrier; when the tallest mountains seem to shrink and dwindle.

"What does it remind me of? Scotland."

"Aye, that's it," he murmured. "The Isles."

Rain blew down the Gulf of Adramyttium towards the Troad. The citadel of Assos, which we could see standing up near the shore, and a white town on the hill behind it, were blotted out for a time, and then, as the rain passed, shone out again washed and clear.

"We might be coming down the Sound of Raasay to Portree," I heard him say. "It's awful like the Isles."

As he talked of his early days at sea and of the old paddle-steamers that once went from the Kyle to Skye, I thought of St. Paul at Troas and Assos, wondering if he had seen waves the colour of lead breaking on the rocks, if he had heard the wind screaming over the heights of Mitylene, and if he had seen the rain-banks scudding down the Gulf.

"The rain's passing," I heard the captain say, and following the direction of his eyes, I saw a patch of blue in the sky. Long before we had turned south round Mitylene, the sun was shining and the sea was the colour of a wood violet.

I have seen the islands of the Ægean dried up like last year's walnuts, seamed and wrinkled by the heat of the sun, their moisture sucked up and hidden in the fruit of the fig-tree, the melon, and the pomegranate. But in the spring these islands sing to the sound of torrents falling through pinewoods to the sea. They shine like emeralds, green with growing corn, with fig-leaves like green fingers held to the sun, with vine-leaves running over the ground like small green fires of the earth. Honeysuckle hangs over white walls; the pale asphodel grows on the hills, and oleanders in the marshy places. Men and women, who in summer-time lie in the shade and sleep the hours away beneath the olive trees, are now busy on the terraced hills; and in the evening the streets of the little white towns ring to the sound of mule-bells as villagers come home from the vineyards.

The islands take on every change of light. In the early morning you will sometimes see them lying with gold clouds above them, their mountains the colour of saffron, the valleys picked out with threads of violet and mauve; in the evening they become purple in the sunset, sharp and hard against a sky in which the first stars burn.

We came in the greyness of morning to the chorus of mountains round Izmir. We saw the town lying far off in the curve of the bay, with the enormous heights towering above it. When the sun rose from behind Mount Pagus, those of us who stood looking towards the land had to gaze through smoked glasses.

I stood on deck trying to convince myself that this was a real morning and that it was really I who should that day see Ephesus. It is curious how names which cast their enchantment over one in childhood sometimes retain their magic through life. There are probably thousands of people who long to see certain foreign places for no other reason except that they invested them with unearthly qualities of beauty. The names which used to enliven the dullest of days for me were: Ephesus, Thebes, Tintagel, La Mancha, Camelot, and Avalon. They seemed to my young mind like trumpets sounding from some hidden world. I had seen Tintagel and Thebes, and Don Quixote's Toboso, on the brick-red plain of La Mancha; and now, on this still morning with the sun rising over Izmir, I was going to Ephesus.

The anchor rumbled into blue water. Little *caïques* moved busily round us, manned by Turks who stood up as they rowed, facing the oars. I was soon speeding across to the landing-steps. I was soon rolling over the cobbles of Izmir to the station, where the post train was waiting to puff away forty miles south, to Ayasoluk, the village for Ephesus.

With a pained shriek, the train set off through a luscious valley planted with fig trees. Since Roman times the figs of Izmir have been famous, and the valley is a great fig-grove where the Republic now decrees that the trees must be pruned and planted in rows, like cherry orchards in Kent. Soon, however, the warm, rich valley is left behind and the train plunges into untamed country where wide marshes lie for miles, haunted by every kind of wild fowl. The blue mountains close in and the way lies between rocky gorges famous for wild pig.

The train came eventually to the terminus station known until recently as Ayasoluk, but which is now called Seljuk in conformity with the Turkish determination to stamp out all Greek names. I think this change of name is a pity. The old name was a corruption of Ayios Theologos, the Byzantine name for St. John the Divine, who lived and died at Ephesus. Still, the Turks are naturally more interested in associating themselves with the Seljuks than in perpetuating a Christian place-name.

The village of Seljuk is a small collection of houses chiefly made of stones dragged from the ruins of Ephesus. The tall piers of an aqueduct attributed to the Emperor Justinian stride gauntly on one side of the village street. Houses have been built between some of the piers, and on the summit of every pier is a stork's nest. These delightful birds had just mated, and I was so amused by their love-making that I sat at the table of a little café, drinking a cup of coffee while I watched them.

Unlike the crane, whose piping was noticed by Euripides and Aristotle, the stork is a voiceless bird. He lives in a dignified silence until he falls in love in the spring. As soon as he finds the female of his choice, he feels compelled to make some audible expression of his happiness, but this is a difficult accomplishment for a soundless bird. He expresses his happiness by leaping a few feet into the air in a gaunt and startling manner, uttering at the same time a bone-like clatter, which he makes by opening and shutting his beak with rapidity.

Every time one of these birds came swooping down on the

nest to meet his adored one after a brief absence, he would lovingly press a frog into her mouth (this is probably not true, but it looked like it), and then, lifting his head, he would clatter his mandibles until the whole village echoed.

2

The ruins of Ephesus lie some distance from the village. The Temple of Diana is about one mile away, and the site of the city itself is another mile or so to the south-west.

I walked along a dusty road. Before this road leaves the village, there is a railed-in garden peopled by about twenty headless figures. They are sadly mutilated statues from the ruins of Ephesus, carefully mounted on plinths and standing with their headless bodies facing the road. They form a ghostly introduction to the dead city.

The road was lined on either side with bean-fields and with fields in which the wheat was already three feet high. Peasants bent over root-crops. Oxen came swaying across the dark earth, drawing ploughs as primitive as any in the tomb-reliefs of Egypt. The country bore that well-washed, brilliant air which follows a week of rain in Asia Minor. The hot sun seemed to say that it would never rain again, and the earth luxuriated in the heat. Poppies waved in the corn. Yellow pea-flowers, wild mustard, anemones, small marguerites and forget-me-nots, grew beside the road and on every space of unturned ground. Wherever I looked, I saw little chips of white marble. There is hardly a wall within miles of Ephesus in which you will not find marble that once formed part of a column or a pavement.

I turned off to the right and followed a narrow path that edged a field of wheat. I came to a big, stagnant pond covered so thickly with a snowy water-weed that at first sight it looked like white marble. As I stood still, the frogs which haunt this

pond by the million set up their *brekekekex co-äx* until the
air rang as if a hundred invisible rattles were being whirled.
The croaking shaped itself in my mind. . . .

"*Great is Diana . . . great is Diana . . . great is Diana
. . . great is Diana . . . great is Diana of the Ephesians . . .*"

That was the phrase which seemed to beat itself into the
sunny air of that quiet forenoon: for this stagnant pond is
the site of the Great Temple of Artemis—Diana of the Ephesians—once one of the Seven Wonders of the World.

Nothing in all my wandering filled me with a deeper sense
of the pathos of decay than this water-logged ruin at Ephesus.
The temple which once rose here, whose ground-plan is to-day
so clearly outlined in stagnant water, was larger and more
famous than the Parthenon. Pausanias said that it "surpassed
every structure raised by human hands." Another ancient
writer said: "I have seen the walls and hanging gardens of
Old Babylon, the statue of Olympian Jove, the Colossus of
Rhodes, the great labour of the lofty Pyramids, and the ancient tomb of Mausolus. But when I beheld the Temple at
Ephesus towering to the clouds, all these other marvels were
eclipsed."

I sat there listening to the chorus of the frogs, wondering
if in two thousand years' time some student of England, wandering among marshes and brambles on Ludgate Hill, would
look in vain for a relic of St. Paul's. Two thousand years ago
Ephesus appeared permanent and invincible. It would have
seemed impossible to anyone of that time that the Temple
of Diana should become a stagnant pond.

When Paul came to Ephesus, this temple and the powerful
organization connected with it were at the height of their
fame. Diana of the Ephesians was known the world over. She
was not the lovely, graceful Artemis of the Greeks, the swift
sister of Apollo: she was a goddess from remote antiquity, a

dark, Asiatic being like some ogre from the past of Man. Like the Aphrodite of Paphos, she was believed to have fallen from heaven, and she may, therefore, have originally been a meteorite invested with miraculous quality by the superstitious mind of early man. There is a statue of the Ephesian Diana in the Naples Museum. It shows a queer, barbaric figure, the lower part swaddled like an Egyptian mummy, the hands and face those of a woman. The upper portion is studded with a number of objects which, in the opinion of Sir William Ramsay, are really the ova of bees. These eggs indicate her function as the goddess of fertility.

The bee was the symbol of Ephesus. It is found on most of the coins and is one of the most beautifully modelled bees in ancient art. The goddess was the Queen Bee, and the temple organization included a crowd of priests or drones, who dressed like women, and a crowd of priestesses known as *melissai,* who represented the worker bees. This extraordinary organization developed in Anatolia from the primitive belief that in the life of the bee was seen the divine intention.

Although the Greeks believed that the Queen Bee was a male, the Asiatics, who evolved the worship of the Ephesian bee-goddess, founded their cult on a true knowledge of the sex of these insects.

The drone-priests and the worker-priestesses were assisted by an immense concourse of flute-players, heralds, trumpeters, sceptre-bearers, thurifers, sweepers of the sanctuary, dancers, acrobats, and robers of the divinity. A special mounted force of temple police patrolled the temple area and maintained order within the territory of the goddess. Among the signs of Hellenization were the annual games in honour of Artemis —the Artemisia—which attracted thousands of pilgrims from all parts of the world. At this time, the harbour of Ephesus was filled with pilgrim ships. No work was done for a month, while the great throng of Ephesians and strangers enjoyed a daily programme of athletic contests, plays and solemn sacrifices. Thousands of silver shrines were purchased by the visitors to take home with them as souvenirs of their pilgrimage.

The temple was visited by awe-struck strangers. An effigy of the goddess rose before the altar, but was usually concealed by a veil which had the peculiarity of being raised towards the ceiling, unlike that of Jupiter at Olympia, which was let down by ropes to the pavement, or the veil in the Temple of Isis, described by Apuleius, which was drawn aside at break of day. Why, I wonder, was Diana's veil drawn upward? There must have been a reason for the undignified procedure of first revealing the feet of the goddess, and then her body, before the head and face came into view.

The statue of Diana was wooden, but the writers of antiquity differ widely on the kind of wood which was used. Some say the image was of beech or elm, some of cedar, while others say that it was made of vine-stock. On most of the coins on which the goddess appears, two lines run from her hands to the ground. These represent rods, probably of gold, which were necessary to keep her in an erect position because of her top-heavy shape. On great festival days a statue of Diana was taken through Ephesus on a car drawn sometimes by mules and sometimes by stags or fawns.

And on these solemn occasions hymns to Diana were sung by day and night, and the streets of Ephesus resounded with the city's cry: "Great is Diana of the Ephesians."

Over sixty years ago, the weed-covered pond revealed its secret to an English architect, J. T. Wood, whose researches were financed by the British Museum. The Temple had been lost for centuries, and Wood sunk experimental pits all over the site for six years without a sign of success. Many a man would have given up in despair; but this was the passion of Wood's life, and he was convinced that he was fated to discover the site. He had been inspired by Edward Falkener's book on the lost temple and by his conjectural reconstruction of it. In the face of such faith and such stubborn determination, difficulties were as nothing.

Wood suffered from malaria, from Turkish interference, from shortage of funds, and from distinguished visitors. Still he persisted year after year, conducting his researches in a stove-pipe hat and a tightly buttoned frock coat, like the hardy Victorian he was. I have seen a faded photograph of him in this unlikely garb, taken at the bottom of a deep pit after his triumph. Wood, bearded and tightly-buttoned, stands with an air of victory, one hand resting on a drum of the discovered Temple. Alas, poor Wood! If only he had known that when the photograph was taken, he was standing immediately above the spectacular foundation deposit of thousands of gold and electrum objects and statues of Artemis in bronze and ivory, now in the museum at Istanbul, which D. G. Hogarth was to discover beneath the altar thirty years later.

Wood's discovery was, however, one of the romances of archæology. After sinking pits all over Ephesus and finding himself no nearer to the Temple, he dug one day in the theatre, the same building in which the riot described in *Acts* occurred, and there he unearthed a Roman inscription. This announced that a certain Roman, C. Vibius Salutarius, who lived in Ephesus about fifty years after Paul had been there, had given to the Temple of Diana many silver and gold images weighing six to seven pounds each. He had also left a sum in trust for the repair of the images and the cleaning of them, decreeing, in addition, that when they were carried in procession from the Temple to the theatre, during the birthday feast of Diana, they were to enter the city by the Magnesian Gate and to leave it, on their return journey, by the Coressian Gate. This wide circuit of the city was doubtless prompted by his vanity: he wanted as many people as possible to see his munificent gift. Wood grasped at once the importance of this inscription. Thanks to the vanity of a man who had been dead for over eighteen centuries, he was given an almost certain clue. If he could find these two gates and the roads leading from them, they would take him to the Temple.

He set to work with redoubled energy, and discovered first the Magnesian Gate, and then the Coressian Gate. Following the roads, he was led on the last day of the year 1869, and at a moment when funds had expired, to the site of the Temple, lying twenty feet beneath the modern ground level. What a moment that was for Wood! He had suffered from fever every night for three weeks, and the excitement was almost too much for him. But he rallied and carried on. He discovered columns, the pavement of the Temple, and the sculptured drums which are an architectural feature distinguishing the Temple of Diana from every other temple of the Greek world. The story of this well-earned triumph is told by Wood in a discursive and readable book called *Discoveries at Ephesus*.

Among his visitors was Dr. Schliemann, who at that time had not discovered Troy. He was drawn to Ephesus by a desire to feel his feet on the pavement of Diana's Temple, and as he looked around him, he remarked, a little wistfully, that Wood had won immortality. It must have been an interesting meeting: Wood, who had realized his ambitions, and Schliemann, who was about to win greater fame by establishing the site of Troy and by putting into operation his uncanny gift of forcing the earth to stand and deliver whatever gold treasure it happened to conceal.

Wood's weighty discoveries were transported to England in a man-of-war. Archæological transport had been one of the Navy's side lines since the time of Lord Elgin. Archæologists, in fact, became slightly petulant when captains refused to enlarge their hatches to accommodate the more massive fragments of the ancient world. Thanks to Wood and the British Navy, the superb artistry of the sculptured drums of Ephesus can to-day be admired in the British Museum. If St. Paul ever mounted the steps of this Temple, it is possible that his garments touched these stones.

3

The city of Ephesus lay a mile or so away from the Temple of Diana. The Temple was built on low-lying ground, and the city occupied the higher ground which sloped upward to Mount Prion.

A walk of fifteen minutes along a lonely road brought me to the most impressive ruins in Asia Minor. Malarial mosquitoes have driven away every human being, and Ephesus stands dignified and alone in its death. Here lie ruins of the kind that Piranesi loved to etch; a melancholy mixture of fractured architecture and clinging vegetation, with no sign of life but a goat-herd leaning on a broken sarcophagus or a lonely peasant outlined against a mournful sunset.

Ephesus is really like that. Few people ever visit it. The Turkish lads who herd the goats of Seljuk sometimes wander through its marble streets, but they are not too fond of doing so. Ephesus has a weird, haunted look.

The sea which once washed the harbour walls of Ephesus is no longer visible from the ruins. It began to recede even in Roman times. The plain on which the Temple and the lower part of the town were built lies to-day beneath twenty to thirty feet of silt, brought down in the course of centuries by the river Cayster. Once a fair lagoon, this huge malarial marsh grows nothing but tufts of wiry grass and beds of reeds that rustle in the lightest wind. The sound of the wind in the reeds of Ephesus can be heard from the hill-tops. It is an eerie memory of that haunted place.

I saw a peasant at work in the great stadium whose bones are still marked in the earth. He looked up, startled, when I walked towards him, as if I might have been some Ephesian who had burst his way from the tomb. Men once fought with beasts in this great, scooped-out oval in the rock, where a peasant now plants his beans.

I looked for traces of the vaults in which the wild animals were kept, but all sign of them has vanished. Paul's reference to having "fought with beasts at Ephesus" is probably a metaphorical reference to the fury of his opponents, for it is unlikely either that a Roman citizen would have been flung to the beasts, or that any man so condemned would have survived. But Paul's metaphor was, no doubt, prompted by some event which had taken place in this arena. That the Apostle was familiar with the procedure during these hideous displays is, of course, natural, but many people miss the point of his reference when he wrote to the Corinthians from Ephesus: "I think that God hath set forth us, the Apostles, *last*, as men doomed to death." The significant word is "last," because those doomed to death, generally condemned prisoners, were always paraded as a grand finale in the amphitheatre. Stripped naked, they came in at the end of a program of boxing, racing, and chariot contests, to face the fangs of wild animals.

I climbed above the stadium to the lower slopes of Mount Prion, so that I could get a bird's-eye view of Ephesus. I saw the high shoulder of Mount Coressus running out towards the sea, a great rampart sheltering the whole city to the southwest, and on the end of this long promontory stands a two-story building of ancient date called St. Paul's prison. I understood, as I looked down from this height, why even in Roman times the silting up of the Cayster plain gave the en-

gineers a lot of trouble. The harbour of Ephesus was an ar-
tificial basin lying within a few hundred yards of the city,
and approached by a canal. I am sure that St. Paul must
have compared it with the man-made harbour of his native
Tarsus. Dredging must have been as necessary at Ephesus as
it is in modern Glasgow, and there must have been the constant fear that ships would desert the long canal, and the
comparatively small land-locked dock, for the magnificent
open harbour of Smyrna, a few miles to the north.

What an astounding view rewarded those who came up this
channel from the sea. The white city lay immediately ahead
of them, spread out in splendour at the foot of Mount Pion
and grouped on the flanks of Mount Coressus: as they
glanced a little to the left, they would see the Temple of
Diana standing in the plain, shining with the brilliant blues
and reds and golds with which her marble was embellished.
This building lay due east and west, so that the approaching
traveller would have a magnificent three-quarter view of it
as the ship came slowly into the harbour of Ephesus.

I spent hours wandering over the ruins, which are spread
over an immense area. Sitting on a fallen pillar, I ate the
sandwiches I had brought with me. A few yards away rose
the stately steps of a temple leading upward to—nothing.
Little yellow flowers grew out of cracks in the marble. A fragment of stone, bearing the name of Augustus Cæsar, lay upside down, and it was scored with hundreds of deep scratches,
as if someone had been sharpening a knife on it. A few paces
away, covered by a screen of tamarisk bushes, were the entrances to vaults. Perhaps they had been a strongroom for
some of the gold and wealth of Ephesus. While I looked idly
at them, I saw the tamarisks tremble slightly as a little brown
animal came out from the darkness. I thought at first he was
a fox, but a second glance showed him to be a jackal. He
lifted his sharp little head and sniffed the air, then he yawned

just like any ordinary brown dog. At that moment, however, a puff of wind blew from the pillar the paper in which my sandwiches had been wrapped. He saw me! I had a brief glimpse of round eyes gazing straight at me, and a small black nose moving as it sniffed the air; and the next moment he had vanished. So lonely, so silent is Ephesus that I was sorry when this little creature had gone.

I remembered these words from *The Revelation*. . . .

"Unto the Angel of the Church of Ephesus write: These things saith he that holdeth the seven stars in his right hand, who walketh in the midst of the seven golden candlesticks. . . . I have something against thee, because thou hast left thy first love. Remember therefore from whence thou art fallen and repent, and do the first works; or else I will come unto thee quickly, and will remove thy candlestick out of thy place. . . ."

I looked towards the tamarisk bushes. I listened for the bittern's call. I heard the chorus of frogs in the marshes. Truly the candlestick of Ephesus has been removed out of its place.

4

I sat in the theatre at Ephesus.

The enormous semi-circle lay below me. The white tiers on which the seats had been set protruded from the covering of brushwood. A fig-tree grew out of a tier several feet below, and I looked over its leaves to the plain, where the ghost of a straight road led through the marsh towards the harbour. There were white ruins to the left of the road, showing in the marsh like the bones of an exhumed skeleton, and to the right were queer shapes hiding under the grass and tamarisks.

This theatre once held an audience of twenty-four thousand people. Although rebuilt after St. Paul's time, the structure is essentially the same as that in which the silversmiths' riot occurred. I opened the New Testament and read the brief account of St. Paul's life in Ephesus.

Paul arrived in the city during the course of his third mission. He had come across Asia Minor from Antioch in Syria. We have already seen how, earlier in the year, he had sailed from Cenchreæ, the eastern port of Corinth, in the same ship with his devoted friends and fellow tent-makers Aquila and Priscilla.

This husband and wife had evidently left Corinth for Ephesus at the call of more profitable work. Corinth may have offered them plenty of coarse work on sails of ships, but Ephesus was famous for the manufacture of luxurious tents and marquees and would have afforded greater scope and prospects. It is probable, too, that they came to Ephesus to prepare the way for Paul's ministry there. He trusted this couple and honoured them with unchanging regard and affection. It has been well said by McGiffert that Aquila and Priscilla "furnish the most beautiful example known to us in the Apostolic Age of the power for good that could be exerted by a husband and wife working in unison for the advancement of the Gospel."

With what joy must these friends have greeted their beloved teacher, when, at last, the Apostle descended the mountain road that led to Ephesus. Somewhere in the humble district of the city they gathered to talk of the progress of the Church; of the Christian instruction which husband and wife had given to a cultured and eloquent Alexandrian Jew named Apollos; and, of course, of the prospects of work. Paul was determined to support himself. He declined to rely on the generosity of his converts. Therefore, side by side with his intense spiritual life existed the harsh fight for material existence. How cruel and harsh this was, can be gathered from words written to the Corinthians from Ephesus: "We both hunger and thirst, and are naked and are buffeted, and have no certain dwelling-place; and labour, working with our own hands. . . ." And later, when saying farewell to the Elders of Ephesus, he proved how deep an impression the hardship of his life there had made on him: "Ye yourselves know," he cried, "that these hands have ministered unto my necessities, and to them that were with me."

Putting away the signs of his craft on the Sabbath eve, he lit the Sabbath lamp, and in the morning went to the synagogue to tell the Jews of our Lord, of His suffering and of His glorious Resurrection. He taught in the synagogue for three months, but the same opposition that had driven him from Pisidian Antioch, from Iconium, from Philippi, from Berœa and from Corinth, soon contrived to close the doors of the synagogue against him. It was the same story over again: the Jews would not accept the Gospel of Christ. It was of the wide opportunities that lay before him, and of his Jewish enemies, that Paul wrote when he said to his converts in Corinth: "A great door and effectual is opened unto me, and there are many adversaries."

Think of the problems that beset this heroic saint. On weekdays he was a workman slaving at his task; on the Sabbath, one of the greatest spiritual teachers the world has ever known, winning new souls to the Faith and planning the organization of the growing Church. As if to try his mighty spirit to the utmost, he was fated to learn at this time of the trouble in the Church at Corinth, which inspired his *First Epistle to the Corinthians*. As we read it, we do not think of some pastor in a quiet study, but of a man fighting for his daily bread and at the same time struggling with all the might of his soul to sow the seeds of faith in hard soil. Many missionaries have since that time performed feats of great bravery and endurance, and each one of them, in his darkest moments, must have drawn comfort from the indomitable courage of St. Paul.

In spite of his hardship, Paul seems to have prospered in Ephesus. When the usual opposition of the Jews was moving towards a breach of the peace, he quietly left them and transferred his preaching to the lecture-hall of a teacher named Tyrannus. There he opened his doors to Jews and Greeks—in fact, to any man or woman who cared to listen.

We are not told whether Tyrannus hired his lecture-hall to St. Paul for money, or whether he freely offered it when he was not himself using it. There is, however, an interesting addition in the famous *Codex Bezæ*, which is not found in the Authorized or Revised Version, which states that St. Paul had the use of the hall "from the fifth to the tenth hour." This would mean that Tyrannus used the room from early morning until eleven A.M., and St. Paul then occupied it until two hours before sunset. This is in perfect accord with the custom of the time. Schools began in the cool hours of the early morning, sometimes before sunrise, and all work ceased during the warm hours of the day, to be resumed again after the sun had lost its strength.

So St. Paul must have preached and made his Ephesian converts not at night, as one usually imagines, but during those hours of the day when most people were enjoying a siesta. Then, his preaching over, he may have gone to some horrible den to labour far into the night to complete a task begun in the fresh hours of the morning.

Or is this too harsh a picture of his life? I am sometimes inclined to think that it may be so. I find it difficult to reconcile work in a mean ghetto of Ephesus with the fact, stated so clearly in *Acts*, that the Asiarchs, "chief officers of Asia," were friends of St. Paul. These officials were the wealthiest men in Asia, elected for a term by various cities, and invested with the honorary title of "high-priest" on account of their willingness to defray, out of their own pockets, certain expenses connected with the gladiatorial shows and games which formed part of the cult-worship of the reigning Emperor. Is it likely that these plutocrats would have been on terms of intimacy with a Jewish craftsman? It is not impossible, but it is surely out of tune with the character of the age. Perhaps St. Paul's material circumstances changed at this period.

However that may be, the Apostle stayed longer in Ephesus than in any other place, with the possible exception of Rome. His teaching in the hall of Tyrannus continued for two years, and during that time he came into inevitable conflict with the magicians of Ephesus. At the outset of his missionary career he had met magic in the person of Elymas, the Sorcerer of Paphos; he had encountered it again in more lowly guise in the demented slave-girl of Philippi; but in Ephesus he was in a very cauldron of black magic. The dark form of the goddess which brooded over Ephesus was associated in the minds of the superstitious with miraculous appearances, with cures, and with divination. Magic was in the very air of Ephesus.

St. Paul's success in preaching, and the reverence with which he was regarded by converts, gave Jewish magicians in Ephesus the idea that they could steal his power, which they assumed to be a powerful spirit named Jesus. Therefore in their invocations they used the name of Christ, with disastrous results, for a demented man rose up and thrashed them, crying: "Jesus I know, and Paul I know; but who are ye?" The effect of this on the minds of certain Christians, who had been dabbling in the "curious arts," was such that they brought together their books of magical recipes, their lists of powerful words and phrases, and burnt them publicly. "So mightily grew the word of the Lord and prevailed."

After more than two years in Ephesus, there occurred the singularly dramatic event which terminated St. Paul's ministry in the city. He had intended to stay in Ephesus until

Pentecost, that is, until the end of May. And the reason is obvious. In this month was held the *Artemisia*, the annual festival of Diana of the Ephesians, which filled the city with strangers from every part of the Ægean and the Mediterranean. What better opportunity could a missionary have had of reaching many countries in one sermon?

What a wonderful picture is unfolded in *Acts* of Paul's last days in Ephesus. We see the forces of good and evil in sharp and terrible conflict. Although Paul had been persecuted in many places by his countrymen, this was the first occasion on which Christianity had challenged the vested interests of a pagan divinity. In the riot of the silversmiths of Ephesus we seem to hear a prophetic rumble of the day, still far off, when gods and goddesses would fall from their pedestals and the altars would no longer smoke: a day when church bells would ring across the world.

It was a silversmith named Demetrius who roused his fellow-workmen to rebel against the preaching of Paul. These men manufactured shrines of Diana which were sold to thousands of pilgrims during the festival of the goddess. They were little replicas of the great shrine of Diana and the pilgrims took them home as a memory of their visit. Yet within sight of the sanctuary, Paul was preaching the Gospel of Christ and telling all men to forsake false gods. What an unconscious tribute to the power of his preaching is this riot of Diana's silversmiths. Their one thought was to drive Paul from the city, or to imprison him, in order that he should not spoil trade prospects at the forthcoming festival.

"Sirs, ye know that by this craft we have our wealth," cried Demetrius. "Moreover ye see and hear that not alone at Ephesus, but almost throughout all Asia, this Paul hath persuaded and turned away much people, saying that they be no gods, which are made with hands: so that not only this our craft is in danger to be set at nought; but also that the temple of the great goddess Diana should be despised and her magnificence should be destroyed, whom all Asia and the world worshippeth."

The answer of the silversmiths to this speech was the city's cry:

"Great is Diana of the Ephesians!"

There are many incidents in *Acts* which clearly indicate that they are the impressions of an eye-witness. But the account of the riot at Ephesus, and the description of the shipwreck at Malta, stand by themselves as pieces of graphic reporting. Although the riot in the theatre is not a "we-passage," and thus does not proclaim the personal testimony of St. Luke, I am sure that he was present and saw the disturbance. I believe that most men who have handled the "copy" of reporters, and have some skill in detecting the work of an eye-witness, will agree with me. There is a marked difference between the report of even a small fire in a woodyard, written by a man who got there in time to see the wood burning, and the account of a less rapid competitor, no matter how skilful, who arrived too late. It is this sharp, inimitable touch of first-hand observation which seems to me to distinguish the description in *Acts*.

The agitators rushed from their workshops to the theatre of Ephesus, the recognized place for demonstrations. On their way they seized two of Paul's companions, Gaius and Aristarchus. The riot was heard all over the city. St. Paul heard it, and wished to go to the theatre to answer the charges made against him. His friends the Asiarchs, knowing well the violence of an Asiatic mob, especially when their financial interests were involved, managed to dissuade him from this gallant action. Meanwhile the tumult increased. The muddle-headedness of this mob, and of all mobs before and after, is wonderfully sketched in a few words: "Some therefore cried one thing, and some another; for the assembly was confused;

and the more part knew not wherefore they were come to-gether."

At this point the Jews, who were terrified that the riot might take an anti-Semitic turn, put forward a spokesman called Alexander (was he the copper-smith mentioned in the second *Epistle to Timothy*, who did Paul "much harm"?); but the rioters, seeing that he was a Jew, howled him down. And here comes a graphic touch, obviously the work of an eye-witness. "And Alexander beckoned with the hand, and would have made his defence unto the people." We can actually see the man waving his hands, unable to make him-self heard above the furious shouting of the mob. So for two hours the crowd drowned all attempts at oratory with the monotonous chant of the city, "Great is Diana of the Ephe-sians!", just as Arabs to-day will keep up a maddening chant during a political demonstration, repeating the same sentence again and again. These Ephesians repeated a common for-mula which, in moments of religious or political excitement, must have been one of the most familiar sounds in Ephesus.

Suddenly the noise dies away. The town-clerk of Ephesus has entered the Theatre. He mounts the stage. He looks round at the crowded tiers of marble seats rising before him in a semi-circle. And he makes a brilliant, typically Greek speech. The cold logic of his words falls like ice on the heated audience. He tells them that the supremacy of Artemis is not in question; that the Christians have neither robbed the temple nor blasphemed the goddess; that the law courts are available for such disputes and that, unless they go away peacefully, the Roman authorities may look upon the inci-dent as a riot and impose the usual penalties. "And when he had thus spoken, he dismissed the assembly."

It would have been pointless for Paul to have remained in Ephesus after this spontaneous outburst of fury. Persuaded, no doubt, by his friends the Asiarchs, he said good-bye to the city which had sheltered him for nearly three of the most triumphant and momentous years in the history of his missionary life. He "called unto him the disciples, and embraced them, and departed for to go into Macedonia."

Sitting in the ruined theatre of Ephesus, this scene came to life again. It was easy to forget the weeds growing between the stones, the trees springing from the seats, the fallen columns of the proscenium and the broken stage. I seemed to see this theatre shining in its glory, the streets no longer white shadows under the earth, but thronged with excited crowds, buzzing with question and answer; and above the noise of the crowd I seemed to hear the shout, "Great is Diana of the Ephesians." Then the whole scene fell apart, and I was sitting in a ruined place with a dead road running into the marsh. But from this road, where green water lies in pools, I heard the same chorus which fills the air at the Temple of Diana, as the high croaking of the frogs shaped itself into a rhythm:

"*Great is Diana . . . great is Diana . . . great is Diana of the Ephesians.*"

The letter known as the *Epistle to the Ephesians* was not written only for Ephesus: it was a circular letter addressed "to the Saints who are at——," with a blank space in which the name of the city could be inserted. In the course of time this general encyclical became associated with Ephesus, in the same way that another circular letter, the *Epistle to the Romans*, became associated with Rome.

As the *Epistle to the Ephesians* does not deal with local conditions, but with theological matters which lie outside the scope of this book, I will content myself with the following comment from the Rev. R. H. Malden's *Problems of the New Testament To-day.*

"This encyclical *On the Church* (Ephesians) forms a natural corollary to the earlier encyclical *On the Nature of the Christian Religion* (Romans) and is the fullest single expression of St. Paul's mind which we possess. Perhaps the world has never had more need to assimilate it than it has to-day. Certainly if the teaching of *Ephesians* had been more thoroughly grasped and had been made the foundations of European civilization, the *League of Nations* would not be required now. Probably no other set of ideas will ever succeed in making the League an effective force."

It is the tradition of centuries, and one which is generally accepted, that the *Epistle to the Ephesians* was written from Rome towards the end of Paul's life, while he was waiting his trial before Cæsar. At the same time he wrote the following letters:

> *The Epistle to the Colossians.*
> *The Epistle to the Philippians.*
> *The Epistle to Philemon.*

These four letters have come to be known as the Imprisonment Epistles. But from what prison were they written? The letters contain no information about this. The suggestion has been made, but has not found much favour, that they may have been written during the two years spent by the Apostle at Cæsarea, before he was sent to Rome. The only other imprisonment mentioned in *Acts* is the night spent in prison at Philippi. But clearly we must allow for other imprisonments during his missionary journeys, for does not Paul himself, in his *Second Epistle to the Corinthians*, written shortly after leaving Ephesus, speak of the number of times he had been imprisoned for the Gospel's sake?

An arresting and in many ways convincing hypothesis, known as the Ephesian Theory, has been developed in the last few years. This theory is based on the belief that at least one, and perhaps more than one, of those imprisonments of which

St. Paul speaks took place during his troubled time in Ephesus; and that it was from Ephesus, and not from Rome, that the four Imprisonment Epistles were written.

The leading exponent of the Ephesian Imprisonment hypothesis in this country is Dr. G. S. Duncan, Professor of Biblical Criticism in the University of St. Andrews. His book, *St. Paul's Ephesian Ministry*, is the fullest statement of the theory in any language. The author quotes Paul's own words, which suggest that the opposition in Ephesus was far more dangerous than might be gathered from the narrative of *Acts*. "If after the manner of men I have fought with beasts at Ephesus." And again: "trouble which came to us in Asia, that we were pressed out of measure, above strength, insomuch that we despaired even of life." These words certainly suggest a more dangerous situation than the riot described in *Acts*.

Professor Duncan follows this up by asking whether the Imprisonment Epistles do not become much more intelligible if we regard them as written from Ephesus rather than from Rome. The *Epistle to Philemon* provides two interesting illustrations. When the slave Onesimus ran away from his master in the little town of Colossæ—only a hundred miles from Ephesus—can we really be satisfied in believing that he travelled across two seas and a thousand miles of unfamiliar roads to Rome, when he might have received all the safety he required in the neighbouring capital of Ephesus, where the Temple of Diana was a recognized "place of refuge" for thieves, debtors and murderers? And when, at the end of the letter, St. Paul asks Philemon to prepare a room for him which he hopes to occupy on an imminent visit to Colossæ, surely, asks the author, the request is more natural if we imagine the Apostle writing from the near by city of Ephesus than from distant Rome; quite apart from the fact that when he was in Rome, Paul desired to press to westward into Spain.

When he analyses *Philippians*, Professor Duncan is bold

enough to claim that the case for dating it from an imprisonment in Ephesus during the Third Missionary Journey is so
strong that it should no longer remain a matter of dispute.
This is surprising to those of us who have always regarded
Paul's mention of the "palace," or Prætorium, at the beginning of the letter, and of "Cæsar's household," at the end, as
certain proof that the letter must have come from Rome. Professor Duncan shows, however, that the Prætorium was the
name given to the headquarters of a Roman provincial governor, a word equivalent to the modern Government House,
and that "Cæsar's household" were a body of civil servants
employed in provincial administration.

If Paul were imprisoned in Ephesus, what was the charge?
Dr. Duncan suggests that the solution is to be sought in a
phrase used by the town clerk in quelling the riot. And on
this he offers the theory that the Jews of Asia built up a singularly ingenious and malevolent case against Paul, charging
him with the serious crime of Temple robbery, of diverting
sums of money which normally would have been sent as an
annual contribution to Jerusalem.

And who was the Roman Governor whose sympathies these
Jews sought to enlist, before whom St. Paul had to appear so
often that his bonds, as he says, became manifest in all the
Prætorium, and who finally decided to dismiss the case? Dr.
Duncan shows that the Proconsul was Junius Silanus. While
at Ephesus, Junius Silanus became the first poison victim of
Nero's reign, because Agrippina saw in him a dangerous rival
to her son for the Principate.

It is an interesting piece of detective work. It adds enormously to the interest of the story of St. Paul if, behind the
narrative of *Acts*, we can trace a plot to charge the Apostle
with a capital charge and its consequent protracted hearing,
the vindication of the victim, and then—the secret poisoning
of the judge!

If this were true, one might ask, why does St. Luke not mention it in *Acts*? Dr. Duncan has an answer. He believes that *Acts* was written as a document in connexion with Paul's appeal to Nero. While it was clearly politic to refer to Gallio, a brother of Nero's "prime-minister," Seneca, it was equally politic to make no reference to Nero's victim, Junius Silanus.

It is all very interesting. But is it convincing? The evidence is largely inferential; but many a man has been hanged on similar evidence. It is a disconcerting theory, like all new theories, for if the Imprisonment Epistles were not written from Rome, but at an earlier period from Ephesus, it greatly reduces our knowledge of the conditions of the Apostle's life in Rome.

I walked back along the dusty road from Ephesus, and when I came to the cornfields beside the road, I took a farewell glance at the site of Diana's Temple.

As I passed through the corn, I heard the frog chorus from Aristophanes in full blast. As I came within sight of the pond, there was silence: they had heard me. Gradually one, then another, gained confidence. . . . "*Great . . . great . . . great . . .*" they piped, not yet quite sure of themselves. Then a bold frog piped up with "*Great is Diana . . .*", and in a second the full chorus was crashing out over the desolate quagmire . . . "*Great is Diana of the Ephesians.*"

5

The ship steamed slowly along the coast of Asia Minor. I could never grow weary of that coast-line, with its indented bays and its mountains lying back from the sea. Sometimes a little Turkish boat, with sails alive in the wind, slanted before us into some mud-banked creek which long ago was a marble harbour holding the triremes of Rome. A lonely, dead world it is, crying out for the spade of the archæologist. Some day, perhaps, those mighty green hummocks near the mouths of silted harbours will be excavated and their story made known to us. I wish I could think it would happen in our time.

I could see with the aid of glasses the malarial marsh where Miletus once stood. The four harbours are silted up, but the largest Greek theatre in Asia Minor still stands there. I longed to go to Miletus. They had told me in Izmir that it would take at least ten days, in the flooded condition of the marshlands, and that there was no certainty of fording the Mæander. So I had been obliged to give up the idea. But how dearly would I like to have stood upon the ground where St. Paul said good-bye to the Elders of Ephesus.

He left the city after the riot and travelled in Macedonia and Greece, then returned to Macedonia. In company with St. Luke, he took a coasting vessel which landed him at Troas, where he spent seven days. While he preached there, far into the night, a young man named Eutychus, falling asleep, fell from the open window to the ground below. They picked him up dead, but Paul ran down and cried, "Make ye no ado; for his life is in him." Paul brought him back to life, and after a time the boy returned to show that he had recovered.

There is an interesting side-light on Paul's extraordinary stamina. After preaching until daybreak, he preferred to walk alone for thirty miles across the Troad to Assos, rather than take the ship which was waiting in the harbour. At Assos he rejoined his companions, and they sailed to Mitylene, Chios, Samos, and Miletus, where St. Paul sent to Ephesus for the Elders.

This is one of the most touching scenes in *Acts*. The deep affection which St. Paul felt for his "children" welled up in his heart as he spoke to them, probably on some lonely stretch of shore outside the city, and his words of farewell were tinged with a foreboding of coming disasters:

"And now behold I go bound in the spirit unto Jerusalem," he said, "not knowing the things that shall befall me there: save that the Holy Ghost witnesseth in every city, saying that bonds and afflictions abide me."

He knew, it seems, that in returning to Jerusalem he was, like his Master, to commit himself into the hands of his enemies.

"And now, behold, I know that ye all, among whom I have gone preaching the kingdom of God, shall see my face no more . . . take heed therefore unto yourselves, and to all the flock, over the which the Holy Ghost hath made you overseers, to feed the church of God, which he hath purchased with his own blood. For I know this, that after my departing shall grievous wolves enter in among you, not sparing the flock . . . Therefore watch, and remember, that by the space of three years I ceased not to warn everyone night and day with tears. And now, brethren, I commend you to God, and to the word of his grace, which is able to build you up, and to give you an inheritance among all them which are sanctified. . . ."

He kneeled down and prayed on the shore, "and they all wept sore, and fell on Paul's neck, and kissed him, sorrowing most of all for the words which he spake, that they should see his face no more. And they accompanied him unto the ship."

In that sorrowful and solemn moment they saw him go, and the great Apostle who had planted the foundation stones of the Christian Church in Asia, in Greece and in Macedonia, turned from them and set his face towards Jerusalem with the knowledge that a chapter in his life was over.

In the morning we came to Rhodes. This is one of the islands which St. Paul's ship touched on its way to Palestine. There is a local tradition that it anchored in a small bay near Lindo, a town on the east of the island. There was just time for me to see this bay before the ship sailed for Haifa.

I went ashore in a rowing-boat which passed between two pillars into one of the loveliest harbours I have ever seen. These pillars were erected by the Italians, who have ruled the island since 1912, and on them they have erected the symbols of Rome and Rhodes: a bronze wolf looks out to sea from one, and a bronze stag from the other.

Near the wolf pillar is the massive fort of the Tower of St. Nicholas, which stands where the Colossus of Rhodes once towered one hundred and twelve feet above the water. This statue was one of the Seven Wonders of the World and has only been rivalled in height by the Statue of Liberty which is about forty feet higher. The Colossus was a nude Apollo who stood, his head surrounded by sun-rays, a torch uplifted in his right hand. A spiral staircase ran up inside the figure to the head, in the eyes of which, it is said, the Rhodians lit beacon fires at night. There was a curious mediæval tradition that the figure straddled the harbour so that ships passed between its enormous legs; but this is not so. Not only would no Greek sculptor design Apollo in this ridiculous attitude, but the engineering problem of erecting so vast a mass of bronze on a rock in the sea was already sufficiently difficult without added complications.

The Colossus only stood for the short space of fifty-six years—from 280 B.C. to 224 B.C. In that year an earthquake brought Apollo crashing into the sea, where he lay for nine hundred years. When St. Paul came to Rhodes, he must have seen this mass of bronze lying at the entrance to the harbour, just as Pliny saw it when he visited the island in the same century.

"Even as it lies," wrote Pliny, "it excites our wonder and imagination. Few men can clasp the thumb in their arms, and the fingers are larger than most statues. Where the limbs are broken asunder, vast caverns are seen yawning in the interior. Within, too, are to be seen large masses of rocks, by the aid of which the artist steadied it while erecting it."

The end of the Colossus of Rhodes was humiliating. When the Saracens took Rhodes in 672 A.D., they sold the statue as scrap-metal to a Jew. He carried off nine hundred camel loads —or about nine hundred tons—of bronze, which was broken up and probably made into instruments of war.

I stepped ashore on a water-front which looks mediæval at first sight, but is really modern. The Italians have poured money into Rhodes and have reconstructed ancient buildings and built new ones to match, with their usual infallible good taste. The walled town of Rhodes became the headquarters of the Knights of St. John after they left Cyprus. I have no idea what it looked like before the Italian occupation, but to-day it has been so perfectly restored that every visitor in modern clothes feels himself to be an unhappy anachronism. So perfect is the Street of the Knights that I had the impression that the Grand Commander and his followers were enjoying a siesta, and might at any moment come out of the houses, buckling on their swords and adjusting the straps of their body-armour.

I motored over hills covered with olive trees to the little town of Lindo, which stands on a hill by the sea, bowered in orange blossom and silver-grey olive leaves. It is a quiet, lovely place, full of butterflies, bees, and curiously silent brown children. Climbing through the narrow white streets, I came to the massive castle which the Knights of Rhodes built on the summit of the Greek acropolis of Lindo. It lies in ruins, but the Italians are putting it in order, treating each stone as if it were a block of gold. I think it was Mommsen who called ancient Rhodes the spoilt child of the Roman Empire; it is certainly the spoilt child of the Italian Department of Antiquities.

From the heights of the battlements, I looked down into the little bay to which the name of St. Paul has clung for centuries. It is about half the size of the Serpentine in Hyde Park, and is formed by the sea breaking a way through the volcanic-looking rocks and forming a miniature harbour, entirely land-locked save for the narrow entrance. It would undoubtedly be a wonderful haven for a small ship. The only indication that life ever existed there is a small Byzantine church, standing in ruins on the shore.

No one could tell me why the name of St. Paul should cling to this little haven. There was a Greek town at Lindo in St. Paul's time and perhaps his ship discharged cargo first at Rhodes and then at Lindo. It is significant that in Byzantine times the Christians of Rhodes should have dedicated a church to St. Paul on the shores of this lonely and deserted bay.

I got back to Rhodes in the afternoon, and stayed far too long in the museum where the Italians display the antiquities of the island. I have never been so near to missing a ship in my life, but reached it as threatening siren blasts were echoing over the island. With the air full of flying ropes and excited shouting, I slipped aboard, guilty, but unnoticed.

And in four days the heat of Palestine came out to meet us, as the headland of Mount Carmel grew out of the sea.

6

I stayed with the Carmelite Fathers at their hospice on the point of Carmel. The monastery is one of the most beautifully situated in the Holy Land. It is perched high up above the Bay of Haifa, with a superb view northward to Acre, and southward along the sandy foreshore to the ruined crusading Castle of Athlit. When mosquitoes and sand-flies are making night hideous in the town, this is the only place in which you can sleep in peace, with a cool sea-wind coming through the window. The monastery is surrounded by a wood where the eyes of jackals sometimes shine in the night like green, quick-moving fires.

There are fifty-four Carmelites of seventeen different nationalities on the headland of Carmel, but the visitor rarely sees them. Even when they go to Mass in the dramatic basilica, where the celebrant moves above the lamp-hung cavern of St. Elias, the brothers are hidden from view in a choir concealed behind the altar. The guest-house, too, is set apart from the monastery, almost on the very edge of the mountain, and the visitor is served by a cheerful and obliging layman from Malta. If you wish to experience real Christian kindness, fall ill in Palestine under the hospitable roof of the Carmelites.

Their history is the wildest imaginable mixture of misfortune, heroism, and saintliness. Mount Carmel has always attracted the hermit, and there seems to have been a flourishing community in Byzantine times. The Latin monks, however, began with a Calabrian crusader named Berthold, who settled there with ten companions in the year 1150. Their life was one of continual prayer, almost perpetual silence, and fasting. By the year 1242, the Order of Carmelites began to spread throughout Europe. The first English monasteries were at Holm, in Northumberland, and Aylesford, in Kent. The members of the Order became known in England as the White Friars.

The parent community on Carmel suffered the first of a long list of tragedies when Saladin captured Acre in 1291. The monks were massacred and the monastery razed to the ground. It lay in ruins for four centuries, until the reforms of St. Teresa inspired members of the Order to rebuild their original home. This was done in 1633, when a Mass, attended only by three heroic monks, formally inaugurated the return of the Carmelites to Carmel. A local war in 1761 caused another massacre, in the course of which the monastery was destroyed. It was rebuilt six years later. When Napoleon besieged Acre in 1799, the monks of Carmel nursed the French wounded: but no sooner had the French ships disappeared than the Turks massacred every monk—save one who managed to escape—and cut the throats of the wounded French soldiers as they lay in bed. Again the monastery was reduced to ruins until 1827, when the first stone of the present building was laid down.

But the troubles of the community were by no means ended. In 1886 certain colonists tried to seize the Carmelite property, and the monks were too poor to defend themselves in the law courts. They were saved by a gift of a thousand dollars collected in the United States. During the Great War of 1914–18, the Carmelites were turned out of the monastery by the Turks, who condemned two Spanish monks to death. The sentence was revoked by the intervention of Pope Benedict XV and ex-King Alfonso, and the two monks were permitted to return to Spain.

During the War the Turks pillaged the monastery, and made a search for hidden ammunition the excuse to destroy the monument to the Napoleonic Frenchmen. It was torn down and the bones scattered over the monastery garden. These were, however, reverently gathered. When at the end of the War, and under the British Administration of Palestine, Father Lamb became the first English Vicar of Mount Carmel since the Crusades, the French monument was re-erected and the original cross (discovered in a garden in Jerusalem) placed above it.

Since 1919 the monks of Carmel have known peace. Father Lamb, who is now in Egypt, has been succeeded as Vicar by Father Edmund O'Callaghan, under whose firm but kindly rule the little league of nations on Mount Carmel grows and prospers. Stella Maris is indeed the right name for that saintly haven. When night falls over the Holy Land, a lighthouse in the monastery grounds sweeps the sea with its beam, a symbol of the Light which burns there perpetually: the light of Christian Faith, of Charity and of Love.

I arrived as the sun was setting. The Maltese servant, who did not know that I was coming and had not seen me for over twelve months, came out at the sound of a car at the guest house and greeted me casually, as if he had seen me only yesterday.

"Good evening. Would you like your old room, or one overlooking the garden?"

"But—aren't you a bit surprised to see me?" I asked.

It is always disappointing to arrive suddenly from a great distance and cause no surprise. It is faintly damaging to one's vanity.

"Surprised? Why should I be? Is that all the luggage you've got?"

And I followed him up the stairs to the little white room.

Father Edmund was away on some mission and was not expected back until late. Brother Sebastian was also away; he had left in the early morning to cross the mountain to the branch monastery on the desolate eastward crest, the traditional place of the Sacrifice of Elias, from whose terrace one looks north over the hills of Galilee, and south over the rolling, brown hills of Samaria. He had taken the mail to the Carmelite sisters. He would be calling at the humble little convent, where a few saintly women work among the wild Druse villagers, setting off once a week on donkey-back with a case of medicine to visit the mothers and the children. I was sorry I had missed Brother Sebastian. He would have taken me with him, as he did once before, and I should have seen a faint light of pleasure on the faces of the nuns as they took their letters, and then gently laid them aside as they offered us a cup of weak tea. There would be a sister engaged in washing the eyes of a baby, while a Druse mother crouched on the ground like a witch. There would be a Druse horseman with a *keffieh* over his mouth, his black eyes blazing above it, cantering his horse to the convent to ask for something. All round would be savage, dark eyes, savage, snarling dogs, little mud lanes; and these frail, elderly nuns, their voices never raised above a whisper, never surprised by anything, never afraid, setting off alone on urgent missions into a country haunted by wolves, wild boars, and hyenas; a country that alarms even the Arabs.

Wandering in the monastery grounds before dinner, I heard the sound of chipping from a long shed and, pushing open the door, I saw old Brother Luigi at work on a tall, marble panel depicting an incident in Carmelite history. He is a Maltese brother, the artist of the community, and his admirable work is to be seen in many Latin churches of the Holy Land.

He stood at work, his skull-cap on the back of his head, his spectacles on the end of his nose, his little grey Vandyck beard and the whole front of his habit powdered with stone-dust. Even the rosary that was looped up under his left arm was a string of dusty beads. He was holding a metal implement in his left hand as firmly as a man holds a dagger, and every now and then knocking it very deliberately with a little mallet. At every third or fourth knock he would retreat from the panel, push up his spectacles, cock his head on one side, and then walk back to work, his sandals crunching on the marble chips.

When he saw me, he nearly dropped the mallet. He looked at me as if I were a ghost. I was delighted. Someone was at last surprised to see me! We sat on a sugar box while he told me all the things that had been happening at Stella Maris since I was last there. . . .

After dinner I sat out on the balcony overlooking the garden and watched how the necklace of light glittered round the dark neck of Haifa Bay. Stella Maris is so high that the sounds of Haifa never invade the mountain. It was still. Bats flickered over the palm trees. The stars were wonderful that night. The Maltese layman tip-toed out to me:

"The police are on the telephone."

"Hallo," said a brisk, English voice, "I understand you want to go to Cæsarea. Arrangements have been made. You will catch the train leaving Haifa at seven-thirty to-morrow morning, and get off at a station called Benyamina, about twenty miles down the line. A police escort will be waiting for you at the station. Pleasant journey. . . ."

Before I went to bed that night, I thought of the events that took St. Paul to Cæsarea. His ship left Rhodes for Patara, where the travellers changed to a ship sailing for Tyre. They sighted Cyprus on their left hand as they sailed to the Syrian coast. The ship was a big cargo boat, for she took seven days to unload at Tyre. During that time, Paul, Luke, and their companions, who carried the treasure chest containing the offering of the Gentile Churches, found lodging with the local Christians. The air was full of ominous foreboding. They feared that Paul was going to his death, and warned him of the danger. They begged him not to go.

When the time came for the ship to continue her voyage, all the Christians, with their wives and their children, went down to the harbour to see their beloved friend on his journey. On the beach at Tyre, on the gold sand scattered with the purple murex shells, the loving company knelt and bade Paul good-bye. It is a lovely scene. It is the only occasion on which we see Paul with little children. Kneeling together in prayer, they bade the Apostle farewell; and the ship continued her voyage to the south. Thus, in a few words, Luke indicates

Paul's lovable personality. At Miletus, the elders had wept at the thought that they should see his face no more; at Tyre they had warned him and had flocked to see him off, watching the sail with heavy hearts until it was lost to sight.

At Ptolemais, which is now Acre, St. Paul, St. Luke, and their company walked forty miles south to Cæsarea.

In this city they lodged with Philip the Evangelist, who was living there with his family. He had "four daughters, virgins, which did prophesy." Once again, Paul was warned of his danger. These four women no doubt joined their entreaties to that of a prophet named Agabus, who, earlier in the narrative of *Acts*, had prophesied the world-wide famine of the period. This prophet took Paul's girdle and, in the dramatic Hebrew manner, bound his own hands and feet with it, declaring at the same time that the Jews would "bind the man that owneth this girdle and . . . deliver him into the hands of the Gentiles." Those who heard begged St. Paul not to risk his life by going up to Jerusalem. "What mean ye to weep and break mine heart?" asked Paul gently; "for I am ready not to be bound only, but also to die at Jerusalem for the name of the Lord Jesus."

Sorrowfully the little party set out for Jerusalem, arriving there, as Paul had intended to arrive, just before Pentecost. They presented the collection from the Gentile Churches. The Mother Church received the missionaries with open arms. But still the Mosaic element was strong. There were some who were suspicious of Paul's method; who considered him a bad Jew. It was suggested that, in order to allay such criticism, he should perform some typically Jewish religious rite: something to prove that although he was a servant of Christ, he still held the faith of his fathers. The rite proposed was a common piety of the time among Jews. It was that he should purify himself with four Jews who had taken a vow, and should, on the completion of the vow, defray the expense of the offerings made by the four men to the Temple Treasury. Paul agreed to this. "Unto the Jews I became as a Jew that I might win the Jews. . . . I am made all things to all men," he had once written to the Corinthians.

So Paul shaved his head and spent his days with the four men in the Temple courts. This was, of course, the most public place in Jerusalem. Every Roman and Greek tourist visited the Court of the Gentiles in Herod's Temple. Thousands of Jews from all parts of the world thronged it at festival times. But beyond this Court, which surrounded the various inner courts and the Holy of Holies, no Gentile was permitted to step; and all strangers were warned, by frequent notices in Latin, Greek and Hebrew, that to do so meant instant death. One of these notices, as curt and definite as a danger signal in a power-station, has been dug up in Jerusalem, and is now to be seen in the museum at Istanbul.

However, Paul had been seen in Jerusalem in company with Trophimus, one of his Ephesian converts. Perhaps he had been seen with him and other Greek converts in the Court of the Gentiles. Among those who observed him and his companions were Jews from Asia, members of the synagogues who had rejected the Gospel and had driven Paul from their doors. At last the hated apostate was in their power. At last he had delivered himself into their hands! They had charged him in the past before Roman governors and magistrates; they had roused up the mobs in Greek cities against him; they had even pursued him from town to town in the hope of slaying him; but he had escaped them, only to offer himself at last in the Temple as a sacrifice to their hatred. Why not accuse him of a horrible crime against the faith? They could say that he had taken Gentiles beyond the barrier into the holy place.

"Men of Israel, help!" they shouted; "this is the man that teacheth all men everywhere against the people and the law, and this place: and further brought Greeks also into the Temple, and hath polluted this holy place!"

The Temple courts were instantly in an uproar. The easily inflamed crowd behaved exactly as a Moslem crowd would behave if they discovered Christians at the Kaaba in Mecca. Paul was dragged out of the Temple by the shrieking mob. Twenty priests put their shoulders to the great doors of Corinthian bronze and closed them in the face of the riot. The Roman guard in the neighbouring fortress of Antonia sprang to arms and came at the double down the steps leading into the Court of the Gentiles, thrusting their way through with spears and shields. The commander of the garrison, Claudius Lysias who was not only wide awake at festival time, but was also on the watch for political agitators, including a dangerous Egyptian who had slipped through the fingers of the police, appeared also to see what had happened. He assumed Paul to be the wanted Egyptian, and, indeed, his shaven head, bared in the struggle, may have given him a certain resemblance to the man. Lysias ordered the guard to handcuff him and take him to the barracks for investigation.

So violently hostile was the crowd by this time that, on the way to the barracks, Paul had to be carried by the soldiers in order to protect him from the hands that would have torn him to pieces. As the guard crossed spears on the barrack steps to prevent the mob from following Paul, able at last to make himself heard, said to Lysias:

"May I speak unto thee?"

"Canst thou speak Greek?" asked Lysias in astonishment. "Art not thou that Egyptian, which before these days madest an uproar, and leddest out into the wilderness four thousand men that were murderers?"

And Paul looked at Lysias and said:

"I am a man which am a Jew of Tarsus, a city in Cilicia, a citizen of no mean city: and I beseech thee, suffer me to speak unto the people."

The guard called for silence, and Paul "beckoned with the hand unto the people" and spoke to them in the Hebrew tongue. At the sound of their own tongue, the crowd became silent. He told them, briefly, his history. He told them of his Orthodoxy. He told them how he had stood by and watched Stephen die; how he had guarded the clothes of the stoning party; and how he had consented as the saint's blood was spilt on the stones of the Kedron Valley. He told them of his conversion on the way to Damascus. He told them that he had seen Jesus and had heard His voice, and that God had sent him into the far places of the world to bear the message of salvation to the Gentiles.

But at the sound of the word Gentiles, a clamour worse than before arose and the Jews shrieked:

"Away with such a fellow from the earth!"

They tore their clothes and threw dust in the air. Paul, Lysias, and the Roman guard gazed down from the steps on this spectacle: then Lysias, angered because he felt that his clemency had only made things worse, took Paul into the barracks and ordered him to be scourged.

As the soldiers were strapping him to the pillar, Paul said to the centurion:

"Is it lawful for you to scourge a man that is a Roman and uncondemned?"

The centurion was frightened. It was, of course, illegal. He might get into serious trouble. He went to Lysias and told him. The commander came himself to Paul.

"Tell me," he asked, "art thou a Roman?"

"Yea," answered Paul.

Claudius Lysias looked at him in amazement. He himself had probably been born a Greek. He had bought his way into the privilege of Roman citizenship. In his astonishment that any man who appeared to be as poor as Paul could afford to be a citizen of Rome, he let slip the thought in his mind:

"With a great sum obtained I this freedom."

Paul answered:

"But I was free born."

In a mood in which fear, respect and gratification were mingled, fear because he had nearly scourged a Roman, respect for Paul who had been born to a condition which he, Lysias, had been obliged to buy, and gratification because he had been prompt to rescue a Roman from the detested Jews, Claudius Lysias convened a meeting of the Sanhedrin. He wanted to hear from the lips of Paul's accusers what the trouble was about.

The meeting, however, was so violent that the guard had to take Paul back to the barracks to protect him. While he was there, a young man called to see him. He was Paul's nephew, the son of a sister who had married and settled down in Jerusalem. This is the only definite mention of any member of Paul's family. It has been assumed that the sister was perhaps married to a member of the Sanhedrin, and was thus in a position to hear all the gossip and to warn her brother of a plot against his life. Paul sent his nephew to Claudias Lysias. The commander "took him by the hand" and asked:

"What is it that thou hast to tell me?"

"The Jews have agreed to desire thee that thou wouldest bring down Paul to-morrow into the council, as though they would inquire somewhat of him more perfectly," said Paul's nephew. "But do not thou yield unto them: for there lie in wait for him of them more than forty men, which have bound themselves with an oath, that they will neither eat nor drink till they have killed him: and now are they ready, looking for a promise from thee."

"Tell no man that thou hast shewed these things to me," commanded Claudius Lysias.

When the young man had gone, he called two centurions.

"Make ready two hundred soldiers to go to Cæsarea," he

ordered, "and horsemen threescore and ten, and spearmen two hundred, at the third hour of the night; and provide them beasts, that they may set Paul on, and bring him safe unto Felix the Governor."

He then took his tablets and wrote a letter to the Procurator, giving him an outline of the trouble, and adding a little touch of self-conceit which rings so truly over a great gap of time. "Then came I with an army," he wrote, "and rescued him, *having understood that he was a Roman.*" St. Luke must surely have heard this letter read out in court, or have otherwise taken a copy of it, because no one writing a résumé of it from memory would have preserved this half-truth.

Having sealed it, Lysias delivered it to the officer commanding the escort; and at the third hour of the night the cavalcade, with its screen of spearmen, jangled out of the sleeping city and took the road that descends from the heights of Jerusalem into the Plain of Sharon.

They travelled in the night thirty-five miles over the hills to Antipatris. They were journeying through brigand country, and that was why Lysias had dispatched such a large force with his prisoner. When, however, they reached Antipatris, which is now Ras-el-Ain, a town on the edge of the plain, the danger of an ambush was over, and accordingly the two hundred spearmen returned to Jerusalem, leaving Paul and his cavalry escort to push on over the remaining twenty-seven miles to Cæsarea.

7

I went down to the station in the freshness of the morning. The train started off on its long daily journey across the Plain of Sharon and the Sinai Desert to Kantara East, where it links up with the Cairo Express. I could have cast a stone into the Mediterranean, which sparkled at the righthand windows;

to the left were hills and a sandy road on which files of burdened camels plodded towards Haifa.

We passed the massive ruins of the Castle of Athlit, the *Castrum Perigrinorum* of the Middle Ages, whose vast honey-coloured walls and bastions rise out at sea, the blue waves thundering perpetually against them, flinging up walls of spray.

Within an hour or so the train drew into the little station of Benyamina. The lines lay on sand. Sand stretched away to the east, and rose inland to slight hills. There were a few wooden sheds round the station, and posts to which sitting camels were tied. As I jumped down on the track, I saw that I was the only passenger for Benyamina. A fair-haired young Englishman in the uniform of a police sergeant came up, tapping his blue puttees with a riding-switch. In the background stood a constable holding two horses, one of them a lovely white Arab mare.

"Good morning," said the Sergeant. "We've got a hot day for it. It will take us a good hour to get to Cæsarea."

We walked towards the horses. In the background, subjected to the stony scrutiny of a group of Arabs, was an odd-looking vehicle drawn by two mules. It was a frail, four-wheeled buggy of the kind made familiar to us in old-fashioned films. It had a canvas hood to shield its passengers from the sun, and a narrow box-seat on which a huge Polish Jew in his shirt sleeves sat holding the reins.

The sergeant cast an apprehensive glance at me and coughed.

"I'm sorry," he began, and stopped.

"What's the matter?" I asked.

"Well, I thought you would be an old man," he said, "so I got a sand-cart for you. We could have done it much quicker on horseback."

I climbed into the sand-cart, which creaked in every joint.

The Polish Jew shouted at the mules, and, lurching violently across the railway lines, we ploughed on over the sand. The sergeant and his constable mounted their horses and trotted up, one on either side. I asked the sergeant if the constable were an Arab or a Jew.

"He's a Jew," he said. "A good fellow, too."

"Why is a police escort necessary for Cæsarea?"

"Well, it's a bit out of the way, you know. It's really perfectly safe. The few Arabs who live there are grand people and never give any trouble, but you're the first person to visit Cæsarea for over three years and I thought I'd like to go with you."

Miniature mountain ranges of fine gold sand fringe the Palestinian coast from the frontier at Rafa almost to Haifa, a distance of about a hundred miles. It has drifted up from Egypt and the Sinai Desert. Sir Flinders Petrie once told me that he found evidence, when dipping in these dunes, that in remote times the district was a Riviera where cities surrounded by palm trees stood on the shore of the sea. Irrigation and palm groves which stop the drift of the sand, would bring this desert to life once again.

My memory of that journey to Cæsarea is of dazzling sunlight, of cactus hedges, of camels, of Bedouin watering enormous flocks of sheep at desert wells, and of the creaking and swaying of the cart as it lurched, sometimes up to the front axles, in the soft sand.

Cæsarea is about five miles from the railhead. It still retains its old name; the Arabs have preserved the pronunciation, Kaisereeyah.

The first sign that we were approaching Cæsarea was a blue sweep of the Mediterranean Sea within a mile of us, and something like a road, which now developed between walls of brown stone. The landscape was strewn for miles with countless roughly-shaped, weathered sandstones, looking like petri-

fied sponges. I realized that these were the remains of the
buildings of ancient Cæsarea. As we continued towards a haphazard Arab village that lay ahead, dozens of small children
ran screaming in front of us as if they had seen the devil. We
came at length to a squalid collection of box-like Arab houses
and barns, a mosque or two, and a mass of ruined walls huddled together on a half-moon of sand on the edge of the sea.

"Here we are," said the sergeant. "This is Cæsarea."

While we were arranging for the stabling of the horses and
the mules, the few hundred inhabitants of Cæsarea gathered
round, the veiled women standing on roofs or peeping from
half-open doors. The leading family of Cæsarea was represented by three slim young Arabs, indistinguishable from each
other save for the fact that one was dressed in a shirt and
trousers, another in shirt and riding-breeches, with bare feet,
and the third in a striped native *galabiyeh*. After the formal
handshaking, the three brothers said that they were proud to
welcome a stranger to Cæsarea and they invited us to eat with
them at any hour suitable to ourselves. We said that nothing
would charm us more than to accept the hospitality of a family
so noted for its kindness. We then shook hands all over again.

I turned to explore Cæsarea. There is little left of the
Roman city except numbers of fallen stones. The once magnificent harbour is now a rocky bay into which a ruined pier
of solid masonry projects for some distance. Walking along the
foreshore, we came to the ruins of a Roman theatre cut in the
rock. It is a small one, probably an odeon, and nothing remains except the curve of the tiers of seats. Roman pillars are
built into many of the Arab houses in the village.

The Palestine Government maintains a guardian of antiquities in Cæsarea. We discovered him, a delightful old Arab
in a black gown, rocking himself to and fro as he pored over
a copy of the Koran, spectacles on the end of his nose. At the
sight of us he rose and slowly strapped on an enamelled armlet;

thus officially attired, he unlocked the door of a shed in which we saw a pathetic assembly of battered marble heads and a few shattered inscriptions.

For miles in every direction the country-side is strewn with stones and chips of marble. Complete pillars are often dug up in the fields, but no systematic excavation has ever been carried out. It is impossible to gain any idea of the ancient city.

Josephus tells us that Herod the Great built Cæsarea as the great port of his kingdom. He called it Cæsarea in honour of Augustus Cæsar. Herod was a master of the art of dedication. Even writers of Georgian days, who are usually believed to have developed the art of flattery to its limit in the hope of favours to come, were children compared with Herod. Under his rule Palestine became covered with new towns, each one carefully named in honour of some member of the Imperial House. Herod spent twelve years in building Cæsarea, and it became the best port and most up-to-date city in Palestine. By sinking enormous stones in twenty fathoms of water, he made a breakwater two hundred feet wide. The harbour was magnificent, and every road led down to it. All the main roads were intersected by broad, parallel avenues, and a system of underground subways connected various quarters of the city with the harbour.

He placed some of his finest buildings along the harbour front. On a platform facing the sea, there was a superb temple of marble so high that it could be seen a great way off by approaching ships, and in this he placed a statue of Roma and another of Augustus. The most luxurious of all the buildings was the Palace of Herod.

After Herod's death, Cæsarea was made the political capital under Roman administration. The Herodian palace was turned into the Roman Government House, in which a succession of procurators, including Pontius Pilate, kept state.

In the course of our walk we left the village and explored the country at the back of it, where a few scattered farms stand among orange groves.

"Are there no Christians here now?" I asked the sergeant.

"There is Father John, a Greek priest," he replied.

At that moment a horseman topped a rise of ground before us. He sat in an Arab saddle and his bridle was a single strand of rope. He wore a pair of striped trousers which had once, in some inconceivable past, belonged to a morning coat. His grey shirt was open at the neck and his feet in Arab slippers were thrust into bucket stirrups. He carried a shot-gun slung across his back. But the most remarkable feature about him was his face, which was as dark as an Arab's. It was a lean, brown face, with the straight nose seen in classical sculpture. His beard grew away from the lips and stood out crisply. His hair was looped up at the back in a gigantic knot that would, if unbound, have fallen below his waist. This impressive person came riding towards us, an odd mixture of brigand and saint.

"Who on earth is he?" I asked the sergeant.

"This," he replied, "is Father John."

The priest apologized for his appearance. It was unfortunate, he said, that I should have caught him at such a moment, but he thought there was a hare in the corn and had been out in the hope that he could offer a stew of hare to the Bishop of Cæsarea, who was coming to stay with him.

"The Bishop of Cæsarea?" I said. "I had no idea there was such a see."

"Ah," he said, "alas, alas, it is an empty title! Look around you. Only the stones remain to us. But there were great bishops here in olden times. Eusebius was Bishop of Cæsarea."

He gave a hitch to his shot-gun.

"The present Bishop lives in Jerusalem and I, Father John, am merely a watch-dog—a caretaker."

"But what do you watch, Father?" I asked.

"I watch a piece of land which the Greek Orthodox Church has possessed since the time of the Byzantine Empire. It is all that is left of our great possessions. All . . . all . . . was once Christian," and he swept his arm to include the stone-scattered hills, "but now . . . well, you can see for yourself!"

"And your Bishop?" I asked.

"Comes to see me when he feels in need of a change," he replied. "I am sorry I could not have shot that hare. I must try again to-night."

"Are there no Christians in Cæsarea to-day, not even one family?" I asked.

"There are four families," he replied, "but they are Latins and Maronites. You, sir, seem interested in such things?"

I told him that I was writing a book about St. Paul. At the sound of St. Paul's name, he slipped a leg over the withers of his horse and jumped to the ground, coming towards me with outstretched arms as if about to embrace me.

"Thrice welcome to Cæsarea!" he cried. "You must come and see my church, which is dedicated to St. Paul."

He held my hands in his. I was as eager to see his church as he was to show it to me. I told him we should come to his house as soon as we had lunched with our Arab friends. Beaming all over his handsome face, Father John leapt into the saddle and, with many a backward wave of the hand, disappeared over the stony hill.

"He's a great character," smiled the sergeant. "And he's a fine shot, too. . . ."

The three brothers were waiting for us in a ceremonial attitude outside a wooden gate set in a mud wall. We shook hands. They opened the gate, exposing to view a little court-yard and a whitewashed house approached by a flight of outside stairs. Mounting them, we were shown into a cool room in which a table was set for a meal. With the exquisite courtesy of their race, they had obviously sacked the town for knives, forks and spoons, in their determination to provide a European meal.

Water was brought and poured over our hands. One of the brothers entered, bearing a tray containing glasses of mulberry syrup. Then coffee was produced. This was followed by cigarettes. Every time I moved to do anything, to change my position or to find a box of matches, the three brothers darted to my side in an excess of troubled consideration. Half an hour passed. Three-quarters . . . one hour. Still there was no luncheon! We had some more mulberry syrup. But at the end of the hour savoury smells of varied pungency began to prance and curvet about the room. There was an encouraging sound of sizzling. A look of polite anxiety would cross the face of a brother, and he would quietly disappear, to return almost immediately, looking gratified. Nothing, evidently, had gone wrong.

Suddenly the door was silently opened and two bare female arms were seen holding a steaming bowl. All three brothers rushed to the door, and the soup was placed on the table. It was chicken broth, and excellent. No amount of persuasion would induce the brothers to sit down and eat with us. They insisted on serving us. We said how excellent the soup was, but they lifted their hands in simulated disgust, and said it was very bad, that the meal was mere makeshift and that had they known of our visit in time, a meal more suitable for such distinguished persons would have been prepared.

Again the two provoking bare arms were seen, grasping a gigantic platter heaped with veal, tomatoes and rice. This also was excellent. We said so. The brothers again lifted their hands and said it was a worthless snack. We were so hungry, and ate so heavily of this, that we hoped it was the end. But no. Once more the door silently opened, and the two female arms were seen for a brief second holding a round dish containing sufficient eggs, minced meat and fried onions to feed twenty starving giants. We protested humorously that it was too much. It was a mere trifle, cried our lavish hosts, piling great mounds on our plates, and bidding us set to with a will and have done with our polite speeches.

"But this is a feast, a banquet!" I said rather heavily.

"It is nothing! It is mere pot-luck!" I was told; and one of the brothers darted over and playfully put two more eggs on my plate.

They sat, irradiated with courtesy, administering devastating hospitality. I began to breathe with some difficulty. I thought that I should never again be able to eat veal, rice, minced meat, eggs or onions. Then I became aware that something awful had happened. The door was open again! The two mysterious arms were there. I could hardly bring myself to look. With a sense of impending doom, I saw that the *pièce de résistance* had arrived in the form of grilled chickens' legs and livers. The slaughter in the poultry-house must have been terrible. There were at least twenty legs. Fortunately, the Jewish policeman had the appetite of Gargantua. He ate—goodness knows how—three chickens' legs and a quantity of liver.

In a silence that had now become sinister, I saw the door softly open, but it was only mulberry syrup and coffee. Luncheon, happily, was over.

Our hosts smoked with us and told me as much as they knew about ancient Cæsarea. I was anxious to find out if any memory of the great city lingers to-day in the songs and stories of the modern inhabitants. I heard a curious and interesting thing. The ruins of the little theatre, which I had seen near the seashore, are called in Arabic "the theatre of the girls," and the ruins of the hippodrome on Father John's land, which I had not yet seen, are called "the place of the horses." Are these names a memory of the Greek plays and chariot races held so long ago?

We said good-bye to the three brothers, in whom I shall always think that the traditional hospitality of the Arab race has attained its climax, and made our way slowly and heavily towards the dwelling of Father John. He greeted us on the doorstep; he was dressed in a long gown and wore the stove-pipe hat of a Greek priest.

"You *must* have something to eat!" he said earnestly.

"No, no, no, we must not!" we cried, as we entered his cool kitchen and sat down. But Father John, a Greek from Cyprus, had his traditions too. He produced coffee and saucers of melon jam.

One of the most difficult things, in those parts of the world where the inhabitants are so accustomed to hunger that generosity consists in stuffing a guest until he can hardly move, is to continue to praise the food. It is etiquette to praise, yet to do so is also to run the danger of a second helping. I was, therefore, grateful to Father John's cat, which at that moment caused a diversion by leaping into a meat-safe that had been left open, and attempting to get away with something that was probably reserved for the Bishop.

"And now come and see the Church of St. Paul," said Father John.

He led the way into his garden, where gold-brown stones of the Byzantine period rise among fruit trees and cabbages. The building is the apse of a cathedral that once stood here. The original stones are still in position for about four courses, but the building has been patched in modern times and a roof put over it.

"This was once the Cathedral of St. Paul in Cæsarea," said Father John, "and it was built, as I will show you, above the prison in which he was confined. But first let us see the church."

He hitched up his cassock and, drawing a key out of his trousers pocket, he unlocked a frail wooden door that he had made to keep chickens and sheep out of the church. We entered a dark little stone cell whose enormous original stones looked strange in so small a building. A wooden table covered with an ordinary table-cloth served as an altar. Two brass candlesticks and a wooden crucifix stood on it. There were several ikons hanging on the stone wall, and lying on ledges was a strange assortment of Roman marbles and Byzantine inscriptions which Father John had, from time to time, dug up on his land.

I have never been in such a pathetically poor little church in my life. It is also the only Greek church I have ever seen without an *ikonostasis*. Every Sunday Father John holds a service there alone. No one ever comes, because there are no parishioners. To this feeble flicker has Christianity sunk in the city of St. Paul, of Origen and of Eusebius.

He opened shutters covered with cobwebs to let in more light, and as he pointed out beauties where none were visible to the eye, I realized that I had been unjust to him. Seeing him on horseback with his gun, I had thought him more interested in shooting a hare or planting a row of beans than in spiritual things: but now, in this pitiful little chapel in which he moved with the ease and confidence of long familiarity, he seemed to grow taller and the dignity of his sacred office made him another man.

"I am a poor priest," he cried. "I have nothing. But if I had something, I should give it all to save from foul desecration the vault—the holy vault—that lies below this church."

I could say nothing in reply. I was so surprised to see this change in him. His eyes blazed. He had suddenly become the church militant.

"Below the church," he continued, "is the prison of St. Paul. You will see for yourself. It is a stable for donkeys and mules. Is that desecration? I say it is desecration, most terrible. It was sold in 1925 to Jews who farm some land here, and they use it so. Let us go and see!"

He strode angrily away, pointing over the waste ground to the stumps and pillars which marked the site of the cathedral of St. Paul. He led us to a long, beautifully built vault in which a farm wagon was standing. The vault is built of huge stones which looked to me of Byzantine date, or perhaps even earlier. It had evidently once formed part of the crypt of the ruined cathedral. The tradition of the Greek Church is that it marks the prison of St. Paul. I was so impressed by the intensity of Father John's emotion that I promised to write on his behalf to the Palestine Government and ask that a competent anti-quary should be sent out to inspect the building. This has been done, and I have heard from the Government that, pending the purchase of the vault by the Greek Orthodox Church, steps have been taken "to induce the present tenant to remove his animals from the vault and to preserve it in a seemly condition."

It took Father John a long time to regain his cheerfulness. He strode ahead in unusual silence. Pushing aside a dense clump of oleanders, he said:

"Here is the hippodrome of Cæsarea."

With a start of amazement, I looked over the ghost of a great arena marked in green grass. In the middle, overthrown and lying on its side, was a massive obelisk of rose-red granite, one of the three *metæ* which marked the starting-point of the chariot-races. Like many such amphitheatres, notably the great stadium at Olympia, the race-course of Cæsarea was cut out of the side of the hill and was not, apparently, covered with marble. That is probably the reason why it has been so admirably preserved: there was nothing worth stealing in it. There can be no doubt that this is the amphitheatre constructed by Herod the Great. "On the south quarter behind the port," says Josephus, "he built an amphitheatre capable of holding a vast number of men, and conveniently situated for a prospect to the sea."

The amphitheatre once seated over twenty thousand spectators, and if the brushwood were cleared away, it would be possible to hold horse-races there to-morrow. Wild lemon trees grow on the banks where the audience once sat, and on the shady side of the course, where the imperial box was placed, stands an enormous fig-tree, as if deliberately marking the spot from which Herod, and, afterwards, the Procurators of Rome, looked down in splendour at the games. . . .

I said good-bye to Father John. The Polish Jew whipped up the mules and we set off at a brisk pace, for it was growing dark. On the way back to Haifa in the night train, my thoughts kept returning to that lonely priest who once a week lights a taper to the glory of God among the ruins of Cæsarea.

8

The Procurator of Judæa at the time of St. Paul's arrest was Antonius Felix. He had been appointed in the year 52 A.D., and had therefore been in office for several years.

He was not a pleasing person. Tacitus said that he "exercised the prerogative of a king, with every form of cruelty and lust, in the spirit of a slave," a sentence packed with bitter innuendo, for Felix was a base-born man who had married three princesses. He was brother of the notorious Pallas, the arrogant freedman of Claudius, whose enormous wealth was eventually the cause of his murder. Through the influence of Pallas, Felix was made Procurator of Judæa; and he was the first freedman to occupy such a position.

His first wife is unknown, but she is believed to have been a princess. His second wife was a grand-daughter of Antony and Cleopatra, and his third wife was a Jewess, the Princess Drusilla, sister of Agrippa I, whom he met shortly after he became Procurator of Judæa. She was the wife of Azizus, King

of Emesa, but Felix took her away from her husband. When
Paul arrived in Cæsarea, she was about nineteen years old.
Although none of this is stated in *Acts*, the character of Felix
and the background of his administration are admirably suggested.

Paul was lodged in Herod's Palace, which, as I have said,
was the Government House of Judæa, and the most splendid
building in Cæsarea. In five days' time the prosecuting party,
headed by the High Priest, came down from Jerusalem with a
lawyer named Tertullus. The trial was inconclusive. The ad-
vocate painted a picture of Paul as a dangerous agitator who
had not only spread sedition throughout the Empire, but had
broken the laws of the Jewish nation. Paul's reply was calm
and adequate. He denied the charges. Felix adjourned the
case, giving as his excuse the non-attendance of Claudius
Lysias, the commander of the Jerusalem garrison.

The case and, no doubt, the personality of St. Paul, had
caused interest in the palace. It was natural that the young
Jewish wife of the Procurator should wish to meet her unusual fellow-countryman. We are told, "when Felix came with
his wife Drusilla, which was a Jewess, he sent for Paul, and
heard him concerning the faith in Christ." It must have been
a remarkable scene: the worldly Roman governor, his sophisticated young wife, in whose veins ran the bad Herodian blood,
and the Apostle of the Gentiles, a man now in the late fifties,
worn with years of endeavour, but still full of vehement fire.
We do not know what St. Paul told them of Christianity, but
we know that, like St. John the Baptist before Herod Antipas,
he charged them with immorality, and his letters of Corinth
suggest that he did not mince his words.

"And as he reasoned of righteousness, temperance and judgment to come, Felix trembled, and answered, Go thy way for
this time; and when I have a convenient season I will call for
thee."

Felix sent for Paul on many an occasion; and for a very interesting reason. He hoped that Paul would offer a bribe for his release. It seems strange that Felix, the Procurator of Judæa, the brother of the fabulously rich Pallas, should have expected money from a man in Paul's humble station. Avarice has no rules, however, and sometimes rich men are delighted with small sums; but it seems more probable that Felix knew that Paul was wealthy enough to give him something worth having. If so, when did Paul become rich?

I have suggested that his material condition may have changed during his three years in Ephesus. When he arrived there, he was a poor tent-maker; when he left, he numbered the rich Asiarchs among his friends. When Paul came to Jerusalem, one of the first suggestions made to him was that he should pay for the vow-offerings of four Nazarites. Felix treated him with marked consideration, and consideration from such a man generally means one thing: that the favoured person is rich. Let us glance ahead a moment. Paul's next move was to appeal to Cæsar. That was not the act of a poor man. It was as expensive to appeal to Cæsar as it is to-day for some person in India or Canada to appeal to the Privy Council. And when he arrived in Rome, Luke makes a point of stating that he lived in "his own hired house."

Had Paul inherited money from his family in Tarsus? Was somebody connected with St. Paul—possibly Luke—wealthy enough to rouse the avarice of Felix? These are questions to which there probably never will be an answer; but I think it will be agreed that the evidence for an altered material position is suggested by the New Testament narrative.

Unable to draw a bribe from his prisoner, Felix allowed the case to drag on for two years. During this long time Fate was preparing to place judge, and not prisoner, in the dock. Riots broke out in Cæsarea between the Jews and the Syrians. Felix ordered out the troops and, in restoring order, many Jews were slain and their homes pillaged. Riots in Palestine always ended in the recall of the Roman Governor. Immediately he used force, powerful Jewish influences were brought to bear with the central authority in Rome, which resulted in his departure, and frequently in his disgrace. It was so with Felix. He was summoned to Rome and accused of misgovernment; but for the intervention of his brother Pallas, he might have suffered banishment, or worse. So he and his young princess disappear from history, save for the belief that Drusilla, and her son by Felix, perished during the eruption of Vesuvius in 79 A.D.

Felix had left Paul in bonds, and one of the first acts of the new Procurator, a just and upright man called Porcius Festus, was to inquire into the obvious injustice of Paul's continued imprisonment.

In ancient times, as in our day, a new governor is often the target for ambitions unrealized during the regime of his predecessor. Old policies and schemes, long since shelved, shake away the dust and emerge from their pigeonholes wearing an air of unnatural innocence. Therefore, when the High Priest and his colleagues greeted the new Procurator, they played on his lack of experience, as the Jews of Corinth had attempted to impose on Gallio, and suggested that Paul should be sent up to Jerusalem. They intended to kill him on the road. But Festus was not so simple. He told them that as he would be returning to Cæsarea in a few days' time, those who wished to prosecute Paul might journey down with him.

In those few days, however, the Jews were not idle. They were able to impress on Festus the value of their goodwill. When eventually Paul was brought before him, the Procurator, realizing that the treason charges were fantastic and persuaded that the root of the trouble was some mysterious, religious dispute more suitable for trial before the Sanhedrin than before a Roman law court, played into the hands of the

Jews with the preposterous suggestion that Paul should agree
to a re-trial in Jerusalem. It is true that because Paul was a
Roman citizen, the Procurator consented to be present to
guarantee a fair trial. But Paul at once saw the hidden hand
behind this proposition.

He then made his famous appeal. He uttered the two words
which any Roman citizen was empowered to say in any part
of the great Empire. *"Cæsarem appello,"* he cried. "I appeal
to Cæsar!"

These words alarmed Festus. They warned him into what
deep waters he had strayed. He had been unable to settle his
first dispute. The "ridiculous" case, which he had hoped to
settle in ten minutes, was to be taken before the judgment seat
of Nero. Bewildered and in doubt, he turned for aid to his
legal advisers, and "when he had conferred with the council
answered: Hast thou appealed unto Cæsar? unto Cæsar shalt
thou go."

Those solemn words defeated the Jews. Their prey was removed from their grasp at the very moment when victory
seemed most certain. But Festus was by no means out of his
difficulty. It was necessary for him to prepare papers called
"letters dimissory," giving a statement of the case for the guidance of the appeal court in Rome. Neither he, nor any of the
Romans about him, grasped the real point at issue, and they
found difficulty in presenting it in terms suitable for a Roman
tribunal.

At this point a new character entered: King Herod
Agrippa II. He had come with his sister, Berenice, to pay his
respects to the new governor. Agrippa was the son of Herod
Agrippa I, and a great-grandson of Herod the Great. Like all
the Herodian princes, Agrippa II was a Roman at heart. He
had been educated in Rome, all his vices were Roman, and
his youth had been spent in the highest circles of Roman society. He looked down on the ruling members of his race as a

set of intransigeant fanatics. It was natural that Festus should consult him about Paul.

When Agrippa had heard the Procurator's account, he said, "I would also hear the man myself," and Festus, delighted, replied: "To-morrow thou shalt hear him."

On the following day St. Paul was the central figure in a scene of splendour. He had stood before four Roman governors: Sergius Paulus in Cyprus, Gallio in Corinth, Felix and Festus in Cæsarea. If Dr. Duncan's Ephesian theory is correct, we must include a fifth: Junius Silanus. Now he was to stand for the first time before an earthly king, the last Herod who appears in the story of Christianity. Herod the Great had attempted to slay our Lord; his son, Antipas, had mocked Him with a mantle before the Crucifixion, and had beheaded St. John the Baptist. Agrippa I had slain St. James, and would have slain St. Peter if he could have found him; and now his son, Agrippa II, sat in state to hear the words of St. Paul.

The audience chamber of the Prætorium was arranged for a state occasion. This was not a trial, as it is sometimes misrepresented: it was the indulgence of a royal whim, and, perhaps, a fortunate excuse for Festus to arrange a brilliant little scene for the visiting monarch. The dignitaries entered the hall, escorted by a military guard and with trumpets sounding. Festus, in his scarlet cloak, was attended by his lictors; then followed the *chiliarchs* of the five cohorts, in their parade armour, the local dignitaries, and visiting officials who had come to Cæsarea to attend the meeting of Agrippa with the new Procurator.

Agrippa and Berenice were, of course, the centre of the stage. He was thirty-two; she was a year younger. Famous for her beauty, Berenice had been many times married and was fated, at the age of forty, to enchain the heart of Titus, son of the Emperor Vespasian. She entered the hall hand in hand with her brother, and was dressed "with great pomp." In order further to emphasize the unofficial nature of the event, it seems that Festus had with a graceful gesture accorded to Agrippa the chief seat, which rightly belonged to Cæsar's viceroy. The trumpets rang out again as the dignitaries took their seats. The air was scented with perfumes, and *flabella* of dyed ostrich feathers moved softly above the heads of Agrippa and Berenice.

Into the expectant silence came a man chained by the wrist to a soldier. What would that gathering have said if, by some miracle, they could have known that in future ages they would be remembered only because they had heard the voice of Paul?

Festus explained the character of the inquiry. Here was a man who clearly should be set free. He had appealed to Cæsar. Could this inquiry extract something definite enough to go down on a charge-sheet? He turned to Agrippa, in token that he might now conduct the proceedings.

"Thou art permitted to speak for thyself," said Agrippa. And Paul stretched forth his hand, as he had stretched it over Asia Minor, over Macedonia and over Greece.

"I think myself happy, king Agrippa," he began, "because I shall answer for myself this day before thee touching all the things whereof I am accused of the Jews: especially because I know thee to be expert in all customs and questions which are among the Jews: wherefore I beseech thee to hear me patiently. . . ."

Eloquently, and with carefully thought-out argument, Paul briefly told the story of his life: first a strict Pharisee, a persecutor of Christians; then, one noon-time on the Damascus Road, brought face to face with Jesus Christ and becoming for ever after a changed man. He told Agrippa, as he had told his converts in the Epistles, and as he had told the raving Jews in the Temple, how the Lord had spoken to him, and how he had devoted his life to preaching the Gospel.

There was silence as he spoke. Festus listened with growing amazement. The passion that shook Paul shocked and frightened him.

"Paul!" he cried, "thou art beside thyself; much learning doth make thee mad!"

"I am not mad, most noble Festus," replied Paul with quiet courtesy, "but speak forth the words of truth and soberness."

Turning again to Agrippa, Paul appealed to the King as a Jew and as a believer in the prophets of his race. But Agrippa was too cunning to be caught in any admission, therefore he parried the question with good nature.

"Almost thou persuadest me to be a Christian," said Agrippa.

Such is the rendering in the Authorized Version. But the original is obscure and it is doubtful if we can now establish the precise meaning. Dr. Moffatt translates it: "At this rate it won't be long before you believe you have made a Christian of me."

Then, with all the passion with which Paul was capable, the words burst from him:

"I would to God that not only thou, but also all that hear me this day, were both almost and altogether such as I am. . . ." Then he dropped his voice and with pathetic dignity indicated the chain on his wrist, adding, "except these bonds."

The inquiry was over. King and Governor rose and went apart, both saying that there was no reason for Paul's captivity.

"This man might have been set at liberty," commented Agrippa, "if he had not appealed unto Cæsar."

But the appeal had been recorded and must stand. Arrangements were made for Paul, accompanied by Luke, to sail for Italy in charge of a centurion named Julius, of the Augustan Cohort.

9

At Haifa it was my good fortune to embark in a British cruising ship which had collected its wanderers—some had even been to Ur of the Chaldees—and was to sail straight to Malta and Naples.

The *Letitia,* having strangely lost her diphthong æ in spite of her profound Hellenization, lay in the sunlight of Haifa like a tremendously reliable slice of Glasgow. The rich voices of the crew sent my memory winging far off to Sauchiehall Street and to the Celtic football ground on a Saturday afternoon. I had never been so delighted with a ship in my life. How fortunate were these voyagers, slipping so comfortably into the interesting places of the world: walking into Athens one morning, into Corinth the next, and, in a few days, Cyprus; but sleeping every night in Glasgow.

I met a man on board who told me an extremely good story. He is a distinguished official who had held an administrative position in the Palestine Government.

"In the Druse country of the Lebanon," he said, "there are many wild-looking men who will astound you by breaking into a few words of American. Some of these tribesmen actually venture to the States, manage to pick up a little money, and then return to boast about their experiences for the rest of their lives.

"One Druse is very fond of telling his friends about the United States. And this is what he says while they sit drinking coffee. 'Now the country of the United States is a very great country and full of men and motor-cars. This nation worships a man called George Washington, who was a great chief. At his birth all the good *djinns* were present to endow this George Washington with the good things of life. They bent over his cradle and gave him, one by one, their blessing. But one bad *djinn* gained admittance, and he took away from this George

Washington the ability to tell lies. Ever afterwards, O my brothers, this great man, this George Washington, could not help speaking the truth.' "

One morning we came within sight of the southern coast of Crete. The island lay for many hours on our starboard bow, immense gold clouds hanging motionless above her mountains. We were near enough to see the sunlight patterning the green and mustard-yellow of the lowlands, and striping the fierce mountains and deep glens and passes with streaks of deepest blue.

Half-way along the distant coastline, a few miles to the east of the outward-jutting Cape Lithinas, I could see through glasses a series of dark bays lying back among the hills. One or two small islands sheltered the entrance to them. Among these bays is the harbour of Kali Limniones—Fair Havens—the harbour in which St. Paul's ship sheltered during the voyage which ended in shipwreck on Malta.

As I watched the waves creaming round the shores of Crete, I thought that love of the sea is a modern sentiment. Such lines as "All I want is a tall ship and a star to steer her by" would have found no echo in the mind of antiquity, while even the Argonauts would probably have turned pale at the sound of "A Life on the Ocean Wave." The people of antiquity were too busy preserving their lives on the sea to pay attention to beauties which delight us.

The Israelites frankly loathed the sea. They thought of it as a monster at war with God. The Old Testament is full of disparaging marine metaphor: the wicked are compared to "raging waves" of the sea, and so on.

If the ancient Greeks loved the sea, they concealed their feelings with some skill, and they never permitted themselves to become sentimental about it. The Romans, on the other hand, voiced in ringing tones antiquity's dislike for the ocean and for ships. The frescoes of Pompeii illustrate Roman feelings about the sea. It must never be rough. It must never be dull. It must never be deserted.

Lucretius saw even in the driftwood of a shore a warning to mortals to shun "the wiles of the sea." Ovid believed that safety ended at the beach; after his exile, his metaphors were often of shipwrecks, and his comments on the sea became more morbid and depressing than ever. Horace, who also hated the sea, said that he thought only greed or poverty could induce a man to make a voyage. Cicero, who did quite a lot of sea travelling, but was rarely out of sight of the land, always felt bored or uneasy. And I daresay the list of sea-haters could be considerably increased.

It is not difficult to understand why the people of the past should have hated and feared the sea. Their ships were small and unsafe. Their coasts were unlighted. They had no compasses, and if the sky became overcast and no land was in sight, they were lost. Reefs were unmarked, and ships frequently struck one in broad daylight. Yet, in spite of these things, and, hating the sea as they did, they were great sailors.

St. Paul's voyage to Rome provides an insight into the peril of the sea in classical times. It is the finest piece of writing in *Acts*, and St. Luke was an eye-witness to everything he described. His account of the manœuvrings of the ship, and of its wreck on Malta, are the most vivid descriptions of such happenings in ancient literature. It is a chapter of the New Testament which has always had a great appeal for sailors, who appreciate not only the workman-like sharpness of the narrative, but also the technical accuracy of St. Luke. It was this twenty-seventh chapter of *Acts* that Nelson was reading on the morning of the Battle of Copenhagen.

Autumn was already advanced when the travellers embarked at Cæsarea in a coasting vessel which was to take them to Myra, on the south coast of Asia Minor. No time was to be lost if they were to reach Italy before the seas were shut for the winter. They made for Myra because it was a port on the route of the Alexandrian corn-ships, and they knew that, with luck, they would be able to transfer to one of the last corn-ships of the season.

It may seem extraordinary to us that Myra, so far, apparently, from the natural route of a ship from Alexandria to Italy, should have been a port of call for these vessels; but ancient navigation routes were determined by factors not, perhaps, obvious to us to-day. During the westerly winds of summer, it was more expedient for a grain-ship to cut across to Myra and then to sail round in the shelter of the south coast of Crete, than to make the direct voyage to Sicily.

The travellers were right in their surmise. A corn-ship was ready to leave the docks at Myra, and into this Julius, the centurion, transferred St. Paul, St. Luke, Aristarchus—one of the Thessalonian converts—and various unnamed and unknown prisoners who were also in his charge. No doubt they felt as the traveller feels to-day when he leaves a humble cargo-boat for a big liner, because the Alexandrian corn-ships were the finest and the largest ships of the time, and their Egyptian pilots were famous on all the seas of the ancient world. The grain-fleet was, no doubt, part of the Imperial service, and subsidized by the Government, because at this period Rome was almost completely dependent on imported wheat. Any delay or hold-up in the service might have had serious political consequences, as Claudius realized when he was mobbed by a hungry crowd in Rome during a bread shortage. In Nero's time some two hundred thousand citizens were on the list of the corn dole, receiving every month six or seven bushels at the expense of the Treasury.

The ship in which St. Paul now found himself was not, probably, one of the largest of the fleet. The new passengers raised the number of persons on board to two hundred and seventy-six. It has been suggested that the crew numbered a hundred, that there were a hundred soldiers, and that the odd seventy-six were prisoners.

Setting sail from Myra, the ship made poor headway against a north-west wind. Two weeks were probably occupied in struggling to Cnidus, where the ship turned south and sheltered in the lee of Crete, slowly beating her way round the north-east of the island into the shelter of the southern coast. It was now obvious to crew and passengers that they were in for a bad time, and it was with great difficulty that they managed to struggle, even in the shelter of the Cretan mountains, to the harbour of Fair Havens. As they waited for the wind to change, a council was held. They had to decide whether they should abandon the voyage and lie up for the winter, and, if so, should they lie in Fair Havens; or whether they should try to find a more sheltered spot.

It is clear that the centurion, as a Roman officer, took precedence even over the master of the ship. He invited Paul to the conference, not, one imagines, from politeness, but because he knew that his prisoner had had a great experience of the sea. Paul's advice was to stay where they were. He prophesied the disaster that would overtake them if they put to sea; but the ship's officers thought otherwise, and the centurion took their advice.

Deceived by the softness of a south wind, they loosed from Fair Havens and sailed for Phenice, which was a better harbour. No sooner had they reached Cape Matala than the danger which Paul had anticipated swept suddenly upon them: a tempestuous wind blew them southward from their course to the small isle of Clauda. While they sailed in the shelter of this island, they managed to pull in the long-boat which had previously been towed behind them, and was now full of water, and they also seized this chance to make other preparations to face the gale in which they were now caught.

Their precautions consisted of an operation known as "frapping" the ship, or saving the strain on her timbers by passing cables beneath her hull and tightening them by means of a windlass. As recently as a century ago, this precaution was taken on wooden ships during dangerous storms.

As they drove before the gale, the fear of all on board was that they would be blown on the Syrtis, a stretch of sandbanks and quicksands off the coast of Tunis and Tripoli, from which no ships ever escaped. In their extremity, they "strake sail," or "lowered the gear," and thus, by slackening their speed, allowed the vessel to drift under as little canvas as possible, perhaps putting the helm as close to the wind as they dared, and changing the course slightly to keep away from the African coast.

The next day they lightened the ship by throwing some of the wheat overboard. Prisoners and crew must have worked together in the scream of the wind. On the third day they threw overboard "the tackling of the ship," or the ship's spare furniture and, possibly, the main-yard, now a useless and dangerous encumbrance. Having done this, there was nothing more to do but to cling to the storm-tossed vessel and to pray for deliverance.

For many days they caught no glimpse of sun or moon. They did not know where they were. They tossed, weak from hunger and fatigue, now swallowed in the mountainous trough of the storm, and now cast up towards the sombre sky. So they resigned themselves to death. Except Paul. As usual, in times of peril, his soul escaped from earth and drew strength and comfort from the Divine. He went about comforting his fellow-sufferers in the same manner that he had exhorted his converts to take heart, and to "build themselves up" in the knowledge of God and in the faith of Christ. The Vision granted to him in times of stress and peril had assured him that they would not die, but would be cast upon a shore and saved. He knew that his destiny was to stand before Nero.

The fourteenth night found them drifting helplessly in Adria, which is not the Adriatic, but the stretch of open sea between Greece and Sicily, and the acute ears of the sailors heard something that perhaps not one of the passengers had detected: they heard the sound of breakers booming on a shore. They took the lead and, casting it, found themselves in twenty fathoms of water; they cast again, and found that they were in only fifteen fathoms. It was dark. They did not know where they were. The moon and the stars were hidden, and the ship was being driven before the storm, possibly to end in splinters on the rocks of some desolate coast. They threw out four anchors from the stern and longed for daylight.

Then the crew, sensing the nearness of the land, plotted to take the long-boat and escape, leaving the ship and the passengers to their fate. Paul saw through their cowardly design, and told the centurion of it in words which have rung down the ages like a tocsin on the Church's unity:

"Except these [sailors] abide in the ship, ye [soldiers] cannot be saved," he said.

The soldiers who were listening immediately drew their swords and, rushing to the stern, hacked at the cables of the long-boat, which drifted into the darkness and the storm.

In the greyness of morning Paul comforted his companions and bade them eat. Half dead with fear, still unable to believe in deliverance, weak from prolonged hunger, these men lay in the tossing ship, within sound of the waves breaking over the coast of Malta. Paul knew that the final effort of beaching the ship would need more courage and strength than they possessed, and he continued to move among them, tender as a woman, pressing them to eat. Strengthened and encouraged, they faced the day. As the light grew, they saw that they were anchored near a rocky island on whose shores white breakers were pounding. Although many of the sailors must have been before to Malta, none of them recognized the desolate northern shores of the island. Looking about, they saw "a place where two seas met," where the current, passing between a small island and the mainland, had caused sand banks to form. It was upon this soft place that they decided to run the ship aground.

The last of the wheat had been cast out, and the ship was light. They rigged up a mainsail and drew in the four anchors. Unlashing the two rudder-paddles, they drove with fury, for the gale was still blowing, straight for the land. As the ship's nose struck the sand, the impact shivered the battered vessel, and, even as the exhausted men were struggling ashore, the breakers began to beat open the raised stern. In the wild confusion of that moment, the soldiers drew their swords and made to slay the prisoners. If Paul had not been there, they would have been put to the sword, as indeed prisoners in such a situation had been killed many a time before. But the centurion sternly forbade them, because he wished to save Paul's life. He ordered that those who could swim were to cast themselves into the sea, and that those unable to swim were to grasp pieces of wreckage and so save their lives as best they could.

And the natives, who had been watching, came timidly down to see what manner of men had come so violently out of the storm. They lit a fire, and Paul helped them. As he was gathering a bundle of sticks, a snake fastened on his hand. He shook it off, and the natives, seeing that no harm came to him, whispered that he was a god.

So, to the thunder of waves and the lash of rain, Paul came to Malta.

10

Malta lay before us in the morning sunlight, a khaki-coloured hump in the sea. Nowhere was a tree visible, and the little villages, dotted with great frequency over the undulating monotony of the landscape, had the sharpness and unnatural clarity of models in an architect's office. I saw through glasses the white town of Valetta and the domes of baroque churches; then, as we slowly approached the harbour, I could hear the solemn "din-din-din" of church bells, which, from Malta eastward, are deeper and more gong-like than the bells of the West.

The harbour was a sheet of intensely blue water in a khaki frame. Battleships and destroyers painted Mediterranean blue, which is really a pale grey, lay apparently at rest; but crossing the line of a signal lamp, one realized that the Fleet was winking all the time in a rather sinister way from bridge to bridge. Naval craft exploded across the harbour water, drawing a line from the Customs House to their respective ships. In the shadow of a liner cruised a number of rowing-boats containing swarthy natives with extended arms, who, at first sight, appeared to be singing, but were really attempting to sell lace to indifferent people far up on the deck of the ship.

As we dropped anchor, an admiral's pinnace—or is it still called a barge?—came sweeping towards us, spotless and perfect. In the little glass cabin in which admirals are smoothly transported from place to place sat an important young flag-officer. Two statuesque bluejackets, standing together with upright boathooks, made a concerted grab at our gangway, and the midshipman saluted; the staff officer leapt nimbly from the white rubber mat of the pinnace to come in search of some passenger, hitherto humble and unspectacular, but upon whom His Majesty's Navy had now cast its reflected glory.

I went ashore humbly in a rowing-boat, and took a car up to Valetta, a town Eastern in colour, whose high, narrow streets opened to squares where large churches stood in the sunlight. A constant stream of women pushed aside the padded mats in front of the doors and disappeared into the tinted gloom beyond.

Among the people crowding the streets, I particularly noticed those nun-like women of the older generation who wear the *faldetta*, a curious black hoop on a whalebone frame, a dress peculiar to Malta. It is commonly said that this veil owes its origin to the habit of Maltese women, during the Napoleonic occupation, of casting their outer skirt over their heads as a protection against the bold eyes of the French soldiers. I believe it more probable that the garment originated with the custom of peasant women in ancient times of covering their heads in church with an old petticoat.

Another curious feature of the Valetta streets are British family groups; a sergeant, his wife and child, walk slowly among the crowds as if they had, in some miraculous manner, been caught up from Brixton High Street and were not aware of it.

I went into the Armoury, once the Palace of the Grand Master of the Knights of Malta, and there I saw what must be one of the finest collections of armour in the world.

Hiring a car, I drove to St. Paul's Bay, which lies about nine miles to the north-east of the island. After running through the outskirts of Valetta, where herds of white and brown goats were being milked on doorsteps, the road sprang into the shadeless heat of Malta and streaked away across a treeless, khaki landscape enclosed by walls of white limestone. Malta may reveal beauty to those who earnestly look for it over a long period of time; but I very much doubt it. What little beauty exists on this brown rock, except for a brief moment of spring flowers, seems to be gathered round the rocky shores, where the sea is blue and warm and the atmosphere is that of a semi-tropical Cornwall. But Malta itself, with the ribbons of road lying ahead across a scorched plain, or over slight brown rises of ground, with nothing to break the monotony but a village on the skyline, cannot appeal to anyone who knows other islands in the Mediterranean. The one fine inland sight of Malta is the town of Citta Vecchia, standing up above the plain.

St. Paul's Bay shares the beauty of all Malta's coastline. As I saw it that morning, the waves were breaking in showers of spray on a wide half-circle of shore enclosed by low, rocky headlands. At the mouth of the bay, separated from the mainland by a narrow channel, is Salmonetta Island, or St. Paul's Island, the scene of the shipwreck. On it is a statue of St. Paul, standing in outline against the sky.

It seemed to me that if I followed the road which I could see running round the northern rocks of the bay, I might be able to descend to the shore opposite the island and perhaps even get across to it, for the distance looked no more than a long jump. After travelling for two or three miles, I left the car and found my way down the volcanic rocks to the sandy beach. But, alas, a wide channel of deep and swiftly-flowing water lay between me and the bleak little rock. It was impossible to get across. Waves were breaking violently on its cliffs, so that it lay in a line of foaming white. The statue of St. Paul, mounted on a massive plinth, shows the saint bareheaded, with his right arm uplifted as he faces the open sea.

The rivalry between Malta and Melita, on the Dalmatian coast, as the scene of the shipwreck has now almost died down, although I do know at least one experienced sea-dog whom nothing, apparently, will convince that the wreck did not take place in the Adriatic. The old argument that Malta could not have been the island, because there are no snakes there, is not considered a serious objection. Malta was not always so bare of trees and undergrowth, and it is probable that there were snakes on the island in ancient times: in fact, I believe there are certain harmless snakes in Malta to-day, but they are extremely rare. There is a local legend that St. Paul with-

drew the poison from the fangs of the Maltese snakes and
transferred it to the tongues of the Maltese people!

The extensive Roman remains in Malta, also the soundings
taken in the bay, which exactly correspond with the conditions described in *Acts*, combined with the fact that the travellers continued their journey in another Alexandria corn-ship
that had wintered in the island harbour, all prove that Malta,
and not Melita (which, although it may beat Malta with ser-
pents, was never on the Alexandrian grain route), was the
scene of St. Paul's shipwreck.

As I sat overlooking this little island, it was easy to visualize
the wreck and to see how the ship was blown by the storm
towards Koura Point, the southern extremity of the bay; how
the sound of the breakers on the high rocks alarmed the sailors, who wisely anchored until morning. Somewhere on the
grey, volcanic rocks, perhaps in some cave among them, St.
Paul and his half-dead companions warmed themselves at the
fire of twigs.

"The chief man" of the island was Publius. He treated the
shipwrecked men with great kindness and entertained them
for three days. Paul's gift of healing was exerted to cure the
father of Publius, and, when this became known, the Apostle
was soon famous throughout the island. In gratitude, the
kindly folk heaped gifts upon Paul and his friends and, let
us hope, repaired and supplemented their wardrobes.

In three months' time navigation began. Ships prepared
for sea. Among them was an Alexandrian corn-ship whose
name was *Castor and Pollux*, the patron gods of Navigation,
whose effigies, no doubt, decorated the vessel. Castor and
Pollux were associated in antiquity with that natural phenomenon known to us as St. Elmo's Fire, a harmless electrical
discharge that, in certain conditions of the weather, becomes
visible at night in the form of balls of light that hover over
the tops of masts or at the end of yard-arms. Ancient seafarers

connected this light with the stars that shone above the heads
of Castor and Pollux during their voyage in the *Argo*, and
considered that its appearance was a sign of good luck.

Therefore, when the Roman soldiers and their prisoners
once more dared the perils of the deep, there must have been
many who derived comfort from the thought that they were
to travel under the protection of "the great Twin Brethren."

On my way back to Valetta, I visited the town of Citta
Vecchia, the ancient capital of the island. From the height of
its ramparts, the lowlands of Malta stretch away into the
distance like a length of fawn-coloured Harris tweed.

The cathedral is dedicated to St. Paul. It contains a remarkable assembly of treasures. There is a picture of the Virgin
attributed to St. Luke, and, as usual, completely encased in
silver. There is a superb processional cross bearing the arms
of Godfrey de Bouillon, and said to be the cross which he
carried into Jerusalem, with the banners of the First Crusade
behind him. Strangest of all the treasures are two massive
gates of Irish bog-oak, which are said to have been brought
to Malta in 1090 by Roger of Normandy, one of the sons of
Tancred. These heavy black gates are magnificent, and are
covered with carving.

Beneath the cathedral is a cave in which a statue of St.
Paul stands impressively behind a grille, illuminated by a
burning candle. The priest who took me down to it told me
that St. Paul lived there during the three months he was on
the island.

Near the cathedral are a series of extraordinary catacombs,
the nearest approach to my idea of the original labyrinth that
I have ever encountered. The long, dark galleries, and the
presence all round of open graves, create an eerie atmosphere
from which it is pleasant to escape.

The real hero of the Apostlic Age in Cyprus is not St. Paul, but the Cypriot, St. Barnabas; in Malta, although St. Paul is deeply revered, the real hero of the island is St. Publius. It is curious that local feeling should be so intense, and should lead men to prefer the lesser to the greater.

11

As a ship enters the Gulf of Naples, the attention of its passengers is concentrated on the smoking cone of Vesuvius. In the intervals between eruptions, there is something about Vesuvius which suggests a locomotive peacefully smoking in a railway station. You expect, at any moment, the sudden, violent puff which precedes noise and movement; and this, I think, is what everyone subconsciously awaits when eyes are fixed in fascination on the slow clouds of smoke and on the long, backward plume of grey.

The smoke of Vesuvius is something that St. Paul did not see as the *Castor and Pollux* sailed across the Gulf to Puteoli. The volcano was at that time a harmless-looking mountain whose southern slopes were thickly covered with vines, and in its shadow Pompeii and Herculaneum were laughing their last years of life away. When Paul sailed past Vesuvius, less than twenty years were to elapse before the lava flowed and hot cinders fell; Drusilla, the young wife of Felix, with whom Paul had talked, was to perish in the horror of that August night.

I disembarked at Naples and, when the eternally boring business of customs and passport was over, paid a swift visit to the magnificent museum, where I saw the statue of the Ephesian Artemis and the uncannily modern objects, especially the kitchen bronzes, discovered at Pompeii. This museum is the only one I know where Roman painting can be properly studied, and as I feel in danger of writing long and enthusiastically about it, I must say nothing at all.

A short drive in a car took me to Puzzuoli, a few miles to the west of Naples. This is the ancient Puteoli, the port in which St. Paul first set foot on the soil of Italy. The town is now a manufacturing seaport on a commanding promontory; the harbour, protected by a long mole, is a reflection of the harbour in which the Alexandrian corn-ships cast their anchors. All ships except these were required to lower their topsails as they approached Puteoli, and in the spring, when the corn-fleet came in with topsails flying, every man, woman and child in Puteoli rushed down to the harbour to cheer the arrival of Rome's bread.

I was told that certain portions of the modern harbour date from Roman times, and that six feet below the water are massive rings to which the galleys were tied. Other Roman remains can also be seen under the water, where they sank in one of the subsidences so common on this coast.

Even though there is little left to-day of ancient Puteoli, it was wonderful to see ships still coming in through the narrow harbour mouth, to unload their cargoes on the quaysides where long ago the Apostle who had written "I must see Rome" came ashore after great perils.

For many years I have longed to see the wonderful things which have been discovered at Herculaneum. Taking a car, I motored along the broad road leading to an ornamental gateway with "Herculaneum" written above it. The path slopes gradually from the modern level to that of ancient Herculaneum; and, as the path falls to a lower level, so do the centuries fall away until you are in the first century, with the streets of a town lying round you as they were in the year 79 A.D.

Pompeii is really a dead city. It is not surprising to see those horrible stone corpses in the museum, lying in the attitudes in which they were smothered so long ago. But Herculaneum looks no more dead than many a town of to-day that, having lost some of its roofs in a tornado, is waiting for the return of its inhabitants. The men who work in the excavations seem more like builders putting the place in order than like archæologists awakening the town from its ancient slumber.

Although Herculaneum and Pompeii were destroyed by the same eruption, the manner of their destruction was different. Pompeii was buried beneath a seven to eight feet fall of pumice-stone, followed by a thick deposit of ashes and water. There was plenty of time to flee and, in fact, most of the inhabitants did escape. It is estimated that only two thousand perished out of Pompeii's population of twenty thousand. There were no red-hot masses of rock and belching flames: it was a horrible, steady drive of dust and pumice, like a prolonged storm of warm hailstones, the size of beans. Herculaneum was destroyed by a swift-moving mountain of warm mud that rolled the five miles from Vesuvius and covered the town and the immediate neighbourhood to a depth of sixty-five feet. So completely were both towns hidden, that they remained unknown through the Middle Ages and were only discovered during the eighteenth and nineteenth centuries. Their discovery established a human link between the present and the past, and proved that the people who lived in the first century bore a remarkable resemblance to those alive to-day.

As I walked through the cobbled streets of Herculaneum, with solid little square houses on each side of me, with streets branching off at intervals, with fountains here and there, I felt that I was really back in the world of St. Paul.

If Paul suffered martyrdom in 67 A.D., only twelve years elapsed between his death and the destruction of Herculaneum. Many of the things one sees in the ruins to-day were there when Paul was alive. Men and women were reading books in the shady little gardens lined with marble porticoes, were admiring the lovely bronze and marble statues that have recently been discovered, looking as if they had just come from the artist's studio, and were passing along the narrow streets to bathe in the sea, which at that time washed the eastern promenade of the town. It must have been very like Juan les Pins, or one of the smaller seaside places in the South of France.

I came to a group of workmen and archæologists who were putting the final touches to a small hotel that they had just dug from a wall of mud. The wooden staircase was perfect, though black and carbonized. Each step had been carefully encased in plate-glass, and, as I mounted them, I was using a staircase that had been there in the first century. In rooms upstairs I saw beds which had been slept in on that tragic August night in 79 A.D., and each bedroom contained a glass case in which was displayed the luggage left behind by guests as they rushed out in alarm. Nothing is allowed to leave Herculaneum for a museum; it must be preserved where it was found.

In a warehouse I saw a wooden capstan and a rope. The rope was still strong and pliable. In another warehouse I saw a wooden press of the type in use to-day in every bookbinder's shop, and exploring some outbuildings which were only partially excavated, I saw a pile of black wheat. Each grain was hard, but light in weight.

The sunlight falls over silent little gardens of Herculaneum in which, after so many centuries of darkness, trees grow again and flowering shrubs attract the bee. You stand in such places, separated by over eighteen centuries from the people who used to live there, yet as near to them it seems, as to a man in whose empty house you wait, expecting him at any moment to return. When you see the brown cliffs of dry mud which still hide so much of this town, you wonder what lies hidden there.

Think what *might* lie buried in Herculaneum. Suppose some Christian, in the year 79 A.D., had left a copy of the Gospel in a metal box that had preserved it, a copy older than any known to us? Suppose some bookman of Herculaneum had treasured not only the lost books of Livy, but also the second volume if such a book ever existed, of the *Acts of the Apostles.*

That evening I took the train to Rome.

12

The compartment was full of Neapolitan business men. Each one carried the badge of the Continental man of affairs, a portfolio of shiny black calf-skin. They pressed back the clasps and drew forth typed papers in which they soon became immersed, and gradually the carriage filled with the smoke of cigars and cigarettes. When I pulled down the window, three men sneezed, and it had to go up again. I went out and stood in the corridor, watching the lights streak past in the dark and wondering what river we had crossed.

I remembered Cardinal Wiseman's description of arriving by road during the last century. There was always a moment when, climbing a rise of ground, the coachman would point with his whip towards the distant city and say: "Ecco Roma!" What a grand moment that must have been. Some day, I told myself, I would approach Rome, not in a train but by road, and I should hear those two words that have thrilled the hearts of generations of pilgrims—"Ecco Roma."

It was six years since I had been in Rome. My last visit had been in February, and Rome lay under a fall of snow. I arrived some time after dark, and set off at once into the white streets. I walked up to the Capitol, where I encountered a crowd of excited young men in the act of rolling a snowball down the hill. And when I went into the Restaurant Ulpia, near the Forum of Trajan, and ordered something to eat, the doors burst open and a number of men ran in holding snow in their hands, which they showed to their friends; and everybody roared with laughter. It was then I realized that snow was something new and wonderful to Rome.

The Colosseum was sheeted in snow. A circle of white lay in the starlight, its awesome silence intensified. The gaunt circle of seats, rising up against the frosty sky, seemed blacker and more threatening. It was strange to stand in the place which I had always thought of as red with the blood of saints, and to find it white, like a traditional Christmas morning.

It was the week that the Lateran Treaty was signed. The streets were full of yellow and white Papal flags. Carmelites, Franciscans, Capuchins, and seminarists from every part of the world, gathered in street and *piazza* to discuss the historic event. I think the most remarkable crowd I have ever seen in my life stood outside the Lateran Palace when the bells rang out to announce signing of the treaty. Japanese stood with Africans, young Scotsmen, Americans, Irish, English, Germans and French formed groups, each wearing the distinctive gowns of the various seminaries. Then, as the bells died away, some monks in the crowd began to intone a Te Deum, and the whole of Rome gave itself over to rejoicing.

I obtained a ticket for the Pontifical High Mass in St. Peter's. Pope Pius XI, no longer "the Prisoner of the Vatican," was to make his first public appearance. The snow had turned to rain. Early in the morning, and in full evening dress, I went to St. Peter's, and never have hours passed so easily, as I sat watching the crowds that swiftly filled the gigantic building. The Vatican Guard patrolled the aisles of the church. They wore bearskins, white doeskin breeches and black thigh-boots and, as their spurs rang on the marble floor, I thought that they might be a squadron that had strayed from history at the time of Napoleon.

The Swiss Guard was on duty round the Baldacchino, which rises above the tomb of St. Peter. They wore their full-dress uniform, which is said to have been designed by Michael Angelo: steel casques, doublets and hose slashed with stripes of red, yellow and blue. Each guardsman grasped a pike. And, as the hours passed, Vatican officials, who might have stepped from the canvasses of El Greco, came softly down the nave to show distinguished visitors to their seats, their pointed white beards lying against starched ruffs, swords slanting against black satin breeches.

Words of command rang out suddenly from some distant archway. Troops all over the church stood to attention with a ring of pikes and spurs. Then through St. Peter's rang a fanfare of silver trumpets at the sound of which, to my amazement, the thousands of men and women rose to their feet and began to cheer.

I looked down the nave towards the great west doors, and I saw what seemed to be the splendour and chivalry of the Middle Ages coming in slow procession up the church. I saw the burnished casques of the Swiss Guards moving slowly above the heads of the standing people. I saw the Papal Body-guard, carrying drawn swords and wearing scarlet tunics and helmets from whose crests hung long plumes of black horse-hair. I saw members of the Vatican Chapter walking two by two, representatives of every Catholic order, and many a monk walking in a brown habit. When the cheering died down and there was a second or two of silence, I could hear the steady tramp and the ring of spurs on marble.

As the procession came at funeral pace up the nave, the great church, lit hitherto by the pale daylight, blazed suddenly with countless lights; and the trumpets ceased their fanfare. The sound of a solemn march now filled St. Peter's, and I saw Pope Pius XI far off at the east end of the church, seated in the state palanquin, the *sedia gestatoria*, clothed in white. There was a jewelled tiara on his head, and he sat motionless, except when he slowly raised his hand to trace the sign of the Cross in the air.

Two *flabella*, great fans of ostrich feathers, moved slowly above the Pope's head, and they reminded me of Constantinople and of the Byzantine emperors, and of the time when the representative of St. Peter ruled the church of Eastern Christendom. There was not one meaningless thing in all this rich display. There was not one piece of embroidery that had not been pinned in position by Time. All the centuries had combined to make this progress of the Pope. St. Peter's was suffocating with its memories. I could not understand how people could find breath to cheer and shout their "vivas." The centuries had flooded the church to the roof, and in that flood the imagination struggled like a drowning man.

People all round me were cheering, but my throat was dry, and I do not think I could have cheered to save my life. Strangely, perhaps, I was not aware of any emotional appeal in the sight before me: the appeal was purely to the mind and imagination. There was an elderly man in white, borne shoulder-high in a chair that trembled slightly as it advanced, but I was looking not at one man or at one Pope: I was looking at all history and at all popes. It seemed to me that everything else in the world was young. I had seen the oldest living thing in the world: I had seen the visible expression of a corporate memory that goes back into the very beginning of the Christian Age.

The great chair was lowered from the shoulders of the bearers. The white figure stepped from it and walked to a white throne under a scarlet canopy. One by one the Cardinals approached and kissed his ring. High voices sounded from the Sistine Chapel, and the Pope rose and knelt before the altar. . . . It was a moment I cannot describe. I saw a line of men kneeling into the dim perspective of the past, and the first in the long line was St. Peter.

"*Tu es Petrus, et super hanc petram ædificabo ecclesiam meam.*"

13

After travelling across the broad plains of the Campania, the train climbed for a long time into hills. Suddenly I saw the sea pounding on the coast to my left; and we ran into the station at Formia. The railway from Naples to Rome which goes through Formia follows for part of the way the route probably taken by Paul on his journey to Rome. The modern Formia is the ancient Formiæ, as pleasant a seaside town to-day as it was when Cicero retired there from the cares of office. It is almost certain that Julius, the centurion, must have rested in this town with his prisoners.

When they reached Terracina, beyond Formiæ, the travellers had the choice of continuing along the famous highway, or of taking a mule-drawn barge along a canal that traversed the Pontine marshes. We do not know which of these ways they travelled, but we are told in *Acts* that they arrived at Appii Forum, which was the north end of the canal and the place where mules were unhitched for the reverse journey. It was a place of low taverns, bargemen, and travellers of every sort and condition.

Standing among the motley crowd at the end of the canal, eagerly scanning the faces of all travellers from the south, were a band of Christians who had marched out from Rome to meet the Apostle and escort him to the capital. How Paul's face must have lit up with joy when he saw the men who had marched forty miles from Rome in order to give him the kiss of brotherhood and to grasp him by the hand!

We may ask ourselves how it was that the Church was so well organized in Italy at this early period; how it was that a Christian community at Puteoli was waiting ready for Paul, and had sent news to fellow-Christians in Rome, telling them that he would be leaving on such a day and arriving on such a day along the "Queen of Roads." Surely St. Peter's presence in Rome is the only possible explanation. It is the tradition of the Church that St. Peter was in Rome as early as 42 A.D., organizing the infant church there.

Paul's Christian welcome on the road to Rome is one of the loveliest things in *Acts*. We have seen him fighting all his life, apparently failing, always opposed, shaken to the depths of his soul by the meanness and the malice of his enemies, slandered and rejected often, but never for one moment unequal to the fight, because Christ lived in him. This meeting on the way to Rome was a reward for his years of struggle. If there was a time in his life when those all-seeing eyes softened and when his face seemed to be "the face of an angel," I think it was the moment when he came to Rome and found a Christian welcome.

Marching beside him as if he were a conqueror and not a captive, those loving children of the early Church uplifted his spirit with news of the little community in Rome, and when they drew nearer to the city, at the place called "Three Taverns," ten miles along the Appian Way, another band of Christians, perhaps older people who could not walk the forty miles to the canal, were standing ready to greet him. When Paul saw them "he thanked God and took courage."

They were now on the most crowded and most famous of the world's highways. They were almost at the gates of Rome. Every step took Paul nearer to the realization of his life's dream. At last he was going to see Rome! He was arriving as a prisoner, but he was a prisoner in triumph, surrounded by the advance guard of that love and affection with which the ages have since dowered his name.

What, one wonders, did other travellers think as they encountered that file of travel-stained prisoners on the road, marching under guard, with one among them who moved in a crowd of happy friends? Surely they must have asked: "Who is that man?" Surely Julius and his legionaries were busy shouting back to curious passers-by: "He is Paul, a citizen of Tarsus, who has appealed to Cæsar."

So they came to Rome. They approached the Porta Capena, whose green stones dripped perpetually with water from a leaking aqueduct which ran above it. They made their way through the crowd thronging the gate, the press of market wagons, the ranks of chair-men, and the carriages which at this point had to put down their passengers during daylight hours; and they entered Rome.

It was once believed that Paul was taken by Julius to the headquarters of the Prætorian Guard on the Palatine Hill. The Greek word used in *Acts* to describe this officer is *Stratopedarch*—Chief of the Camp. Such a title is too modest for the Prefect of the Prætorian Guard. The great historian, Theodor Mommsen, with the help of an old Latin version in which the title is given as *Princeps Peregrinorum*—the Chief of the Peregrini—has told us who this officer probably was, and in doing so has cast an entirely new light on Paul's reception in Rome.

As I have mentioned earlier in this book, the *Peregrini* were a special corps of Imperial messengers—a military postal service—with a chief of their own and special headquarters. Although members of the corps were drawn from legions stationed in the provinces, they were relieved from ordinary military duties, passing from their camp in Rome to distant missions, and returning to the city to wait for further orders. Julius "of the Augustan band" was not, therefore, an ordinary centurion who was told by his commanding officer at Cæsarea to take Paul and other prisoners to Rome: he was a member of the *Peregrini* who had probably arrived at Cæsarea with dispatches from Rome, and was waiting to make his usual return journey. The camp of the *Peregrini* was not on the Palatine Hill, but on the Cælian. Therefore those who have imagined Paul passing into the heart of Rome on his first entry are in error. It is more probable that the little group turned to the right immediately they entered the Porta Capena, and made their way to a barracks just within the city walls.

Reading between the lines of *Acts,* it is perfectly clear that Julius cherished a deep respect for his prisoner. We may imagine that if the documents from the Procurator of Judæa had survived the salt water, they would have been produced before the Chief of the *Peregrini* accompanied, no doubt, by an account of Paul's courage during the shipwreck, and of his service to the centurion by warning him of the plot to abandon ship.

Paul was received with marked courtesy. He was a prisoner on bail. He had, therefore, the choice of taking a house of his own, if he could afford to do so. He could also live as he pleased, with the natural restriction that he was under military supervision and must always be ready to appear when wanted. It is on this note that St. Luke ends his *Acts of the Apostles.*

"And Paul dwelt two whole years in his own hired house, and received all that came in unto him, preaching the kingdom of God, and teaching those things which concern the Lord Jesus Christ, with all confidence, no man forbidding him."

The scattered lights of farmsteads on the Pontine Marshes were visible on the left, and, as the train rushed on towards Rome, the gentle outline of the Alban Hills rose on the righthand. Lights became more frequent. They formed double chains that were streets. Soon we arrived in Rome. I stepped out into streets where fountains flung their jets high in the lamplight.

14

I rang up an Italian friend who is concerned with the care of ancient monuments. He said that he was free to dine with me. When we met, he was maddeningly mysterious, withholding some great secret from me until the end of dinner.

"You have come to Rome on the right night," he said. "You shall see!"

I gave up trying to extract his secret. I described my journey and the object of it, and I explained that I was interested only in first century Rome: the Rome that Paul had seen.

"Then, my friend, very little above ground exists for you. St. Peter's does not exist. St. John Lateran does not exist. The Vatican Museum does not exist. Even the Fontana Trevi does not exist! My friend, you have come to see the cellars of Rome."

"That is true."

Then his irritating humour returned.

"Ah, but you have come on the right night," he cried, "and I shall soon put you out of your misery by telling you why."

When the coffee arrived he leaned back, put his head on one side and asked:

"Have you ever been in the Forum at night?"

"No, it is always locked."

"You have never been there in moonlight? Well, we shall go to-night. I am going there to supervise the flood-lighting of the forum for some celebrations next week. You will come, and you can go off by yourself and think of first century Rome. You will find more there than anywhere else. It's nearly time. Let us go."

The moon was not full and was obscured from time to time by banks of high cloud. My friend had to meet a number of electricians at the entrance to the Forum, near the Arch of Titus. We arrived too soon and walked down the slope into the Colosseum.

"No building carries such a heavy weight of memories," said my friend. "The air is heavy in this place."

The moonlight was sufficient to whiten the immense oval of masonry, so that it seemed to be shining again with its lost marbles. Two or three other visitors tiptoed about the arena, gazing into shadows which are more sinister here than in any place in Rome.

"Even the Colosseum does not exist for you," whispered my friend, "because St. Paul never saw it."

Yes; even the Colosseum did not exist for me! It was built probably five years after Paul's death. In his time it was an ornamental lake in the gardens of Nero. Among those who laboured to make it were twelve thousand Jews who were sent to Rome in chains after the Fall of Jerusalem.

As we walked about the haunted place, we stood beneath the Cross which commemorates those who received martyrdom in the Colosseum. I think it is one of the most dramatic Christian memorials in the world. It is said that the first Christian to die there was the venerable St. Ignatius, Bishop of Antioch, who has always been claimed by Eastern tradition as the little child whom Jesus placed in the midst of his disciples as a model of innocence. It is related of him that so great was the purity of his life that he was granted the privilege of hearing the song of angels, and that is the reason why he introduced responses into his church service: it was an attempt to reproduce on earth the heavenly choirs answering one another's hymns of praise. The poor old saint was dragged across the world by brutal soldiers, happy only in the thought of his approaching martyrdom and in expectation of his meeting with his Master. Surely even the mob in the Colosseum hid its face in shame as the lions pulled his feeble body to the sand.

My friend looked at his watch and said that we must go. We mounted the slight rise of ground from which the Arch of Titus surveys the ruins of the Forum. This Arch is another relic of Imperial Rome which Paul did not see. It commemorates the downfall of Jerusalem and is a testimony to the fulfilment of our Lord's prophesy that "thine enemies shall cast a trench about thee, and compass thee round, and keep thee in on every side, and shall lay thee even with the ground."

The words of Jesus are a literal description of the methods employed by the Roman armies in the course of the most terrible siege in history. Titus ordered an immense trench to be dug all round Jerusalem, so that the cast-up earth might be built into a rampart which encompassed the city completely; and behind it the legions waited until Hunger sat grinning on the walls. In the final assault, although Titus wished to preserve Herod's Temple, a flaming brand was cast into it and the building was burnt to the ground.

The sculpture on the arch pictures the triumph which Titus enjoyed when he returned home with his victorious forces, bringing with him, as curiosities to parade through the streets of Rome, the seven-branched candlestick, the golden table of shew-bread and the silver trumpets. These are all clearly visible on the sculpture, which, by a fortunate chance, was placed in the interior of the arch and has thus been preserved.

While we waited, we looked over the fence into the dark trench of the Forum, lying sixty feet or so below the level of modern Rome. Every evening at dusk a guardian locks a gate across the Sacra Via and the heart of the ancient world is silent and deserted until morning, a haunt only of bats and owls. We could see the ghosts of temples and roads gleaming like the bones of a skeleton.

A group of men arrived and unloaded boxes from a van. The gate was unlocked, and walking together ahead of the others, flashing an electric torch on the Sacra Via, we descended into the silence and the shadows.

"Is it not wonderful?" whispered my friend.

"Many years ago," I whispered back, "when I was a young reporter, I had to attend an exhumation in a country church-yard. It was like this . . . whispering . . . men carrying things in the dark . . . white stones lying all round . . ."

And indeed, as we stumbled down the slope of the Sacra Via and came to the general ground level of the Forum, the resemblance to some vast cemetery, with its headstones shining in the starlight, was even more remarkable. For a thousand years this cemetery had been the centre of the civilized world.

The yellow disc of my friend's torch wavered over shattered columns, hovered over bushes growing from slabs of marble, moving here and there, up and down, picking out some fallen architrave, and encountering two or three complete columns standing erect, more spectral than if they had been over-thrown.

"That is the Temple of Romulus," he said, pouring a line of light into the darkness, "and that,"—pointing in the opposite direction,—"is the Temple of Vesta and the House of the Vestal Virgins, which, by the way, was centrally heated with hot-water pipes. Right ahead you can see the columns of the Temple of Antoninus and Faustina."

The chill of the grave-yard lay over the ruins. Was this the place where the destinies of the world were once discussed? The only sound was the tramp of the men behind us and the sharp click of a stone kicked down a slope; and again I thought that our stealthy progress could not have been more like that of men about to open a vault.

"This is where we begin our work," said my friend. "I shall now leave you to decide for yourself how much of this comes within your Rome. You will need this."

He handed the torch to me, and I walked off into the darkness. Near the Rostra, where every orator of Rome had spoken, I startled the only living creature in the Forum. I think it was one of the lean cats which haunt the ruins of Rome.

How much of the Forum had Paul seen? He saw it before the Fire, in all its glory, as Augustus and his successors had left it. And I imagine that he gazed on it with less disapproval than he had gazed on the Acropolis. There were statues by the hundred to offend him and gods by the score, but there was something else which must surely have appealed to his practical mind: there was the inspiring atmosphere of the centre of the world. It was the heart of the world he had set forth to conquer. When he stood at the golden milestone, Paul was standing at the spot from which the distance was measured to Jerusalem on the east; to Londinium on the west. St. Paul the Christian scorned the idols of the Acropolis; St. Paul the statesman cannot have looked unmoved upon the Forum.

His two years in Rome are years of provoking mystery. Luke tells us no more than that he lived in his own "hired house," preaching the Word to all and sundry, and no one interfered with him. He lived there for two years, waiting for his appeal to come before Cæsar. He was under military supervision. That is all we know.

If we accept the theory that the Captivity Epistles were not written from Rome, our material for a reconstruction of his life in the capital is, of course, curtailed to some extent. But the traditional view is that he wrote these letters from his "hired house" in Rome, and on the strength of that tradition we are entitled to build up a picture of his activities. The "hired house" must have been a busy place. If we accept these Epistles as having been written from it, we have an impression of men coming and going, bringing news of the distant churches and returning with the wise words of their founder. Some of the many friends who visited Paul in his house begin to take shape before our eyes, though perhaps we may feel surprised that so many have come all the way from Asia.

Luke, the beloved physician, is there, and Aristarchus, both of whom had travelled with Paul from Cæsarea. Epaphras of Colossæ arrives, and Epaphroditus from Philippi; Tychicus, who was to be the bearer of letters to the churches in Asia; Demas, a Gentile Christian, whose faith was not to stand the strain of sharing to the end the Apostle's afflictions; and Jesus, called Justus, a Jewish Christian of whom we know nothing but the name. There are, however, two visitors of exceptional interest: John Mark and a slave called Onesimus.

How good it is to know that John Mark has made his peace with St. Paul, and visits him in Rome as the shadows are beginning to draw around the Apostle. It is pleasant to imagine Paul "the aged" sitting in Rome, talking with Mark about Barnabas, about the house in Jerusalem of his mother, Mary, where the Church used to meet in days that seemed long ago. Mark must have talked much of St. Peter and have told St. Paul of the Gospel he had written, or was about to write, in which he had put down some of St. Peter's memories of the Lord. I wish some great painter had left for us a picture of Mark reading his Gospel to Paul in the "hired house": Mark reading how the cock crew thrice and how the crowd about the fire in the courtyard of Caiaphas turned to Peter; and Paul leaning forward eagerly, listening to every word.

Then Onesimus. He was a slave belonging to a Christian named Philemon of Colossæ. He had run away from his master. Life was dangerous for a runaway slave in the first century. He was a hunted criminal. If caught, he could be branded and even killed. Possibly this poor creature, finding freedom not as he thought it would be, sought out Paul, whose name he may have heard in his master's house. He must have known that, in a world of enemies, Paul at least would be kind. The very fact that a man so hunted and so low in human estimation should have flung himself on Paul's charity, surely speaks worlds for the sway exercised by the Apostle over the hearts and affections of men.

Paul grew to love this slave. He showed him a new heaven and a new earth. He brought him to a knowledge of Jesus Christ. Paul would like to have kept Onesimus, but his rigid morality could not countenance such an action. The man must go back to his master and the master must be persuaded to forgive him. That was Paul's decision. He therefore wrote a letter called the *Epistle to Philemon*, in which he placed not only the slave, but himself, on the mercy of the slave's master.

If there is anyone who thinks of St. Paul as a hard, stern schoolmaster, let him read this short letter to Philemon, the only letter of Paul's written about a purely personal matter which has survived the wreck of Time. It is as if a window were opened for us into his soul.

". . . as Paul the old man, who nowadays is a prisoner for Christ Jesus, I appeal to you on behalf of my spiritual son, born while I was in prison. It is Onesimus (Worth)! Once you found him a worthless character, but nowadays he is 'worth' something to you and me. I am sending him back to you and parting with my very heart. I would have liked to keep him beside me, that as your deputy he might serve me during my imprisonment for the gospel; but I did not want to do anything without your consent, so that your goodness to me might come of your own free will, without any appearance of constraint. . . . You count me a partner? Then receive him as you would receive me, and if he has cheated you of any money or owes you any sum, put that down to my account. This is in my own handwriting: 'I, Paul promise to refund it'—not to mention that you owe, over and above, your very soul. Come, brother, let me have some return from you in the Lord! Refresh my soul. . . ."

In *Philippians*, if it were written at this time, there is a hint of spiritual tension. "My strong desire is to depart and be with Christ," he writes, "for that is far the best. But for your sakes it is needful that I should live on here below . . ." Perhaps these moods of dejection accompanied the "thorn in the flesh." Yet even in *Philippians* we must note that the predominant tone is one of hope and joy: "Rejoice in the Lord always; I will say it again, 'rejoice.' "

In nearly all reconstructions of the Apostle's two years in Rome, you will find it stated that he was chained day and night to the wrist of a soldier. Can we really believe this? Does it sound humanly possible that this solemn farce of chaining an old man, who had not the slightest intention of escaping, would have been kept up day by day, month by month, for two years? It is true that when Agrippa the elder was under detention, he was chained by the wrist to a soldier, and his friends went to Macro the Prefect and asked that only well-spoken and humane soldiers should be detailed for this purpose. But Agrippa was an important state prisoner. Paul was not a prisoner in the same sense. He was merely a man detained on bail, awaiting an appeal.

I suggest, with due humility, that Paul enjoyed much greater personal freedom than some scholars have imagined. There are eight references to his "bonds" in those letters which are traditionally connected with Rome, but, in view of the happy picture given in the closing words of *Acts*, may they not be regarded as figures of speech? If I know anything about soldiers and military regulations, the task of guarding Paul became a matter of form, and developed rapidly into that kind of sinecure which was no doubt as popular with soldiers in the first century as it is to-day. Paul must have encountered many members of the Guard; he probably met different soldiers every day. But I have a strong feeling that had you or I been orderly officer, we should have discovered on many occasions that the man who was technically chained to Paul was really playing knuckle bones in a tavern.

It has often been suggested that Paul and Seneca met. There is nothing inherently improbable in the meeting, except their relative positions. Seneca was Prime Minister to Nero. He was the brother of "sweet Gallio," before whom Paul had been charged at Corinth. He was also a great admirer of Paul's fellow townsman, Athenodorus the Stoic. We know from the letters of Cicero the kind of gossip that circulated from the seats of the mighty. Why should not Gallio have written to his brother, describing his arrival at Corinth and the ugly reception which the Jews had prepared in the hope of catching a new governor napping? It would, in fact, be unusual if such a letter had not been written.

Therefore it is probable that Seneca had already heard about Paul. As Prime Minister he would have to give some thought to Paul's case, affecting, as it did, the attitude of the Imperial Government to the new form of religion. The Stoic philosopher would moreover find that he had much in common with the Christian Apostle. To their cultured outlook they added, each in his own way, the concern of men conscious that a world morally bankrupt must find a new way of life. It is tempting to imagine those occasions on which Seneca may have passed from his covered litter into the "hired house" of St. Paul.

What was the result of Paul's appeal? There are some who believe that he was condemned to death at the end of the two years and was executed, probably in the year 61 A.D. There is, however, a strong tradition, which is supported by the three

Pastoral Epistles, that Paul was released, and that he set out on a further period of missionary activity.

He may have gone to Asia. He had asked Philemon to prepare a lodging for him. He may have visited Ephesus, here he had left Timothy to supervise the church. He may have gone to Crete. He had left Titus there to organize a church. All this is conjectured from the Pastoral Epistles. There is, in addition, a very ancient tradition that Paul visited Spain. He is said to have carried the Gospel to "the boundary of the West," and many people like to believe that this means that the Apostle visited Britain. It is, however, considered more likely that it means Spain, although it is curious that no legend of Pauline churches survives in that country.

While Paul was at liberty, the Fire of Rome broke out on the night of June 18, 64 A.D. Nero's plans for the rebuilding of his capital had been opposed by priests and owners of slum property, whose shrines and hovels congested certain areas which he wished to demolish. It is suspicious that it was among these tightly packed quarters near the Circus Maximus that the fire began. The flames got out of hand, destroying three, and partially destroying seven, of the fourteen regions of the city. Nero was not in Rome when the fire broke out, but he rushed to the Capital in time to see the last of it. Rome, stunned by the disaster, looked round for a victim. The same thing happened in the England of Charles II's reign, when the blame for the Great Fire of London was placed on the Catholics. As whispers in Rome began to implicate Nero, he cleverly deflected the fury of the populace upon the Christians. Thus began the first great persecution of the Church.

The flames of burning Rome are vividly reflected in those verses of *Revelation,* in which the merchants and the shipmasters of Ephesus are depicted weeping and wailing round the quays of their city.

"And the merchants of the earth shall weep and mourn

over her; for no man buyeth their merchandise any more: the merchandise of gold, and silver, and precious stones, and of pearls, and fine linen, and purple, and silk, and scarlet, and all thyine wood, and all manner vessels of ivory, and all manner vessels of most precious wood, and of brass, and iron, and marble, and cinnamon, and odours, and ointments, and frankincense, and wine, and oil, and fine flour and wheat, and beasts and sheep, and horses, and chariots, and slaves, and souls of men. . . .

"The merchants of these things, which were made rich by her, shall stand afar off for the fear of her torment, weeping and wailing, and saying, Alas, alas, that great city, that was clothed in fine linen, and purple, and scarlet, and decked with gold, and precious stones, and pearls! For in one hour so great riches is come to nought. And every shipmaster, and all the company in ships, and sailors, and as many as trade by sea, stood afar off, and cried, when they saw the smoke of her burning, saying, What city is like unto this great city! And they cast dust on their heads and cried, weeping and wailing, saying, Alas, alas, that great city, wherein were made rich all that had ships in the sea by reason of her costliness! for in one hour she is made desolate."

The year in which Paul was arrested, to suffer death during the general persecution that followed the Fire, is not known. An ancient tradition states that St. Peter and St. Paul received martyrdom on the same day, and the date given is the year 67 A.D.

It is to this period of his second detention in Rome—no longer a formal "prisoner" as on his first residence, but as a hated Christian—that his last epistle is attributed. This is the second *Epistle to Timothy*. We learn from it that Paul has been forsaken by many of his old friends. He wishes Timothy to hurry to him and to bring with him a cloak and some parchments which he had left at Troas in the house of Carpus. Does this suggest that he was in a cold dungeon? Did he want a travelling cloak, a *kepenik* of close-woven Cilician goat's hair, to save his aged bones from the chill of a Roman cell? And why did he want the parchment? Was his indomitable spirit dreaming, even in his last extremity, of new letters to the churches?

He says pathetically that "only Luke is with me." At the same time he sends greetings from Eubulus, Pudens, Linus and Claudia. Does this mean that he and Luke were incarcerated in the same dungeon? And despite the fact that he asks for his cloak and his parchments, an air of approaching tragedy underlies the whole letter. It is the letter of a man in great danger, who cannot say what the next hour may bring forth. Paul, the greatest missionary the world has known, lifts his voice in a last call to the Christian Church.

"Now you, who have followed my teaching, my practice, my aims, my faith, my patience, my love, my steadfastness, my persecutions, my sufferings—all that befell me at Antioch, Iconium and Lystra, all the persecutions I had to undergo, from which the Lord rescued me. Yes, and all who want to live the religious life in Jesus Christ will be persecuted. Bad characters and impostors will go from bad to worse, deceiving others and deceived themselves; but hold you to what you have been taught, hold to your convictions, remember who your teachers were, remember you have known from childhood the sacred writings that can impart saving wisdom by faith in Jesus Christ Jesus . . .

"In the presence of God and of Christ Jesus Christ, who will judge the living and the dead, in the light of his appearance and his reign, I adjure you to preach the word; keep at it in season and out of season, refuting, checking, and exhorting men; never lose patience with them, and never give up your teaching, for the time will come when people will decline to be taught sound doctrine and will accumulate teachers to suit themselves and tickle their own fancies; they will give up listening to the Truth and turn to myths.

"Whatever happens, be self-possessed, flinch from no suffering, do your work as an evangelist, and discharge all your duties as a minister. The last drops of my own sacrifice are falling; my time to go has come. . . ."

Then St. Paul, having issued a call to all the missionaries of the Christian world, past, present and to come, took up the pen and wrote his own epitaph:

"I have fought a good fight, I have finished my course, I have kept the faith."

That is the last letter written by St. Paul. A chain of men extending back through Time to that moment—a chain which we call the Tradition of the Church—states that ten days later he was led out of Rome along the Via Ostiensis and beheaded under a stone pine on the Via Laurentina, at a place called Aquæ Salviæ.

I went out on the following morning to see the tomb of the Saint whose steps I had followed for so long across the ancient world.

It was early in the morning. Rome was not yet awake. The sun was shining, and the shadows of that early hour lay strangely over the quiet streets. This, I think, is the most wonderful moment in Rome's day. The wine-carts come in from the country, some drawn by white oxen, others by mules. And Rome is so quiet at this time that you can hear the sound of the fountains. The air is full of the whisper of falling water: water flung in white jets, water gushing from the jaws of lion and dolphin, water escaping from the embrace of naiad and triton, and water sliding over the rim of marble basins.

In a little time the church bells ring for early Mass. Sleepy sacristans glance down the street as they arrange the mats at the church door, and you meet stray breaths of incense at the street corners. And as I listened to the bells of Rome, I thought of Lystra and of Derbe and of Konya, far away on the wild uplands of Asia Minor, and of Philippi, lying cold in the morning sunlight of Macedonia, far from the houses of men. I thought of ancient Corinth, lying dead on a plain between two seas.

God was remembered in those places for a little space—for centuries are a little time except to men—and now they have fallen into silence and their story is told. The thought came to me that their churches are alive still in the sound of the bells of Rome. I fancied that they were ringing not only for Rome, but also for the Galatians, the Ephesians, the Colossians, the Philippians, the Corinthians, and all those dead and solitary places where bells have long since fallen into silence. For the bells of Rome, and the bells everywhere of the Christian world, are in a very true sense the voices of St. Peter and of St. Paul ringing down the centuries; and I thought how right were the bell-founders of the Middle Ages to give the names of the Apostles to their finest work.

A little later the streets and the squares of Rome are filled with marching squads of seminarists. They parade like soldiers. They line up and march away to their studies, with one umbrella between every two students. When I saw these young men, many of them learning to be missionaries, I thought: "I wonder what Paul would have said to see these young 'soldiers of Christ'—probably like Timothy or Titus—walking through the sunlight of a Roman morning."

I crossed the Tiber by the Ponte Sant' Angelo and went into St. Peter's. When I came out again, Rome was awake; for I had been there a long time. I had been down into the crypt and I had been up to the roof. Then I set out to find those few places in Rome associated with the memory of St. Paul.

The Rome of St. Paul lies from thirty to sixty feet beneath living Rome. Its guardians are venerable monks or guardians, who grasp keys in their hands and lead the way down long flights of stone steps. The keys sometimes stick in damp and rusty locks. The doors of crypts open, and a breath of chilled air comes out to meet you. Holding a taper above your head, you go in and glance round a rough vault from which daylight has been excluded for centuries. It smells of the grave. There is a heavy silence in the air. The light of the taper wavers over a rock-cut tomb. There is often a fading fresco on the wall. You can see, perhaps, a hand or a head. The monk will tell you the sacred associations of the crypt, but your mind will all the time wander from his words into the past, struggling to reach out into the distant time when this dark place was alive with light and human voices, when it had a door which men and women opened, and windows which let in the sun.

There is a church in the Via Urbana, at the foot of the Esqueline, which is, perhaps, the oldest church in Rome—St. Pudenziana. Steps lead down from the street level. The outside is modern except for a pretty campanile, which dates probably from the ninth century. The church has been restored from time to time, but it contains over the tribune the oldest mosaics in Rome, still in position as they were erected in the third or the fourth century. I was interested not only in their beauty, but also because they show one of the earliest mosaic portraits of St. Peter and St. Paul. The Apostles are seen on either side of our Lord, who is seated on a throne. St. Peter, who is on the left hand of Christ, wears a travelling cloak, and St. Paul, who is on the right, holds a manuscript in his hand. Both Apostles are pictured as men of about the same age, both are bearded, but St. Paul, although not bald, has a very thin covering of hair, which bears out the ancient tradition about his appearance.

"There is no doubt," wrote Professor Lanciani, "that the

likenesses of St. Peter and St. Paul have been carefully preserved in Rome ever since their lifetime, and that they were
familiar to every one, even to school-children. These portraits
have come down to us by scores. They are painted in cubiculi
of the Catacombs, engraved in gold in the so-called *vetri cemeteriali,* cast in bronze hammered in silver or copper, and designed in mosaic. The type never varies. St. Peter's face is full
and strong, with short curly hair and beard, while St. Paul appears more wiry and thin, slightly bald, with a long pointed
beard. The antiquity and genuineness of both types cannot
be doubted."

The *vetri cemeteriali* were glasses placed with the dead in
the catacombs of the second and third centuries, many of them
stamped with the heads of the two Apostles in gold leaf on the
flat bases. Out of three hundred and forty of such glasses published by Garucci, eighty bear portraits of St. Peter and St.
Paul. These heads never vary. They conform so rigidly to an
established type that it is obvious they originate from genuine
portraits known to everyone, and that a departure from the
real portraits, or an attempt to idealize them which became
the fashion in later times, would have been vigorously resented by early Christians, who were still near enough to the
Apostles to remember their true likeness.

People who will not believe anything unless it is written
sometimes find difficulty in believing that a description of a
person or an event can be handed down for two or three centuries, although nearly every old family can testify to the
fidelity of verbal tradition. I think Monsignor Barnes, in his
fascinating book, *The Martyrdom of St. Peter and St. Paul,*
has put this matter admirably:

"Many are apt to forget that the memory of an individual
as to any outstanding event may extend over a very long period, and that besides this there is such a thing as a corporate
memory in a community, especially if it be stimulated and

kept in being by a ceremony of annual recurrence. Yet this must certainly have been the case with regard to the martyrdom of the two Apostles. Rome simply could not forget at least the main facts of the tragedy.

"The present writer comes of a long-lived family, and need not go beyond his own family circle for instances to illustrate what he is saying. His mother died at a great age in 1927. She could remember clearly to the last, how she was taken to hear Princess Victoria proclaimed Queen in June 1837. There we have a clear memory, of an event only of secondary importance, extending over ninety years. There was another old lady he was often taken to see as a child. She could remember the French Revolution and the execution of Marie Antoinette. As a child she had lived in Philadelphia, where her father held a high legal position, and she had known Benjamin Franklin. But Benjamin Franklin was born in 1706, three years before Dr. Johnson, and eight years before the death of Queen Anne. If the present writer equals the years of his mother, an improbable supposition, no doubt, but not an impossible one, there would be a stretch of 250 years covered by three lives. It would have been possible for Franklin to have told the old lady in question of some event of his early childhood—the great fire, perhaps, in Boston in 1711—and for her to have passed on the account. Just in the same way it would have been possible for a Christian child in Rome in the year 67 to have been actually present at St. Peter's martyrdom and to have seen him nailed to the cross, and still to have been alive and able to tell the tale in 150. And the child to whom he told it then could have told the story again in his extreme old age to one who lived to see the peace of the Church in 312 under Constantine. Is it conceivable, considering what the deaths of the Apostles meant to Christianity in Rome, that Rome could have forgotten? Did the Royalist child in London who knew how Charles I was beheaded outside the Banqueting Hall in Whitehall, on 30 January 1648/9 forget in later years when and where it had happened? Did the Royalist child in Paris who saw and heard the tumbrel roll past with Marie Antoinette going on her way to execution, forget in after-life when and where that had happened, and whether it was before the fall of Robespierre or after? Just in like manner, while there are some points in those early days where tradition may fail us, the date and place of the martyrdom of the two Apostles cannot be among them. On those points the Roman tradition, the Corporate memory of the Roman Church concerning the most tragic and terrible moment of her life, must be allowed to be of overwhelming value and undoubted accuracy."

The portraits of St. Peter and St. Paul in the Church of St. Pudenziana are therefore of supreme interest. There are, of course, earlier portraits, but these are, I believe, the earliest large mosaic portraits in existence. I have said that St. Peter is shown on the left of our Lord and St. Paul on His right. This is interesting. I must again quote Monsignor Barnes:

"Many modern writers have been puzzled by the fact that where both Apostles are represented together, especially in the oldest examples of all, it is St. Paul who is generally depicted on the right and St. Peter on the left. They have argued from this circumstance that St. Paul in the earliest ages was regarded in Rome as the superior even of St. Peter. A little knowledge is often a dangerous thing. They were unaware that in Rome from the earliest times, and for many centuries after, although in the time of Augustus the greater dignity of the right was already creeping in from Greece, the Roman place of honour was always on the left. There are abundant instances to be found in Rome even up to the thirteenth century. On the altar lately found at San Sebastian on which our Lord and St. Peter are represented as the Good Shepherd it is our Lord who is on the left, St. Peter on the right. On some official Papal Seals even to-day St. Paul is on the right and St. Peter on the left. To this day the whole Latin Church makes the sign of the cross from left to right while the Greeks make it from right to left. . . . In dealing with works of art of the first four centuries this question of right and left often tells us whether or not the artist was under Greek influence."

When I went down into the crypt of this church, I understood the importance of the site to any student of the Apostolic Age. It is a brick house of the first century, evidently one of some size and consequence, for its foundations extend under the neighbouring buildings. It was always the tradition that the church above occupied the site of the house of a Roman Christian called Pudens, who had entertained St. Peter and St. Paul, and was the Pudens mentioned in St. Paul's second letter to Timothy. In 1870, men digging under the church broke their way into this Roman building.

There can be no doubt that this house existed when St. Paul was in Rome. It is possible that he entered it and that the very walls which rise up round one in the dark echoed to the sound of his voice.

A fascinating wealth of conjecture has been built up round Pudens. Some believe that he was the same Pudens to whom the poet Martial wrote an epigram on the occasion of his marriage to a British princess who changed her name to Claudia. Both Claudia and Pudens are mentioned by Paul in his letter to Timothy. Martial says in his epigram:

"Although Claudia Rufina may be a blue-eyed Briton born, how much has she the disposition of the Latin race! What a graceful figure! The Italian matrons might believe her a Roman, those of Attica of their country. The gods bless her in that she proves fruitful to her pious husband."

If the Claudia and Pudens of Paul's letter are the Claudia and Pudens of Martial's epigram; if the Pomponia Græcina, the wife of Aulus Plautius, who had commanded the Roman forces in Britain, was, as many think, a Briton and a Christian, then we can indulge in the pleasing reflection that among the members of the Christian community in Rome who knew St. Peter and St. Paul were some natives of these islands.

I went to another church in Rome which interested me enormously because of its association with those two devoted friends of Paul, Aquila and Priscilla. This is the Church of St. Prisca, on the Aventine. A tradition extending possibly to Apostolic times claims this church as the site of the house of Aquila and Priscilla. There is nothing spectacular to see there, as in the Church of St. Pudenziana, but there is, however, a curious mystery connected with this church which deserves the attention of archæologists. In the year 1776 a subterranean oratory was discovered near the Church of St. Prisca. The walls were decorated with fourth-century frescoes. Without even drawing a plan or copying the frescoes, the discoverers apparently walled up the oratory again. There is little doubt that this was the original site of the house of Aquila and Priscilla.

The only notice of this extraordinary discovery is written on a scrap of paper preserved in the Bibliothèque Nationale in Paris, signed by a man named Carrara and addressed to the Treasurer of Pope Pius VI. So far as I know, no attempt has been made since that time to uncover the oratory. If it were discovered, surely we might have a relic of the Apostolic Age as interesting and as precious as the crypt of St. Pudenziana.

There is a tradition, though only of the tenth century, that St. Paul's "hired house" stood in the Via Lata, and there is another tradition that places his final place of confinement in the notorious Mamertine Prison, near the Arch of Severus. The upper portion is occupied by the Church of San Giuseppe dei Falegnami, but the sacristan leads the way down into a barrel-shaped vault which is claimed to be the prison of St.

Peter and St. Paul. It is obviously part of the horrible old prison whose very stones reek of tragedies. It has been transformed into a chapel, and above the altar, set back behind a grille in the rock, are effigies of the Apostles. Before the electric light was installed, this crypt was said to be the gloomiest and the most tragic in Rome.

It is the tradition of the Church that St. Peter and St. Paul were in prison for nine months and were led out to death in the year 67 A.D.

St. Peter was crucified in Nero's Circus, a site now partially occupied by St. Peter's, and St. Paul, because he was a citizen of Rome, was led outside the walls to be beheaded with a sword. The road along which he was taken was the Via Ostiensis, the busy road to the port of Ostia. It is now called the Via Ostiense; and beside the Gate of St. Paul, by which this road enters Rome, stands the Pyramid of Cestius. The Pyramid was standing there when St. Paul was led to his death, and it was one of the last famous monuments of Rome upon which he gazed.

He was led to the third milestone along this road, a road surrounded to-day by a new industrial suburb, by market sheds and factories. When St. Paul walked along it to his death, it was probably, like all the roads outside Rome, a place of tombs. They came at the third milestone to a side road at a place called Aquæ Salviæ, and there they ordered St. Paul to prepare for death. According to a Greek *Acta*, the scene of his death was a pine-wood which grew beside the road. Picturesque writers of a later time said that as his head struck the earth it bounced three times, and at each place rose a spring of sweet water: and the place of execution became known as Tre Fontane—Three Fountains.

The Abbey of the Three Fountains stands to-day on the site of the execution. It is a picturesque group of three churches, with their outbuildings, approached by a grove of eucalyptus trees, and enclosed within a wall entered by a gatehouse roofed with tiles. In the little church of St. Paul of the Three Fountains they show the Salvian Springs, which were, of course, in existence long before the Apostle's death, and they show also the fragment of a marble column to which, it is claimed, he was tied before his execution.

Until the year 1875, it was assumed that the writer of the ancient Greek *Acta*, who mentioned that St. Paul had died in a pine-wood, had exercised his imagination and that this was merely a picturesque touch. In 1875, however, Trappist monks who then inhabited the abbey were digging the foundations of a water-tank behind the chapel. They came upon a mass of coins of Nero, and with them a number of pine-cones, hardened to the consistency of stone by age and the earth's pressure.

The bodies of St. Peter and St. Paul were lovingly guarded by the members of the Church. There seems to have been an attempt on the part of certain Jewish Christians to steal them and carry them to the East, but this was frustrated, and, for a time, the two great Apostles met again in death when they occupied a niche in the "marble tomb," the Platonia, beneath the Church of St. Sebastian on the Via Appia. This place was called by the Romans of the first century *ad catacumbas*—"in the hollows"—probably a reference to the nature of the ground. The word "catacomb" originally referred only to this tomb. It was not until the Middle Ages that the word assumed its present meaning and was applied to every underground cemetery in Rome.

When Constantine the Great gave peace to the Church and honoured her saints, the body of St. Paul was lying in a Roman tomb, in what had once been a vineyard situated in an angle formed by the meeting of the Via Ostiensis with a small side road which provided a short cut to a tow-path on the banks of the Tiber. Constantine enclosed the Apostle's body in a case of metal and placed upon it, as he had done upon the body of St. Peter, a heavy cross of gold. He then built a church above the grave.

This was the first church of *San Paolo fuori le Mura*—St. Paul's-without-the-Wall. The building was enlarged and re-built in succeeding reigns. St. Paul's-without-the-Wall and St. Peter's became the two grandest basilicas in Rome. A splendid colonnade of pillars, roofed with lead, ran for two miles from the church to the city gate; of these not a trace remains. Two of the tragedies of all time were the demolition of old St. Peter's in 1506 and the destruction by fire of St. Paul's-without-the-Wall on the night of July 15, 1823.

It was the night that Pope Pius VII lay dying. He had been a monk at St. Paul's and he loved this church, which was the most magnificent early Christian church in Rome. No one dared to tell the dying Pope that the flames were devour-ing the precious frescoes and the mosaics; that the superb columns taken from the Forum in Rome, and the other treas-ures which made this church unique, were crashing down in ruin. In the morning the basilica had been almost gutted. Fortunately the arch above the Apostle's tomb had done good service, and the tomb itself was almost the only uninjured object in the church.

The present St. Paul's, constructed on the design of the ancient basilica, took thirty years to rebuild. Kings sent mar-ble pillars to decorate it, and among those who contributed rare marbles was Mehemet Ali, whose birthplace was Kavalla, in Macedonia where St. Paul first set foot in Europe.

Despite the barbarian hordes which have sacked Rome in the course of centuries, it is believed by such archæologists as Lanciani, and by such authorities as Monsignor Barnes, that the bones of St. Paul still lie in the vault beneath the high altar, enclosed within the metal sarcophagus in which they

were placed by Constantine the Great. In fact it is not very
widely known that St. Paul's coffin has been seen in modern
times; though in unfortunate circumstances and by people
whose emotion, or whose fear, prevented them from leaving
an adequate account of their brief examination. It happened
that during the rebuilding of St. Paul's Church, it was necessary to dig new foundations round the altar, in the course of
which an opening was accidentally made into the vault on
July 28, 1838. This was kept very quiet. Even the Vatican
was not told about it. The two men who looked through the
aperture were Vespignani, the architect, and an aged priest,
Abbot Zelli of St. Paul's. Years afterwards Vespignani used
to boast that he had seen the coffin of St. Paul. He said that
he had seen "a cage of iron bars." An unsatisfactory sketch
of these "iron bars" was found among his papers when he
died. Monsignor Barnes describes this sketch as showing "a
strong lattice of metal bars crossing each other so as to give
squares of 4 or 5 inches opening, with some ornamental detail
as they cross. It is built into a framework of stone, so as to make
panels or windows in the structure. The 'cage' in fact would
seem to have been of stone, with large apertures closed by
metal lattices."

A similar account was given by the Abbot to a monk,
Brother Grisar. This monk left an account in which he states
that Abbot Zelli confided to him that he had peeped into St.
Paul's tomb and had seen that the saint was buried on the
paving stone of a Roman lane, and that the "edificio" of the
tomb itself was surrounded by bars of iron (bronze?), very
ancient. Monsignor Barnes, who has investigated all the evidence with great thoroughness, sums up:

"St. Paul lies in a stone coffin immediately under the High
Altar. If the little round passage from the 'billicum' under
the present altar were reopened, we could once more lower
objects into the vault, and perhaps, with modern appliances,

obtain photographs of what is below. What we should expect to find is a vault about 20 feet by 17, with the coffin in the centre, probably raised above the ground. We should expect to find this coffin enclosed and hidden away in a structure of stone, with large gratings of bronze. This structure would go right up to the roof of the vault, and would be designed to strengthen the roof so that it would be able to support the weight of the great stone altar above. Above the coffin there might, or might not, still be the great cross of gold, 150 pounds in weight, which Constantine is said to have placed there, and which would alone have justified the provision of the metal lattice and the stonework which protects it."

One feature of the tomb, revealed by the fire of 1823 and since kept visible under the high altar, is an inscription carved on several large stones which form a slab about seven feet long and four feet wide. The inscription reads:

PAVLO

APOSTOLO MART . . .

The last word is incomplete because the portion of the stone containing the last three letters is missing. The complete word was, of course, "martyri." On December 1, 1891, Professor Lanciani let himself down on hands and knees through the *fenestrella* under the high altar in order to examine this inscription. He stated that it is formed "in large letters of the time of Constantine." This great authority also believed that the tomb is intact.

"The grave of St. Paul has come down to us, most likely, as it was left by Constantine the Great, enclosed in a metal case. The Saracens of 846 damaged the outside marble casing and the marble epitaph, but did not reach the grave. As to the nature of the grave itself, its shape, its aspect, its contents, I am afraid our curiosity will never be satisfied."

It is interesting, in view of the nebulous suggestion that St. Paul visited Britain, and in view of the fact that the only great church of St. Paul outside Rome is St. Paul's Cathedral, London, that the church in which the Apostle lies buried was, before the Reformation, under the protection of the Kings of England. In the shield of the Abbot of San Paolo fuori le Mura can still be seen an arm grasping a sword, and the Riband of the Garter with the motto: "Honi soit qui mal y pense."

St. Paul's Church stands on the ancient Via Ostiensis some two miles from Rome. I thought that I might be standing in some palace of Imperial Rome. This church has the peace of great dignity, the majesty of perfect proportions; and its ancestors are the palaces of the Cæsars and the law-courts of the Empire.

A bare expanse of shining marble sweeps to the high altar, smooth as a windless lake. The reflection of a forest of columns is mirrored in its surface as lake-water holds the images of trees. This accident of light is beautiful, for it reminds you that the Saint walked to the spiritual conquest of the world beneath the pine-trees of the Cilician Gates, taking with him a message preached beside a lake.

I approached the high altar, where, beneath a canopy upheld by four columns of the purest alabaster, is the vault of Roman times in which St. Paul lies buried. Through the kindness of those who guard his tomb, I was allowed to kneel at the *fenestrella* and to gaze for a moment into that dim space below, where the words, "Pavlo Apostolo Mart . . .", are written on a stone.

As I knelt there, I remembered a pious legend which the Church has preserved. It is said that St. Peter and St. Paul received martyrdom on the same day and were led out together through the Ostian Gate, until they came to a place which is to-day occupied by the little wayside Chapel of the Parting. At this point they separated, St. Peter for Nero's circus; St. Paul for the Salvian Springs. The Apostles did not say good-bye. St. Peter said:

"Go in peace, Preacher of glad tidings, Guide of the just to salvation."

St. Paul replied:

"Peace be with thee, Foundation of the Church, Shepherd of the flock of Christ."

So they went to their martyrdom, in the year 67 A.D. Less than forty years had passed since that night in the Upper Chamber in Jerusalem; less than forty years since the Agony in the Garden and since the Cross had been lifted on Calvary. In that little time the grain of mustard seed had taken root, and the shadow of God's Kingdom was upon the earth.

APPENDIX

A PRECISE statement of Pauline chronology is impossible. We sometimes know that one event took place so many years after another (his own statements in *Galatians* i. 18 and ii. 1, or the information given in *Acts* that he spent a year and a half at Corinth and three years at Ephesus—*Acts* xviii. 11, xx. 31), but wide divergence of opinion exists on the question of the exact date of certain events. A fixed date, however, is now provided by an inscription recently found at Delphi, which indicates that Gallio, before whom St. Paul appeared at Corinth, was proconsul of Achaia in 50–51 A.D.

The conversion of St. Paul is variously dated between 30–35 A.D. It was followed by a long period (12–17 years) of which we have little detailed information, beyond the fact that the first 2–3 years were spent in and near Damascus, with a visit to Arabia, and the subsequent years in Cilicia (Tarsus) and in Syria (Antioch). The table that follows, which is based on Professor C. H. Turner's article *Chronology of the New Testament*, in Hasting's *Dictionary of the Bible*, Vol. I, may be accepted as a guide for the important dates in St. Paul's life:

A.D.

St. Paul called by Barnabas to supervise the work in Antioch 47

FIRST MISSIONARY JOURNEY.—Cyprus and Galatia . . . 48–49
(Many scholars place at this point the *Epistle to the Galatians*.)

Apostolic Council at Jerusalem 49

SECOND MISSIONARY JOURNEY.—Galatia, Troas, Philippi, Thessalonica, Bœotia, and Athens 49–50

In Corinth 50–52
(I and II *Thessalonians written*.)

Visits to Jerusalem and Antioch 52

THIRD MISSIONARY JOURNEY begun 52

479

Later developments in St. Paul's life are obscure. Some scholars believe that he suffered martyrdom after he had been in Rome for two years, which would date his death at 61 A.D., others believe that his appeal to Nero resulted in an acquittal at the end of two years, and that, after his release, he embarked on a further period of missionary activity. There is a tradition that, during this journey, he visited Spain. It is to this period that critics assign I and II *Timothy* and the *Epistle to Titus*.

In 64 A.D. the Fire of Rome took place, which was followed by the Christian persecution under Nero. A strong tradition states that St. Peter and St. Paul suffered martyrdom during this persecution in 67 A.D. St. Peter was crucified; St. Paul, because he was a Roman citizen, was executed with a sword.

THIRTEEN LETTERS WRITTEN BY ST. PAUL (TO CHRISTIAN COMMUNITIES AND TO INDIVIDUALS) HAVE BEEN PRESERVED. *THE EPISTLE TO THE HEBREWS*, THOUGH HIS NAME IS ATTACHED TO IT IN THE HEADING OF THE ENGLISH BIBLE, DOES NOT CLAIM TO BE BY ST. PAUL, AND IS NO LONGER COUNTED AMONG THE PAULINE LETTERS. THE OCCASION, AND PROBABLE SEQUENCE, OF ST. PAUL'S LETTERS ARE AS FOLLOWS:

Galatians. The Roman Province of Galatia (Asia Minor) included the towns of Pisidian Antioch, Iconium, Lystra and Derbe, which were visited by St. Paul and St. Barnabas on their First Missionary Journey; and it is probably to the Christians of that region that this epistle was addressed. It was written to counteract the doctrines of certain Judaistic missionaries who, after the departure of the Apostles, had attempted to undermine the teaching and the apostolic authority of St. Paul. There is much dispute as to the date of this letter. If, as many scholars believe, it was written immediately after the First Missionary Journey and before the famous Council of Jerusalem, it is the earliest of the Pauline letters, indeed the earliest portion of the New Testament. If, however, it is assigned to a later date, then that honour must be given to the First Epistle to the Thessalonians.

Thessalonians I and II. These letters to the Christians of Thessalonica (modern Salonica) were written from Corinth about the year 50 A.D. In them St. Paul shows his concern to establish the friendliest relations with a congregation which circumstances had forced him hurriedly to desert; to answer questions and correct misconceptions about the Coming of Christ and the End of the World (which first century Christians expected in their life-time), and to give converts guidance in Christian living.

Corinthians I and II. Of the two Epistles to the Corinthians, the first was written towards the end of the Apostle's long stay at Ephesus, the second shortly afterwards, when he was on his way through Macedonia to Greece. During his absence the

Corinthian congregation had been divided into factions, and pagan immorality had revived in various forms. In the first epistle, St. Paul deals with a succession of problems affecting both faith and conduct; in the second he deals resolutely with the creators of dissension. The crisis at Corinth evoked four letters from the Apostle; two, however, have been lost, though it is widely believed that part of one of them is to be found in Chapters x–xiii of II *Corinthians*.

Romans. This epistle was written apparently from Corinth, towards the end of the Third Missionary Journey, to prepare the way for the visit which St. Paul hoped to pay to the Imperial capital. In this letter he surveys the needs, not of one particular congregation, but of the world as a whole. His aim is to show that, apart from a revelation of the true God, humanity is in a state of bankruptcy, and that such a revelation has now been given in Jesus Christ.

THE IMPRISONMENT EPISTLES

Under this title are included Philippians, Colossians, Ephesians and Philemon. The problem whether these letters were written from Rome, while the Apostle was waiting the issue of his appeal to Cæsar, or at an earlier period, during his stay at Ephesus and its neighbourhood, has been dealt with on pages 337–339.

Philippians. This letter to the church at Philippi was written during a time of great personal anxiety, to cheer a congregation which had always shown concern for the Apostle's welfare and the progress of his work, and to encourage among its members a spirit of Christian brotherhood and self-abnegation. It is a letter whose dominant note is joy.

Colossians. Written to the Christians of Colossæ, a town in Asia Minor, about a hundred miles from Ephesus, to counteract a type of false teaching which had become current under Jewish influence.

Ephesians. Written at the same period as the above, and bearing marked similarities to it. This letter is really a general letter to the churches in Asia Minor. The reason why it is called Ephesians is because the copy sent to Ephesus is the only one that has been preserved.

Philemon. This charming letter stands by itself as the only purely private letter written by St. Paul. It was written to Philemon, of Colossæ in Asia Minor, to ask him to forgive a runaway slave.

THE PASTORAL EPISTLES

Under this title are included the two letters to Timothy and the letter to Titus—so called because they deal with the pastoral oversight of the congregations. There is much discussion as to whether, in their present form, they are the work of St. Paul, though parts of them are unquestionably genuine. Assuming their Pauline authorship, we must place them late in the Apostle's life, at a period subsequent to his first Roman imprisonment. On that view, they shed light on a period of missionary activity in the East, on which St. Paul was enabled to embark after his appeal to Cæsar had ended in acquittal.

Timothy I. This letter was written by St. Paul to his faithful assistant, Timothy, who was administering the church at Ephesus on behalf of the Apostle. St. Paul gives him practical advice and warns him to beware of false teachers and heretical doctrines.

Titus. A similar letter. addressed to his devoted assistant, Titus, who was organizing the Church in Crete. Titus is frequently mentioned with appreciation in St. Paul's letters, though, strange to say, his name does not appear in *Acts*.

Timothy II. The last letter of St. Paul, written from his prison in Rome at some time shortly before his martyrdom. It is a letter of admonition and advice, written in the shadow of the Saint's approaching death.

BIBLIOGRAPHY

Anderson Scott, C. A. *Saint Paul: the Man and the Teacher.* (Cambridge University Press, 1936.)

" " *Foot-notes to St. Paul.* (Cambridge University Press, 1935.)

Arundell, F. V. J. *Discoveries in Asia Minor.* (2 vols. Richard Bentley, 1834.)

Barnes, Arthur Stapleton. *The Martyrdom of St. Peter and St. Paul.* (Oxford University Press, 1933.)

" " " *St. Peter in Rome.* (Sonnenschein, 1900.)

Bate, Herbert Newell. *A Guide to the Epistles of Saint Paul.* (Longmans, Green, 1936.)

Carpenter, Rhys. *Ancient Corinth.* (American School of Classical Studies at Athens, 1933.)

Chandler, Richard. *Travels in Asia Minor.* (Oxford, 1775.)

Conybeare and Howson. *The Life and Epistles of St. Paul.* (Longmans, Green, 1862.)

Conybeare, F. C. *Philostratus: the Life of Apollonius of Tyana.* (The Loeb Classical Library, Heinemann, 1912.)

Deissmann, Adolf. *St. Paul.* (Hodder and Stoughton, 1912.)

" " *The New Testament in the Light of Recent Research.* (Hodder and Stoughton, 1929.)

Duncan, G. S. *St. Paul's Ephesian Ministry.* (Hodder and Stoughton, 1929.)

" " *The Epistle to the Galatians.* (Hodder and Stoughton, 1934.)

Foakes-Jackon, F. J. *The Life of St. Paul.* (Jonathan Cape, 1933.)

Fouard, Abbé Constant. *St. Paul and his Missions.* (Longmans, Green, 1911.)

Glover, T. R. *The World of the New Testament.* (Cambridge University Press, 1933.)

"   "   *Greek Byways.* (Cambridge University Press, 1932.)

"   "   *The Ancient World.* (Cambridge University Press, 1935.)

Gunnis, Rupert. *Historic Cyprus.* (Methuen, 1936).

Hastings, J. *Dictionary of the Bible.* (5 vols. T. and T. Clark, 1905.)

"   "   *Dictionary of the Apostolic Church.* (T. and T. Clark, 1915.)

Hausrath, A. *A History of the New Testament Times.* 6 vols. (Williams and Norgate, 1895.)

Hobhouse, J. C. *A Journey through Albania, etc.* (James Cawthron, 1813.)

Hogarth, D. G. *Excavations at Ephesus.* (British Museum, 1908.)

James, M. R. *The Apocryphal New Testament.* (Clarendon Press, Oxford, 1926.)

Knox, Wilfred. *St. Paul.* (Peter Davies, 1932.)

Lake, Kirsopp. *Paul: His Heritage and Legacy.* (Christophers 1934.)

"   "   *Landmarks of Early Christianity.* (Macmillan, 1920.)

Lanciani, Rodolfo. *Pagan and Christian Rome.* (Macmillan, 1892.)

Lewin, Thomas. *The Life and Epistles of St. Paul.* 2 vols. (George Bell, 1890.)

Lowther Clarke, W. K. *New Testament Problems.* (S.P.C.K., 1929.)

Lucas, E. V. *A Wanderer in Rome.* (Methuen, 1930.)

Malden, R. H. *Problems of the New Testament To-day.* (Oxford University Press, 1923.)

Miller, William. *Greece.* (Ernest Benn, 1928.)

Moffatt, James. *A New Translation of the Bible.* (Hodder and Stoughton, 1936.)

"   "   *The New Testament.* (Parallel Edition.) (Hodder and Stoughton, 1922.)

Moffatt, James. *Introduction to the Literature of the New Testament*. (T. and T. Clark, 1920.)

Mommsen, Theodor. *The Provinces of the Roman Empire*. (Richard Bentley, 1886.)

Pewtress, Leslie S. *Saul who is also called Paul*. (Marlborough, 1923.)

Rackham, Richard Belward. *The Acts of the Apostles*. (Westminster Commentaries. Methuen, 1912.)

Ramsay, Sir William. *Luke the Physician*. (Hodder and Stoughton, 1908.)

" " *The Church in the Roman Empire*. (Hodder and Stoughton, 1893.)

" " *Pauline and other Studies*. (Hodder and Stoughton, 1906.)

" " *The Cities of St. Paul*. (Hodder and Stoughton, 1907.)

" " *The Teaching of Paul in Terms of the Present Day*. (Hodder and Stoughton, 1913.)

" " *Historical Commentary on the Galatians*. (Hodder and Stoughton, 1899.)

" " *St. Paul the Traveller and Roman Citizen*. (Hodder and Stoughton, 1896.)

" " *The Historical Geography of Asia Minor* (*Royal Geographical Society. Supplementary Papers*, Vol. IV, 1890.)

" " *Studies in the History and Art of the Eastern Provinces of the Roman Empire*. (Aberdeen, 1906.)

Schurer, Emil. *The Jewish People in the Time of Jesus Christ*. (T. and T. Clark, 1896.)

Skeel, C. A. J. *Travel in the First Century*. (Cambridge University Press, 1901.)

Smith, James. *The Voyage and Shipwreck of St. Paul.* (Longmans, Green, 1866.)

Stirling, J. F. *Philips' Atlas of the New Testament.*

Stuart and Revett, *The Antiquities of Athens.* (London, 1787.)

Tucker, T. G. *Life in the Roman World of Nero and St. Paul.* (Macmillan, 1910.)

Wade, J. H. *New Testament History.* (Methuen, 1932.)

Wheler, George. *A Journey into Greece.* (London, 1682.)

Whibley, Leonard. *A Companion to Greek Studies.* (Cambridge University Press, 1906.)

Wood, J. T. *Discoveries at Ephesus.* (Longmans, Green, 1877.)

GUIDE BOOKS

Guide to the Holy Land, by Father Barnabas Meistermann. (Burns, Oates and Washbourne, Ltd., 1923.)

La Grège. (Les Guides Bleus, 1932.)

Greece. (Murray's Handbook, 2 vols., 1884.)

Asia Minor. (Murray's Handbook, 1895.)

The Handbook of Cyprus. (Christophers, 1930.)

INDEX

CLASS

ACC

CLASS

Morton

(LAST NAME OF AUTHOR)

In The Steps of Saint Paul

(BOOK TITLE)

ISSUED TO

DATE DUE

CLASS

ACC.

Morton

(LAST NAME OF AUTHOR)

In The Steps of St. Paul

(BOOK TITLE)

Roadside Chapel

STAMP LIBRARY OWNERSHIP

BROADMAN
B P
SUPPLIES

CODE 4386-03
CLS-3   MADE IN U. S. A.

Date Due

Code 4386-04, CLS-4, Broadman Supplies, Nashville, Tenn., Printed in U.S.A.

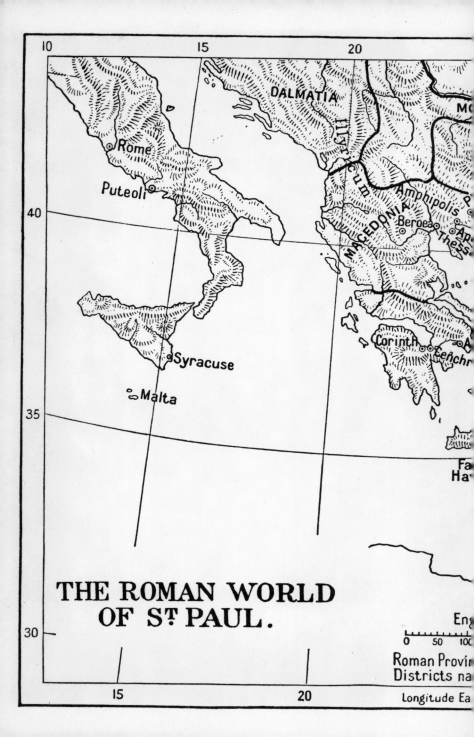

THE ROMAN WORLD
OF St PAUL.